THE END OF
CATHOLIC
MEXICO

THE END OF
CATHOLIC
MEXICO

Causes and Consequences
of the Mexican Reforma
(1855–1861)

DAVID GILBERT

VANDERBILT UNIVERSITY PRESS
Nashville, Tennessee

This book will be made open access within three years of publication thanks to Path
to Open, a program developed in partnership between JSTOR, the American Council
of Learned Societies (ACLS), University of Michigan Press, and the University of
North Carolina Press to bring about equitable access and impact for the entire scholarly
community, including authors, researchers, libraries, and university presses around the
world. Learn more at https://about.jstor.org/path-to-open/.

Library of Congress Cataloging-in-Publication Data

Names: Gilbert, David, 1958– author.
Title: The end of Catholic Mexico : causes and consequences of the Mexican
   Reforma (1855–1861) / David Gilbert.
Description: Nashville : Vanderbilt University Press, 2024. | Includes
   bibliographical references and index.
Identifiers: LCCN 2023049636 (print) | LCCN 2023049637 (ebook) | ISBN
   9780826506436 (paperback) | ISBN 9780826506443 (hardcover) | ISBN
   9780826506450 (epub) | ISBN 9780826506467 (pdf)
Subjects: LCSH: Mexico—History—1821-1861. | Mexico—History—War of
   Reform, 1857–1861—Causes. | Church and state—Mexico—History—19th
   century. | Catholic Church—Mexico—History—19th century. |
   Constitutional history—Mexico—19th century. | Mexico—Church
   history—19th century.
Classification: LCC F1232.5 .G55 2024 (print) | LCC F1232.5 (ebook) | DDC
   972/.06—dc23/eng/20231025
LC record available at https://lccn.loc.gov/2023049636
LC ebook record available at https://lccn.loc.gov/2023049637

Front cover image: *Plaza de Santo Domingo*, colored lithograph by John Phillips, ca. 1847–
1848. National Museum of History, Ministry of Culture. INAH. Credit: Fideicomiso
Centro Histórico de Ciudad de México

In memory of Charles A. Hale
(1930–2008)

A model scholar and a generous teacher

Contents

Acknowledgments

I wish to express my gratitude to all those who have supported me in this project over the years. In the beginning, Dr. Charles A. Hale encouraged me to pursue the topic of the Mexican Reforma, and the history department at the University of Iowa made my initial investigations in Mexico possible. My research there was always facilitated by patient and helpful staffs at all the archives I consulted. Above all, the cooperation and hospitality of the personnel at the Biblioteca Eusibio F. Kino in Mexico City will never be forgotten. More recently, the project has been supported in various ways by Clayton State University where I teach.

I am also grateful for Clyde Feil's careful reading of an early draft and Kevin Schmiesing's sharp critique. I am further indebted to Zachary Gresham and the anonymous readers for their valuable insights. I also thank the other editors at Vanderbilt University Press for all their hard work preparing the manuscript for publication. But above all, my heartfelt gratitude goes to my friend and colleague Adam Tate, for his steadfast help and encouragement along the way.

The Reforma
as Culture War

Of all the beautiful streets in Mexico City, by far the most spacious and elegant is the grand Paseo de la Reforma. Modeled on the Champs Elysées in Paris, the emperor Maximilian originally built it to connect his residence, the Castillo de Chapultepec, with the National Palace five kilometers away.[1] Originally named Paseo del Emperador, Maximilian later changed its name to "Avenue of the Empress," in honor of his wife. But after the fall of the monarchy in 1867 it was rechristened Calzada Degollado in memory of a fallen liberal hero.[2] Finally, in 1872 liberals changed the name again to commemorate what they considered their most important achievement: the Reforma. Initially, the "Reformation" was understood to mean the liberal modernization program implemented in Mexico between 1855 and 1861. But like the avenue itself, the period encompassed by the Reforma has expanded over time. Today, the execution of Emperor Maximilian in 1867 is often marked as the definitive end of the reform era. On the other hand, some historians use the term Reforma to designate the entire period of liberal political ascendancy, which lasted until Porfirio Díaz established his dictatorship in 1876.[3] A casual trip down this historic road, however, belies the convulsive nature of the transformation it commemorates.

In polite company, modern commemorations of the Reforma often elide its essential character. Without a doubt, this period was a watershed in the development of the modern Mexican state. Politically, the reform program stood for federalism and constitutionalism, although these ideals existed more in theory than in practice. Economically, the reforms were intended to strengthen the middle class and laissez-faire capitalism, which also did not happen. Socially, the liberal plan reorganized the army and abolished the special legal privileges formerly enjoyed by the military and the clergy. Ultimately, however, the main impact of the Reforma was religious: the total exclusion of the Roman Catholic Church from the public life of the nation. For the liberals of the nineteenth century, this was the ultimate meaning of their triumph: *Écrasez l'infâme!* Once the greatest success story of the Church's evangelization campaign in the Americas, after 1861 Mexico was a secular state, ruled by the most anti-Catholic government in the hemisphere. Formally ubiquitous religious rituals were now confined within the walls of churches, and religious teaching was banished from Mexican schools. Catholic hospitals, orphanages, and other charities also disappeared. Even monasteries and convents, once the glory of Catholic Mexico, were forbidden.

Naturally, such a radical cultural change evoked resistance from many sectors of Mexican society. From the beginning, popular protests greeted every new law affecting the Church, and there were frequent revolts against the liberal government. This standoff culminated in a fratricidal civil war, lasting from January 1858 to December 1860. In fact, the War of the Reforma, also known as the "Three Years' War," was one of the most ferocious wars in Mexico's history, during which most of the punitive measures against the Church were enacted. Liberal secularization projects were also carried out in other Latin American nations during the nineteenth century, but the Mexican Reforma remains unique for the level of violence it generated and its ruthless implementation.

Paradoxically, although a clash of religious ideals was at the core of the liberal-conservative conflict, it is this aspect that has received the least attention in the standard histories of the period. Indeed, many historians are hesitant to describe the Mexican Reforma as a religious conflict at all. Patricia Galeana de Valadés expressed the common view when she wrote, "The Mexican liberals were in the majority believers . . . they never thought to persecute the religion that they themselves professed. [The Reforma] was a political struggle, not a war of religion."[4] Those who conflate these two elements—politics and religion—according to Benjamin Smith, simply overlook "the thin line between the anticlerical and the antireligious."[5] Or, as another historian has pointed out, "both liberals and conservatives prayed to the very same Virgin of Guadalupe."[6] From this perspective, a true religious conflict could not occur in Mexico, since protagonists on both sides of any political battle belonged, at least nominally, to the same Catholic Church.

But internecine conflict does occur within a single religious community, perhaps especially when religious identity is the main vehicle of social unity and cultural expression. In the mid-nineteenth century the Catholic Church was still a fundamental part of Mexico's national identity; culture and public space were by and large still dominated by religious rituals and images. Indeed, it is hard to ignore the religious dimension of a struggle in which even the sacraments became potent political weapons. This is why the Mexican Reforma can be best understood as a confrontation between two opposing political-religious visions fighting for the control of religious symbols and institutions, "a war of political convictions, but also a war for Catholicism and the signs it represented."[7] Precisely because both sides claimed membership in the same religious body, the conflict between traditionalist and revolutionary religious factions became a battle for the soul of the nation, without which no political program could hope to succeed. In any event, although Mexicans might have belonged to the same spiritual community at the beginning of the Reforma, this was no longer true when it ended. In this way, the Mexican Reforma parallels the original European Reformation, which likewise generated social conflict and sectarian violence.

Instead of a religious conflict, the Reforma has traditionally been viewed as a classic nineteenth-century political struggle. In both style and substance, this pervasive interpretation of the Reforma is part of a much wider "master narrative" of nineteenth-century history, celebrated as a period of progress and the triumph of reason. This template was applied immediately after the Reforma in Mexico, where the victorious liberals became its official interpreters. For example, José María Vigil was a member of a militant student group and editor of a radical newspaper during the 1850s. Three decades later he contributed a history of the Reforma to Vicente Riva Palacio's monumental *México a través de los siglos* (Mexico across the centuries).[8] According to this influential interpretation, the Reforma was a struggle of reason and justice against the forces of obscurantism and privilege. Unsurprisingly, the villains in this story were the conservative elites, *latifundistas*, upper clergy and military officers, who manipulated the endemic religious fanaticism of the masses "in order to save Mexico's past from Mexico's future."[9]

After 1926, when Wilfrid Hardy Callcott published his *Church and State in Mexico:1822–1857*, this interpretation also became dominant in the United

States.[10] In Callcott's retelling of the story, the Reforma became a struggle of "the masses," championed by liberal heroes, against "the classes," composed of the usual conservative suspects, especially the clergy. His interpretation, which treated a topic heretofore little studied north of the border, resonated with progressive-era elites and thus had a lasting impact on subsequent English-speaking interpretations.[11] This explanation was revived in the later twentieth century by US scholars applying a "nation-building" model to Mexican history.[12] At the same time, the development of improved methods for quantitative analysis coincided with the opening of Mexican archives containing some 1,936 bundles of documents relating to the disentailment and nationalization of Church property. This generated a spate of economic histories of the Reforma that complicated but did not challenge the received interpretation.[13] Eventually, however, new perspectives did begin to appear. For example, some researchers also turned their attention to the long-term consequences of the liberal project for peasant society in Mexico, employing a Marxist rather than the classic liberal model of class conflict.[14] More recently, new regional histories have revealed the complexity of the Reforma as it was experienced at the local level.[15]

Building on this previous scholarship, Will Fowler has recently published two books focused on the civil war that erupted during the Reforma. The first, *La Guerra de Tres Años: El conflict del que nació el estdo laico mexicano*, provides a much-needed, updated narrative of the military conflict.[16] In his second book, published in 2022, Fowler creates a multidisciplinary template of typical civil wars and then uses the Three Years' War as his illustrative case study. *The Grammar of Civil War: A Mexican Case Study, 1857–61* adds new dimensions to the study of this conflict by emphasizing the complex origins and global context of every modern civil war. Also relevant are Fowler's claims that cycles of violence ultimately have a logic of their own, that political actors often have mixed motives, and that fanatics exist on both sides of such struggles. On the other hand, although he eschews a "cooking pot" model, he believes that civil war in Mexico was "inevitable" once all the necessary conditions were in place.[17] In his interpretation, religion appears as the crucial flashpoint, but not the only cause of the war.[18] Instead, Fowler asserts that it was primarily the "toxic interference of the Vatican" that in "numerous instances" turned a political conflict "into one of religion."[19] But he also blames the "intransigent" Mexican bishops whose "clerical worldview" made compromise unthinkable.[20] Just like the army, Fowler argues, the clergy supported the conservative cause in order "to defend their privileges and wealth." He does concede they might also have "genuinely believed their sacred religion was being attacked."[21] But in the face of the utopia promised by liberals, the clerical posture appears clearly misguided.[22] Predictably, as in the earlier works on which it is based, Fowler's exclusive focus on the clergy reduces the religious question to a power struggle between an institutional Church, wedded to a colonial past, and an enlightened liberal state marching resolutely toward the future.

The surprising persistence of this Manichean model in the historiography of the Reforma owes much to the powerful and popular "secularization theory," a paradigm that automatically denies the validity of any religious motives or explanations in the modern age. This theory holds that religious disestablishment and secularization are necessary and inevitable stages in the development of every modern nation. Its key tenets are summarized by Jeffery Cox as follows:

> The spread of scientific knowledge, along with technological change and its associated values of instrumental rationality, have undermined the plausibility of religion in the modern world, displaced churches and other religious institutions with specialized social institutions based on the principles of means/ends rationality, and consigned religion to the status of the marginal, the purely private, or the anti-modern reactionary.[23]

From this perspective, no other explanation is ever needed or expected for the decline of religion in the modern age, and any attempt by actors in the past to withstand this iron law of progress deserves only pity or derision. Although this model is "teleological, Eurocentric, deterministic and deceptively value-laden," according to Cox it continues to influence historical interpretations because its assumptions remain largely hidden.[24] Like other unidirectional historical models, it has been challenged by scholars in recent years.[25] But it continues to function as an unconscious explanation in the absence of other interpretive frameworks.

Although largely unknown in the United States, a counter-narrative of the Reforma has also long existed along the ideological margins of Mexican society.[26] Already in the nineteenth century, conservative historians like Niceto de Zamacois penned their own accounts of the Reforma, usually presented as a social and cultural disaster imposed by force on an unwilling population.[27] In both conservative and self-identified Catholic narratives, liberal reformers appeared not as progressive benefactors of humanity, but as impious and dangerous demagogues. From the religious point of view in particular, the Reforma was explained as another unfortunate episode in the perennial war of unbelievers against the Church. This view was also reinforced by the violent anti-Catholic persecutions that occurred in Mexico during the 1920s and was a central theme in the histories written by Mariano Cuevas, SJ, during this period.[28] But although the theme of religious war is not absent in these treatments, there was still no analysis of underlying causes and conditions. Instead, like the liberal narratives they contested, these authors tended to rely on ahistorical models of monolithic and unchanging institutions achieving foreordained purposes over time.

The Reforma is also the focus of a new generation of scholars in Mexico, whose approach to the topic appears more nuanced and comprehensive than earlier treatments. For example, Marta Eugenia García Ugarte's *Poder político y religioso* still presents the Reforma as part of an extended power struggle between two rival institutions. But drawing on new sources gleaned from Church archives, her analysis reveals a more pragmatic, rather than reactionary, response by Church officials in Mexico.[29] Other recent works also highlight the moderate and rational positions often adopted by the ecclesiastical hierarchy.[30] Ironically, this trend corresponds with a recent emphasis on the moderate goals of most liberals. For instance, Brian Connaughton notes that "the project of separation of Church and State, the official removal of religion as foundation of the nation, appears during the decades after independence in the dream and goal of very few."[31] He also insists on the religious sincerity and Christian sensibilities of liberal activists during the conflict.[32] Considering the alleged moderate goals of both the bishops and most politicians, the Reforma might appear as merely a tragic misunderstanding. However, it was precisely the moderate Catholics and Catholic liberals who disappeared from the pages of Mexican history as a result of the ensuing conflict.

In the end, it was the program of the most radical political faction that triumphed in the Reforma, dramatically transforming the economic, political, and cultural landscape of Mexico.[33] Likewise, although clergy in Mexico may have exhibited a variety of reactions toward the liberal project, over time the conservative cause came to be identified with the most uncompromising expression of Catholic identity. But neither an institutional power struggle nor a class conflict model can adequately explain this extreme outcome, much less an appeal to ahistorical theories of progress. To break this interpretive logjam, new sources were needed that could reveal the more popular dimensions of the conflict. These could then be integrated into a more comprehensive narrative, one encompassing more voices from both sides of the struggle.

My search for such material began in one of the lesser-known archives in Mexico City, the Biblioteca Eusebio F. Kino. This library contains a massive collection of historic documents, including a large deposit of nineteenth-century materials. Most important was the extensive pamphlet collection amassed by the Father Basilio José Arrillaga, SJ, during the 1850s and 60s.[34] Here I discovered political tracts, petitions, essays, sermons, and speeches, reflecting the ideas and aspirations of the Reforma and its opponents. Because they were still uncatalogued at the time, many of these sources had been overlooked by previous writers. Other gems in this repository were literary works used as propaganda, including forgotten plays and novels. These are of special interest because, even as fiction, their dialogues echo the conversations and concerns of the day. Combined with similar materials from other nineteenth-century collections, a distinct image of the dynamics of the Reforma began to appear.

As it turns out, many of the events recorded in these underutilized sources do not appear in the standard narratives of the period. Nevertheless, these documents reveal a host of highly charged incidents that mark key turning points in the fatal polarization of Mexican society. Invariably, these symbolic episodes were reported from partisan perspectives, reflecting incompatible worldviews and visions for Mexico's future. Over time, these interpretations motivated other provocative acts, generating more popular reactions, until the cycle culminated in civil war and the Carthaginian peace that followed. Tracing these events allowed me to create an alternative chronology, which also provided a new context for analyzing the competing ideologies at the heart of the Reforma. At the same time, these ideas spread to wider audiences through sermons, speeches, and the print media, and were carried into the streets by public protests and demonstrations. Because ultimately the entire population participated in the struggle, identifying such symbolic moments is essential for connecting the theological and political rhetoric of the elites with the popular emotion that galvanized the conflict.

Based on these considerations, this book provides the first complete narrative of the Reforma in English in over forty years.[35] More importantly, it is the first to employ a culture war paradigm to explain the rapid polarization of Mexican society in this period. This model allows us to trace the hardening of ideas and attitudes on both sides of the conflict, to recognize the agency of a wider range of actors, and to explore the unfolding of events without anticipating their final denouement. The concept of culture war, widely applied today, was first defined by the American sociologist, James

Davison Hunter in the 1990s. A true culture war, according to Hunter, is a certain type of ideological struggle that produces drastic social change. Unlike class- or ethnic-based forms of social conflict, however, it is a competition among elites themselves for control of the terms by which public life is organized.[36] Furthermore, a culture war cannot be reduced to a dialectic between "liberal" and "conservative" political actors. To conceptualize the problem as merely a "political squabble," Hunter points out, "would imply that each side shares the same ideals of moral community and national life." Instead, during a culture war "each side operates within its own constellation of values, interests and assumptions," operating on separate planes of moral discourse. Ultimately, it is this "mutual moral estrangement" that precludes the possibility of conciliation or compromise, since "*each side of the cultural divide can only talk past the other*."[37]

The development of opposing worldviews sets the stage for social conflict, but according to Hunter, a true culture war only exists when these "competing moral visions are sustained by a rhetorical structure and discursive environment that operates according to its own imperatives." First, there is a "pattern of image building and accusation shared by both sides of the cultural divide." In particular, rhetorical hyperbole is employed to "stretch, bloat, or conflate realities in order to evoke a visceral response from the listener." Eventually, this inflated rhetoric becomes "institutionalized," creating "dominating and virtually irresistible categories of logic." At the same time, moderate positions are pushed "into the grid of the extremes" and "public discourse is reduced to reciprocal bellicosity."[38] This process was certainly at work in Mexico during the Reforma. As Enrique Krause has written, "Between 1858 and 1860, as López Velarde would portray it, 'the Catholics of Peter the Hermit and the Jacobins of the Tertiary age' came face to face, hating each other 'in good faith.' Good faith that was bad faith, bad faith that would consist in no dialogue, no discussion, no listening, no negotiation."[39] According to Hunter, "It is at this level that the term culture war—with the implications of stridency, polarization, the mobilization of resources, etc.—takes on its greatest conceptual force."[40]

Significantly, a culture war model has already been employed to understand religious-secular conflicts in nineteenth-century Europe.[41] Many of the most contentious issues in Europe were the same as those in Mexico, including secular education, civil marriage, and clerical participation in politics. But one additional factor makes the Mexican Reforma unique: the eruption of ideological difference into bloody conflict. In Europe, the "culture wars" of the nineteenth century remained wars in the metaphorical sense. "Although there were certainly episodes of physical violence against people and property," Christopher Clark and Wolfram Kaiser observe, "these wars were primarily fought through the cultural media: the spoken and printed word, the image, the symbol."[42] In Mexico, however, the rhetorical conflict became a military one of a particularly violent nature. In order to understand this anomaly without recourse to essentialist arguments, the historical context of Mexico's ideological struggle must also be taken into consideration.

In Mexico, the ideological culture war was exacerbated above all by the psychological trauma resulting from the country's recent war with the United States (1846–1848).[43] Following crushing defeats on the battlefield, Mexico was compelled to forfeit half of its national territory to the enemy. After this disaster, the traditional consensus among elites dissolved and longstanding political differences were intensified. "Both liberals and conservatives, in viewing the impotence of their country in 1847, asserted their former programs with increased vigor," wrote Charles Hale.[44] Richard Sinkin concurs: "the debate became more intense, positions became hardened, and political ideologies—which had hardly existed prior to the war—became polarized into irreconcilable visions of the solutions to Mexico's problems."[45] This ideological division is reflected throughout the rhetoric of the Reforma, but particularly in the opposing attitudes toward the United States.

As it turns out, the rapid political polarization of elites after the Mexican-American War exactly reflects the dynamics described by Wolfgang Schivelbusch in his book, *The Culture of Defeat*. To explore the psychological impact of war on defeated societies, Schivelbusch analyzed the devastating defeats suffered by the Confederate States of America, the Second French Empire, and Imperial Germany in 1865, 1870, and 1918, respectively. In the process, he also identified the two common reactions that develop in response to such "national trauma." First, an enemy's "unworthy" victory can be attributed solely to material and economic factors. Then, as Schivelbusch explains, the "one great consolation for the defeated is their faith in their cultural and moral superiority."[46] True to form, after Mexico's defeat many conservatives embraced the nation's Hispanic and Catholic heritage with a new intensity, a counterpoint to Yankee materialism and greed.[47] Conspicuous in this position was an unqualified support for the Catholic Church, its traditional privileges protected and its moral monopoly guaranteed.[48] On the other hand, defeated nations also show a tendency to adopt and imitate the traits of the victors. "Losers imitate winners almost by reflex," Schivelbusch explains.[49] Mexican liberals were no different, and the United States quickly became the template of the future they envisioned for Mexico. "The contrast between the dynamic, aggressive, prosperous economy of the United States and the stagnant, decaying economy of Mexico stood out in sharp relief to the development-oriented liberals," notes Donathon Olliff.[50] According to Schivelbusch, these postwar reactions are "psychological mechanisms for coming to terms with defeat." Not surprisingly, in Mexico those most in need of such "protective shields . . . against a reality unbearable to the psyche" were the elites, those most involved in the nation-building project from the beginning.[51] It is also not surprising that religion became the casus belli for the clash of these exigencies, since it was so deeply embedded in ideas about the past and hopes for the future of Mexico. This is how a crushing military defeat turned traditional political tendencies into a high-stakes culture war in Mexico.

A similar perspective is offered by the literary scholar, Jaime Javier Rodríguez, who locates Mexican responses to defeat under the headings of righteousness and agony. He uses these two terms to capture the dominant sentiments that he uncovered in his analysis of postwar literature in Mexico: elite reactions to "the invasive, destructive actions of the United States," once viewed as a model democracy and now revealed as "just another tyrannical imperial power." Here the term righteousness refers to the "greater, truer morality to be found in Mexico when compared to its northern neighbor," an idea that Rodríguez, however, believes was shared by both conservatives and liberals. For conservatives, accusations against the US also implied a vindication of Mexican identity and culture. According to Rodríguez, this posture was more complex for liberals, who had always "elevated the United States to an exemplum of liberty." But faced with its "greed" and "perfidy," they could still embrace righteousness by insisting that since the US had betrayed its own ideals, so Mexico "would have to be the *true* democratic republic." On the other hand, many liberals also turned their anger inward, experiencing agony as they contemplated the national failures that explained Mexico's defeat. This position entailed a more complete rejection of the past, but all liberals agreed that "Mexico's loss revealed the need to reform Mexican society and start anew." In every case, according to Rodríguez, Mexico's defeat "left a profound scar on the Mexican national psyche, or at least on members of the intelligentsia."[52]

In this toxic environment, the culture war of the Reforma could only be a zero-sum conflict. Inflamed elite discourse, incarnated in symbolic confrontations, pushed political options to the extremes. This process was exacerbated by the hatreds spawned in a civil war that no one wanted, culminating in a religious solution that no one had expected when the struggle began. Because of the dramatic changes that followed, the Reforma is included, along with the struggle for independence from Spain and the 1910 Revolution, in the "trinity of historical processes" that created modern Mexico.[53] In this sense it is still celebrated in textbooks, monuments, and even street names throughout the republic. But also important is the legacy of bitter struggle in which the reform laws were forged. Even today, the social and cultural ramifications of that conflict, in particular the official marginalization of religion, resonate in Mexican society. Or to put it another way, "the wounds of the Reforma still have not healed."[54] Rereading the Reforma as a culture war generated by a post-traumatic reaction can shed new light on the contingent and unpredictable nature of the entire reform process. At the same time, and even more importantly, it may also increase our appreciation for the human drama that accompanied Mexico's great leap into modernity during the middle of the turbulent nineteenth century.

CHAPTER 1

The Road
to the Reforma

The Mexican Reforma officially started in 1855, but the conflict reflected decades of growing political and religious tension. On one side of the ideological divide was the legacy of Spanish anticlericalism inherited from the eighteenth-century Bourbon monarchs. After independence these tendencies had been further exacerbated by the spread of Masonic ideals among Mexican elites. Increasingly, the progressive ideas of the political class clashed against the massive weight of Mexico's traditional Catholic culture. Although slowed by this formidable obstacle, the liberal agenda still seemed to be gaining ground every decade. Challenging this trend, however, was a growing Catholic revival among some sectors of the population. In Mexico as in Europe, the dogmatic orthodoxy and religious zeal of earlier centuries were discovering new life in the theological and devotional innovations of the nineteenth century. This movement became even more important when many Mexicans turned inward following the trauma of the war with the United States. Because political differences were increasingly expressed in religious terms, disagreements between Church and State took on an even deeper meaning than they might otherwise have warranted. Rather than merely power struggles between an expanding state and entrenched clerical interests, they reflected the evolution of the two competing visions of modernity that shaped the underlying culture war of the Reforma.

The relationship between religion and society in Mexico was always complex, beginning with the theocratic Aztec empire that flourished before the arrival of Hernán Cortés in 1519. After the Spanish Conquest, religious and secular authority in New Spain were also united in the form of the *patronato real* (royal patronage). Since the popes of the sixteenth century could not directly oversee missionary activity in the distant Indies, they allowed the Spanish crown to control many aspects of ecclesiastical life in its colonies. Under this pragmatic arrangement, Hapsburg monarchs in Spain sponsored a massive evangelization campaign and the erection of religious institutions throughout the Americas. This model was particularly effective in Mexico, the most populous and highly developed of the newly conquered territories. In return, the Church provided a unifying culture for the disparate peoples of the empire and lent legitimacy to the colonial social and political order.

After more than two centuries of cooperation, the first major crisis in this symbiotic relationship occurred in the eighteenth century, precipitated by the ideas of the French Enlightenment. The rationalism of the philosophes crossed the Pyrenees with the Bourbon dynasty, and soon the newly enlightened Spanish monarchs were using the power of the *patronato* not to spread the faith, but to curb ecclesiastical power and promote secularization in government and education across the empire.[1] The most dramatic example of this policy was the expulsion of the powerful Jesuit order from Spanish territory in 1767.[2] But while such measures may have been popular with liberal elites in Spain, by and large this kind of reform was unwelcome in Mexico. In fact, resentment generated by royal assaults against the privileges of the clergy was a significant factor in the 1810 revolt against Spanish rule.[3]

The Mexican revolt against Spain was initiated by a creole priest, Miguel Hidalgo, in 1810, and continued by a mestizo priest, José María Morelos, after the execution of Hidalgo in 1811. Throughout the ten-year struggle for independence, both sides utilized religious symbols and rhetoric in an effort to gain popular support and legitimacy for their cause.[4] But in the end it was a new wave of liberal legislation emanating from Spain that convinced Mexican loyalists to join the insurgents in their struggle for political autonomy. In particular, traditionalists in Mexico distrusted the mildly anticlerical Spanish Constitution of 1812, and feared the social chaos it might unleash on the colony. When King Ferdinand VII accepted the controversial document in 1820, many conservatives withdrew their support for Spain. That is why one of the chief elements of this unlikely liberal-conservative alliance was a commitment to the perpetuation of Catholic religious hegemony in Mexico and the preservation of clerical immunities. Under the leadership of General Agustín de Iturbide, a united "Army of the Three Guarantees" finally achieved Mexican independence in 1821.[5]

Although the Catholic hierarchy had vocally opposed the revolt against Spain, the Church itself emerged from the conflict comparatively unscathed. There were changes at the highest level to be sure, but most of these had no immediate impact on the daily religious life of the nation. The moribund office of the Holy Inquisition finally disappeared, and some of the bishops appointed under the *patronato* returned to Spain. But the vast majority of lower clergy remained at their usual posts. Since the crown always advanced moderates in the ecclesiastical hierarchy, however, the end of royal appointments may have contributed to the development of a more conservative Mexican hierarchy over time.[6] Although the loss of *peninsular* members of the religious orders would eventually weaken the Church's influence in society as political power shifted to the less organized secular clergy, the importance of this change was not immediately apparent. In fact, after the war the Church appeared more stable and powerful than ever, since competing civil institutions were still weak or nonexistent in the new nation. Thanks to the "Three Guarantees," the church also enjoyed the unqualified protection of its rights for the first time since the days of the Hapsburg kings.[7] "The religion of the Mexican nation is and always will be the Roman, Catholic, and Apostolic," the Constitution of 1824 proclaimed. It also promised that the government would protect the Catholic religion "with wise and just laws and prohibit the exercise of any other."[8] At the same time, the constitution confirmed the *fueros*, the exemption from civil trials enjoyed by members of the clergy and the military, the traditional first and second estates.

Just as in the colonial period, the new state benefited immensely from its identification with the Church. Above all, religion played an indispensable role in the formation of an independent Mexican national identity. First, the Catholic faith distinguished Mexico from its heretical neighbor to the north, an obvious difference that helped perpetuate in the populace an inherited sense of Hispanic pride. But religious discourse also helped legitimate the break with Spain and even generated support for a republican form of government after 1823.[9] Throughout the 1830s, nationalist rhetoric relied heavily on Catholic themes that described Mexico as a privileged nation, chosen by God for a unique mission in the world. The theme of "providential nation" was especially connected to the cult of the Virgin of Guadalupe, whose image had been emblazoned on Hidalgo's rebel banner.[10] Ultimately, politicians realized, it was the Church that gave meaning to the concept of "Mexican nation" and provided a substitute for the former ideals of royal and Spanish sovereignty.[11] Furthermore, the Catholic religion was widely recognized and appreciated as the chief guarantor of the social order and the bulwark of public morality.[12]

But in spite of the clergy's support for the republican regime and the government's promise of favor, the relationship between the two powers was not entirely smooth. Spain, still hoping to recover its American possessions, had insisted that the pope appoint no new bishops for its break-away colony, which might be interpreted as formal recognition of its sovereignty. Although the Holy See attempted to mediate the Spanish-Mexican stand-off, by 1829 there was not a single bishop remaining in the country, and the number of clergy was starting to decline without new ordinations. Just twenty days after becoming pope in 1831, however, Gregory XVI defied the Spanish crown and confirmed six new bishops for the country.[13] On the other hand, freed at last from the meddling of the Spanish crown, Mexican churchmen were nevertheless still haunted by the specter of the *patronato*. The Archbishop of Mexico City had pronounced the arrangement ended in 1822, but this did not prevent the 1824 Constitution from conferring the monarch's traditional powers on the new state. Opponents argued that a royal prerogative, granted personally by a pope to the kings of Spain, could not be unilaterally appropriated by a republic. Politicians, however, were reluctant to forfeit this advantage and the issue was not finally resolved until 1851.[14]

Notwithstanding these tensions, religion was still not a divisive factor in Mexican politics at this time. Due to their shared background and culture, the creole and mestizo upper class tended to share similar social attitudes regardless of their political views.[15] While their level of religious commitment varied, they all embraced the Catholic "family values" of New Spain: respect for the father, for authority, and for private property.[16] Politically, there were real divisions between the Federalists and Centralists during the 1830s and 1840s, but both factions were equally committed to ideals of progress and modernization. The real debate in this period was not whether social or economic reform was desirable, but over the speed at which changes could be implemented. After Mexico achieved independence from Spain in 1821, the philosophical differences that had emerged during the eighteenth century were still contained beneath an external Catholic conformity. Indeed, before the Reforma publicly denying the Catholic faith in Mexico would have been political and social suicide.[17] Foreign observers, like the Scots-American Fanny Calderón de la Barca, were often surprised by the pervasive Catholicism they encountered in Mexico.[18] Living in the capital from 1839 until 1842 as a diplomat's wife, she reported that here "the *padres* have still an overweening influence, and the superstition of all classes is perfectly astonishing in this 19th century."[19]

In spite of this unpromising context, liberal ideas were nevertheless embraced by many elites in Mexico before and after independence. As in Europe, the liberal program in Mexico was based on the ideas of the French Enlightenment and stressed the themes of progress, human perfectibility, and autonomous individualism. In general, these positions entailed a rejection of the Christian doctrine of original sin as well as the need for divine grace. The existence of God might not be denied, but rather than the Trinity of Christian theology, "God" became an immanent force, sometimes identified with nature, human consciousness, or the universe itself. Although sometimes packaged as a kind of "reformed" Catholicism, this model also deemphasized the key Christian dogmas of the Incarnation and the divinity of Christ, which present Jesus as the sole mediator (and redeemer) between God and humanity.[20] A purely "spiritual" relationship with the "Supreme Being" also had no need for a sacramental economy or a liturgical/devotional program to unite believers with Christ, making the Catholic priesthood redundant at best.[21] But by renouncing the clergy instead of Christ, progressives could, for a time, remain within the Church they ultimately hoped to replace. For example, one Mexican liberal prophesied that the Christian ideal of the future would be "liberty, equality and fraternity." Its focus would become "philosophical without ceasing to be Catholic," transforming men through the ideas of love and social progress, rather than divine grace, prayer, or the sacraments.[22] Such a vision explains how the most radical members of the liberal party, the *puros*, could embrace the anticlerical agenda and language of the Masonic lodges while still insisting on their Catholic credentials.[23]

Another cause of anticlerical sentiment among Mexican elites was the professional rivalry between educated laymen and priests for social power and control in the new republic. As Anne Staples has observed, "The priest's influence stood in stark contrast with the weakness of those new to public life—the young lawyers, military officers, doctors, and gentlemen—trying to piece together a modern state. . . . The relative power of the groups in contention—clergymen vs. civilian politicians—was quite clear, and it was evident in public affairs large and small."[24] On the other hand, the complaint of professionals about the excessive numbers and influence of the clergy may have reflected their own perceptions rather than objective reality. In 1852, for example, there were only about 3,320 secular and 1,295 regular clergy in Mexico, serving an estimated population of 7,860,000.[25] The ratio of less than one priest for every two thousand Catholics was well below that of Europe, where there was an average of one clergyman for every one hundred parishioners. On the other hand, the concentration of clerical establishments in major urban centers may have contributed to the impression of an overabundance of priests.[26]

As far as the secular clergy was concerned, the conciliar seminaries that replaced the Jesuit colleges after their suppression were full. But during this period the seminaries also admitted lay students who needed a higher education as preparation for the secular professions, especially law. The presence of so many worldly students, however, inevitably undermined the ecclesiastical discipline and spiritual formation of the candidates for the priesthood. At the same time, many of the non-clerical graduates complained about the rigid devotional atmosphere they had to endure during their education, an experience that did nothing to hinder the growth of anticlerical sentiments among the professional elites. For example, according to Pablo Mijangos y González, reforms in the diocesan seminary in Morelia reflected "curricular innovations and scientific rationality." Nevertheless, he adds, "it is quite probable that the cloistered atmosphere of the seminary was the origin of many anticlerical careers in Michoacán."[27] Meanwhile, a study of the clergy in the Diocese of Yucatán shows a decline in the "quality" of priests during the same period, as clerical careers became less attractive to educated elites. According to Raymond Harrington, this decline in class status naturally contributed to a decline in clerical influence and power.[28]

Rather than professional envy or class snobbery, however, many liberals in Mexico attributed their hostility toward the clergy to its alleged moral failings. In fact, a denunciation of clerical greed, hypocrisy, and immorality was a fundamental feature of most anticlerical rhetoric. However, this problem also seems to have been greatly exaggerated. A study of clerical life and training in Mexico by Dennis Ricker did not reveal any pattern of egregious behavior on the part of priests during this period. Instead, his examination of secular and ecclesiastical court records from 1821 to 1857 suggests that clerical misbehavior was actually quite rare. Problems did exist, and from time to time a small number of priests were charged with drunkenness or accused of sexual immorality.[29] But Ricker also found that evidence of dedication, competence, and hard work was more common. Ninety-nine percent of the lower secular clergy could be classified as "good ministers of religion," he concludes, leaving little basis to support the contention that "the personal lifestyles of the lower clergy were in some way responsible for the development of anti-clericalism."[30]

As in Europe, anticlericalism in Mexico was a complex phenomenon. In Spain, the Bourbon monarchs had combined a commitment to rationalism with a pragmatic appreciation for the social benefits of religion. As heirs of this eclectic model, Mexican elites in the new republic usually expressed their desire for social reform in anticlerical—but not explicitly anti-Catholic—terms. This discourse was also heavily influenced by eighteenth-century Jansenism, which supported the use of the secular arm to reform "corrupt" religious institutions, and the French Gallican tradition, which advocated independence of national churches from Rome. The influence of Jansenism was especially marked in the moral sensibilities of the reformers, who appealed to an ideal of primitive Christianity in order to attack the alleged excesses of the Baroque Church.[31]

Wherever it appeared, however, anticlericalism reflected an ideological commitment that was not necessarily a response to any particular actions by the clergy. That is why, in evaluating the phenomena in France, James McMillian warns against "taking anticlerical spokesmen at their own evaluation as men of science and progress and the rationalist enemies of bigotry and obscurantism." Like anti-Semitism, he explains, nineteenth-century anticlericalism had a "mythical and fanatical dimension" with "its own internal logic and internal dynamics."[32] José Sánchez concurs that the "myth of clericalism" was one of the most widely propagated legends during the nineteenth century.

> Its chief tenet was that the clergy were a self-seeking group, usually an obstacle to progress, constantly fomenting superstition, obstructing knowledge and human wellbeing, and not above plotting civil rebellion to maintain themselves in power.[33]

Other scholars agree that anticlericalism owed more to the psychological mechanisms of scapegoating than to empirical reality and often increased in response to entirely unrelated social frustrations or during periods of political despair.[34] Such ripe moments were certainly not lacking in the first half-century of the Mexican republic.

Whatever its justification, antipathy toward the clergy was especially pronounced in the Masonic lodges, which dominated the first decade of political life in independent Mexico.[35] The constant rivalries between the

Scottish and York rites resulted in the creation of an independent Mexican lodge in 1825, but this did not diminish the anticlerical influence of European Masonry. Although all of its members professed the Catholic faith, the official charter of the new "National Rite" publicly denounced the clergy as "a permanent obstacle to all reform in the social order." Furthermore, the lodge complained, priests were a threat to the very existence of the republic because of their special privileges and "tendency toward domination." The first general assembly of the new rite even attacked the Church's "pernicious" monopoly on education, because of its alleged desire "to maintain men in ignorance and superstition."[36] Perhaps even more urgent, the Catholic monopoly on public worship prevented economic growth by deterring Protestant immigration. That is why the official program of Mexican Masonry included, among other goals, the abolition of the clerical *fuero*, the suppression of monastic institutions, the secularization of public schools, and religious toleration.[37]

Not all Mexican liberals, however, were so fanatically anticlerical. In fact, this issue was a main cause of the division between the *puros* and the *moderados*, between the radicals who wanted to destroy the Catholic Church and the moderates who desired to reform it.[38] For the former, "without the destruction of [the Church's] public authority, it would be impossible to create a modern, secular society committed to the principles of the French Revolution." Alternatively, moderates "favored a purified form of religion and indeed argued that 'the liberal party is the true observer of the Gospel.'"[39] A description of moderate European liberals of the time could also be applied to many *moderados* in Mexico. Unlike their radical colleagues, they were characterized not by revolutionary rage but by "a polite skepticism as well as a wistful sympathy, a self-doubting faith, a scholarly questioning, a highly developed private conscience, a romantic pantheism." Like their European counterparts, they might also exhibit "religious devotion," a "traditional piety," and "a strict moral discipline."[40] Such attitudes, however, were scorned by the *puros*, who accused moderates of being indecisive, if not entirely misled by their early religious training.

The first attempt to implement the Masonic program in Mexico occurred in 1833, just one year after General Antonio López de Santa Anna overthrew the centralist regime of Anastasio Bustamante. Although the victorious general was elected president after the coup, he left the running of the government in the hands of his vice president, Valentín Gómez Farías. Influenced by the writings of the radical priest and liberal theorist, José María Luis Mora, the new cabinet immediately began to enact legislation designed to reduce the power of the Church in Mexican society.[41] First, the California missions were secularized and their property nationalized, a measure later extended to all the remaining missions in the republic. At the same time, some smaller religious houses were also confiscated and closed. Next, civil enforcement of religious vows was declared unlawful and the government administration of the agricultural tithe was abolished. For the first time, the state also assumed direct control of all public education. The University of Mexico, a clerical stronghold, was suppressed and its assets seized. Finally, preferring an Erastian solution to the lingering *patronato* debate, the president and governors of the states were given authority to make all ecclesiastical appointments. Plans to extend the reforms even further, including a program to disentail Church property, were only thwarted when a coalition championed by Santa Anna himself overthrew his own government in May 1834.[42]

Santa Anna may have reappeared under the banner of "*Religión y Fueros*," but at this point his public posture did not necessarily signify a lack of sympathy with the ideals of the reformers. And while the *santanistas* promised support for the Church's privileges, they also demanded a series of loans with which they could finance their own projects, especially the resurrection of the army. Like many politicians during this period, Santa Anna favored the preservation of essential Catholic social values along with a program of incremental secularization.[43] That is why his cabinet reversed only a portion of the anticlerical legislation of the previous administration. For instance, the mission system was never reestablished, and the tithe remained a voluntary contribution.[44] The University of Mexico was reopened but was not returned to ecclesiastical control. And the secularization of schools continued apace. Whereas the Church controlled most of the education system before 1833, only twenty-one of the nation's 1,310 schools were still in its hands by 1842.[45] Nevertheless, in keeping with Santa Anna's moderate approach to reform, Christian doctrine remained part of the curriculum in the new secular institutions.[46]

The secularization of the missions, a process that actually began under the Bourbons, was a major blow to the male religious orders in Mexico. These had already been weakened by the loss of peninsular funding and Spanish superiors after Independence.[47] Now, with the loss of their missions, hundreds of previously active friars were returned to the cloister. Deprived of their traditional apostolic work, the religious zeal of the missionary orders could not be maintained. In the next decades, the Franciscans in particular faced "declining vocations, deterioration of religious discipline, and decline in public esteem."[48] Eventually even Rome recognized that men's religious life in Mexico was in disarray, for in 1854 the Bishop of Michoacán, Clemente de Jesús Munguía, was delegated to investigate and correct the situation. The much-needed reforms, however, were preempted by the outbreak of the Ayutla Revolution.[49]

After a decade of relative calm, the next crisis in Church-State relations occurred as a consequence of the Mexican-American war, which began after the United States annexed Texas in December 1845. A liberal plan to develop this part of the State of Coahuila by encouraging massive Anglo immigration had backfired when the settlers revolted against the central government in 1836.[50] Lorenzo de Zavala, one of the early promoters of the settlement scheme, even joined the rebels in creating an independent republic.[51] Ten years later, a dispute over its actual borders created a diplomatic crisis when Texas became the twentieth-eighth state in the union.[52] The US finally declared war on May 13, 1846, after Mexican troops entered the disputed region and clashed with American forces. The fall of Monterrey in September 1846 was followed by the shelling and seizure of Veracruz in March 1847. US troops also moved into New Mexico and California. After the assault on Chapultepec Castle, defended by young cadets, on September 13, 1847, Mexico City was occupied by US forces and the war came to an end. Mexico's resounding military defeat was followed by the signing of the Treaty of Guadalupe Hidalgo on February 2, 1848, in which Mexico ceded fifty-five percent of its territory to the United States.

As previously discussed, the political scene in Mexico became fatally polarized in the aftermath of this national humiliation. Searching for scapegoats, liberals were quick to blame the clergy for their military defeat. As it turned out, the start of the war had also brought Santa Anna back to power in another coup in 1846. And once again he placed Gómez Farías in charge of the government, this time while Santa Anna devoted himself to the defense of *la patria*. But a crisis ensued when this same vice president attempted to appropriate 15 million pesos for the war effort by a forced sale of Church property. As in 1834, clerical resistance was followed by a military revolt, and Santa Anna was once again moved to oust his own government from power.[53] The president subsequently negotiated a loan of 1.5 million pesos from ecclesiastical coffers to pursue the war, and the clergy continued to preach resistance to the invaders. But many liberals insisted that the Church's refusal to hand over the original amount on demand was further proof of clerical self-interest and venality.

Ironically, liberal complaints about the clergy were shared by some of the invading enemy forces. For example, during the occupation of Mexico

City, Captain Robert E. Lee penned the following plan for Mexico's salvation to a friend: "Open the ports of European immigration, introduce free opinions of government & religion. Break down the power & iniquity of the church. It is a beautiful country & in the hands of proper people would be a magnificent one."[54] The first tentative steps in that direction followed immediately after the US troops were withdrawn. First, liberals exacted a measure of revenge on the clergy by passing a new bill that required the Church to pay a tax on the products of the now-voluntary tithe. Soon afterward, delegates from Veracruz introduced legislation to end the Catholic monopoly in public worship. It is not surprising that the first calls for freedom of worship came from here. The city of Veracruz was the main Atlantic seaport and commercial entrepôt for the nation. Thus, not only were *veracruzanos* exposed to many outside influences but a significant number of influential non-Catholic foreign nationals also resided there.[55] However, the premature proposal generated a flood of anti-toleration petitions from other areas in the republic, and the proposal was easily defeated. Nevertheless, the fact that it appeared at all caused alarm among conservative Mexicans.

Three years later, the still unresolved issue of the *patronato* generated an even more sustained confrontation between the Church and the government in the western state of Michoacán. According to Mexican law, Clemente de Jesús Munguía, bishop-elect of the local diocese, was required to take a civil oath before consecration to his episcopal see. Neither civil nor ecclesiastical authorities anticipated any problems with this formality, and the ceremony was scheduled for January 6, 1851, at the governor's palace in Morelia. When Governor Juan Bautista Ceballos administered the oath, however, he added an unexpected phrase at the end: "Do you swear to keep and confirm the constitution and general laws of the United Mexican States, *now subjecting yourself to those which the* patronato *of the federation shall frame?*" Munguía hesitated, and then shocked the assembled dignitaries with his response: "No, because this formula prejudices the rights and liberties of the Church."[56]

Munguía was the government's own choice for the bishopric of Michoacán, and his refusal to take the oath startled the politicians in Mexico City, who claimed that previous bishops had sworn to the formula without qualms. Newspapers debated the matter for months, eventually compelling Munguía to publish a detailed manifesto in defense of his unpopular stand. He had consulted his own conscience when the oath was read, he recalled, and concluded that he could not swear to uphold laws that were as yet undefined. Furthermore, having been trained as a lawyer, he considered the formula itself unconstitutional. But the center of his argument was an insistence on the juridical independence of the Church, and everyone understood that this was the real issue at stake in this debate. Ultimately, Munguía did take the oath and took possession of his diocese on Christmas Eve 1851. But this was only after the president of the republic, Mariano Arista, clarified that the indefinite terms of the formula were to be understood in a sense "fixed by law," which Munguía chose to interpret as meaning "subject to a concordat with the Holy See."

Although the government had not conceded any of its own claims during the Munguía affair, militant liberals were still annoyed by this unprecedented challenge to supremacy of the state. This was why Melchor Ocampo, a senator from Michoacán, orchestrated a cause célèbre of his own during the standoff. According to him, a peon in the town of Maravatío had been refused burial by the local priest because his widow was unable to pay the customary fees. In response, Ocampo not only covered the mortuary expenses himself, but also began a crusade to abolish the "stole fees" paid to priests altogether. In Michoacán, the sliding fees set for baptism, matrimony, and burial dated from 1713, and the schedule was already the subject of legislative attention before Ocampo's intervention. But according to Margaret Chowning, Ocampo seized upon this issue "as the best means yet to force the church to bend to the will of the government, as well as to impress upon the pueblo the extent to which the government, and not the church, had its best interests at heart."[57] More importantly, his petition to the state legislature to this effect touched off a national debate on the controversial issue of clerical wealth and initiated a nine-month polemic with an anonymous "Priest of Michoacán" in the national press.[58] Although the state legislature eventually agreed to allow the Church to revise its own fee schedule without interference, the highly charged rhetoric surrounding the Munguía affair is likely to have contributed to the fall of the Arista presidency in 1853.[59]

The first officially conservative party in Mexico had only emerged after 1848, in the aftermath of the war with the United States. But conservative ideas were certainly present among many elites in the previous decades. For some, conservative attitudes might merely reflect personal temperament, or perhaps an inherited pride in Hispanic culture and accomplishments. It was often associated with the professional army, whose corporate structure was anathema to liberal principles. When the conservative party finally emerged, its undisputed champion was Lucas Ignacio Alamán y Escalada (1792–1853), who wrote two series of books on Mexican history from a conservative perspective.[60] Throughout his life he was also keenly interested in Mexico's economic development, investing in both mining and textiles. As minister of the interior and external relations (1830–1832), he created Mexico's first bank to promote investment in national industry.[61] But although he was as dedicated to modernization and progress as any liberal, his approach to Mexico's economic problems was "pragmatic" rather than ideological.[62] The same thing might also be said of his attitude toward the Church. His sentiments on this topic were expressed in a letter he sent to Santa Anna on March 23, 1853. "The first thing is the conservation of the Catholic religion," he advised, "because we believe in it, and because even if we did not take it for divine, we consider it as the only common bond that unites all Mexicans, when all the rest have been broken, and as the only thing capable of sustaining the Hispanic-American race, and that is able to save it from the great dangers to which it is exposed."[63] After Mexico's defeat in 1848, even more elites embraced this position, perhaps in spite of any doubts they may have harbored about the divine nature of the Church and its doctrinal authority.

On the other hand, many Mexicans of all classes, including elites, did accept the Church's official dogmas and put their religious faith above other political or pragmatic considerations. These men and women understood their lives in the light of the teaching of the *Doctrina Cristiana* of Padre Jerónimo de Ripalda, SJ (1536–1628). This was the basic catechetical text used throughout the Spanish-speaking world since the seventeenth century and its contents were familiar to most Mexicans. Here the purpose of human life was summarized in two simple questions and answers:

Q. What is the primary obligation of man?
R. To seek the ultimate end for which he was created.
Q. What is the ultimate end for which he was created?
R. To serve God [on earth] and enjoy Him [forever in heaven].[64]

From this eternal perspective, the Church, its teachings, sacraments, and devotions, were not optional, but essential. This worldview was the opposite of the utilitarianism of the liberals, who adopted "the greatest happiness for the greatest number" principle as their only metric for determining right and wrong.[65] Traditional Catholics, then, were necessarily supporters of the clergy, and evaluated political and social policies in the light of their impact on the Church. So, although the views of pragmatic or political conservatives and the body of orthodox believers may not have always been identical, they were clearly on the same side of Mexico's growing cultural divide.

Ultimately, a pragmatic alliance between Mexican conservatives and the *santanistas* toppled the liberal Arista government in 1853, bringing Santa Anna back to power for the last time. In the past, the general liked to portray his military interventions as a nonaligned alternative to factional politics. But the political landscape of Mexico was now dramatically different than it had been before Mexico's defeat and there was a much wider gap between the opposing political factions. This clash of visions had been summarized in a conservative essay published in 1850, just two years after the war. There were now only two positions in Mexico, the writer explained. On the one hand were those who were determined to "die a thousand times before allowing the barbaric Anglo-Saxon democracy to plant its foot on the neck of the Spanish race." To that end, they were determined to preserve the religion, "that came from our fathers, that made our grandparents famous and good, that is the consolation of so many unfortunates today, and is the only bond that unites this society, although it is being whittled away; that conserves the rights of property, of the family, of man and citizen and finally, that preserves national independence." Their opponents, on the other hand, were characterized as "annexationists," afflicted with "*nortemania*." Even if they denied that they wanted Mexico to become a state in the American union, they still pursued policies that made that fate inevitable, given the greed of "the eagle of the north that stalks us, with its talons always bared over us." But their "enthusiasm and admiration for the model republic" blinded these adorers of the US idol to the dangers of imitation, driven by "their foolish itch to imitate the republic of the north, to apply here the utopian fantasies of modern philosophism." From this perspective, the battle lines were already drawn. Mexico's options were either order, based on its Catholic and Hispanic heritage, or religious and social anarchy, based on the revolutionary ideas of the pro-US demagogues.[66]

Now, thanks to a deal mediated by Alamán, the new government headed by Santa Anna created Mexico's first officially conservative administration. Reflecting this ideological orientation, the government immediately centralized political power in the country. It also reformed the tax system and expanded the army to an all-time high of 900,000 troops. There was even a move to repeal more of the anticlerical legislation that Santa Anna had ignored in 1834. Perhaps the most dramatic sign of the new era dawning in Church-State relations was a decree allowing the Society of Jesus to return to Mexico.[67] Only a few Jesuits were available to take advantage of this unexpected opportunity, but the symbolism of the act, including the restoration of the Colegio de San Gregorio to its original owners, was much more important than its practical effect.[68]

For a while, Santa Anna's autocratic tendencies were restrained by his new cabinet, consisting of Alamán as minister of foreign relations; a moderate liberal, Antonio Haro y Tamariz, as minister of finance; and the old *santanista*, José María Tornel y Mendivil, as the minister of war. But the death of Alamán in June of 1853, followed by the resignation of Haro y Tamariz and the death of Tornel in August, ended the brief conservative experiment. From this point until his overthrow in August 1855, Santa Anna's rule simply degenerated into a personal dictatorship, characterized by censorship and the exiling of political enemies.[69] The old general also lost popular support after his controversial sale of the Mesilla Valley to the United States in December 1853.[70]

Eventually, a liberal opposition movement began to take shape and the Plan of Ayutla was proclaimed on March 1, 1854.[71] Although this manifesto contained no specific social or religious agenda, the conservative press warned that liberal intentions in these areas were already well known. In particular, it predicted that once in power the revolutionaries would demand religious toleration, confiscation of Church property, and the end of the clerical *fuero*. "This program of the demagogues," the conservative newspaper *El Universal* declared, "encompasses the destruction and overthrow of all the fundamental principles that constitute our society," and would include "the persecution of the Catholic clergy and the theft of its property."[72] On the other hand, when the former minister Haro y Tamariz joined a separate rebellion centered in the state of Michoacán, he issued his own plan promising "total protection and respect" for the military and the clergy.[73]

The Ayutla Revolution triumphed when Santa Anna fled the country in August 1855, leaving political power in the hands of the liberals. At this point, even conservatives took measures to distance themselves from the dictator, since association with him might prevent their participation in the new revolutionary government. For example, an anonymous pamphlet appeared claiming that the administration of Santa Anna was, in fact, not conservative at all. This tract, entitled *El partido conservador en México*, insisted that true conservative principles were ignored after the death of Alamán and that the party could therefore not be held accountable for the policies and behavior of the discredited regime. In any event, it proclaimed, "No ideas, including those of conservatives, should be excluded from a democratic and representative government."[74] Although conservatives maintained that their exclusion from government would be "illegal, absurd, and impossible," many liberals, embittered by the persecutions they had so recently endured, did not agree.

At this point, political tensions between liberals and conservatives were at an all-time high. Members of the two parties disagreed on many critical issues facing the nation, including economic policy, the organization of the military, and the structure of the federal government. Above all, each side had reacted differently to Mexico's humiliating defeat in 1847 and the psychological imperatives of their positions resonated deeply with conflicting religious agendas. Encouraged by his conservative supporters, Santa Anna had generously supported the Church and effectively silenced its critics during his final administration. The clergy, often enough, had responded in kind, with lavish ceremonies and copious benedictions. In his last months, a few leading churchmen had finally spoken out against some of Santa Anna's more excessive policies.[75] Nevertheless, many liberals identified the entire clerical establishment with the hated regime and now that the dictator was gone, they could give free rein to their pent-up frustrations. Ideological anticlericalism, in both its radical and moderate forms, thus became the central motivating force for the entire Reforma program. Post-war liberals, anxious to join the modern world represented by the United States, were now even less tolerant of obstacles to their utopian plans. Having seen their reform plans thwarted in 1833 and 1847, they were now determined to eliminate the "theocratic power" from Mexico once and for all.

Traumatized conservatives, on the other hand, took refuge in the Hispanic past and their Catholic identity. Energized by an international Catholic revival, they were also less willing to compromise on issues related to the faith. In fact, just as liberals across the world were confidently predicting the imminent transformation (or final destruction) of Catholicism, the Church of the nineteenth century was actually entering into a new period of growth and vitality. Austen Ivereigh, among others, argues that the essential religious conflicts of this period were never between an outdated, decaying religious establishment and a dynamic modern version of the state. Rather, "as it 'came of age,' the liberal project collided with another modern success story: the Catholic revival." Furthermore, he explains, both sides were equally modern and employed similar tactics to achieve their goals, resulting in "a lengthy and unusually intense conflict over public space." Above all, "there were issues of ideology and language," which invested the conflict "with all the venom and bitterness associated with a war of religion." "Only if we grasp this picture of a Church that was popular and in expansion," Ivereigh writes, "can we begin to understand the nature of the conflict between Church and State, Liberal and Catholic, in the nineteenth century."[76] According to Christopher Clark, this "New Catholicism, with its networks of voluntary associations, newspapers, mass-produced imagery and mass demonstrations" was as much an artifact of political modernity as "liberalism, anticlericalism and socialist secularism." Rather than a "confrontation between 'modern' and 'anti-modern' forces," he argues, these were "competing programmes for the management of rapid political and social change."[77] As Mijangos y González observes, in Mexico it was not the Church's "supposed attachment to a foregone past," but rather its modern self-definition that generated its new conflict with liberalism. "Without a careful consideration of the complex ecclesiastical response to the mid-century liberal revolution," he writes, "historians have not yet been able to explain why Catholicism became such an explosive and divisive issue after decades during which it had provided a powerful social bond and perhaps the only common ground for national self-definition."[78]

One key to the Catholic revival in the nineteenth century was the spread of the ultramontane movement and the reinvigoration of the papacy it inspired. Favoring papal supremacy over national or diocesan authority, the term ultramontane (beyond the mountains) referred to fact that for the French, Rome was on the other side of the Alps. Evolving in a European context, ultramontanism was primarily a strategy used by Catholics after 1789 to protect religious liberty from the encroaching secular state. But ultramontanism was also embraced by those longing for a church militant to combat the intellectual errors of modern society. Along with this emphasis on doctrinal orthodoxy, the ultramontane movement also contained a vibrant emotional component centered on the diffusion of new popular devotions and an unprecedented attachment to the person of the pope himself. "Perhaps never before," writes Raymond Grew, "had Popes been so widely known to the faithful, so consistently seen as the embodiment of a Church under siege, and so loved as spiritual leaders."[79] Ultramontanism reached its apogee during the pontificate of Pius IX (r. 1846–1878), who became an uncompromising opponent of modern liberalism in all its forms.[80] Paradoxically, some scholars argue that by resisting the autocratic tendencies of the modern secular state, Catholic opposition to liberalism actually contributed to the development of democracy and political liberty in Europe.[81]

Thanks to the intellectual capacity and moral leadership of its new bishops, the Mexican church was also experiencing a period of vibrant growth and renewal when the liberal assault began. It was also deeply affected by the religious fervor associated with the ultramontane ideas emanating from Europe.[82] The Church-State confrontation in Michoacán, for example, was provoked by Bishop Munguía's insistence on the freedom of the Church, but his position also presupposed papal supremacy in all ecclesiastical affairs. Pope Pius IX, in particular, seems to have inspired devotion in many Mexicans, especially after he himself became a victim of Italian nationalism and anticlericalism. For example, when the pope fled the hostile forces occupying Rome in 1848, some prominent Mexicans wrote him letters suggesting that he seek refuge in Mexico. Then president José Joaquín de Herrera had even issued an invitation, promising the pontiff that in Mexico he would find "seven million sons full of love and veneration toward your sacred person, who would consider themselves fortunate to receive a paternal blessing directly from your own hands."[83] This growing pro-Roman sentiment was also evident in the jubilant crowds that greeted the arrival of Msgr. Luis Clementi, the first apostolic nuncio appointed to the republic, in Mexico City on November 11, 1851. "It was reserved to this supreme pontiff to concede to afflicted Mexico the inestimable remedy of grace for its spiritual maladies," gushed one observer. "The great Pius IX, who with a single glance has understood the situation of the whole Christian world, and saw the terrified nations, trembling at the clamor of those new doctrines that seem to want to invalidate everything, heard this part of his flock pleading for help, and the holy Shepherd has deigned to send us a representative, to see firsthand the necessities of the Mexican Church."[84] Opposition to the Vatican envoy by anticlerical members of congress, including Melchor Ocampo and Miguel Lerdo de Tejada, prevented his official recognition for over a year. But on the recommendation of an investigative committee, which included José Joaquin Pesado and Bernardo Couto, President Arista finally accepted the papal delegate, with certain restrictions, in March 1853.[85]

Another event, the papal declaration of the dogma of the Immaculate Conception in 1854, also seems to have had a galvanizing effect on Mexican believers.[86] For an entire year, extravagant public celebrations were staged to celebrate the decree, producing "an unusual excitement" and "general delight" throughout the country. At Zacatecas, for example, the papal decree arrived in a coffer of gold, "accompanied by various friars and a multitude of people." The city, adorned with drapery and streamers, greeted the document with the tolling of bells, music, and fireworks. In honor of the occasion, a new Confraternity of the Sacred Heart of the Virgin was instituted and hundreds of enthusiastic citizens enrolled. A few days later the corporation of lawyers staged another "brilliant display" of their own.[87] Lavish celebrations were also held at the Universities of Mexico and Guadalajara. Ironically, at the latter institution the radical student José María Vigil won a poetry contest for his verses entitled "To the Mother of God in her Immaculate Conception."[88]

In addition to the important Marian dimension of these events, such extravagant religious theater, so inimical to the sober ideals of the reformers, also served as mass public demonstrations of loyalty to Rome. "No, do not believe, my brothers, that in the solemn spectacles that are now being celebrated in all the Catholic world we are only confessing the Immaculate Mother of God and her Conception," exclaimed one famous preacher in Mexico City. "We are also here to recognize the legitimate authority of the Vicar of Jesus Christ and accept all of its ramifications."[89] Some churchmen even held that the promulgation of this doctrine was a powerful rebuttal to the entire philosophical basis of liberalism. As a priest in the Cathedral of Durango declared, the pope wrote this "ingenious manifesto" touching on original sin because the denial of this doctrine was at the root of all the errors of the rationalists.[90] Indeed, the Enlightenment belief in human perfectibility was one of the key ideas dividing liberals and conservatives in Mexico.

Along with an emphasis on doctrinal orthodoxy, fidelity to the pope and new devotional expressions, historians note that the nineteenth-century religious revival in Europe was also characterized by the foundation of new religious orders, including many active orders for women, and the creation of an entire network of welfare institutions, hospitals, orphanages, and schools. Similarly, orders dedicated to charitable work, like the Daughters of Charity and the Vincentian order of priests, also appeared in Mexico during this period. But the increased fervor among Catholics was chiefly expressed by an increased involvement of the laity in new charitable and devotional initiatives. The most striking example of this trend was the spread of the Society of St. Vincent de Paul, a lay organization for the relief of the poor. The first conference of the Society met in Mexico City in 1844, and by 1851 there were sixteen conferences located in six cities across the country. In her study of this movement, Silvia Arrom stresses the "modern" character of its approach to charity, and the widespread participation of social elites as well as less affluent members in its activities.[91] Another important movement that spread widely in this period was the *Vela Perpetua* (Perpetual Vigil), a daily prayer vigil in rotating shifts usually lasting from 6:00 a.m. to 6:00 p.m.[92] Given the temper of the times, this devotional practice might also have subtle political undertones. For example, in 1854 the Bishop of Guadalajara mandated that it be observed in all the parishes of his diocese, as reparation to God for the "horrible blasphemies of the impious." If practiced conscientiously, he promised, this devotion would bring about "the correction of customs, the prosperity of the people, the peace of the republic, and the permanence of the holy and divine religion that we profess."[93] Other signs, like the increased popularity of local shrines, also highlight the vitality of religious life in rural areas.[94]

In spite of the short reprieve provided by Santa Anna's pro-clerical dictatorship, by 1855 many orthodox Catholics were convinced that their religion was under siege. In particular, the public debates surrounding the premature Veracruz bill for toleration and Ocampo's attack on stole fees had caused anxiety among supporters of the clergy. And after the fall of the dictatorship unshackled the anticlerical press, the specific nature of the threat became even clearer. At the same time, the ultramontane movement, with its explicit criticism of the entire liberal project, provided Catholics with an ideological vantage point from which to interpret and combat the secular menace. But while not all conservatives were driven by the logic of ultramontanism, they were willing to employ its rhetoric in their antiliberal crusade. During the Reforma, the vocabulary of Catholic orthodoxy would become a powerful weapon in the hands of the conservative opposition.

Meanwhile, for liberals, the psychology of anticlericalism provided an alternative religious aspiration as compelling as that of their opponents. Many were no doubt inspired by their own vision of a reformed church that might serve as a cultural conduit for disseminating progressive principles into Mexican society. The historic discourse of Jansenism and Gallicanism supported the notion that such a program was in fact a legitimate, if not superior, expression of the Catholic faith. But if some Mexican liberals did not embrace this particular religious vision, they all shared an unshakable faith in the inevitable march of progress. Even more importantly, they were all convinced that the clergy was in some way to blame for Mexico's lack of development, not to mention its terrible defeat in 1848. Thus, the impending clash between liberals and conservatives was also a confrontation between two mutually exclusive religious ideals: anticlericalism, with all the heterodox interpretations this term implied, and the new orthodoxy of ultramontanism. At its deepest level, then, the struggle for Mexico's political destiny was simultaneously a culture war to define the religious character of the nation.

CHAPTER 2

The Radicalization
of the Ayutla Revolution

Along with the liberal and conservative split in Mexican politics, the period of the Reforma was also complicated by a serious division within the liberal party itself. The devastating outcome of the Mexican-American War had convinced liberals across the country of the need for immediate and sweeping reforms. But although they all shared similar anticlerical ideas, there was still deep disagreement over the scope and pace of desired social and ecclesiastical reforms. The more radical members of the party, the *puros*, demanded a complete secularization of Mexican society. The moderate wing, on the other hand, was more willing to work slowly and even countenanced pragmatic compromise when required. Many *moderados*, in fact, were still practicing Catholics who hoped to use a rationalization of the Church itself as a mechanism for change. However, it was the radical faction that seized the initiative in the first weeks after the collapse of Santa Anna's dictatorship, creating a confrontational atmosphere that polarized the nation from the outset of the new liberal regime.

Although members of the *puro* faction were active throughout the country, the most critical phase in the radicalization of the Reforma occurred in Guadalajara, the capital of the western state of Jalisco.[1] Guadalajara pronounced for the Plan of Ayutla on August 13, 1855, and was occupied by rebel forces on August 22. After taking possession of the city, the *moderado* General Ignacio Comonfort withdrew on September 13 to attend a conference in Lagos (Jalisco) aimed at reconciling the remaining revolutionary factions.[2] On leaving Guadalajara, he named José Nemesio Francisco

("Santos") Degollado Sánchez, a *puro* from Michoacán, as governor and military commander of the state. Within days of this transition, radical groups in Guadalajara became involved in a series of clashes with the Church that would impact the ideological climate of the entire nation. Coinciding with the liberal seizure of power, these incidents exposed the underlying religious character of the political conflict ahead.[3]

Because of an internal power struggle between revolutionary factions, Mexico was without an official head of state from September 12 to October 4, 1855.[4] Elements of the triumphant liberal party, nevertheless, took advantage of the national holidays that fell during this period to publicize their political ideas. The Independence Day festival on September 16 was a particularly important forum for Mexican politics, and patriotic discourses delivered on this day were an important gauge of the national political climate.[5] Falling on the heels of the liberal victory, the speeches in 1855 naturally sought to identify the Ayutla rebels with the heroic insurgents of Mexico's earlier struggle against Spain. Vilification of the Santa Anna regime by the orators was likewise to be expected. But some speakers went even further and took this opportunity to attack their main nemesis, the Roman Catholic clergy. Introduction of this theme at such an early stage in the liberal consolidation of power, however, did not bode well for the future of the religious establishment.[6]

The first salvo against the clergy was delivered by the *puro* politician Guillermo Prieto Pradillo during the patriotic celebrations in Mexico City on September 16. Prieto was an important man of letters whose oeuvre included poetry, history, drama, social commentary, and books on economic reform. But on this day he used his considerable gifts to praise the revolution and demand the abolition of *fueros*. Clearly, the *fuero* offended the democratic principles of liberalism and calls for their abolition were as old as Mexican independence. Now, in the Alameda of Mexico City, Prieto prophesied that a future of equality and liberty would follow the fall of Santa Anna, but only if this legal anachronism was eliminated. To preempt any clerical opposition to his program, Prieto also proclaimed that the true essence of Christianity was a revolt against privilege. The Gospel was revolutionary, he declared, because it preached liberation, equal rights for all and universal democracy "for the people and by the people." At the same time, he praised the "bloody but triumphant and irresistible" French Revolution, *inter alia*, for restoring these ideals. He punctuated his speech throughout with the cry of "Liberty and Reform!" and in keeping with the patriotic theme of the celebration, he even claimed that Father Hidalgo had wanted to abolish the privileges of the army, the clergy, and the upper classes when he began his uprising against the Spanish in 1810.[7] Meanwhile, at the public celebrations in Guadalajara, the twenty-five-year-old Ignacio Luis Vallarta Orgazón, Degollado's personal secretary, called on the youth of the city to imitate the revolutionary spirit of the heroes of independence and inaugurate needed changes in the country. But in order to take advantage of the opportunity provided by the fall of Santa Anna, he explained, Mexico needed "new men, new institutions, and new laws." The first step in this transition, he insisted, was the abolition of *fueros*.[8]

One Catholic newspaper later dismissed the Independence Day speeches as "outlandish," "ridiculous," and "fodder for jokes."[9] But although the discourses on September 16 were provocative, they were quickly submerged in the wake of one delivered in Guadalajara on the following day. The civic festival held on September 17 was a patriotic extension of the Independence Day celebration and a commemoration of the translation of the relics of the insurgent leaders, known as "martyrs of the fatherland," to the Cathedral in Mexico City on that date in 1823. As such, the occasion often lent itself to hyperbolic rhetoric about the "price of freedom."[10] In 1855, Miguel Cruz-Aedo y Ortega, a well-known radical, was chosen to deliver the patriotic address before a gathering of dignities in Guadalajara. This oration, more than any other, exemplified the anticlericalism of the most radical wing of the liberal party. Whereas the previous speakers had argued from democratic principles and targeted only clerical privilege, Cruz-Aedo insinuated that the real problem in Mexico was the clerical establishment itself.

At twenty-nine years of age, the tall, dark-eyed Cruz-Aedo was already a figure of some importance in the liberal party in Jalisco. He was a graduate of the Conciliar Seminary in Guadalajara and had privately studied literature under the famous Carmelite priest, Juan Crisóstomo Nájera.[11] Whatever religious impressions he received from this association, however, were erased after he entered the university to study jurisprudence. During that period, he acquired radical ideas from reading eighteenth-century philosophes. In 1849 he joined a literary society named Esperanza (Hope) and in 1850 he helped found another, the Falange de Estudio.[12] Among these "fiery students" Cruz-Aedo was recognized as "perhaps the most radical, fervent, the most daring and the most Jacobin."[13] When the members of the "Student Phalanx" abandoned their academic pursuits and joined the Ayutla Revolution, he quickly rose to the rank of colonel. On September 11, 1855, he became an official in the secretariat of the new liberal government in Jalisco. Along with Vallarta, Emeterio Robles Gil and the twenty-six-year-old José María Vigil, he also founded the radical newspaper, *La Revolución*.[14] The anticlerical mission of this paper was clearly articulated in its first issue, published on August 28, 1855. Its goal, the editors declared, was "to wound in the heart, with a mortal blow, the Jesuitical party" and to exhort the people "to shackle forever the ecclesiastical class, because it is a contradiction to civilization and a monster of humanity."[15]

Cruz-Aedo's speech was destined to have a lasting impact on the unfolding of the entire reform program, because as a representative of the liberal party, his remarks were regarded by many as tantamount to an official declaration of war against the Church.[16] Ostensibly, his target on this occasion was conservatives, who he claimed were responsible for the regime of the late dictator. Indeed, his discourse began by comparing Santa Anna to a long list of tyrants drawn from history, after which he turned his attention to that "assembly of corrupt men" he identified as "the conservative party." History, both ancient and modern, provided the speaker with an entire catalog of crimes that he attributed to the perfidy of this party, from the death of Socrates to the execution of Hidalgo. According to Cruz-Aedo, humanity owed to conservatives "its most cruel misfortunes and the blackest pages of its history." "Is not that the party that proscribed reason, the child of heaven," he demanded, "substituting authority for it, the offspring of man?" "Is not that the same party that abjured the Gospel, divine code of love, ordering intolerance as a maxim of the Divinity?" It was this party, he claimed, that "condemned liberty and political equality, emanations of nature, with anathemas." For example, "conservatives" had preached the crusades, installed the Inquisition, enslaved the Indians, and persecuted the Jews. Torquemada, the speaker proclaimed, was one of the saints of the conservative calendar. In Mexico, conservatives had preached "the religion of peace at the point of a sword" and on Bishop Zumárraga's order destroyed "the ancient monuments and history" of the Aztecs, building "monuments to its pride" on the ruins of the conquered civilization.[17]

Mexico's premier Catholic newspaper, *La Cruz*, later complained bitterly about Cruz-Aedo's speech and its real objective. "Empty words and more words, names and more names, curses and more curses form that incomprehensible gibberish that our *famous* academic tries to call a discourse," the editors lamented. Nevertheless, the meaning of Cruz-Aedo's diatribe was clear: "Even in the midst of this muddle and obscurity . . . it is enough to comprehend that under the name 'conservatives' he wants only to signify the ministers of the Church."[18] Liberals often used "clerical party" as a term of derision for conservatives. In this case, using the term "conservative" as a euphemism for the clergy allowed Cruz-Aedo to avoid charges that the Catholic Church was his real target. Nevertheless, at times it was impossible to mistake the clerical identity of the villains in his presentation. For example, even wealthy politicians in Mexico were not known to wear purple, but the members of this party "go around dressed in purple and insult the poor with their luxury." Likewise, in an anachronistic allusion to the sale of indulgences, he charged that conservatives "put spiritual goods on auction, selling the inheritance of heaven; trafficking with human weakness and crimes; making a speculation of the sacraments."[19] Cruz-Aedo also compared conservatives to nocturnal birds, having "eyes to read consciences" in the dark, an obvious reference to the role of the priest in the confessional. This sinister capacity, clearly unrelated to any political power or office, allowed these "night creatures" to "slip into the interior of families in order to overhear their intimate secrets and disunite them."[20] Even more explicitly, he excoriated the "foreign despot" in Rome, whom he identified as the Antichrist, the harlot of the Apocalypse, sitting upon seven hills. Those who followed this monster he called "sacrificers to the Beast."[21]

It was shocking, *La Cruz* declared, that on a day dedicated to national celebration and reconciliation, "a rabid dog was thrown into the arena, reviving ancient hatreds and false grievances." But in spite of his not-so-subtle attacks on the clergy, Cruz-Aedo insisted that his goal was not "to renew musty hatreds." "My banner is of the people,' he had proclaimed, "and on it are written these holy words: 'Love your neighbor as yourself.'" In contrast to the perfidious conservatives, he suggested, the Ayutla revolutionaries were the real Christians. Like the martyrs of independence, they were dedicated to "building the temple of charity, the distinctive symbol of Christianity." In spite of inevitable delays, Cruz-Aedo promised that once "the dikes of fanaticism, corruption and ignorance" were destroyed, there would be a dawn of true liberty "in which all the members of the human family, obeying the laws of nature, common for all, recover their rights and recognize themselves as brothers because of their origin, instincts, and destiny." When this "universal republic, one and undivided" finally arrived, he predicted, "its reign over the earth will never end."[22]

Over the next few weeks, the conservative press mercilessly attacked Cruz-Aedo's discourse, and especially its negative characterization of the Catholic clergy. A more impartial review of history, the papers argued, would recognize the great contributions of the Church and her ministers to civilization. One of the most creative of these rejoinders came in the form of an imaginary conversation between two friends. In a series of pamphlets entitled *Dialogue between Martin and Juan Diego*, Martin appears as a representative of the new class of self-styled enlightened men of reason, "that harmonize with the spirit of the century."[23] As a representative of that group, he enthusiastically quotes slogans from the inflammatory speech, convinced that these ideas will bring a new golden age to Mexico. His remarks, however, provoke his more reflective companion, Juan Diego, to point out the fallacies of his borrowed ideas.[24] Throughout this anonymous work, the protagonist dissects Cruz-Aedo's claims to expose the contradictions of liberalism and to express a more orthodox viewpoint on the controversial issues of the day. In discussing Mexican history, for example, Juan Diego argues that rather than destroying a valuable culture, the Church actually transformed the Aztecs from a people "that offered thousands of human sacrifices" into a virtuous Christian nation. Significantly, Juan Diego is also never presented as a member of any political party, but simply as a man of common sense and integrity.

For conservative Catholics, Cruz-Aedo's appropriation of religious language and imagery was one of the most dangerous aspects of his rhetorical strategy. It was therefore crucial for their cause that a clear distinction be made between faithful believers and the liberal reformers. The *Diálogo* accomplished this goal in a simple and straightforward way. "Don't go around telling the simple people that you and your comrades are Christians," Juan Diego warns Martin. "Your Christianity is that of the sectaries Luther and Calvin, of those that learned to call Catholics *sacrificers to the Beast* and hold that the Holy Apostolic See is *the whore that sits on the seven hills of the Apocalypse*." Everyone knew the catechism's definition of a Christian: "the man who has the faith of Christ that he professed at his holy baptism." Part of that profession of faith, Juan Diego reminds Martin, was a belief in the Holy Catholic Church, defined as "the congregation of the faithful, ruled by Christ and by the pope his vicar."[25] Reflecting the view of many traditional Catholics, Juan Diego concludes in the end that the liberal crusade against "fanaticism" was in reality just a covert war against the Church.

Although Cruz-Aedo's ideas were not new, conservatives were particularly concerned because they seemed to reflect the official views of the new revolutionary government. In Guadalajara, witnesses testified that throughout his speech the orator exchanged knowing glances with Governor Degollado. It was also reported that when Cruz-Aedo had finished speaking, the governor embraced him and congratulated him on his theological erudition.[26] When the inflammatory discourse was subsequently reproduced on government presses, the Bishop of Guadalajara, Pedro Espinosa y Dávalos, lodged a formal complaint. In his letter to the governor, Espinosa expressed his concern over the disrespect shown toward religion in the speeches of Vallarta and Cruz-Aedo, both of which he had personally attended. He also requested that further publication and circulation of materials that insulted the Catholic Church and its ministers be prohibited.[27]

Sixty-year-old Bishop Espinosa was well prepared for his role as defender of the faith against the new liberal opposition. A native of Tepic, in the Nayarit district of Jalisco, Espinosa held a number of important jobs in the Diocese of Guadalajara before becoming its bishop in 1853. He had also gained political experience serving as vice president of the Jalisco Chamber of Deputies and was co-editor of a popular Catholic newspaper called *Defensor de la Religión* from 1827 to 1830. Well educated, he taught both in the seminary and as a Doctor of Theology in the university. Cruz-Aedo had attended both of these institutions during Espinosa's tenure, so it is possible that the two adversaries were at least acquainted. In the spirit of the times, he opened free elementary schools in the parishes of his diocese and placed its two hospitals under the care of the Daughters of Charity.[28] He was also deeply devout and zealously orthodox.

In response to Bishop Espinosa's complaints, Degollado defended his choice of orators and the sentiments that they had expressed. Like his protégé, he defended the fine distinction between anticlericalism and anti-Catholicism. "I assure you," he replied sarcastically to the bishop, "that notwithstanding that the reading of dogmatic books has been the frequent object of my studies . . . I did not notice the enumeration of any proposal or doctrine anathematized by the Church of Jesus Christ." Cruz-Aedo's use of figurative speech meant that Degollado was technically correct in stating that no dogma of the Church had been attacked directly. However, this defense was not well received by Catholics, who seem to have been even more offended by the hubris of non-clerics who felt themselves qualified to pontificate on religious issues. For instance, Degollado's claim to theological expertise irritated one cleric, who wrote:

This was an unfounded boast to try and give lessons in ecclesiastical material to our wise bishop; it was a hypocrisy to show off to the people. It was, finally, a ridiculous lie that rather showed off his ignorance, all his bad faith, and all the resolution that he had to be an accomplice to the aspirations of Protestantism. Because if he had really studied dogmatic books, he would have known that no Catholic could accept Cruz-Aedo's proposition that *reason ought to dominate authority.* [29]

In any event, Degollado maintained, it would be unfitting for a civil official to become involved even if any anti-Catholic statements were uttered in his presence. Such a display of inappropriate religious zeal, he explained, "is rightly regarded in a layperson as a symptom of hypocrisy and of disguised individual interest." Not surprisingly, the governor also flatly refused to censure anticlerical publications, pointing out that neither was Espinosa making any attempt to curtail antigovernment sermons in his diocese.

In fact, anti-liberal and anti-government sermons were becoming more common at this time, much to the consternation of the would-be reformers. It was reported, for example, that Cruz-Aedo's speech had alarmed the priest of Zapotlán (Jalisco), who denounced it from his pulpit as "impious and heretical," adding that "it should be burned so that it does not spread among us." But according to the delighted correspondent, the ten copies on sale in the town had sold out quickly and spread even among the Indians, who were asking for more copies.[30] Other liberal newspapers eagerly shared similar stories, like the one claiming that a priest in Mexico City had admonished some nuns to pray "that all those who planned to attack the ministers of the Church should be exterminated, along with those that read liberal periodicals."[31] Or the news that a priest in Morelia had preached that judgment day must be near since Mexico was now ruled by liberals, "and they are *heretics*."[32] But these reports were invariably accompanied by vehement condemnations of priests who "turned their pulpit into a political podium."[33] The editors also demanded that the government intervene and stop these "imposters." Certainly, Degollado was already well aware of clerical criticism in Jalisco. Conservatives even claimed that "the governor dispersed some of those that composed his clique and they attended all the sermons of the priests to listen, secretly denouncing those that spoke against impiety and in favor of the rights of the Church."[34]

Santos Degollado himself had a long history of radical political ideas and of personal conflicts with the clergy. When his father died leaving the family destitute, the young Degollado, along with his mother and brother, was forced to move in with a maternal uncle, an Augustinian priest and ex-military chaplain. A "nervous, rickety, irascible" boy, Degollado experienced a rather severe upbringing in the clerical household, first in Mexico City and later in the parish of Cocupao in Michoacán. After attending a military college, he succumbed to pressure from his uncle and married at the tender age of seventeen. At eighteen he drifted to Morelia, the capital of the State of Michoacán, where experience in his uncle's parish and his excellent penmanship gained him a job as a scribe. He spent the next twenty years as a clerk in the tithing offices of the Cathedral of Morelia, where, ironically, he was reported to have been a favorite of the priests in charge. In his free time, however, he engaged in physical exercise and the private study of Greek, Latin, Hebrew, French, mathematics, physics, and theology. Clearly, Degollado was preparing himself for greater things than a future as a minor clerk in the vast ecclesiastical bureaucracy.[35]

Perhaps because of his years subordinated to priests, Degollado very early developed a pronounced rebellious and anticlerical attitude. From his perspective, the clergy were "corrupt" and "ravenous bankers" without nationalistic sentiment, "hypocritical Pharisees that invoke the religion of Jesus Christ without believing in it nor observing its maxims of fraternity and peace." At the age of twenty-four he was already involved in the radical political group centered around Melchor Ocampo and was twice jailed for anti-government activities. After 1846 he served as director of education in the first Ocampo administration. He also joined in the governor's famous polemic with Bishop Múnguia in 1851. He was elected to congress in 1855 but then joined the Ayutla rebels instead. Because of his intelligence and fervor, he rapidly worked his way up to the rank of general. He was only forty-three when he was appointed military governor of Jalisco. A dedicated reformer, he has been credited with the foundation of more than four hundred elementary schools during his brief tenure.[36]

Although formally respectful, Degollado's response to Bishop Espinosa also contained serious recriminations and threats, reflecting the writer's underlying hostility toward the ecclesiastical hierarchy. For instance, he sarcastically suggested that those who dared to accuse the present government of anti-religious tendencies should be considered in the same way as those who blamed the Church for all the excesses of the Santa Anna regime. The Church, he claimed, was unwilling to take any blame for the "murders, assassinations, robberies, confiscations, and burnings" that occurred under the dictator, even though some priests had openly supported him. By analogy, the government in Guadalajara was not disposed to accept any responsibility for the actions of anticlerical youths in the present situation. On the other hand, Degollado warned, the clergy had always emerged "less pure, less strong, and less respected" whenever religious questions had produced revolts. Should there be a civil war provoked by charges of official impiety, he predicted, Mexico would "fall into a lamentable state of religious indifference or schism from which it will not be able to recover."[37]

Unsurprisingly, reports of the governor's adroit reply to the prelate emboldened the young radicals in Guadalajara, who immediately accelerated their anticlerical campaign. For example, on one occasion members of the Falange hoisted an effigy of the bishop, complete with miter, embracing a female figure in his arms. Attached to the amorous figures were signs proclaiming, "Death to religion!" and "Death to Espinosa!"[38] At the same time, the group began to deliver daily speeches in the main plaza and to make political addresses at the weekly assemblies of local artisans.[39] But these speeches, "ridiculing the pope, the bishops, friars, nuns, and all the practices of religion," were not always welcomed, and sometimes bystanders tried to drown out the speakers with whistles or run them out of the plaza with stones. On one occasion some *falangistas* even occupied one of the cathedral towers, tolling the bells to call attention to their demand for the reopening of the Instituto de Ciencias del Estado de Jalisco.[40] Apparently this violation of church property and decorum was too much even for Degollado, since he personally reprimanded the youths and apologized to the bishop.[41] Nevertheless, they continued to organize bands of musicians and singers who toured the barrios at night singing scurrilous anti-Catholic songs. Inebriated groups of these minstrels especially targeted the homes of priests and even entered the atriums of convents, shouting "Death to the Pope!" and "Death to the Clergy!"[42]

Not surprisingly, many citizens in Guadalajara were highly alarmed by these activities, and signs reading "Wake up Mexicans! Our religion is being lost!" began to appear throughout the city.[43] In response to the deteriorating situation, Bishop Espinosa issued a pastoral letter on September 29, to be read at Mass throughout the diocese on the following Sunday. "The most bitter sentiments have penetrated our heart," he began, "on seeing in our city and in our people the horrible unleashing of passions, the corruption of customs, and the insults of some toward the holy religion of our fathers, the one true Church, the representative of Christ on earth, and the venerable clergy." In particular, he complained, the "nightly orgies" of the Falange had created a real crisis in the city. In these scenes of drunken youths shouting anti-religious epithets, the prelate felt he heard an echo of the mob that had cried "Crucify Him!" on the first Good Friday. But in spite of his recent unpleasant exchange with the governor, the bishop insisted that his letter was not an attempt to meddle in political affairs, which he agreed were not the business of the clergy. It was, however, his duty as a bishop to defend the Church and to combat evil doctrines. Therefore, he directed his remarks to those who believed, "in order to support them in their faith," as well as to the unbelievers, "so that they abandon their error and return to the way of truth."[44]

Like the other members of the Mexican hierarchy, Bishop Espinosa firmly held the principle that one could not attack the Catholic priesthood without assaulting the Catholic faith itself. From his perspective, the real goal of those who slandered the clergy was simply the destruction of the Church. As he pointed out, this was what Jesus meant when he said, "Strike the shepherd and the flock will be scattered."[45] The bishop also marshalled a plethora of scriptural quotations to demonstrate the supernatural origin of the Church and the divine mandate of its leaders. Furthermore, he added, because of its sacramental nature, there could be no Church without a clergy, and no unity in the Church without the papacy. Those who cried "Death to the Pope!" or who called him the Antichrist were as bad as Protestants, he insisted. Everyone knew the catechism's definitions of a Christian and of the true Church. Dissenters belonged instead to the "Synagogue of Satan."[46] On the other hand, the bishop also eschewed retaliation against those who attacked the clergy. Rather, Espinosa exhorted believers to follow the example of Christ and the saints by loving their enemies and praying for those who blasphemed God and persecuted the Church.

Bishop Espinosa's missive produced a strong reaction from the radicals in Guadalajara, who claimed that "the spirit of the pastoral letter is nothing more than the old tricks of the conservative party." In spite of its charitable appeal, the pastoral's real goal, La Revolución alleged, was to incite priests to preach "a crusade against the republicans in place of the Gospel; to preach anarchy in the name of order, rape in the name of fraternity, ostracism in the name of humanity, war in the name of peace."[47] A few days later, six members of the Falange, including Cruz-Aedo, Vallarta, and Vigil also signed an open letter in which they denied the implication that they were heretics and accused the bishop of "bad faith and other dark machinations." Convinced that they were riding the tide of history, they wrote: "But it is already late, your Excellency, for we are in the middle of the nineteenth century, a time in which thought is being transmitted from one end of the earth to the other at the speed of light. Millions of thinkers are tirelessly occupied with the future of the world, and they will jeer and shatter to bits any imposter that tries to deceive the people with disguised self-interest."[48] "Thus some insolent boys treated the wise, virtuous, and venerable Sr. Espinosa," one clerical observer lamented, "with the acquiescence, or better said, permission of Santos Degollado."[49]

But although conservatives loudly condemned the activities of the Falange, there was no denying the impact of their message. "A hundred thousand ignorant troublemakers escaped from prison," one citizen complained, "are not as frightening as two or three perverse students who have acquired a bit of knowledge and want to get ahead in politics without the light of faith." Whereas the former dishonored vice by their behavior, he explained, a few students "may with their seductive writing make vice adored by many, and lead to the ruin of an entire society."[50] In response to this growing threat, the editors of Guadalajara's Catholic newspaper, *La Voz del Pueblo* (The voice of the people), launched a new program to protect the city's impressionable youth. Officially, their plan was to hold frequent public meetings in order to foster "true knowledge of the arts and science." However, the real goal of the program was to provide young people with the moral inspiration and training in religious apologetics that would help them to combat the anti-Catholic sentiments of the liberal press. "What of our innocent youth," the sponsors of the initiative asked, "if they follow the road that is being presented to them as full of flowers, flattering their passions so that they will end up the victims of vice?"[51]

The danger that liberal ideas posed to Mexican youth was always a major concern for conservatives. Because of their association with modernity, progressive ideas were naturally appealing to the younger generation. More serious Catholics and conservatives, however, connected the liberal program not with fresh ideas but with moral corruption. This explanation of liberalism was most clearly articulated in another fictitious dialogue eventually published in 1860. *The Lighthouse of Youth* was the story of a student named Laureano, "in whom instruction and talent were happily united by the careful education that he received from his pious parents."[52] Unfortunately, Laureano suffers from a painful and protracted illness, and is being attended by a young doctor named Eduardo. The book consists of a series of long conversations in which these two characters debate the burning religious issues of the day. Over the course of seventeen chapters, Eduardo, a liberal and unbeliever, is slowly converted by the example of Laureano, who ably defends his orthodox opinions in the face of all rationalistic objections.[53]

A warning to youth, *The Lighthouse* was also a cautionary tale to parents who neglected the religious training of their children or exposed them to liberal ideas. In the story, after Eduardo has realized the error of his ways, he is led to trace the origin of his unbelief, which Laureano had erroneously supposed was simply due to the reading of bad books. "What is equally true," Eduardo observes, "is that the disorder of my ideas began in the first years of my youth." Eduardo then describes his father, a dedicated military man but one indifferent to the upbringing of his children. In his childhood,

Eduardo explains, he had "obtained all the liberty necessary to pervert my-self," and as a young man he was sent to a college where his character and bad habits only grew worse. He also inherited, from his father's books and example, a liberal philosophy that greatly contributed to his moral decline. "Oh, if I had only had a father similar to that which ministered those pre-ventative instructions to you, that antidote or anti-venom!" he exclaims to Laureano. But because his father did not provide this protection, Eduardo confesses that he has been miserably unhappy and given over to unnamed vices since his youth. Liberalism in this context appears as a sort of poison, the moral effects of which are worse than the physical disease suffered by Laureano.[54] This diagnosis in particular may have resonated with the many Catholic champions who were themselves repentant liberals who had also tasted the bitter fruit of religious rebellion in their youth.

News of the confrontation between Bishop Espinosa and the Falange in Guadalajara, spread quickly throughout the country, contributing to con-servative anxiety about the future of religion under the new liberal order. Meanwhile, their worst fears were realized when the well-known radical, General Juan Álvarez, was named interim president of the republic at a conference in Cuernavaca on October 4, 1855.[55] Since Álvarez handpicked the delegates who attended this meeting, it was no surprise that it was dominated by Freemasons and *puros*.[56] But in spite of the temporary accord achieved at the Convention of Lagos on September 16, not all the Ayutla revolutionaries were happy with this outcome. Many less doctrinaire liber-als had hoped that General Ignacio Comonfort, a *moderado*, would be cho-sen as interim president instead of Álvarez. At the same time, according to James Gadsden, the US minister to Mexico, "The triumph of Revolution in favor of the Plan of Aytula and the unexpected election of Alvarez, when all the moral force of the country seemed to be with Comonfort including Alvarez's own predilections, for he did not aspire to the Presidency, has alarmed the [European] Allies, least [sic] Mexico might fall into the hands of the liberals with American sympathies."[57] Instead, Comonfort was ap-pointed to the new president's cabinet as minister of war. The other five members of the cabinet were all *puros*.[58] In Cuernavaca there were celebra-tions after the new president took office, and as was customary, Álvarez even attended a Te Deum in the local church. The reaction in Mexico City, however, was muted by conservative dissatisfaction. There, troops from the garrison removed the clappers from the bells of the cathedral to prevent the tolling that traditionally followed inaugurations and prevented citizens from discharging fireworks in the streets.[59]

In Guadalajara, on the other hand, Álvarez's presidency encouraged Cruz-Aedo and his colleagues at *La Revolución* to launch their most daring attack on the clergy to date. This was the publication of five inflammatory articles under the title "El poder teocrático" (The theocratic power). This series, which began to appear only four days after Álvarez became president, again attacked the lavish lifestyle and indolence of priests, whom it characterized as ignorant, lazy usurers, living in concubinage and "dancing the fandango in the midst of their [illegitimate] children." The articles also railed against nuns and demanded that no new candidates be allowed to enter religious life. Even the popular nursing sisters, the Daughters of Charity, were denounced as "the vanguard of Jesuitism and backwardness." Furthermore, the writers claimed that the clergy's refusal to invest its resources in factories and mines or in building new roads was the main reason the country remained underdeveloped. The clergy were also denounced because of their alleged "intrigues against established governments."[60]

In Guadalajara, there was a mass demonstration in support of the clergy on the evening of October 8, the day the first installment appeared. On that occasion, Bishop Espinosa, returning from a sick call, was cheered by a large crowd of people, some carrying torches. They also began chanting "Long live religion!" and "Death to the impious!" Liberal newspapers, referring to the event as a "disturbance," claimed that the demonstrators had also shouted "Death to the Republic!" "Death to the Federation!" and "Death to Degollado!" Furthermore, they insisted that the shouts came not from "the people" but from paid fanatics, and they demanded harsh punishment for the offenders.[61] *La Revolución* added that it was also a scandal that a "humble bishop" was given such adulation, which rightfully belonged only to the "Supreme Being." It also blamed the bishop, who if not the instigator of the "riot," had condoned it by his silence.[62]

News of the disturbances in Guadalajara spread quickly, along with the contents of *La Revolución's* attacks on the clergy. In Mexico City, the French ambassador even heard that the demonstrators had turned violent and attacked the home of Governor Degollado, who was forced to seek refuge in the bishop's residence.[63] On October 16 José Ramón Malo recorded in his diary that "in Guadalajara there has been a popular commotion, for having wanted to criticize the clergy." The next day, he reported, Mexico City also awoke to find papers "very injurious to the clergy" displayed on the street corners.[64] This tract, *El Clero — La Religion*, repeated many of the key points from "The Theocratic Power." But they were quickly torn down and replaced by posters cheering the pope and the priests, or with "rude expressions against the revolution," according to different sources. The liberal press blamed "the clerical party" and their agents, the "sacristans and altar boys," for this action and claimed that "sensible people tore down those nasty papers" in turn.[65]

On October 28, *La Revolución* finally concluded its provocative series with a detailed proposal for the reform of Mexican society.[66] This sixteen-point "anti-theocratic program" was designed to transform the country and "place it at one leap to the level of more advanced nations." But this could only be accomplished, its authors believed, if the clerical "cancer" was excised once and for all from Mexican society. The list of needed reforms began with a cry for another expulsion of Jesuits from Mexico, reflecting liberal paranoia toward this "highly noxious" order.[67] The second point was an appeal for religious toleration, in the sense of allowing public worship for members of any religion. There was also a demand for the suppression of all monasteries and convents and for an end to the clerical *fuero*. Further proposals included the confiscation and sale of ecclesiastical properties and the state control of marriage, cemeteries, and the registry of vital statistics. As usual, this plan was presented as an effort to eliminate "abuses" and not as an attack on religion per se. Nevertheless, these were still revolutionary ideas at the time. In 1855 few Mexicans could have anticipated that within six years all but one of these policies, the one recommending state payment of clerical salaries, would have become the law of the land.

During the height of the controversy over "The Theocratic Power," the Álvarez administration made its own move against the clergy with a decree that excluded priests and religious brothers from the body politic of the nation. According to the Plan of Ayutla, the most urgent task of the interim president was the convocation of a constitutional convention.[68] The first step in this process was the promulgation of an electoral law to provide for the election of delegates to the extraordinary congress. Prior to 1855, Catholic priests, highly educated as a class, were regularly elected to legislative positions in Mexico.[69] The *convocatoria* issued by President Álvarez's cabinet on October 16, however, excluded males under eighteen, felons, vagrants, and the clergy from all aspects of the political process.[70] Henceforth priests and members of religious orders could neither vote nor be elected to any political position. According to the French ambassador, the administration originally planned to include the military in the new law as well. But this led a certain angry general to offer his resignation, claiming that since he was not a citizen, he had neither the right nor the obligation to continue serving. Realizing the potential for disaster should this sentiment spread, Álvarez promptly removed the army from the list of proscribed classes.[71]

At the same time, other liberals urged the government to disenfranchise all "conservatives, *santanistas*, deserters, and reactionaries" from any participation in public affairs.[72]

Conservatives were outraged by this symbolic demotion of the clergy and quickly published condemnations of the new law. The newspaper *La Patria*, for example, touched off a flurry of editorials when it printed a headline declaring that, since only one of these had the right to vote in Mexico, "A Common Laborer is Worth More than an Archbishop!"[73] But liberal newspapers claimed that this "malicious exclamation" was intended to fan discord and "to make others believe that liberals disparage the clergy." Good Catholics, one editor retorted, preferred priests that administered the sacraments rather than "clergy that deliver political pronouncements." Nevertheless, *La Cruz* expanded the argument by claiming that priests in Mexico were now in the same position as slaves in the United States or pariahs in India, neither having political rights in the land of their birth. Liberals always insisted that the exclusion of clerics was justified by Christ's claim that "My kingdom is not of this world." But *La Cruz* countered that it was "for hatred of religion and not to mark out a dividing line between Church and State that certain innovators want the ministers of religion to take no part in political or civil matters." Were this not true, it claimed, the liberals would follow the logic of their position and refrain from meddling in spiritual affairs.[74] The clerical exclusion was also vehemently denounced in the pulpit as an injustice and a sign of the nefarious intentions of the new regime.[75]

In spite of this barrage of criticism, the new government made an even more controversial move against the clergy less than six weeks later. After a prolonged delay in Cuernavaca, Álvarez and his retinue had finally reached Mexico City on November 15, 1855. On their arrival, liberals staged demonstrations of support for the president, and a belated Te Deum was sung in the Metropolitan Cathedral. Five days later, the president ordered the arrest of Father Francisco Javier Miranda y Morfi for alleged antigovernment activities. Miranda, officially attached to the *sagrario* of the Puebla Cathedral, was a tireless worker on behalf of the conservative cause.[76] Ignoring his bishop's reprimands, he had remained heavily involved in politics even after the fall of Santa Anna. After the arrest at his home in Puebla, the priest was taken to Mexico City and imprisoned under armed guard at the San Hipólito barracks. In response, the Bishop of Puebla protested vehemently to the local governor for this breach of the clerical *fuero*. In addition, he complained of the unprecedented lack of respect shown toward the Church by the government's refusal to notify him in advance of its intentions toward one of his priests. But in spite of his bishop's objections, Miranda was held in custody and then deported without trial a few weeks later.[77]

Three days after Miranda's arrest, however, the real significance of the government's unusual action became clear. On November 23, 1855, Benito Pablo Juárez García, the new minister of justice and ecclesiastical affairs, issued a preliminary decree against the *fuero*. For the moment, church tribunals and courts martial could still try their own members for common crimes, but this right could be renounced by the accused if the defendant preferred to take his chances with civilian justice in any particular case.[78] Although liberals had always complained that "benefit of clergy" violated the democratic principle of equality before the law, since the fall of Santa Anna the radical press had also begun to denounce the privilege because of the alleged corruption and vice it might conceal.[79]

The Archbishop of Mexico City, Lázaro de la Garza y Ballesteros, was the first churchman to lodge an official protest against the *Ley Juárez*.[80] On November 27, 1855, he sent a letter to the minister of justice rejecting the government's decision and promising that any cleric who attempted to renounce his *fuero* would be subjected to canonical penalties. Instead of debating the merits of the law, however, he simply explained that because of the oaths taken at his episcopal consecration he was unable to consent to the elimination of this or any other ecclesiastical prerogative protected by canon law. Mexican bishops were entirely dependent on the pope's decision in this matter, he wrote, "it being impossible for us to work against the general laws of the Church, or to fulfill any orders that contradict them." In light of *puro* animus toward the papacy, the prelate's appeal to the minister's "true religiosity" and his "love and respect for the Holy See and for its venerable head, the Roman Pontiff" seems somewhat disingenuous, but his recommendation that Juárez negotiate directly with Rome was sincere. Radicals in the liberal party, however, deeply resented this suggestion. According to one report, the archbishop's letter "produced a profound commotion" in the capital, with some "fanatics" demanding his arrest and expulsion from the country.[81]

The sixty-nine-year-old archbishop, a native of El Pilón (Nueva Leon), was born in 1785. His formative years and education were therefore primarily spent in the *ancien régime*, during the waning years of the viceroyalty. Ordained a priest in 1815, Garza earned a doctorate in canon law in 1819 and a degree in civil law in 1830. After a series of administrative, teaching, and pastoral appointments, he was consecrated Bishop of Sonora in 1837. The diocese was in disrepair when he arrived, having suffered a long vacancy after the war for independence. Garza dedicated himself to its rebuilding, devoting himself especially to education, the reformation of the clergy, and the founding of a seminary for the training of new priests. Thanks to his reputation for hard work, he was chosen as the Archbishop of Mexico City in 1851. There he became renowned for the simplicity of his personal life and his generosity, donating almost all his personal resources and income to charitable projects. After the liberal ascendancy, he became equally famous for his uncompromising defense of the rights of the Church. Liberals interpreted this steadfastness as obstinacy, and even his friends recognized the limitations of his temperament. As one biographer noted, "by his habits and natural character, he did not possess the flexibility, permitting the phrase, that was necessary in order to overcome difficulties smoothly and make the concessions that his obligations allowed."[82]

But although Juárez reacted negatively to the suggestion of papal intervention, Garza's appeal to the pope should not automatically be read as further proof of clerical intransigence. Both conservatives and liberals were aware of recent negotiations between Austria and the Holy See, and of the compromises reached in other recent concordats.[83] An appeal to Rome was therefore not necessarily a claim that nothing could change in the religious situation in Mexico. Rather it represented a universal vision of the Catholic Church that prevented unilateral local modifications. It is in this sense that an article in *La Cruz* could claim that the *Ley Juárez* was a breach of international law, "in the point of introducing variations *without the consent of both parties* to that which was established with the consent and mutual accord of the Apostolic See and the government of Mexico."[84]

La Cruz dedicated numerous articles to *Ley Juárez*, whose symbolic value was ultimately far greater than its practical consequences. In the context of recent events, however, the editors were certain that the real aim of the law was not political equality. "The attacks on ecclesiastical privileges and immunities do not have any other goal but to destroy first the independence of the Church in order to later destroy the Church itself." Beginning with Martin Luther, the newspaper proclaimed, the enemies of the Church had always used similar tactics.[85] Above all, the "monstrous contradiction" between the *convocatoria* of Álvarez and the *Ley Juárez* revealed the real intentions behind the legislation. First, *La Cruz* complained, the enemies of the clergy "deprived priests of their character as citizens, excluding them from voice and vote in popular elections." Now, however, the government claimed that in a republic all citizens must be subject to the same laws and demanded that the clergy be tried in ordinary courts. But if the priest is an ordinary citizen, this article asked, why does he not have the same civil rights as his fellows? If the spiritual nature Christ's kingdom excluded priests from mundane politics, why were they being submitted to secular judgments? "Either concede to the clergy the vote in elections or let them retain the *fuero*," the journal demanded.[86]

In spite of widespread liberal support, the promulgation of the *Ley Juárez* created tensions in other segments of Mexican society as well. The Supreme Court, for instance, which had not been consulted on the measure, lodged a protest against its provisions and declared itself in recess until the legal issues related to the changes could be resolved. In reply, Álvarez simply replaced the nine defiant justices with more compliant jurists. The measure also served to alienate a substantial portion of the military from the new revolutionary regime. Above all, according to one observer, "the Catholic people that composed the majority of the country believed that they detected in that law the first of others against Catholicism and showed themselves highly alarmed."[87]

A petition signed by twelve hundred laymen in Puebla on November 30, 1855, seems to support the editor's assertion that a "large part of society clamored against this law."[88] Puebla was well known as a conservative and Catholic city, so a negative response to the new law there was not surprising. But the petition also represents the skillful use of political action in the service of the conservative/religious cause. Furthermore, it shows an acute awareness of the power of the media to shape public perceptions and political events. In fact, popular petitions were the most direct form of civic participation in Mexico at this time, since elections rarely reflected the will of any majority.[89] The *poblano* petition also indicates that, initially at least, citizens were still hopeful that the fall of Santa Anna might bring about a more democratic and lawful regime. "We that subscribe to this protest had believed, lamenting in silence, that the evils in our unfortunate country were produced in great part by the abuses of the press," the petition began, "We consoled ourselves in considering that the multitude of immoral and irreligious writings were viewed with horror by the greater part of Mexicans." Initially, the petitioners claimed, they were unwilling to believe that the government was involved in this "merciless war" against the Church and its ministers. But the promulgation of the *Ley Juárez* crushed this fond illusion. "It is not hard to see that these dispositions attack the immunity and privileges of the ministers of Jesus Christ very directly," they argued, "and any consent to this attack turns one into an enemy of the Church."[90]

As in Guadalajara, the identification of the priesthood with the Church itself appears as the most salient difference between conservative and liberal approaches to this religious question.

Unwilling to consent to what they considered an assault on their religion, these citizens made a "solemn protest" against the new law as well as a declaration of obedience to the "dispositions of the Holy See." At the same time, however, they insisted that their protest was not an act of insubordination against the government, which they would continue to respect and obey. On the contrary, if "sovereignty resides in the people; if those that govern in a republic are only representatives or empowered by the people . . . then we do not believe that our leaders will charge us with a crime when we declare our will to them." These principles, they asserted, gave them the right, if not the obligation, to voice their concerns to their "representatives." Some inhabitants of Mexico City, however, chose a less civil way to express their displeasure with the *Ley Juárez*. On December 3, the walls of the capital were again plastered with large signs reading "Long live religion!" and "Long live the archbishop!" or alternatively, "Death to Álvarez!" and "Death to the *puros*!"[91]

At this point, some moderate liberals decided to take advantage of the widespread discontent generated by the government's recent actions. Manuel Doblado, the *moderado* governor of Guanajuato, was one of the signatories of the Plan of Ayutla at the Lagos Convention. Nevertheless, he revolted against the Álvarez government on December 6, demanding the installation of General Comonfort as president. "Before seeing the Plan of Ayutla shattered by those who call themselves its supporters, and before consenting to the breaking of the religious bond, the only element that unites all Mexicans," he declared, "I have resolved to resist and to pit the resources of this state against that authority that today is found in conflict with the principal classes that form our society." Just as in 1833 and 1847, he explained, the revolution was being hijacked by extremists and falling into "the excesses of libertinage and demagoguery." The recent laws issued by the government were proof that "under the pretext of reforming the clergy, it is trying to introduce into the republic an even more dangerous Protestantism, no matter how it is disguised."[92] Although Doblado's revolt probably owed as much to personal political considerations as religious conviction, the sentiments he expressed highlight the effectiveness of Catholic rhetoric in the wake of *Ley Juárez*. His call to arms, for example, assumes that a substantial part of the population was already convinced that the government's actions constituted an attack on the Church and as such posed a serious threat to the nation.[93]

Doblado's ambitious revolt was ultimately a part of the ongoing power struggle within the liberal party, but the *puros* were quick to blame its outbreak on the clergy. After all, his political plan included the promise to maintain Catholicism as the official and exclusive religion of Mexico. It is true that Doblado had been in contact with Bishop Munguía, whose diocese of Michoacán included the State of Guanajuato.[94] But although other bishops, including Espinosa in neighboring Jalisco, expressed vague support for his ideals, when solicited they all refused to contribute ecclesiastical funds to his military campaign. Nevertheless, Degollado, the governor of Jalisco, declared that the clergy were personally responsible for the insurrection. According to a declaration of the Guadalajara City Council, Doblado had been "seduced by the glitter of the gold with which the anarchical clerical class abounds." In the pages of *La Revolución* Cruz-Aedo added, "The clergy and the army, that double monster bristling with aspergillums and bayonets, are the authors, the means and the end of the counter-revolution." In fact, he alleged, Doblado's "theocratic-military" movement was the direct result of that "seditious and rebellious" protest lodged by the Archbishop of Mexico City against the *Ley Juárez*.[95]

From the conservative point of view, the anticlerical orientation of the Ayutla Revolution was revealed almost as soon as the new political order began. In particular, protected by Governor Degollado in Guadalajara, Cruz-Aedo and the "Student Phalanx" had been able to express the most extreme anticlerical sentiments. The early actions of the Álvarez administration, including the *convocatorio* and the *Ley Juárez*, also seemed to reflect a similar orientation. Perhaps as much as the measures themselves, the preemptory fashion of their implementation, without negotiation or even advance warning to the ecclesiastical establishment, indicated a new adversarial relationship between the government and the Church. Above all, the heated rhetoric generated during the first few months of the liberal regime was already encouraging many Mexican Catholics to adopt extreme positions that they may not have otherwise considered. Although the Doblado revolt eventually forced Álvarez to resign as president of the Republic, the spiral of ideological polarization had already begun.

CHAPTER 3

La Cruz and the Formation of the Catholic Reaction

Although numerous national, and even international, forces contributed to the unfolding of the Reforma, the central conflict expressed itself most saliently as a clash between two incompatible religious ideals, an increasingly militant anticlericalism and an emerging ultramontane expression of the Catholic faith. Understandably, the Roman Catholic clergy was unwilling to relinquish its power and social influence without a struggle. Priests thundered against liberal reforms from the pulpit, and the Mexican hierarchy issued a record number of official protests and pastoral letters defending the church's traditional prerogatives. But opposition to the Reforma also relied on a more self-consciously Catholic laity in Mexico, permanently alienated from the revoltionary project of the liberal reformers. To a large extent, the diffusion of this new religious consciousness was the work of a handful of Catholic laymen who wrote pamphlets and published newspapers to combat the spread of anticlerical ideas. In a series of celebrated polemics with the liberal press, these writers challenged liberal assumptions about society, the Church, and even the meaning of modernity. In the process, they also helped to relocate the social and ideological boundaries of the Catholic Church in Mexico.

The active participation of laymen in the field of religious apologetics was another example of Catholic innovation in the face of nineteenth-century social realities.[1] In the anticlerical atmosphere of the era, reliance on lay apologists was something of a practical necessity for the Church. In fact, it was Pope Pius IX who recommended that bishops "exhort men of outstanding talent and sound doctrine to publish appropriate writings with which they might enlighten the minds of the people and dissipate the darkness of creeping errors." In particular, he suggested that bishops encourage those who, "animated by a Catholic spirit and educated in literature and learning, will endeavor to write books and publish magazines."[2] Such an appeal, by its very nature, reflected a new appreciation for the importance of forming public opinion in a democratic society. One of the best examples of the type of journalist project the pope had in mind was *L'Univers* (1843), produced by a French layman, Louis Veuillot.[3]

In Mexico, two "Catholic" newspapers appeared briefly after the Mexican-American War, their religious self-designation a response to the crisis created by the congressional proposal to introduce public worship for Protestants in 1848. But after the toleration bill was defeated, the embryonic religious press abandoned its polemic focus. *La Voz de la Religión* (The voice of religion), for instance, advertised itself as a religious, social, scientific, literary, and fine arts magazine.[4] After the foundation of the conservative party in 1849, its newspapers monopolized the anti-liberal discourse until the end of the Santa Anna regime. The presses of *El Universal*, founded by Lucas Alamán, were destroyed by a liberal mob on August 13, 1855.[5] But *La Voz del Pueblo* in Guadalajara and *El Omnibus* both survived the dictator's fall, and were joined by two other conservative journals, *La Verdad* (The truth) and *La Patria* (The fatherland), before the end of the year.[6] These four journals were sympathetic to the Church and promoted themselves as defenders of religion, but this was only one part of their larger political agenda.

In the 1850s newspapers still served as the central vehicle for expressing political and philosophical ideas.[7] At this time, "the press was not conceived as an enterprise or a business, but as a mouthpiece for those who struggled for an ideology or represented power."[8] And the Reforma, in particular, "was a period of major periodical production."[9] In this context, freedom of the press was an article of faith for liberals, and the Plan of Ayutla specifically condemned Santa Anna for his "obvious disdain of public opinion whose voice was suffocated beforehand by means of hateful and tyrannical restrictions imposed upon the press."[10] But these restrictions fell along with the dictator, and for a brief period Mexicans enjoyed complete liberty in publishing. Liberal organs, both radical and moderate, proliferated rapidly after the triumph of the Ayutla Revolution and soon heavily outnumbered conservative publications, which were concentrated in the capital.[11] Now uncensored, it immediately released a flood of attacks on the privileges, lifestyle, and political influence of the clergy.[12]

The first periodical in Mexico dedicated exclusively to the defense of the Catholic faith was the weekly journal *La Cruz*, published continuously between November 1, 1855, and July 25, 1858. Produced in Mexico City, it was apparently the brainchild of Clemente de Jesús Munguía, the foremost intellectual in the Mexican episcopate and the Bishop of Michoacán since 1851. According to its masthead, it was "established *ex profeso* in order to spread orthodox doctrines and vindicate them against dominant errors." In the prospectus of the first issue, Munguía declared that since the Church was now under constant attack, it was the duty of all Catholics to prepare themselves for ideological and moral combat. The choice of the journal's title, *La Cruz* (The cross), was particularly significant in this regard. The cross signified both the person of Jesus Christ and the crusading spirit, a dual focus also represented by its motto, "*Fides, Fidelitas.*"[13] For both practical and strategic reasons, Munguía handed over its direction to one of his lay collaborators, José Joaquín Pesado y Pérez, two months after its inauguration.[14]

In many ways, Pesado's life reflected the ideological evolution of many of the young men of his generation. Born in Orizaba in 1801, he was raised in a traditional atmosphere by his mother and educated exclusively at home. Pesado's father had died suddenly when he was only seven and his mother remarried three years later. But his doting stepfather was killed in 1811 by Father Hidalgo's insurgents, who mistook the fair-skinned *hacendado* for a Spaniard. As a teenager, Pesado joined the men of his town in a popular Franciscan *cofradía* (confraternity), even wearing the habit of the order in funeral processions for his confreres. But in the political excitement that followed Mexican independence, the twenty-year-old embraced republicanism, federalism, and the other liberal ideas of the day. In 1833, he was elected to the legislature of the State of Veracruz, during the most radical phase of the Gómez Farías administration. Veracruz enthusiastically supported the reforms emanating from the capital, and at Pesado's suggestion, introduced additional restrictions on religious orders in the state. Acting as lieutenant governor in March of 1834, Pesado personally ordered the closure of Franciscan and Augustinian houses, including the convent of San Juan de Gracia in Orizaba. When the religious were allowed to return after Santa Anna's coup three months later, the population celebrated by breaking the windows of Pesado's home and shouting, "Down with the [Masonic] lodge of Don Joaquín Pesado!"[15]

Temporarily out of politics after Santa Anna's return to power, Pesado nevertheless continued his political activism for a time. He was co-editor of the liberal newspaper *La Oposición* (The opposition), until the government shut it down in November 1835.[16] Then, in 1836, he became a member of the new literary salon at the Academia de San Juan de Letrán. The membership of this group, a veritable who's who of nineteenth-century Mexican letters, met weekly for the next twenty years to share their literary compositions and discuss the principles of art and culture. Along with his poetry, written in a neo-classical style, one of Pesado's earliest offerings was an anticlerical novel entitled *El inquisidor de México* (The inquisitor of Mexico).[17] In this setting, Pesado honed his literary style and became acquainted with characters of all political persuasions, many of whom would play an important role in the political future of the nation. It was also here that he first encountered the formidable priest Clemente Munguía.

In 1838, Pesado signaled a modification of his political ideas by accepting a cabinet post in the administration of the centralist president, Anastasio Bustamante.[18] At about the same time, his religious opinions also changed dramatically. This change of heart may be connected to his intellectual contacts in the Academia, or the reasons may have been more personal, such as the dream that he later described in a poem entitled "La Visión." In these verses he recounted a nocturnal visit from his deceased mother, who chided him for wandering from the principles of his earlier religious upbringing. "Repent, my dear son," this messenger from beyond the grave pleaded, "my cold lips recall your former lessons. Blessed will you be if you put them into practice, but woe to you if you forget my words!"[19] In any event, at the age of thirty-eight, Pesado joined the growing ranks of those disillusioned with liberal political projects and disturbed by the growing secularization of Mexican society.

After his conversion, Pesado remained a member of numerous intellectual and literary associations but also began to cultivate relationships with the pious minorities within each group. In the Academia, he gravitated toward Manuel Eulogio Carpio, a renowned physician and poet, who shared his interest in Church history, Catholic mysticism, and the Bible. These enthusiasms were reflected in their writings from this period, which were saturated with religious and biblical themes.[20] During the 1840s, in a somewhat unique manifestation of religious sociability, the two men even constructed an elaborate cardboard and paper mâché model of Jerusalem in a spare room in Pesado's home, where they delivered detailed archeological tours of the Holy City to astounded visitors. Guillermo Prieto's memoirs also provide an interesting insight into the atmosphere at the Academia during this period, including the impression made by the religiosity of Pesado and Carpio. Although he was highly critical of Pesado's style, he admits that the humble character of both men made a profound impression on the other members of the group. "The incessant reading of the holy fathers and the mystics affected [Pesado's] conversation so that one almost caught glimpses of David, St. Teresa and St. John of Cross," he recalled. [21]

Over the years, Pesado became friends with other conservative writers who also shared his religious ideals. During the 1840s Pesado and Carpio became members of El Ateneo Mexicano, a cultural center where they associated with Lucas Alamán, the chief theorist of the conservative party; Vicente Segura Argüelles, a conservative publisher; and Juan Rodríguez de San Miguel, who wrote an important defense of the clergy in 1848.[22] They also met regularly with other like-minded individuals in the famous library of José María Andrade, on whose presses La Cruz was later produced. In addition, this group included other writers such as Alejandro Arango y Escandón and the poet José Sebastián Segura.[23] Another Pesado protégé and a fellow poet was his lifelong friend and future biographer, José María Roa Bárcena. Born in 1827, the self-educated Roa Bárcena was the youngest member of the group.[24] Ultimately, this informal network became an important vehicle for "Catholic Action" when many of Pesado's associates became contributors to La Cruz. Although Pesado was recognized as the central figure in its production, more than a dozen other laymen also produced articles for the journal, and another fifty submitted literary compositions for inclusion in its pages.[25] During the critical years of its publication, Pesado, Carpio, and the celebrated jurist, José Bernardo Couto, met every night to discuss the events of the day and plan an appropriate response.[26]

Unsurprisingly, Couto's political and spiritual evolution paralleled that of Pesado since they both shared similar reactions to the disappointments of Mexican history. Fast friends and former colleagues in the legislature of Veracruz, Pesado and Couto were also first cousins.[27] Like Pesado, Couto had been an ardent liberal in his youth but became disillusioned with politics over time. Both men were also deeply affected by Mexico's defeat in 1847. In fact, Couto was one of the three delegates chosen to negotiate the terms of surrender. He signed the humiliating Treaty of Guadalupe-Hidalgo on February 2, 1848, he later explained, only to assure the survival of his country and prevent even more extensive territorial acquisitions by the United States. The two friends became even more depressed when this trauma was followed by news of the bloody revolutions in Europe in 1848. According to Andrea Acle Aguirre, at this point "Couto and Pesado advanced to a moralistic interpretation of the national disaster."[28] This means that they blamed Mexico's failure on its flirting with alien philosophies and believed that a return to traditional faith and values was the only hope for its future.

Munguía's choice of Pesado as his successor to run the magazine was a fortunate one. As a former associate of the Academia, Munguía was well aware of Pesado's intellectual capabilities. Pesado himself did not hesitate to take up his pen in defense of the Catholic faith, since by this time he was convinced that the liberal ascendancy was a lethal threat to both the Church and the nation. In addition, he wished to atone for his own former anticlerical activities, and "to give more solemn testimony to the rectification of his own [ideas]."[29] Pesado was also able to enlist collaborators from among his former colleagues in literary and cultural societies for his new apostolate. Furthermore, as literary figures, these recruits could draw on their extensive journalistic and publishing experiences for the production of *La Cruz*.

The mission of *La Cruz*, to preserve the Catholic faith in Mexico, was reflected in every aspect of the journal, from the content of its articles to its strategic design. In order to establish a firm philosophical foundation for its positions, every issue opened with a section called "Esposición" that dealt with "those points of doctrine that seem to us most urgently required by the present circumstances." "The lack of solid religious instruction, even in the comfortable classes, is one of the evils that afflicts our society," the editors complained, "and thus we never lack topics for our exposition section."[30] After the first eight issues, Pesado was the author of almost all the essays in this section. These covered a wide range of topics, from proofs for the existence of God and the divine creation of the world, to the immortality of the soul, the nature of original sin, the process of redemption, and the foundation of the Church. Here the principal errors of rationalist philosophy were also exposed, especially those related to the structuring of society. As Roa Bárcena later explained, this section offered Mexican readers "a complete course in Christian philosophy."[31]

Following "Esposición" was another regular feature entitled "Controversia." Less theoretical, it sought to apply Christian principles to the social and political problems of the day. Because it addressed specific issues as they arose on the contemporary scene, "Controversia" probably had a more immediate impact in the ideological war against liberalism. For instance, Catholic positions on questions of the clerical *fuero*, disentailment of ecclesiastical property, and religious toleration were all developed in this section. Again, Pesado produced the bulk of the articles under this rubric, although other writers made occasional contributions. Since the culture war in Mexico was analogous to that in Europe during this period, translated works by European Catholic polemicists were also often serialized here. For example, in the face of the growing number of attacks on religious orders, *La Cruz* ran, in twenty-five installments, a translation of Clemente Grandcourt's monumental work, *The Influence of Religious Orders on Society and the Necessity of their Reestablishment in France.*[32]

Following the apologetic and polemic sections, each issue of *La Cruz* contained a regular segment called "Literatura y Variedades." Although this segment ostensibly focused on the arts, it also had a serious didactic purpose. It usually included inspirational religious poetry, compositions in the neo-classical or romantic style, often by Pesado, Carpio, or Arango y Escandon. There were also weekly installments of novels with a religious or moral theme. Although Mexican writers were preferred, at times other European authors were also introduced in its pages. In fact, in this section the journal often produced the first Spanish translations of significant French, German, and Italian works for a Mexican audience.[33]

A good example of the literary strategy utilized by *La Cruz* was a novel by Roa Bárcena that appeared just after the promulgation of the 1857 Constitution. On the surface, *La Quinta Modelo* (The model manor) is a tale about the ruin of a family whose head had abandoned the Catholic faith.[34] In reality, it was a satire on the condition of Mexico itself in 1857, exposing the underlying causes and ultimate consequences of the new liberal regime from a conservative point of view.[35] The novel tells the story of thirty-eight-year-old Gaspar Rodríguez, a radical landowner who exemplifies the excesses of the *puros* in Mexico. Naturally, given his hatred of the Church, Gaspar writes anticlerical articles for the newspapers on all the hot topics of the day. But when Santa Anna exiles him for his political views, he tours the major cities of the United States and becomes smitten with Anglo culture. After the fall of the dictator, he is elected (by fraud) to the constituent congress, where he presents the US Constitution and Rousseau's *Social Contract* as models for Mexico's future.[36] On the floor of the chamber, he also delivers an obvious parody of Cruz-Aedo's Independence Day rant. But after his radical agenda is thwarted by *moderados*, he decides to implement his ideals on his own estates instead. There, the land is divided, work is made optional, and a school is opened for the peons. Of course, Gaspar blames the inevitable failures of his commune on religion, so the hacienda's chapel is wrecked, and the chaplain expelled. Ultimately, he even exiles his reactionary wife and daughter from the estate. He is supported only by his teenage son, Enrique, who is placed in charge of the school where he teaches atheism and communism to the reluctant students.

Throughout the novel, Roa Bárcena caricatured the *puros* and their agenda through the attitudes and behavior of Gaspar.[37] At the same time, Enrique represented the much-feared moral corruption and tragic fate of Mexican youth under liberal ideas. For example, at the age of fourteen Enrique had been enrolled in a liberal school where the boys mainly learned to drink, smoke, gamble, and swear. Here the students also spoke only French, since they were taught to despise Spanish, although Gaspar himself preferred English, "the language of the future." In the climax of the story, Gaspar loses his mind when he finds the body of his son, killed by one of his own henchmen during a card game. The story concludes with the return of the women, the priest, and the overseer who restore order and tradition. In this scenario, only the radical Gaspar, his wits restored, does not live happily ever after, perhaps a poignant echo of the restoration fantasies harbored by conservatives before their defeat in the Three Years War.[38]

In addition to literature, per se, other educational items appeared in the "Literature and Varieties" section as well. There were historical and liturgical studies, biographies of important Catholic figures in Mexico's history, as well as architectural essays on great Mexican churches, complete with lithographic illustrations. Because of these features, *La Cruz* has been described as "the most attractive literary magazine of its time."[39] In keeping with the purpose of the newspaper, this celebration of Mexico's cultural patrimony was primarily intended to emphasize the link between the Catholic Church and national identity. The last section of *La Cruz* was dedicated to "Noticias," a summary of edifying Catholic news from around the nation and the world. Even here, every item was carefully chosen for its polemic potential. For instance, reports of the mistreatment of Catholic minorities in countries like the United States or Great Britain were particularly prized as conclusive evidence of the dangers of religious pluralism. Stories of the conversion of prominent Protestants were also popular since they exemplified the appeal of the Catholic faith even in so-called progressive countries. Finally, each issue closed with a weekly schedule of the major religious festivals and devotions taking place in and around Mexico City. A practical calendar for the observant Catholic, this feature also served as an endorsement of particular cultural and religious activities by the editors of the journal.[40]

Ironically, although explicitly dedicated to defending the Church in Mexico, the religious image reflected in the pages of *La Cruz* would probably have been unfamiliar to many Mexican believers, especially among the rural masses. While the journal frequently praised the piety of the common people, in reality, it completely ignored many of their characteristic beliefs and devotional practices. Special features celebrating the liturgical seasons, for instance, always focused on the artistic beauty of the official liturgy in the great churches of the capital rather than the less edifying popular customs connected with the holidays. Authorized devotions such as Eucharistic adoration and the rosary were promoted along with the official sanctoral cycle, but no notice was given to the myriad of competing folk rituals. "Literatura" regularly included poems on biblical themes and elegant verses dedicated to the Virgin of Guadalupe or to the Immaculate Conception, yet no mention was ever made of the miraculous or apotropaic attributes of other local images and shrines.[41] Conservatives were always insistent that the Catholic faith was a unifying bond among Mexicans of all classes, and at a broad level this was true. However, *La Cruz* was also part of an elite discourse, and its presentation stressed a refined and somewhat romantic representation of Catholicism. Obviously, this was in part because the intended audience for this vision of Catholic life was the educated classes, whose opinions carried the most political and social weight.[42]

Today, it is not possible to determine the exact circulation of *La Cruz*, but the remarkable number of surviving copies suggests that it was quite large.[43] According to its editors, the periodical circulated "in every corner of the republic and is requested and read with appreciation by every class of persons, even those that would seem to be most antithetical to it because of their political ideas."[44] Judging from the amount of liberal criticism it generated, its impact must have been substantial. "They (conservatives) wrote long articles in order to prove the divinity of the Catholic religion," Vigil later complained, but their real purpose was "to fuel the bonfire of passions" against liberal ideas.[45] In his foundational history of Mexican politics, Justo Sierra also credited "the eloquence of the distinguished writer José Joaquín Pesado and the dry and precise logic of Bishop Munguía" with stirring up "terrible polemics" after the promulgation of the 1857 Constitution.[46]

Pesado himself was viciously attacked in a satirical play produced by liberals during the height of the Reforma War, where he was presented as one of the ringleaders of a secret conservative conspiracy. In one scene, Pesado brags that his articles in *La Cruz* are worth much more than all the secret meetings he attends. "By stirring up the worst emotions of the masses and turning them into fanatics," his character declares, "I serve my party more than any other clerical busybody."[47] This play is also revealing for its depiction of a fictitious conservative cabal, reflecting liberal suspicions that their enemies were organized into a kind of anti-Masonic lodge. Liberals even claimed to have discovered its actual rulebook, which they published along with annotations and commentary. As one editor insisted, this document confirmed that conservatives were more of a *cofradía* than a political party.[48]

Although its enemies always considered *La Cruz* a tool of the conservatives, its editors insisted that they did not "take the uniform of any party."[49] Truth, justice, and decency were their only political opinions, they proclaimed, and their only enemies were anticlericals and the impious.[50] But even the editors recognized that the newspaper's religious message had inevitable political implications. "There is not an error in politics that does not emanate from some religious error," Pesado wrote, "nor is there any political error that does not disfigure the idea of God in the human mind."[51] Or as Munguía more succinctly put it, "At the heart of every political question, one always encounters a theological one."[52] Obviously, many links also existed between the newspaper and the membership and ideals of the conservative party. Indeed, one of the chief dynamics of the Reforma was the collapse of a meaningful distinction between "Catholic" and "conservative," since anyone who defended the Church automatically found themselves aligned with the so-called "clerical party." Nevertheless, where religious issues formed the central core of an individual's political concerns, even party affiliation can be seen as just one strategy among many in the defense of a more spiritual ideal.

Along with its reputation as an organ of the conservative party, *La Cruz* was also denounced as the work of reactionary priests, even after Munguía was no longer associated with its production. When it first appeared, remembered Roa Bárcena, its opponents "were determined to dress and decorate the editors of *La Cruz* with cassocks and miters."[53] It was simply inconceivable to many liberals that laymen could display such theological erudition or express such unequivocal support for the clergy. Later, when a law was passed that required every published article to carry its author's signature, critics were shocked to find the names of some of Mexico's most respected literati in the pages of the journal.[54] Afterward, its opponents still insisted that the paper was secretly funded by the clergy, but this was a charge that the editors consistently denied. In fact, the editors boasted that the large number of subscriptions easily covered all their expenses, so that there was no need nor desire for any clerical funding.[55]

In the final analysis, *La Cruz* was founded in response to the anticlerical challenge and this reality colored all the positions that the journal adopted. In particular, its editors were anxious to demonstrate that authentic Catholic ecclesiology preempted the reformers' project by undermining its epistemological claims. It is therefore not surprising that the first edition of "Exposition" addressed the all-important question of religious authority. In an article subtitled "Teaching Authority of the Catholic Church," Munguía sought to alert the Christian community to the dangers posed by self-appointed liberal reformers posing as Catholics. Unlike the eighteenth-century philosophes, he explained, Mexican liberals did not dare to deny the existence of God, the divinity of Christ, or the authority of the Bible openly. Instead, they had "changed their strategy and placed themselves under the Christian banner in order to destroy the reign of Jesus Christ." "This class of adversary is more difficult to combat," he declared, "because they are inside the house; they pretend to profess Catholicism and they present themselves as ardently desirous of returning to primitive times."[56]

According to Munguía, the Church's monopoly on religious truth granted it immunity from rationalist criticism and secular interference. Only the Catholic hierarchy had the right to govern and reform the Church, he explained, because Christ himself had given to Peter and the apostles, and to their successors, his own divine authority. They alone were "sent" to teach and preach, to speak authoritatively on matters of dogma and morals, and to explain the true meaning of sacred scripture. In spite of the human failings of its representatives, he explained, Christianity's divine mandate was the guarantee of the dogmatic authority of its ministers. It was therefore illegitimate for liberals or any others to attempt to use the power of the state to reform the Church. In response to rationalist critics like Cruz-Aedo, Munguía insisted that the only "true Catholics" were those who understood the Gospels and the holy scriptures as the Church explained and taught them, and who recognized that there could be no Church without the priesthood and no priesthood without the pope. To reject these truths, he declared, was to "deny Jesus Christ and his religion" and to identify oneself as a Protestant, an apostate, an infidel, a materialist, and an unbeliever. Although they might claim to be Catholics, he warned, by relying on their own opinions in matters of faith, liberals joined those other apostates who had placed themselves outside the body of the Church.

Although the editors of *La Cruz* may have preferred to contain the clerical issue within the theological context of Catholic ecclesiology, their opponents preferred a less theoretical approach to the topic. Liberal anticlerical rhetoric was focused on what they considered to be concrete manifestations of the "clerical problem," and *La Cruz* eventually had to confront these charges. The first installment of "Controversy," in fact, was a reaction to the anticlerical tirades of the Guadalajara Falange. "In civic discourses, in articles in periodicals, and even in documents that call themselves official," it began, "we see the spirit of impiety raising its head in terrible and threatening posture, taking advantage of the unfortunate crisis that has enveloped the country." Under the cloak of reformism, this impiety "thundered furiously against the popes, exaggerated the vices of the Catholic priesthood, lavishly praised its persecutors, and called it the enemy of civilization and progress and the friend of tyranny and of ignorance, and finally attributing to it all the disgraces that the world has suffered, and particularly that has been suffered by Mexico." The author of this piece (probably Munguía) admitted that it was possible that "the corruption of the century has penetrated at times even into the sanctuary." It was simply not possible to deny that some unworthy priests existed. But the faults of a few all-too-human clerics did not justify the hatred heaped upon the entire clergy by their enemies. The real goal of liberal anticlerical rhetoric was to destroy Catholicism in Mexico, he wrote, "and for that reason even good Catholic priests are smeared and vilified."[57]

The intended target of this article became even clearer in the next issue, when *La Cruz* responded directly to *La Revolutión's* inflammatory series, "The Theocratic Power."[58] In contrast to the brash and aggressive tone of their opponents, the editors adopted a modest posture from the beginning of their response. After considering all the slander hurled against the clergy by Cruz-Adeo and his colleagues, they explained, they considered abandoning "such a distressing task." But in spite of the "bitter conviction" that their "weak voice" would not be able "to quench that tumultuous clamor that has been raised against the sanctuary and its ministers," the editors sallied forth, relying on the power of Christ's light to "dispel the darkness of error."[59]

Perhaps in imitation of Cruz-Aedo's rhetorical technique, the editors began their defense of the clergy with an appeal to history, comparing *La Revolución's* position with that of other heretical reformers over the centuries. "Since the time of the life of Jesus Christ," they began, "it was the tactic of the enemies of the Church to attack the conduct of the ministers in order to tear down the holy edifice." Then, as now, these foes claimed that they themselves were religious, that they were enemies only of abuse. But *La Cruz* denounced as disingenuous the liberal disclaimer that no harm was intended toward the Catholic faith. In fact, it claimed, the articles displayed "a profound spirit of hatred toward the clergy and Catholic worship, a critical spirit toward religion and little respect for society." Strategically, none of the specific complaints against the clergy made in "The Theocratic

Power" were addressed directly and the sixteen-point liberal plan, with which everyone was already familiar, was simply summarized as "tyrannical, anti-social, unjust, and sacrilegious."

According to *La Cruz*, the true intentions of the authors of "The Theocratic Power" were revealed by their reference to the glories of the French Revolution. In particular, the journal attacked *La Revolución* directly for its approval of the French triumphs over the theocratic power" in 1789. By praising the French Revolution, Vigil and Cruz-Aedo may have only intended to celebrate the secularization of French society and the elevation of rationalism to the status of state religion. But the specter of the Terror, with its frenzy of bloody persecutions, still haunted Catholics on both sides of the Atlantic. That is why *La Cruz* denounced all those who, because of audacity or ignorance, had dared, "to raise this execrable idol in the midst of a Catholic nation."[60] Radicals such as the members of the Falange, the journal implied, were awaiting an opportunity to unleash a similar holocaust in Mexico.

In the context of this rebuttal, *La Cruz* also articulated a clear position on the pressing question of ecclesiastical reform. According to "Dominant Errors," the authentic Catholic position rested on three theological truths. First, "the holiness of the Catholic religion is independent of the conduct of its ministers." This axiom, stretching back to the Donatist controversy of the fourth century, was an essential—and handy—element of orthodox ecclesiology.[61] Secondly, "one could not attack the priesthood without attacking the Catholic faith itself." According to Catholic teaching, the hierarchical and sacramental nature of the Church made its mission inseparable from the role and function of its ministers. This claim helps explain the Church's persistent rejection of the distinction that liberal polemicists tried to posit between the clergy and the Catholic faith. The final and most important point followed from the first two principles: "all reforms that are attempted without the authority of the Church are wicked."[62] By reasserting the illegitimacy of secular interference, this third point sought to preempt the type of forced overhaul of the Mexican Church that these reformers envisioned. These three pillars, as enumerated by *La Cruz*, were the foundation of the orthodox critique not only of "The Theocratic Power," but of the entire liberal anticlerical program.

The response of *La Cruz* to "The Theocratic Power" immediately established its reputation as the champion of Catholic orthodoxy in Mexico. But just one week later the editors became embroiled in an even more important controversy, one that was destined to become the longest and most celebrated in the journal's thirty-two-month career. This polemic began in response to an article called "State of the Republic" written by Juan Bautista Morales. Whereas writings by members of the Falange reflected the ideas of the younger, more radical elements of the liberal party, the series by the venerable Morales represented the thinking of the more numerous *moderados*. At sixty-seven years of age, Morales also symbolized political experience and the long liberal tradition in Mexico.[63] His first article, which appeared on October 6, 1855, in Mexico City's premier liberal newspaper, *El Siglo Diez y Nueve*, inaugurated an exchange that would continue to have ramifications even beyond his death on July 29 in the following year. Although many newspapers became involved in the crucial debate, *La Cruz* was recognized as the premier defender of the conservative Catholic position.[64]

Morales, a native of Guanajuato, had a long and illustrious career in Mexican politics. He had been a supporter of independence and a federalist opposed to the monarchy of Iturbide in 1821. Because of his influential writings during the *patronato* controversy, in 1835 he was appointed to the chair of canon law at the College of San Ildefonso. Even more significantly, in that year he also wrote his famous "Dissertation against Religious Tolerance" to combat the writings of Vicente Rocafuerte, the anticlerical ex-president of Ecuador living in exile in Mexico at the time. Morales became a magistrate of the Supreme Court in 1837, and its president in 1850, although Santa Anna relieved him of this post in 1853. At one time he was co-editor of *La Voz de Religión*, and he was also a long-time contributor to *El Siglo Diez y Nueve*. Ironically, in 1835 Morales had attacked Rocafuerte's *Essay on Religious Toleration*, which presented the United States as the ideal country on Earth and asserted that Protestants were always more industrious and richer than Catholics.[65] Twenty years later, in the aftermath of Mexico's humiliating defeat by the United States, Morales had reversed his earlier position.

Because they reflected more moderate sentiments, the positions taken by Morales were perhaps even more threatening to the conservative cause than the crass anticlericalism of radicals like Cruz-Aedo. First, in his "State of the Republic" Morales criticized the clergy based on what he saw as the practical consequences of their political behavior. He was disturbed, he claimed, by the tendency of the clergy to advance issues relating to their own interests as if they were dogmatic truths. This led him to enter the current debate, in spite of a certain anxiety about addressing sensitive religious topics, "not because of what might upset men, but what might, without being intended, offend God." Although still a practicing Roman Catholic,

Morales nevertheless presented three propositions that were highly insulting to many of his co-religionists. First, he candidly declared, "it is an undeniable fact that the Catholic countries are the most backward in all areas." In Mexico this meant that many people believed that in order to be materially successful they must renounce the Catholic faith, he explained. "Wanting therefore to better their fortune and that of their compatriots, they not only become unbelievers, but desire that everyone else does too in order to be happy in this life." This was the how the antireligious spirit had become a political platform in Mexico, he concluded. In his second proposition he blamed the clergy for this state of affairs, stating, "it seems that ecclesiastics have been born exclusively in order to serve as vassals of despotism and to preach and sustain despotism." The only remedy for this situation, he exclaimed in his final point, was for the clergy to "abjure despotism and tyranny and to unite themselves with liberals." Otherwise, Mexico, like other Catholic countries, would always lag behind. "Are the Catholic peoples perhaps condemned to be the dregs of the human race?" he wondered.[66]

For Mexican liberals, the economic disparity between the US and Mexico had to be addressed in light of the debacle of the recent war. In general, Morales explained, he was profoundly disturbed by the economic position of Hispanic countries compared with that of the Anglo-Saxon world. For example, British businessmen and investors had replaced Spanish merchants after independence and now dominated the business and commerce sectors throughout the country. As in the rest of Latin America, signs of ostentatious British wealth, protected by diplomatic concessions, were evident everywhere. Many Mexican elites were also aware of the historical theory recently articulated by Thomas Babington Macaulay, who identified material progress exclusively with Protestantism.[67] But while enthusiasm for the ideals and institutions of their northern neighbor was at an all-time high among Mexican liberals, conservatives dreaded further US political and cultural hegemony over Mexico. Many were even convinced that the liberals wanted to see Mexico entirely annexed by its former enemy. Indeed, among a few liberals "sentiment in favor of a foreign protectorate surfaced as part of post defeat disillusionment."[68] Persistent rumors of government plans to hand the nation over to the United States probably explain why in his later remarks Morales emphasized British rather than American achievements as the model that Mexico should follow.[69]

Unlike his more radical colleagues, Morales did not harbor any dogmatic animosity or personal resentments toward the clergy. Nevertheless, the second pillar of Morales's argument was an attempt to demonstrate a connection between clerical political influence and the problem of chronic underdevelopment in Catholic countries. The alleged clerical support for despots was a common anticlerical theme, Morales noted, because religious display was always more extravagant under despotic governments. Although this hardly proved that "ecclesiastics have been born exclusively in order to serve as vassals of despotism," this sentiment would have resonated with all those who suffered under the final Santa Anna administration and resented his support for and from the Church. Considering his own political fortune under the pro-Catholic regime, for Morales this point probably had personal significance. His final proposal—that the clergy could remedy this situation by allying themselves with the liberal party—may not have been as unrealistic as it now appears. It was well known that Charles de Montalembert, an indefatigable defender of the Church in France, was advocating Catholic acceptance of many liberal principals and the creation of "a free Church in a free State." By resisting necessary reforms, the French marquis had argued, Catholics were "isolating themselves from the social movement and political activity of the country."[70] Morales would also have been in contact with many progressive Mexican Catholics through his association with *La Voz de Religion*. In Mexico, however, the demonstrations of radical hostility toward the Church that had occurred in Guadalajara had already convinced more conservative Catholics that no compromise with liberalism was possible.

In response to the Morales propositions, a spirited defense of Catholic culture and civilization began in the pages of *La Cruz* on November 29, 1855. This series of rebuttals began with an attack on Morales himself. "There is almost no public writer," the first installment announced, "that does not believe himself authorized to put forth his ideas respecting what are called the abuses of the Church and its ministers." Now even the famous Morales had joined the ranks of these critics with his three propositions, which because of his prestige were likely to make a big impact. But these propositions were so shocking, *La Cruz* suggested, that their author has been damaged "not only in his reputation as a Catholic, which we are sure he does not want to lose, but also in his political and literary reputation." By expressing sentiments held by the majority of the *moderados*, the editors of *La Cruz* implied, Morales had discredited himself both intellectually and religiously.

Conservatives recognized that a perception of cultural inferiority was a potent argument against the Church in the pragmatic and nationalistic

nineteenth century. As Morales pointed out, personal and economic ambitions informed the liberalism of many moderates, who tended to idolize
Anglo-Saxon accomplishments. Combating the notion of Catholic backwardness was, therefore, an essential element of the *La Cruz's* defense of
the clergy. In this regard, France, "the vanguard of European civilization,"
was offered as proof that "Catholic peoples march at the front of human
progress."[71] But even outside of France the Church had always been an instrument of human development, the journal claimed. It was undeniable
that everywhere the faith had been planted,

> it has improved the social condition of man at the same time that it
> opened to them the gate to heaven; that in its shadow the slave broke his
> chains, woman entered into the possession of her rights, arts and science
> spread their light over the world, and humanity came to its state of true
> civilization.

How could Catholics be "the most backward" of all peoples, it asked, compared to those who lived under Islam and "other types of religions that leave
man in a truly abject and miserable state?" Although he had not said so,
obviously Morales considered Catholic nations inferior only to those "that
once belonged to the Roman communion and that more or less recently
separated themselves from the Catholic Church: in a word, the Protestant
countries."[72]

As a challenge to this seductive Whig interpretation, the editors of *La
Cruz* also presented an alternative, Catholic version of European history.
In this view, the Protestant Reformation was not the beginning of Europe's
emancipation and social progress, but a "great retrograde step." Among
the authors cited to support this position, the most frequently and ex-
tensively quoted was the Spanish priest and philosopher, Jaime Balmes.
In *European Civilization: Protestantism and Catholicity Compared*, Balmes had
argued that whatever progress Europe had made was due to its Catholic
heritage, not to the "dissolvent" principles of Protestantism. He pointed
out, for instance, that all the great European universities began as Catholic
institutions. On the other hand, the foundations of Protestantism, which
Balmes summarized as the principle of private interpretation and the denial of human free will, were not a creative force. "Protestantism in general
has blocked," *La Cruz* quoted, "the progressive march of humanity, and in
particular the countries that have fallen under the shadow of its doctrines."
Writing to combat anticlericalism in Spain, Balmes also pointed out the

many similarities between the sixteenth-century reformers and nineteenth-century liberals: "Hatred of authority is the eternal and infallible character of every erroneous sect," he declared.[73]

The polemic against the propositions of Morales continued for many months in the "Controversy" section of *La Cruz*, during which the reflexive conservative defense of Hispanic culture was on full display. In some articles, the attack on the Whig version of history was also connected to a critique of the very ideal of Anglo-Saxon progress. For example, this theme was expressed in an anonymous letter to the editors signed "Catholic in Jalisco." Catholics must recognize, the writer asserted, that "at the heart of most of the attacks against religion are questions of political economy, and that it is necessary to accept the challenge in this field." It was true, he admitted, that Protestant countries were ahead in "comforts of life, industry, and material wealth," he wrote. But "the richest nations are not always the most civilized." As far as the United States was concerned, its own authors admitted that "the hunger for gold has killed the love of art, truth, the good and the beautiful" in that country. Reflecting on this "curse of Midas," one US commentator had even complained that "if intemperance in drink is a vice that degrades the greater part of our citizens, *the intemperance of money* sickens just as many, and usually it is difficult to say which is worse!" In spite of the intellectual, moral, and cultural accomplishments of Catholic countries like France, there was no denying that Great Britain excelled in "the advance of the mechanical arts, the spirit of association and of work, and the accumulation of wealth resulting from the practice of economic doctrines." But the implementation of these doctrines had also led to "horrible consequences" there. In that country, the writer reported, "man is considered as a machine, to the point of seeing in him nothing but muscle and bone, as a machine is made of wood and iron." It is because humans are treated merely as a means to a material end that the cancer of pauperism affects one-sixth of the population of that unhappy island, he declared.[74]

After Morales indicated that Great Britain was the country he had in mind when evaluating Mexico's progress, *La Cruz* also expanded its exposé of the actual conditions in that model country. Numerous European authors were enlisted to give testimony of the miserable conditions in England at this early stage of industrial development.[75] Observations by the Italian Givoanni Perrone, for example, highlighted the dangerous conditions in English factories and coalmines. According to Perrone, two-thirds of the thousands of children "condemned to consume their tender years in fetid factories" did not live to reach adulthood. The spiritual condition of the working class, which he described as semi-pagan, was also a cause of concern: "Without instruction, without sacraments, without spiritual consolation, buried in vice, they live and die in the crassest ignorance of their eternal destiny and in the most profound moral degradation."[76] Excerpts from the French writer Jean Guame also focused on similar Dickensian images of the British life. "We go to Birmingham, Manchester, Liverpool; we enter into these vast factories, through dense clouds of black and infectious smoke, and we see thousands of helots work like machines: this is the English people," he wrote. Guame also condemned an alleged English practice of selling the labor of wives and children in payment for debt, which he thought reflected the extreme corruption of society and family life in England. Rather than ameliorating such conditions, he claimed, the established Protestant church only contributed to the egoism of the privileged classes.[77] In sum, all those horrors of industrial capitalism publicized by Karl Marx during this same period were presented to the Mexican readers of *La Cruz* in order to highlight the social and spiritual advantages enjoyed by putatively "backward" Catholic nations.

Morales's second and third propositions did not receive as much attention from the defenders of the clergy as his denigration of Catholic culture. His claim about the clergy's political tendencies was summarily dismissed: It was ridiculous to say that clerics were "born" supporters of despotism, since priests were called to the ministry out of the whole of society and no one entered the world as a cleric. As far as the proposal that the clergy should join forces with liberals, Pesado pointed out that the party actually consisted of two warring factions, the *moderados* and the *puros*. As the principles of both groups were vague and undefined, how could priests know with which they were supposed to affiliate? In any event, he explained, "the clergy, we have said, and we repeat it, ought not to be tied to any political party. . . . It is 'Catholic,' that is to say, universal, and under this aspect is indifferent to the forms of government that rule in human society: all that work for justice are good."[78]

By the end of 1855, the liberal administration was no longer willing to tolerate the consequences of its own free-press ideals. On December 28, the new minister of the interior, José María Lafragua, issued a controversial law regulating all publications in the country. Because of the role played by newspapers in exacerbating partisan passions, the new law forbade the publication of any libelous material or of anything that disturbed the public order. In particular, the *Ley Lafragua* outlawed criticism of the government and attacks on religion, although in keeping with liberal thinking, this prohibition did not apply to criticism of the clergy.[79] For the next two years editors of all political persuasions suffered fines and imprisonment for violations of the law, and printing presses of both parties were suspended or permanently shut down on a regular basis. Thanks to its unusually elevated and civil tone, however, *La Cruz* was one of the few journals never prosecuted under this law.

La Cruz represented a new initiative in the long struggle against liberal anticlericalism in Mexico. It appeared in response to the threatening attacks on the church that characterized the first months of the new liberal regime. Perhaps more than any other publication, this journal was in the vanguard of the uncompromising Catholic identity that characterized the ultramontane reaction. In the Morales debate, the journal defended both Catholic identity and Hispanic culture. But over time defense turned to offense, and the polemics in which its editors participated also played an important part in the polarization of Mexican society during the Reforma. In some respects, the ideological stalemate that followed was a testimony to the effectiveness of Catholic newspapers in the face of the numerical superiority of the liberal presses. But success in the long run was only relative. Rivers of ink were spilled on each side of the religious debate, but it is doubtful that any committed anticlerical or ultramontane believers were converted by the arguments of the opposing side. Instead, the exclusionary discourses that all parties employed only hardened the political and theological positions of their readers and further alienated their foes. During 1856, this escalating rhetoric combined with a series of highly symbolic confrontations that seemed to confirm the worst suspicions of each side. Ultimately, this process created a zero-sum game that neither Catholics nor anticlericals would be able to win on their own terms.

CHAPTER 4

Resistance and Retribution (1856)

Liberal and conservative rhetoric was an essential element in the polarization of society during the Mexican Reforma. In a politically charged atmosphere, however, actions usually speak louder than words. Even minor events often could take on an ideological significance out of all proportion to the empirical facts of a case. The participation of a single priest in a military revolt, for example, might be used as conclusive evidence that the entire clergy was involved in a vast antigovernment conspiracy. On the other hand, even practical and moderate reforms were often read as proof positive of a sinister campaign to destroy the Church. If nothing else, the cycle of symbolic provocation and dramatic response that characterized the Church-State relationship in 1856 highlights the contingent nature of the whole reform process. In the hostile discursive environment created by anticlerical and ultramontane polemics of 1855, interpretation became much more important than the actual intentions or behavior of individual protagonists on either side of the ideological divide.

By December 1855, the Ayutla Revolution was in trouble. After the Manuel Doblado *pronunciamiento*, other local revolts also broke out in protest against the actions of the new liberal regime.[1] To save the movement, General Álvarez resigned as "temporary president" on December 8 and named Ignacio Comonfort as "substitute-interim president" in his place. One of the military heroes of the Ayutla Revolution and a well-known moderate, General Comonfort was also—important from a political point of view—still a practicing Roman Catholic and known to be on friendly terms with the archbishop. *Moderados* hoped that these traits would reassure the population of the benevolent intentions of the new government and help diffuse the partisan tensions created during its first months in power. The *puro* faction, however, was not pleased. Although both factions shared the same basic agenda, they disagreed on the speed with which reforms should be implemented. This is why some *puros* referred to Comonfort's supporters as the "not yet" party. According to Vigil, "The radical party viewed his elevation with a total lack of confidence, fearing that he had neither the conviction nor the decisiveness needed to accomplish the great reforms they awaited."[2]

One of the most intimate portraits of Comonfort comes from the memoirs of Guillermo Prieto. He had come to know Comonfort well at the soirees held at the home of the liberal politician and writer, Mariano Otero, before the latter's death in 1850. Here, Prieto recalled, Comonfort recounted stories of his life, including his impoverished childhood. He had attended the Colegio de Pueblo as a servant/student, under a scholarship scheme developed to educate the poor, but there he had been badly treated and undernourished. He was devoted to his mother, and Prieto remarked that he conversed easily with old ladies and children. Although his mild temperament and gentle manners seemed most suited to the domestic sphere, there was "an incredible transformation" when the subject of government, the budget, or war came up. Then Prieto encountered "a shrewd man, an ardent patriot of firm principles," but alas, one who was also "unable to shake the mystical upbringing of the people of his era." This remark reveals the fundamental split between the Catholic *moderados* and the *puros*, for whom religious faith could only be seen as an outdated superstition. Above all, the radical Prieto complained, as a moderate and conciliator Comonfort "vacillated" and "zig-zagged" between positions. Nevertheless, his true character was seen on the battlefield, where he took "farsighted and astute action" and demonstrated a "tranquil and impressive serenity while bullets roared around him and the ground, sown with cadavers, shook in the tumult of the struggle."[3]

Because of the divisions within the liberal ranks, the situation in Mexico City was tense following Comonfort's appointment. Anticipating a possible coup, some of Álvarez's troops and members of the national guard stationed themselves on the domes and in the towers of the cathedral and some of the other major churches in the city. On the evening of December 10 members of the radical political clubs also took to the streets, chanting "Down with the moderates!" "Death to Comonfort" and "Long live Álvarez!"[4] Some protesters, along with members of the national guard, occupied a few government buildings and demanded arms from the governor of the Federal District, Juan José Baz, which were refused. At that point rioters attempted to break into an arms store to gain the weapons for themselves. The main group of demonstrators was finally dispersed by the regular army, although there were also other demonstrations in front of the presidential palace, around the university and in other locations. Along with denunciations of Comonfort, some groups were said to have cried "Long live the Americans!" while others yelled insults against the bishops and other "alarming blasphemies."[5] There were even reports of residents being threatened by a mob, led by a few "democrats in frock coats," shouting "Death" to religion, the Pope, the Holy Trinity, and even the Immaculate Conception![6] The liberal press, however, vehemently denied that anyone had cheered the Americans.[7] The coup having failed, Comonfort took office on December 11 and afterward attended a Te Deum sung in his honor in the Metropolitan Cathedral. However the *puro* faction's dissatisfaction with the new president was confirmed by the complete absence of radicals and Freemasons in his new cabinet, appointed on December 13.[8]

At the same time another disturbance, and possibly another attempted coup, was taking place in Puebla, less than ninety miles away. It occurred on December 12, the feast of the Virgin of Guadalupe, a major religious festival with deep patriotic overtones. Many people would have been in the city for the celebrations that day, which was also a national holiday. Just after evening prayers a rumor began to spread that the governor planned to seize and deport the local bishop, Pelagio Antonio de Labastida y Dávalos, because of his recent protest against the *Ley Juárez*. An early report blamed members of a dragoon regiment for "deluding" the population in service of a pre-planned conservative conspiracy. But *El Monitor Republicano* insisted that the "criminal mob" had been incited by a friar, leading only some poor women, some gullible souls and a "very few" soldiers.[9] In any event, as word of the government's alleged intentions spread, the bells of the city's numerous churches began to toll the alarm, and the clamor continued until the next day. Excited crowds gathered, and there was even an attempt to seize the barracks, aided by dragoons of General Francisco Güitián's brigade from nearby Amozoc. However, they were forcefully repelled by national guard troops under the command of General Juan Baptista Traconis. Meanwhile, defenders of the bishop had surrounded the episcopal palace, shouting "Long live religion!" "Long live the bishop! And "Death to the impious!" They dispersed on the morning of the 13th but calm was only restored after Bishop Labastida published a statement reassuring the population that he was in no danger.[10] Nevertheless, here the violence was much greater than in Mexico City, and some reports placed casualties from the clash with government forces as high as one hundred.[11] Meanwhile, General Güitán and his troops marched toward Zacapoaxtla, where he had previously been ordered to put down another rebellion already in progress.

Zacapoaxtla, with a population of 23,500, was made up of four municipalities in the northern highlands of the State of Puebla. The revolt there began when a local priest, Francisco Ortega y García, called upon his Indian parishioners to rise up in defense of "Religion and *fueros*."[12] On December 10, the liberal press reported an Indian uprising in the area that had already resulted in "horrible atrocities," including the burning of some houses belonging to "whites" and the death of more than twenty people. Rather than a revolt in favor of religion, however, the newspaper claimed that this was actually a "caste war" aimed at the extermination of the white population, provoked by alleged "conservative" oppression of the natives.[13] Subsequent events, however, do not support this interpretation. On December 12, the revolt became official when the priest held a meeting of local notables and proclaimed the "Plan of Zacapoaxtla."[14] The rebel manifesto, later modified, was endorsed by the local military commander, Colonel Lorenzo Bulnes, and signed by 3,678 local inhabitants. When General Güitián's troops arrived a few days later to suppress the supposed Indian uprising, they joined the revolt instead.[15] This action, along with the behavior of his troops during the disturbance in Puebla, suggested to many that he was already part of a larger regional conspiracy.[16]

Bishop Labastida was quick to denounce the revolt in Zacapoaxtla, which, given the makeup of the population of Sierra del Norte, he feared might indeed escalate into a caste war.[17] He must have also been nervous about the involvement of a priest, since this would only serve to confirm liberal conspiracy theories about the clergy. In a letter written on December 19 he asked the inhabitants to lay down their arms and "recognize the present government, hoping from its enlightenment and religiosity all manner of good for this unhappy country." This appeal was accompanied by an order to Father Ortega y García, demanding that he end the rebellion, "tranquilizing that neighborhood and exhorting it to return to order and the required submission to the national government." Once this was accomplished, he was commanded to appear before Labastida for a hearing on his conduct. But although the priest acknowledged receipt of the documents, he did not comply.[18]

The thirty-nine-year-old Bishop Labastida was a relatively recent arrival to Puebla. A native of Zamora (Michoacán), he was ordained a priest at twenty-three and consecrated bishop of the Diocese of Puebla on July 8, 1855. Both a lawyer and a doctor of canon law, he held many ecclesiastical posts in the Diocese of Morelia prior to his episcopal appointment, including a position as rector of the seminary reformed by Bishop Munguía. A few years later the Emperor Maximilian noted privately that in Labastida, "all the world recognizes a superior intelligence joined to a profound erudition, which is the cause for the rapid advancement of his career."[19] Very different in temperament from Archbishop Garza, his colleague in Mexico City, Labastida was described in 1856 as "still young, relaxed in the good sense of the word, gifted with a peaceable and conciliatory character, and without political passions of any kind, without having figured until then in any political party, and without decided affections for any of them."[20] In spite of these traits, the new bishop found himself unwillingly drawn into the political arena by events over which he had no control.

On the same day that the bishop's appeal for peace was delivered to Zacapoaxtla, the leaders of the combined rebel forces issued the definitive version of their political plan. Like the Doblado proclamation, the document decried the betrayal of the ideals of the Ayutla Revolution, the pending danger of national anarchy, and the illegitimacy of the current administration. The reasons listed for the revolt, however, were entirely political: "the lack of guarantees for citizens, the most rigorous exclusivism in administration, and the unfairness in the distribution of national income."[21] The plan therefore proposed a return to the political arrangements of 1843 and called for the election of a president who would represent all parties and segments of society. The absence of any mention of religion or *fueros* in the list of grievances may have been calculated to avoid giving the movement too much of a clerical tone.[22]

In spite of the omission of explicitly Catholic language from the Zacapoaxtla manifesto, and the hierarchy's opposition to the revolt, religious emotion remained a potent force in the progress of the movement. Whatever the political motivations of their leaders, many rebels still believed that they were fighting to preserve the Catholic faith in Mexico. For example, the four hundred rebels that seized the town of Teziutlán on December 18 wore crosses and images of saints around their necks and had signs pinned to their hats proclaiming: "Religion or death!"[23] Even more telling was the defection of government troops that occurred on the day after Christmas. An army under General Ignacio de la Llave, José Joaquín

Pesado's former brother-in-law, had been sent into Puebla to put down the rebellion.[24] But when the federal soldiers encountered the self-styled "Sacred Legion," almost the entire brigade spontaneously defected, shouting, "Long live religion!" De la Llave was obliged to abandon the field in order to save his own life.[25]

In the face of these unexpected reversals, the government moved to extinguish other possible threats to its hold on power. Thus, the year 1856 opened with a roundup of potential conservative conspirators.[26] Among the suspects arrested were Antonio Haro y Tamariz, one of the signatories of the Lagos accord, and two other generals. In spite of the charges against him, evidence has never been produced that implicated Haro y Tamariz in an anti-government plot at this time. On the other hand, some moderates considered him a possible presidential candidate, and Comonfort, who had unexpectedly excluded him from the cabinet, may have feared his ambition. Thanks to a carriage accident, Haro y Tamariz managed to escape from custody three days later while being transported to Veracruz. Soon afterward, he found his way to Zacapoaxtla. Although his affiliation with the rebels there was unplanned, after his arrival he was offered command of the entire movement.

The presence of Haro y Tamariz in the insurgency seems to have reassured other federal officers of its moderate character and chances for success. Determined to crush the growing threat to his government, Comonfort sent a second battalion from Mexico City to subdue the rebels in early January. This force encountered the insurgents at San Juan de los Llanos on January 12. But when the officers under General Severo de Castillo discovered that Haro y Tamariz was at the head of the opposing forces, the entire army again deserted en masse. Because of General Severo's national prestige and former loyalty to the regime, his loss was a severe blow to the government.[27] "This defection raised the wrath of the enemies of the army," Zamacois recalled, "without having in mind that perhaps they, with their impudent writings, had provoked it."[28] Refreshed by this new influx of troops, Haro y Tamariz led an attack on Puebla, his hometown, under a banner with the ambiguous slogan, "Liberty and Order." The city surrendered and was occupied by the rebel forces on January 23.

After he entered Puebla, Haro y Tamariz finally clarified the personal reasons for his impromptu participation in the rebellion. In typical military fashion, he issued a *pronunciamiento* to the inhabitants of the city in which he explained that after helping to expel "the cruel tyrant," Santa Anna, he now found himself "a victim of persecution by dictatorial power and unrestrained demagoguery." Therefore he had abandoned the pleasures of private life "to deliver my dear country from the disasters of immoral libertinage."[29] As in the formal articles of the Plan of Zacapoaxtla, religious motives were conspicuously absent from his explanation. In phrases similar to those that had been used by Doblado in Guanajuato, however, another general, young Luis Gonzaga Osollo, rose to praise the Catholic faith for its unifying effect on the nation.[30]

Following the defection of General Severo, Mexico City found itself in a precarious situation.[31] Without adequate military protection, Comonfort was forced to reorganize the defense of the capital "with radicals and beggars," in the words of the French ambassador.[32] When the rebel forces did not move, however, the president took advantage of the opportunity to collect funds and draft soldiers for a new army.[33] Félix María Zuloaga, an old *santanista* general who now supported the Ayutla Revolution, was placed in command. Among the other officers recruited from the states was Governor Manuel Doblado, reconciled with the government after the appointment of Comonfort and now strangely silent on the issue of the *fuero*. On January 27, the Archbishop of Mexico City publicly blessed the banners of eight new battalions of the regular army and the national guard in a ceremony held in the military college at Chapultepec Castle.[34]

The administration now turned its full attention to the defeat of the rebels occupying Mexico's second largest city. During the ceremonial opening of the constituent congress on February 18, 1856, the president seemed preoccupied with the struggle being waged only eighty miles away. In his address to the delegates, Comonfort described the rebels as enemies of "liberty, progress, justice, order, and morality" and denounced the way they had "forced a part of the army into a most shameful defection." He also pledged that the government would "consecrate all its forces to suffocate the reaction." In a similar vein, Ponciano Arriaga, the newly elected president of the congress, assured the assembly that "a handful of men blinded by personal ambition, deceived by illegitimate hopes" could never prevail against "the sovereign people."[35] In fact, after their defeat at the Battle of Ocotlán on March 8, the conservatives capitulated under a deal brokered by Bishop Labastida on March 22, 1856.[36] Needless to say, many citizens who had not openly supported the rebels were nevertheless disappointed in the final victory.[37]

Although Comonfort may have been initially disposed to benevolence toward the defeated rebel army, some radicals considered the lenient terms of surrender to be a sign of weakness. The defection of over three thousand troops was an embarrassment for the government, so the administration's official position was that conservative officers had deceived and misled the rank and file. According to the terms of surrender, repentant soldiers were returned to the regular army; those wishing to leave military service altogether were discharged. Meanwhile, rebel officers were to be relocated until the government could determine under what terms they might be retained in military service.[38] The liberal press, however, reacted to these efforts at conciliation with concern. For instance, *El Siglo Diez y Nueve* insisted, "We do not want vengeance, nor reprisals; we ask for justice. We do not suggest shootings, but we do believe that prudence is dictating certain precautions."[39] Other liberals openly regretted that the entire conservative force had not been entirely annihilated in battle.

On March 25, in response to growing threats from the *puros*, Comonfort passed sentence on more than three hundred of the rebel officers.[40] Taking advantage of the ambiguous language in the surrender agreement, commissioned officers were reduced to the rank of private and assigned to the infantry—generals for three years, subalterns for two. Those who had been distinguished for service in the war for independence or during the US invasion were sentenced to a single year.[41] Meanwhile, the actual leaders of the revolt, including Haro y Tamariz, had escaped from the city before its fall. Although Comonfort published a ban against any who aided or abetted the fugitives, on April 27 they managed to sail out of Veracruz on a French ship.[42]

As a warning to future rebels, Comonfort's punitive decree was fixed on the walls of the major cities under a bold headline announcing "JUSTICE." As the condemned officers were related to a great many of the elite families, its harsh sentences caused widespread distress in the upper levels of Mexican society. Even many loyal officers considered this action a betrayal of the terms of surrender and an assault on the class structure of the military.[43] Stories circulated that the prisoners were marched south, "on foot, naked, without food, and treated as inhumanely as possible." There they were handed over to the tender mercies of General Álvarez, who was reported to have announced that if they starved, "it should not be regarded as vengeance, but simply because he could not feed them."[44] In the face of massive public disapproval and appeals by more moderate politicians, Comonfort mitigated the punishments on April 27.[45]

Rebel officers were not to be the only target of liberal retributions. Many radicals insisted that the military victory would be worthless unless the clergy as a whole, whom they blamed for the rebellion, was also punished. In particular, they saw this as an opportunity to strip the Church of the economic resources that allowed it to foment reaction. Masons of the National Rite, both inside and outside of the constituent congress, were among the most adamant and outspoken on this point. This also seemed to be the perfect opportunity to initiate more of the reforms that the radical press had been demanding. On March 26, Comonfort toured the captured city and attended a Te Deum in the Puebla Cathedral to celebrate his victory. Five days later he decreed the confiscation of ecclesiastical assets throughout the entire diocese, which included the states of Veracruz and Taxcala, even though these areas had not participated in the revolt.

The confiscation decree, issued on March 31, enumerated the charges that justified the government's reprisal against the Church. According to Comonfort, some of the rebels had tried to give the revolt "the character of a religious war." Furthermore, "public opinion" held that the clergy had fomented the war by every possible means.[46] Most damning was the claim that the clergy had used ecclesiastical resources to support the rebel army. Thus it was only fair that Church wealth should be used to repay the nation for the costs of the war, to indemnify loyal citizens for damages, and to pension the mutilated, widows, and orphans. As the decree explained, the clergy had been able to mislead the people "by a spirit of sedition" because they belonged to those classes of society that "exercise a great influence due to their wealth." Depriving the Church of its resources would eliminate its capacity for mischief, Comonfort implied.[47] In hindsight, however, it is clear that the punishment of the Puebla Diocese was intended to be "a test case for the forceful and exemplary implementation of the liberal reform program."[48]

Unknown to the public, there were other pressures that also might have influenced Comonfort's decision to move against the Church at this time. The French ambassador, Alexis de Gabriac, reported that the administration needed the assets of the Puebla Diocese as collateral for a loan of ten million pesos it was seeking from the United States. The ambassador also reported that the Americans were taking advantage of Mexico's situation to demand the expulsion of the papal nuncio. Gabriac was a monarchist who supported the conservatives in the hopes of a future alliance between Mexico and France. Although he also harbored anticlerical sympathies of his own, he recognized the political importance of Mexico's Catholicism. He therefore interpreted the American demand as a threat to both Mexican sovereignty and French influence. The Americans wanted Mexico to break its ties with the papacy, he explained to Comonfort's foreign minister, "because Catholicism is the only and the most powerful barrier that exists in Mexico against an invasion of Yankees, atheists, and Mormons."[49] Nevertheless, in response to US pressure, the Mexican government initiated a review of the Vatican envoy's credentials.

In a speech after his return to Mexico City, Comonfort again defended his measures against the army and his decision to punish the Puebla Diocese. "Only severe punishments, but neither bloody nor cruel," he proclaimed, "are able to reestablish peace and order and prepare for radical reforms." In spite of rumors to the contrary, he insisted, the Catholic religion was not the target of his punitive program:

> Even if religion was invoked as a pretext for the war that is now happily ended, even if a few men became fanatics with religious ideas, the nation is already enlightened enough to know that representative democracy, a democracy without turbulence or disorder, is not incompatible with Christianity, and that the greatest progress, the most important social improvements, can be realized without violating what is truly sacred or immutable in the religion of our fathers.[50]

Ultramontane Catholics, however, were not reassured by the president's apparent usurpation of the authority to decide what was "truly sacred" and unchanging in the ancestral religion. For them, such distinctions were the prerogative of the clergy, not the secular government.

As might be expected, liberals and conservatives reacted very differently to the news of the punitive decree. On the front page of *El Siglo Diez y Nueve*, under bold headlines proclaiming "REPARATION! JUSTICE!" Franciso Zarco argued that since the great wealth of the clergy had been diverted by rebellious priests, the government's action was "politic, moral and just." Furthermore, religious services had been used to recruit men to the cause and nuns had distributed crosses and religious medals to the soldiers. It was high time for Comonfort to show that his government was not a joke, Zarco concluded. Another long article in the same issue blamed the "satanic fury" of the so-called "defenders of religion" for the recent bloody conflict. "Damnation upon such horrible, criminal entities," it thundered.[51] On the other hand, more conservative Mexicans interpreted the confiscation as an unjustified assault on their religion and Gabriac reported that much of the nation was "profoundly wounded" by the decree.[52] The Catholic sense of the sacrilege involved in the seizures was also reflected in rumors surrounding the intervention. According to one story, of the first three administrators appointed to make the inventory of Church funds, "one went crazy, one committed suicide, and the other dared not execute the order."[53] Clearly, some people believed, or hoped, that divine retribution awaited anyone who participated in the illicit government action.

Sentiments such as these ensured that implementation of the decree would not go as smoothly as the president had planned. As much as possible, the clergy utilized passive resistance, or "the force of inertia," to delay the required inventory and requisition of assets. But the government was not deterred. For instance, when the official *interventor*, Col. Juan Duque de Estrada, appeared at the diocesan tithing offices in Puebla on April 8, the canons refused to hand over the keys. He returned the next day with a force of twenty-one men and sacked the building, threatening with death anyone who tried to stand in his way. News of this action, however, provoked a mass demonstration in the city, where it was reported,

> Men, women, and children armed themselves to resist the government's measures; priests of the Most High commanded the mob, brandishing the crucifix in place of a sword; some military officers also appeared in the crowd, inciting reaction anew; force was mingled with exorcisms, lamentations with cries of exasperation.[54]

The appearance of General Traconis restored order, but resentment and resistance continued. Over the next few days, a number of *poblanos* were arrested for "murmuring against the robberies," and in Orizaba, two scribes were jailed on April 22 for refusing to notarize the inventory in their district.[55]

Bishop Labastida did what he could to prevent the plunder of his diocese. Rather than comply with the presidential decree, he declared his willingness "to suffer whatever comes upon me before making myself an instrument for the alienation or despoilment of the goods of this Church, whose protection has been entrusted to me."[56] He also wielded the spiritual weapons at his disposal and in accordance with canon law, excommunicated the governor for violating the sanctions protecting Church property. When Governor Francisco Ibarra y Ramos was replaced by the more ruthless General Traconis, the prelate excommunicated him as well. Enraged by this demonstration of ecclesiastical cheek, the new governor threatened to bomb the city if the censure was not removed.[57]

Labistida's most enduring legacy during this crisis was a series of letters he exchanged with government officials in defense of the Church in Puebla.

The entire diocese, he insisted, could not be blamed if some rebels chose to call their movement a crusade. "Public opinion" notwithstanding, only the priest of Zacapoaxtla and "four or five other restless ecclesiastics" were known to have supported the uprising. Furthermore, this participation was expressly against his wishes, and he had ordered the priests to desist their political activity on more than one occasion. Yet the current law attacked all the clergy and religious without distinction, for what were the private acts of a few.[58] This argument against collective punishment was reprinted by the conservative newspaper *La Patria*, which rhetorically demanded, "Were all the apostles traitors because Judas was?"[59]

The government's response was presented in a letter to the bishop written by the minister of justice and ecclesiastical affairs, Ezequiel Montes. The thirty-six-year-old *moderado*, a native of Guanajuato, was well suited for his post and his new role as defender of the government's punitive action. After admission to the bar in 1852, Montes served as professor of law at San Ildefonso until 1854. According to Vigil, Montes "united all the qualities of a great orator: prodigious memory, vast and profound classical erudition, correct and elegant expression, logical rigor in thought."[60] In this case, all these gifts were employed to demonstrate that the president's punishment fit the Church's crime. After all, Montes explained, rebel soldiers had carried holy relics into battle and some wore crosses fashioned by sympathetic nuns.[61] In addition, he noted, during the siege of Puebla, special prayer services for victory had been held in the city's churches.[62] Furthermore, Father Ortega y García not only incited his parishioners to revolt but even joined the insurgents on the front lines; whether as combatant or chaplain was not specified. For the government, this was incontrovertible evidence of a widespread clerical conspiracy. Along with these accusations, Montes also sent the bishop an elaborate treatise that questioned the Church's legal right to own any property at all.[63]

In spite of Montes's efforts, Bishop Labastida remained resolute. Using scripture, Church history, and canon law, he argued that the character of the Church's own sovereignty and independence gave it full property rights, including the faculty to dictate the rules concerning the collection, conservation, or investment of its own goods. If in extraordinary circumstances it ever became necessary for rulers "to stretch out a hand to the goods of the Church," papal authorization would be required. On his own, he argued, an individual bishop was simply unable to authorize such an action.[64] Some liberals considered this an insolent reply, and one that proved the bad faith of the clergy. In his history of the Reforma, Vigil argued that Labastida's recourse to Rome was an important turning point in government attitudes toward the Church. How could anyone, he asked, have seriously expected the chief magistrate of a republic to appeal to a foreign power for permission to punish a crime, knowing that such permission would not be granted? "Undoubtedly no sane spirit would harbor such a belief, it being obvious at the time that in taking this position the clergy had closed the way to any possible conciliation, provoking revolutionary reprisals in consequence," he wrote.[65]

The government's most serious charge, and an article of faith among the liberals, was that the clergy had actually bankrolled the rebellion. In this instance, however, Labastida could only defend the Church on a technicality. Although no ecclesiastical funds had ever been given to "rebels," he claimed, a small loan had indeed been provided to Haro y Tamariz. But this had occurred only after Governor Ibarra y Ramos had officially handed over the city, and the municipal authorities had recognized the occupying army as the legitimate government. The bishop argued that despoiling the Church for this insignificant loan was unjust; such transactions were common in Mexico. Montes, however, replied that after the overthrow of Santa Anna, the only legitimate government was that of the liberal regime in Mexico City, and as such only it had the right to demand loans from Church coffers. Because the clergy had provided a loan to Haro y Tamariz, he concluded, it had financed the killing of government troops and helped sustain the war. In spite of the bishop's excuses, the loan was proof enough that the Church was guilty and deserved to be punished.

In the end, Labastida offered a compromise. The confiscations, he claimed, would punish the innocent more than the handful of actually guilty persons. Orphans, the sick, and the very poor all depended on the charity of religious institutions for their care. The president had claimed that a primary motive for the confiscations was so that Church funds could be used to provide pensions for the victims of the war. Therefore, the bishop suggested that the Church itself take over their care and support, thus ending the need for government interventions. This proposal, however, was rejected out of hand, which reassured conservatives that the president's motives "were not as philanthropic as they might have seemed."[66] In fact, the intervention did have an impact on the charitable works of the Church. For example, on July 9, the Daughters of Charity, whose funds had been confiscated, took to begging alms in the streets to keep their orphanage afloat.[67] Public worship was also affected, and from Orizaba it was reported that the Carmelites could no longer pay their bellringer and some parishes could not even afford the oil to keep the sanctuary light burning before the tabernacle.[68]

Although the government tried to restrict its circulation, the correspondence between Bishop Labastida and Montes was published widely in the conservative press. *La Cruz* reprinted all the documents relating to the affair in a special fifty-two-page supplement on May 10, 1856. By way of justification, the editors described the situation in Puebla as "without doubt one of the gravest that has presented itself to Mexican society, due to its nature, its circumstances, and its consequences."[69] The conservative newspaper *La Patria* had already been shut down for its editorial remarks that followed its publication of part of the bishop's defense. To avoid a similar penalty, *La Cruz* published the letters without comment.[70] The documents were accompanied, however, by the reprint of an exposition written by the Bishop of Sonora against the confiscation of Church property in 1847. Zamacois later wrote that the circulation of Labastida's protest caused "a profound sensation among the Catholic people."[71] Part of the impact seems to have been a general conviction that the bishop won the debate with Montes, hands down. Reflecting on the outcome of this exchange, the French ambassador observed that, "Montes does not understand the futility of debating with the Church in writing."[72]

In Mexico City, the Comonfort administration began to fear that Labastida's intransigence would inspire further reaction against the government. Reports from Puebla claimed that priests were publicly denouncing the intervention from the pulpit, and that those who counseled compliance with the decree were labeled "heretics" and "Protestants." Liberal newspapers in Mexico City also reported that the bishop himself was counseling disobedience. The incriminating evidence, relayed by an unknown informant, was an inflammatory remark alleged to have been made by Labastida in a sermon on May 4. "With much sorrow I have seen the Christian people indifferent to attempts being made against the goods of the Church," he was reported to have said.[73] In response, the bishop was finally arrested at his home on May 12. Although it was escorted by a military contingent, huge crowds pressed upon the carriage that carried him away, making it difficult for the vehicle to move. This "sorrowful multitude," it was reported, followed the entourage to the gates of the city, Labastida extending his arm through the window of the coach to bless the crowd. Afterward, armed troops patrolled the streets to prevent disturbances, and some clergymen who publicly lamented the arrest were placed in custody.[74] On the other hand, an editorial in *El Monitor Republicano* applauded his arrest, asserting that there was no doubt the clergy had instigated and supported the previous revolt. In spite of the government's mild measures in Puebla, it opined, the bishop was again trying to foment a rebellion and deserved to be punished.[75]

After a brief imprisonment, Labastida was expelled from the country without trial, sailing from Veracruz on May 21. On June 16 he published a letter to Montes from Havana in which he denied all the charges against him. In particular, he claimed, more than a thousand people had attended his sermon on the Immaculate Conception in the Church of the Holy Spirit when the offending phrase was supposed to have been uttered. All of these witnesses could testify that he had never spoken the words attributed to him. The real motive for his arrest, he believed, was the effectiveness of his reasoning in the debate with Montes, "in which I victoriously dissected, in my humble opinion, all the reasons and authorities that you expounded to me." Nevertheless, if he was to be punished for having successfully defended the Church's position, he stated, "I am resigned to suffer it along with all the other privations that they want to impose on me."[76]

In response to their bishop's exile, the citizens of Puebla presented another petition to President Comonfort, this time demanding a revocation of the expulsion decree. This document began with a preamble in which the *poblanos* again claimed their democratic right and duty to speak out on recent events. "Will a free and sovereign people doubt," it asked, "that it is permitted to direct its voice to its representatives, to the trustees of their power, in order to manifest to them what in their opinion could harm the common good and ask that it not be done?" As eyewitnesses to the bishop's words and behavior, the citizens denied that he had ever uttered anything "inflammatory, subversive, alarming, offensive to the authorities, etc." Instead, they rehearsed his good works and charity, and asked for his immediate restoration "for reasons of public utility." "A general mourning reigns in the unhappy Diocese of Puebla since that fatal moment [of Labastida's arrest]," they claimed, "and only a handful of extreme liberals live with joy." The petition also demanded an end to the unjustified confiscation of Church property in the diocese, which was causing serious economic problems for the inhabitants. This petition, however, did not alter the administration's policy toward Puebla or the exiled bishop.[77]

The deportation of Bishop Labastida is a clear example of the impasse already reached between the revolutionary government and the Church. Although the prelate had studiously avoided politics, his refusal to recognize the state's rights over ecclesiastical property made him a de facto enemy of the regime. On the other hand, his firmness also made him a hero to the Catholic resistance. According to one *moderado*, "his sermons caused the friends of the government to quake, at the same time that they filled its enemies with joy, and all those who were looking for an occasion to start riots."[78] The need to silence this voice of opposition, therefore, out-weighed questions of judicial evidence or due process in this case. According to Vigil, although probably innocent of any specific offences, Labastida's "obligations as a prince of the Church have prescribed a course of conduct that could not be reconciled with his obligations as a citizen."[79] According to this view, obedience to the laws of the Church would henceforth be seen as incompatible with the duties of Mexican citizenship. Perhaps even more than a policy to isolate dangerous influences, the physical expulsion of ecclesiastical dissenters symbolized their unworthiness for membership in the republican community.

At this point, since new censorship laws prohibited overt criticism of the government, the editors of *La Cruz* had to contrive a less direct way to express their sentiments about the turn of events in Puebla. So the day after the bishop's deportation, the newspaper began the serialization of an obscure fourth-century Latin text by a Christian writer named Lactantius. *On the Death of the Persecutors* described in grisly detail the horrible and pain-ful deaths suffered by all those Roman rulers who had attacked the Church before the time of Constantine. By publishing its translation at this mo-ment, *La Cruz* was plainly suggesting a connection between Comonfort's recent actions and the violent persecution of Christians in the Roman Em-pire. Furthermore, the moral of Lactantius's work was clear: although the Church had suffered grievously, it still survived and prospered. Even more importantly, according to the Roman chronicler, "Those who had out-raged God lie prostrate; those who had overturned his holy temple have themselves fallen in even greater ruin." Lactantius himself had explained that he recorded these occurrences so that posterity might learn "both that there is one God and that he as judge imposes punishments which are clearly deserved on the impious and on persecutors." For bewildered Mexican be-lievers, this text also contained a promise of ultimate vindication. For the enemies of the Church, as Lactantius expressed it, "their punishment has come late, but it has come heavy, as it deserved to be."[80]

Like the Pueblo petition, the veiled threats of divine retribution also had no effect on the liberal program of the Comonfort administration. Having weathered the Zacapoaxtla revolt and the Puebla intervention crisis, a few weeks later it delivered another devastating blow to the Church. This was the daring *Ley Lerdo*, issued by President Comonfort on June 25, 1856, and named for Miguel Lerdo de Tejada, the minister of the treasury who drafted it. Containing thirty-six articles, this law made it illegal for any ecclesiastical or civil corporation in the country to own real estate. Although the vast holdings of the Church were the chief target of the new legislation, actual convents, churches, clerical residences, and educational or charitable institutions were exempted from its provisions.[81] Furthermore, designated properties were not confiscated, but rather were to be sold to the public with the proceeds returned to the owners. At this stage the government's goal was not to bankrupt the Church, but to transform its rural and urban real estate into liquid assets within a period of three months. Comonfort promised that these adjustments in ownership would bring great economic benefits to the nation, "considering that one of the major obstacles for the prosperity and aggrandizement of the nation is the lack of movement or free circulation of a great part of its property, the fundamental base of public wealth."[82]

Although the *Ley Lerdo* was relatively mild by the standards of the Church's experience in Europe, events of the previous months had not disposed conservative Catholics to a benign interpretation of the law. Instead of recognizing the generous concessions of the new legislation, some re-christened it the "Lerdo Theft Law," and many were convinced that this measure was just a prelude to a complete despoliation of the Church.[83] Even in the absence of further legislation, most Mexican churchmen in the mid-nineteenth century were simply unable to imagine the survival of the Church as an institution without its landed properties. Furthermore, the unilateral nature of the state's action implied a basic disregard for the Church's rights and a profound disrespect for its mission. In spite of its moderate reputation, the government had made no attempt to notify the hierarchy or negotiate any compromise before its abrupt abolition of the Church's entire fiscal regime.

In keeping with his position as the chief pastor of the nation, the Archbishop of Mexico City was the first to protest the government's action. He expressed his misgivings to the president on July 1, explaining that he preferred not to "enter into disputes with the supreme government, which I sincerely respect." Nevertheless, he felt compelled to speak out and ask for a revocation of the decree. Taking a pragmatic approach, Garza at first raised technical questions about the economic utility of the decree. But he also touched on its spiritual implications, making it clear that the bulls of his consecration forbade participation in any alienation of Church property. As a citizen of the republic, he had sworn to obey the law. But since the law now conflicted with his duty to God, the archbishop announced himself ready and willing to suffer the penalties mandated for noncompliance.[84] As an expert in canon law, it was Ezequiel Montes who again responded in the government's name to Garza's objections. As in the debates with the Bishop of Puebla, he used his background to draw upon canon law and Church history to argue for the legitimacy of the government's claims.

As Montes was surely aware, only the pope could authorize a sale of ecclesiastical property such as the *Ley Lerdo* was now demanding. Therefore, as in the earlier *fuero* debate, the archbishop suggested that direct negotiation with the Holy See was the only possible solution to the legal and canonical impasse created by the government's action. Apparently, Garza's proposal had widespread public support. Later in the month, for instance, a petition signed by five hundred and eighty residents of Querétaro proclaimed in bold letters: "THAT THE POPULATION OF THIS STATE, WITH RARE EXCEPTIONS, DESIRES THAT NO INNOVATIONS IN THIS MATTER [of Church property] BE INTRODUCED WITHOUT THE DECISION OF THE HOLY SEE."[85] On August 28, the archbishop even notified Montes that he was willing to ask Rome to excuse Mexicans from the canons regulating Church property if the government would postpone the deadline for adjudications by six months. However, Benito Juárez, the current minister of justice and ecclesiastical affairs, dismissed the appeal to Rome as another obstructionist ploy.[86]

The government's assault on the financial structure of the Church created an unusual solidarity among the Mexican episcopate, which was usually characterized by a certain localism and regional isolation.[87] Receiving no reply to his initial complaint, the archbishop sent a more strongly worded statement on July 7, reminding the government of the canons of the Council of Trent directed against those who took unauthorized possession of Church property. This was immediately followed by a protest from the cabildo (cathedral chapter) of Mexico City. Bishop Munguía came out against *Ley Lerdo* on July 19. Because of his outspoken opposition to the law, he was finally removed from his diocese on September 13 and his movements restricted to Mexico City.[88] The Bishop of Chiapas issued a pastoral letter against the law on July 20 and the Bishop of Guadalajara did the same on July 21.[89] The Bishop of San Luis Potosí added his voice on July 24 and the exiled Bishop of Puebla, who received the news of the decree in a Spanish port, published his response on July 30.[90] In spite of his public opposition, *El Monitor Republicano* later reported that Bishop Espinosa had given consent for the alienation of property in the Diocese of Guadalajara; this rumor, however, was officially denied by diocesan authorities.[91] In fact, because they interpreted the forced sale as a species of illicit appropriation of Church property, the bishops also threatened excommunication for anyone who attempted to purchase adjudicated buildings or land.[92]

Apparently, the collective outcry by the Mexican hierarchy worried liberal leaders, since they made strenuous efforts to impede the circulation of the episcopal statements. In the State of Michoacán, the printer who published Bishop Munguía's protest was prosecuted on August 16 and on September 4 some priests were fined for having read it from the pulpit. On September 6 Comonfort announced that governors could restrict the printing or public reading of pastoral letters in any state, and on September 12 Governor Doblado forbade the publication or distribution of episcopal statements in Guanajuato. The State of Chiapas passed a similar ban against protests on October 18. Officials there described the pastoral letters as "subversive" because of the "germ of sedition that their rash opposition implied."[93]

The position taken by the bishops against the *Ley Lerdo* divided Mexican society at a deeper level than any of the previous liberal-conservative confrontations. For the first time, conflicting ideologies pitted issues of conscience against personal economic interest for even non-political citizens. Many Mexicans did take advantage of the program to purchase real estate; in 1857 Lerdo announced that the law bearing his name had created nine thousand new property owners in Mexico.[94] Liberal newspapers like *El Monitor Republicano* also published updated lists from the government sales "so that the great success of the Lerdo Law might be seen."[95] Naturally, as in sixteenth-century Europe, those who benefited financially from the ruin of the Church would also become ardent supporters of the new order.[96] But at least half of the population opposed the measure on moral grounds, and this group "looked with horror" on those who participated in the forced sale. In some places tenants refused to pay rent to new landlords that they considered impious and illegitimate.[97] To ensure that no one escaped the ignominy of their actions, *La Cruz* and other Catholic newspapers also regularly published the name of the purchaser of each adjudicated property.[98] In response to this pressure, the government added new fines and restrictions for anyone attempting to retract their purchase of Church property. In one case, the governor even removed the priest of Irapuato (Guanajuato) from his parish for daring to hear the confession and public retraction of a remorseful buyer on his deathbed. On the other hand, there was also a report that priests were refusing to hear the confessions of wounded soldiers unless they first promised not to continue serving a government that was trying to seize the property of the Church.[99]

Although the principals involved in this standoff might have seemed clear, their application was not as obvious in individual cases. In fact, Catholic theologians in Mexico disagreed over the extent to which the faithful could cooperate with purchasers of ecclesiastical properties. Most held that paying rent to the new owners of adjudicated properties demonstrated cooperation with the despoliation of the Church. The archbishop held this view but was willing to allow tenants to pay until they could find alternative housing. The former head of the Jesuits in Mexico, Basilo Arrillaga, however, disagreed. He argued that since the law affected approximately 30,000 people, it would be impossible for all of them to find new dwellings. He therefore concluded that this impossibility exculpated those who unwillingly found themselves under new landlords. As one later Jesuit historian quipped, "this time, at least, the liberals would not object to Jesuit casuistry."[100] As a last resort, many elites that had purchased properties "in good faith" appealed to Rome for clarification, hoping for a dispensation that would remove the canonical penalties the Mexican bishops had imposed. However, after the "Holy Congregation of Extraordinary Ecclesiastical Affairs" investigated the issue, it concurred with the interpretation of the Mexican hierarchy.[101]

Naturally, the liberal press blamed the self-serving clergy for the negative popular reactions to Ley Lerdo. Along with the circulation of forbidden episcopal pronouncements, priests were accused of using the pulpit and the confessional to denounce the law and intimidate prospective buyers.[102] In one official statement José María Lafragua, the minister of the interior, charged that priests had "disfigured the worship of the God of peace" by the "expositions, circulars and discourses with which throughout the republic they have tried not only to discredit the law of June 25, but to raise all the classes of society against the government." The law had been intentionally mischaracterized by "indiscrete ecclesiastics and agents of the reaction" as an attack on the religion of Jesus Christ, he charged, "and many of its ministers, straying in every way from the teaching of the Divine Master, fomented the elements of disorder with the breath of their mouths, wickedly employed in defending earthly interests, in mixing the chaff with the wheat of good doctrine and in inciting the people to rebellion." Although they accused the government of being the "enemy of the Church," he wrote, "the present administration is just as Catholic, if not more so, than those pharisaical defenders of religion."[103] Liberals also charged that too often it was trusted laymen who purchased ecclesiastical properties, leaving practical ownership and control in clerical hands. On the other hand, there were also numerous cases in which unscrupulous government officials were able to manipulate the law to illegally seize property for themselves. Conservative critics also alleged that much of the alienated property was grabbed by foreigners.[104]

As social tensions rose in the aftermath of the implementation of the new law, liberal fears of new conspiracies also grew. As usual, the clergy and religious were the targets of most of this paranoia.[105] Following accusations by Guadalajara's *La Revolución*, Governor José Ignacio Herrera y Cairo arrested the superiors of the Dominican, Franciscan, Augustinian, Carmelite and Mercedian orders in the city on July 11: "He publicly reprimanded them saying that they helped the enemies of the government with their sermons, their secret meetings and their money."[106] In this case, however, the clerics convincingly denied all the charges and were set free. In Puebla, where religious emotions were running even higher, suspected subversives were not allowed to defend their innocence. On July 17 Governor Traconis arrested seventeen prominent citizens and churchmen, among them a general, three physicians, the prior of the Carmelites, the prior of the Dominican monastery, the Franciscan provincial, and the dean of the cathedral, Ángel Alonso y Pantiga, "a venerable old man of 80 years."[107] Accused by a liberal newspaper of plotting against the government, they were all exiled from the country without formal charges or a hearing, in spite of a written appeal to the president for justice.[108]

By the end of July, the government's penchant for summary justice had created a sense of panic among conservatives. The French ambassador captured the desperate atmosphere in the country in his sensational dispatch on July 26. "The alarm is general," he wrote,

and the irritation against the government is such that from one moment to the other it might fall. The prisons of Puebla are overflowing with honest men and priests; the upper class is fleeing the city. [In Mexico City] the prisons are equally full. Even the least influential members of the clergy are persecuted. The minister of justice has prohibited any priest to express even the slighted discontent in his parish; the governor has arrested even sacristans and vergers for allowing the posting of handbills in the churches or circulating them among the faithful, in which they make a call against the radicals and the excommunicated. [109]

The situation in Puebla grew even worse after the government levied a new fine of one million pesos against the diocese on August 16. That same day the new prior of the Dominican monastery and four other notable citizens were taken into custody and exiled. Four more Dominicans were arrested there on September 4.[110]

The government's crackdown on suspected clerical conspiracy reached its apogee with an assault on the Franciscan monastery in Mexico City on the night of September 14, 1856. At eleven o'clock, having been informed that some friars were involved in an anti-government plot, officials broke into the cloister and arrested nine men that they discovered meeting in one of the cells. The search continued until noon the next day, but no incriminating evidence or arms were ever found. Nevertheless, six friars, a visiting priest, and twenty-one servants were brought in for questioning. On September 16, the annual celebration of Mexico's independence, Juan José Baz, governor of the Federal District, ordered the destruction of part of the monastery for reasons of "public utility," ostensibly in order to open a much-needed new street.[111] Work began at midnight the next day, since it was feared that a riot might break out if the demolition was carried out in broad daylight. On September 17, Comonfort also decreed the suppression of the religious community itself and confiscation of all its goods, alleging that sedition had been uncovered in the cloister.[112]

The suppression of San Francisco, the most famous monastery in Mexico, was a blow to many Mexican Catholics. It was the national headquarters of the Franciscan order, which still had seven hundred and sixty-three friars scattered around the country. The earliest missionaries in Mexico had founded this sprawling complex in 1525, and friars trained here had been sent as far away as California and Japan. Many illustrious names, such as that of Bernardino de Sahagun, had been attached to this community, and for many people the convent of St. Francis symbolized the entire history of Christianity in Mexico.[113] Along with the other social and spiritual services it provided, the monastery also operated a school with one hundred students and housed a library, open to the public, with over 20,000 volumes. The Franciscan church, once the subject of a special feature in *La Cruz*, was also the preferred site for religious functions for many social groups in the capital.[114]

For Catholics, the fate of the monastery buildings also became a potent symbol of the lethal danger posed to the Church by the liberal regime. One writer compared this event to the destruction of the historic and irreplaceable Church of St. Denis by radicals during the French Revolution.[115]

More immediately, this new "sacrilege" was used to inflame passions against the Comonfort government. One of the posters produced on conservative presses during this period expressed the outrage generated by this action:

> Attention Mexicans! Alert! You see with amazement how the tyrannical government of Comonfort has calumniated the innocent priests of Saint Francis for no other reason than to grab the church plate, to begin destroying our religion, and to profane those holy places that even Martin Luther and Peter [*sic*] Calvin respected. Mexicans, do not permit this; better death than that they destroy our religion. Eternal hatred to tyrants! May the curse of God fall on those men of abominable memory! On those sacrilegious thieves! Cursed be all the *puros*, by God and by man! Long live the immunity of the Church![116]

Henceforth, the theme of "destroyed temples" joined the litany of reproaches against the liberal "demagogues" in seditious literature and numerous rebel proclamations.[117]

According to many conservatives, the charges of conspiracy were only a "pretext for the demolition of part of the convent."[118] In fact, evidence suggests that the destruction of portions of the monastery may have been part of an ongoing liberal campaign to reduce the physical presence of the religious orders in Mexico.[119] After all, these massive buildings were a constant reminder of the power of the Church, and of the spiritual ideal of monasticism rejected by liberalism. Critics also claimed that the buildings hindered urban development. As early as 1846, Baz had unsuccessfully pushed for the partial demolition of La Profesa, a historic Jesuit religious complex in Mexico City then under the care of the Congregation of the Oratory.[120] Now, however, charges of conspiracy provided sufficient justification for the removal of the unwanted buildings. The day after demolition began on the Franciscan monastery in Mexico City, laborers were also sent to dismantle a portion of the Dominican convent in Puebla. This action, recklessly carried out in broad daylight, created much excitement in the city, with crowds of women "wailing and crying in the surrounding streets" and men shouting threats against the government.[121] On September 22 and November 3, 1856, the Augustinian convents in Morelia and San Luis Potosí fell victim to the same "mania for new streets," as it came to be known.[122]

Ultimately, the government was unable to prove any of its charges against the friars in Mexico City. Yet many liberals, predisposed by their own anticlerical rhetoric, continued to believe in the truth of the accusations. *El Tribuno del Pueblo*, one of Mexico City's most anticlerical newspapers, even reported that the friars and their co-conspirators had already pronounced against the government when they were apprehended. Only timely intervention had prevented their calling for reinforcements to begin an armed uprising, the editors claimed. The newspaper even informed its readers that the slogan of the aborted revolt had already been chosen: "Long live religion and death to the *puro* heretics!"[123] So convincing were such stories that twenty-five years later, when he was writing his own history of these events, Vigil still believed that the friars were guilty.[124]

In fact, another revolt did occur during the next month, orchestrated not by priests but again by disaffected military officers. The second rebellion in Puebla broke out during the night of October 19, when rebel forces under colonels Joaquín Francisco Orihuela and Miguel Miramón seized control of the city. This time, however, the religious element in the uprising was more pronounced. In the following weeks, the *Ley Lerdo* was suspended in areas of the state controlled by the rebels, and on one occasion three priests led a huge demonstration to rally the troops, waving a white flag with a large red cross and shouting "Long live religion!" and "Death to Comonfort!" A massive government force finally quelled the rebellion on December 5, with over a thousand casualties reported between the two sides.[125] During the conflict a scandal had arisen when a local priest refused the sacraments to two seriously wounded federal soldiers unless they promised to stop fighting on the government side. Although another priest was found to attend to the soldiers, the original offender was still arrested, and enraged liberals began to demand long prison sentences or exile for such "pharisaical priests."[126]

Looking back on the events of 1856, conservatives could only see a series of defeats and disasters for their country. This mood was reflected in Malo's diary entry on the first day of 1857. The year that has just ended, he recalled,

> saw Puebla destroyed by two sieges in which many people and valiant leaders died. It saw the expropriation of the goods of the civil and religious corporations, the exile of a bishop and various high-ranking churchmen, of generals, chiefs, and officers in the army and of many individuals; the extinction of the convent of our father St. Francis, a street being opened that divided it in half, and a decided persecution against religion and its ministers . . . God permit that the present year will be less calamitous for the unfortunate Mexicans![127]

However, the New Year began almost immediately with new anticlerical legislation by the Comonfort administration, indicating that Malo's wish would not be fulfilled.[128]

The interior minister, José María Lafragua, issued the first of the new controversial decrees on January 27.[129] Historically, the imposition of a civil registry has always been an important milestone in the consolidation of a secular state. Traditionally, priests recorded local baptisms, deaths, and marriages in the parish register, thereby associating the major events of every Christian's life with the Church. But the new "Law of Civil Registry" stated that henceforth all vital statistics in Mexico would be recorded, for a fee, by functionaries of the secular government, automatically expanding the state's dominion into all these areas of life. The new law, which would take effect six months after its promulgation, required the secular registration of births, adoptions, marriages, deaths, and the taking of religious vows or ordination. At the same time, stiff fines were leveled on those who failed to comply. Even worse, a marriage that was not registered within forty-eight hours of the religious ceremony would be considered invalid by the state. The benefits and requirements of matrimony would not be legally recognized, the children of such unions would be considered illegitimate, and both parents and children would automatically lose the right of inheritance in such cases. In order to help ensure compliance by the citizenry, priests were also required, under penalty of heavy fines, to report every baptism, marriage, and funeral at which they officiated. In a similar vein, on January 30 the government issued a decree that placed cemeteries under the authority of the Department of Public Hygiene. In the case of graveyards, the imperative of medical science, not politics, was the main justification offered for the further curtailment of clerical jurisdiction and the extension of government oversight even to the final resting place of the dead.[130]

Although conservatives argued that the new law was both redundant and oppressive, the clergy explained that the Church was not necessarily opposed to a civil registry per se. However, some of the articles in this particular organic law were, they pointed out, implicitly hostile to the Catholic faith and constituted undue secular interference in the exercise of religion. First, the legal non-recognition of unregistered marriages called into question the entire Catholic understanding of the sacrament of matrimony. Also, requiring priests to inform the secular authorities of every baptism, marriage, and burial they performed made them (unpaid) agents of the state as well as unwilling accomplices in the enforcement of law. This was ironic, Munguía pointed out, since politically the clergy were still classified as non–citizens.[131] Most offensive of all, however, were the provisions of the new law that regulated entrance into the religious life.

To many Catholics, it seemed obvious that the liberal government was attempting to discourage monastic life in the republic under the pretext of recording religious vows. In particular, the special attention paid to nuns in the law suggests that hoary myths about convent life, common to liberals and Protestants worldwide, played a large part in its formulation. For instance, soon after the triumph of the Ayutla Revolution, the radical press began to agitate for the liberation of the many "poor women" who, they claimed. had been coerced into taking religious vows and were "condemned body and soul" to life in the convent.[132] Now, although the canons of the Council of Trent permitted females to enter a convent at sixteen years of age, Article 79 of the new decree required a woman to be twenty-five years old before she could enter the novitiate of any religious order.[133] Although no age limitation was specified for male postulants, both men and women were also required to receive parental consent and appear before an official of the state and two lay witnesses before taking religious vows, or in the case of male candidates for the priesthood, before receiving ordination to the subdeaconate. Likewise reflecting liberal suspicions about religious life was Article 80, which specified that this interrogation be held privately, without the attendance of any religious figures or family members who might try to influence the outcome of the process. In addition, Article 81 made generous provisions for those who might choose to leave the religious state, even after final vows.[134]

As one priest explained, all these regulations suggested that the Church was dishonest in its recruitment and took no care to ensure the liberty or suitability of candidates for its religious orders. The author of this anonymous work, who refers to himself only as "an obscure priest," argued that the Church had already established the age for females entering religious life and the state had no power to overrule the decision of a general council of the Church. Furthermore, he declared, Church regulations already ensured a prudent examination of all candidates, and their personal freedom of choice was guaranteed by canon law. The Church was very careful in these matters, he argued, if for no other reason than that the presence of an unhappy or unsuitable monk or nun would be detrimental to the common life of any religious community. "This law is not about liberty," he wrote, although it tried to "hide itself" under this pretense. "Its real object," he avowed, "is to degrade and humiliate the authority of ecclesiastical superiors."[135]

Conservative complaints notwithstanding, the decrees that transferred the control of vital statistics and cemeteries into the hands of the state were still relatively moderate measures. After all, although the government could now claim some control over certain details of monastic and family life in the republic, it was still assumed that only priests would officiate at marriage ceremonies and burials. Religious vows were restricted, but at this point still not entirely forbidden. It was not the letter of the new laws that was threatening, however, but the anti-Catholic bias they were alleged to conceal. The cumulative effect of all the real and symbolic attacks on the Church since 1855 had already convinced many Mexicans of the sinister intentions of the reformers. At the same time, the acrimonious debates surrounding the 1856 constituent congress added a new ideological dimension to institutional conflicts between Church and State in Mexico. It was there, on the floor of the congress, that the gap between the liberal and conservative versions of the nation's past and visions for its future became too obvious for anyone to ignore.

CHAPTER 5

Debating the Religious Future of the Nation

Of all the unsettling developments of 1856, none had a more lasting impact on the nation than the meeting of the constituent congress whose task it was to write a new constitution for the nation. Convened within the context of military revolts and rumors of anti-government conspiracy, liberal deputies often felt themselves at war with a reactionary power attempting to undermine their most cherished goals. Meanwhile, conservatives were disturbed by a number of proposed articles that were clearly detrimental to the interests of the Church. Perhaps more than any other event during the Reforma, the proposal to introduce religious toleration highlighted the existence of two competing visions for Mexico's future, both reactions to Mexico's humiliating defeat by the United States less than a decade before. At this juncture liberals saw an opportunity to eliminate the influence of an outdated theological paradigm once and for all. More importantly, they hoped to transform the country by flooding it with more enlightened and productive Protestant immigrants. Conservatives, on the other hand, also wanted to modernize and strengthen the country, but they were even more committed to preserving its Hispanic heritage and culture. During a summer already made tense by reactions to recent anticlerical decrees, the debate over Mexico's religious future reflected and intensified the ideological conflict already occurring outside the walls of the legislative chamber.

Elections for the constituent congress were held on December 17, 1855. Through a three-tiered system of primary, secondary, and departmental elections, one delegate was to be chosen for every 50,000 inhabitants in each state. For the first time, property and residence requirements were eliminated; only criminals, vagrants, and members of the clergy were excluded from the process. But according to some reports the elections were marred by irregularities.[1] It also appears that liberal clubs dominated local elections with their political machinery and effectively eliminated almost all known conservative candidates from the final ballots.[2] With only two notable exceptions, all of the one hundred and fifty-four elected delegates were liberals, a majority with radical *puro* tendencies.[3]

The demographic profile of the candidates chosen under these circumstances was also highly significant for the final outcome of the congress. Almost a third of delegates were relatively young, and an overwhelming majority of them, one hundred and eight, were lawyers.[4] Because of their great numbers and appetite for office, lawyers were sometimes vilified as the "beggars" or "Jews" of Mexico City. The French ambassador claimed that there were 2,500 of them established in the capital, compared with only eighteen engineers.[5] Because of a perpetual shortage of clients, most found themselves employed as bureaucrats. This group dominated the liberal party, and along with a few other public employees and military officers, filled the seats of the constituent congress. In the absence of industrialists or businessmen, the few landowners elected to the congress were in no position to balance the influence and ideological interests of this political class.[6]

In order to avoid the conservative influence concentrated in Mexico City, article sixty-six of the Álvarez *convocatoria* had dictated that the 'extraordinary congress' should hold all its deliberations in the patriotic town of Dolores Hidalgo. But Comonfort amended that rule on December 26, 1855, and relocated the congress to a spacious hall on the second floor of the presidential palace. He officially inaugurated it there on February 18, 1856. On this occasion a speech was also delivered by Ponciano Arriaga, a *puro* delegate from Jalisco who had been elected president of the congress. Both discourses noted the rebellion still raging ninety miles away in Puebla but promised a swift victory and a glorious future for Mexico under a new constitution. At the end of the ceremony, the galleries of the chamber erupted with cries of "Viva Comonfort!" "Viva Arriaga!" "Long live liberty!" and "Death to the reactionaries!"

This feeling of unity between the moderate president and the radical congress, however, did not last long. In fact, differences of opinion and style between them appeared the very next day. According to custom, the administration issued a decree asking that special prayers be offered for the success of the congress in all the cathedrals, parishes, convents, and monasteries of the country. Religious and civic leaders were asked to join together at these services, "in order to implore Almighty God that the legislators decree what is just and for the success of the sovereign congress, the reestablishment of peace and for the happiness of the nation." On February 19, Comonfort's minister of the interior, José María Lafragua, delivered a formal invitation to the congress requesting that a representative deputation join the president and his cabinet at a special liturgy in the Metropolitan Cathedral. After a brief debate, however, the delegates refused to attend the religious functions on technical grounds. Although it was only a minor incident, the rebuff was noted by those observers who were looking for signs of congressional animosity toward the Church.[7]

In fact, the congress exhibited a marked anticlerical bias even before a draft of the new constitution was revealed. For example, on April 22, 1856, the delegates voted, eighty-two to one, to approve the *Ley Juarez*, the initial catalyst for the Zacapoaxtla revolt.[8] Many supporters of the Church had hoped that this law would be repealed once the more moderate Comonfort solidified his political power base. Now that the congress had embraced the measure, however, a reversal seemed impossible. In his diary, Malo lamented this development and recalled how the bishops protested the law when it was issued five months before. "Now we do not know what they will do, since it is prohibited to write against the measure or even publish what the bishops say about it," he complained, "The enemies of the clergy can freely say whatever they please."[9] On the other hand, Francisco Zarco's memoirs of the congress recorded the liberal exaltation: "No more *fueros*! No more privileges! No more exemptions! Equality for all citizens! Justice for all!"[10] Following the logic of the Álvarez administration, however, the congress simultaneously denied members of the clergy the right to vote or hold any political office. On May 26, it approved the revised "Provisional Organic Statutes," whose article 24 restated this exclusion.[11]

In its first months, the congress also adopted controversial legislation that many considered detrimental to the country's religious orders. Because of the former dictator's public support for the Church, such moves were not outside the purview of the congress, in spite of its temporary nature. Along with creating a new national charter, the Plan of Ayutla also charged the delegates with reviewing all the acts of the previous administration. Santa Anna himself had revoked anticlerical laws from the Gómez Farías period, which liberals were now able to revive.[12] In part, their decision to reverse the *santanista* legislation favorable to religious orders was motivated by a desire to erase all memory of the hated dictator. But liberal beliefs about the inutility or even dangers posed by religious life were also very important in the debates that surrounded the revision of these laws.

Religious orders in Mexico had been a constant target of attacks in the liberal press since the fall of Santa Anna. In spite of efforts by Catholic newspapers like *La Cruz* to combat this negative publicity, on April 26 the Congress voted to restore a statue that denied official recognition or legal support for religious vows. This measure, ostensibly a sign of the state's noninterference in religious matters, was also meant to encourage anyone with doubts about his or her religious vocation to leave the cloister.[13] Nuns in particular were often described by liberal journalists as "victims of fanaticism and ignorance," unhappy women who had been lured into the convent as young girls.[14] There are, however, no reports at this time of any religious, male or female, taking advantage of the new provision made for their relief. On the contrary, some convents in Mexico City staged elaborate public ceremonies in which their members voluntarily renewed their original vows.[15]

Although there were only a dozen Jesuits in Mexico at this time, calls for their expulsion were also insistent since the triumph of the Ayutla Revolution.[16] For conservative Catholics, the news that the congress was considering such an action was "sad and disheartening."[17] To liberals, however, the alleged involvement of clergymen in the Zacapoaxtla revolt made suppression of this infamous order imperative. "The existence of the Society of Jesus in our country," declared one liberal newspaper, "would be a perpetual threat and a constant danger for its liberty, progress, and enlightenment."[18] In spite of requests for a public hearing on the matter, the congressional debates took place in closed session.

On June 5, the commission of ecclesiastical affairs for the constituent congress presented its report recommending suppression. The committee argued that because of their notorious reputation, Jesuits should not be allowed to exist in an ultra-Catholic country like Mexico, one where religious sentiment was easily exploited by "an already superfluous number of clergy and religious."[19] Among the respondents, only Marcelino Castañeda spoke against the expulsion. The liberal agenda, he pointed out, promised complete liberty, freedom of religion and conscience, and an end to educational monopoly. In denying Jesuits the right to exist in Mexico, all these principles would be violated. How, he wondered, could the entire congress be so frightened by twelve priests, reduced in Mexico to "the humble position of schoolteachers?"[20]

In the end, this appeal to liberal ideals could not overcome the deep-seated prejudice and fear of Jesuits in the anticlerical party. In response to Castañeda's argument, Ignacio Vallarta, one of the young members of the Falange de Estudios and now a deputy from the State of Jalisco, rehearsed the entire history of philosophe and Bourbon opposition to the order. Summarizing more than a century of anti-Jesuit paranoia, he declared, "the Society of Jesus, vicious in its own constitution, dangerous in its spirit, of fatal consequences in its development, enemy of governments, provocateur of civil and religious war, tenacious in its projects, fearful in its inexhaustible resources, the Society of Jesus, I repeat, damned by history, cannot be planted in a country that has the felicity of lacking these domestic enemies."[21] Under no circumstance should such agents of reaction be allowed to continue the instruction of youth in Mexico, he added. Immediately after this speech, the Congress voted, seventy-seven to eighteen, to suppress the order.[22] A few days later Governor Traconis also expelled the Vincentian fathers from Puebla because, as one conservative sardonically reported, "they looked like Jesuits."[23]

Many Catholics were devastated by the news of the suppression. The Bishop of Puebla, who had been waiting in Havana for a reply to his appeal, received the news of the suppression on June 9. Recognizing the tenor of the new government in this decree, he abandoned hopes for a hearing on his case and immediately left for Rome. According to Zamacois, "the resolution of the government to extinguish the few Jesuit priests that exist in the country was seen by the Catholic people as further proof of a government-sponsored war against Catholicism."[24] Malo, whose name appeared on a petition supporting the Jesuits in 1855, recorded that "all sensible people have received this news with much bitterness." "How long, O God," he wondered, "will you restrain your hand and suspend your anger against this disgraceful country?"[25] On July 10, La Cruz began an eight-part series refuting all the charges leveled against the proscribed order by the members of congress. Having hoped, the editors lamented, that the liberals would respect individual rights, including the freedom of conscience, the right of free association, and freedom of education, "We have been sadly disappointed."[26]

Four months after its inauguration, the congress finally turned its attention to approving a new constitution. Although some delegates made a motion to simply reinstate the federal charter of 1824, this plan was rejected, and on June 16 the drafting committee presented its first proposal for the "Project of the Constitution" to the nation.[27] Disappointed that his ideas on land reform had not found a place in the proposed draft, on June 23 Arriaga delivered an impassioned discourse on "the great abuses introduced in the exercise of the rights of private property."[28] The anxiety that his socialist schemes created among landowners in various parts of the country was reflected in the petitions in defense of property they later submitted to the congress, but no action was ever taken on his actual proposals.[29] Five days later, however, the deputies did approve a resolution in favor of the *Ley Lerdo*, which outlawed the owning of real estate by any civic or religious corporations.[30]

The debate over the Lerdo Law occurred on June 28, 1856, only three days after the law first appeared. Since no congressional action was required to make the law effective, the main purpose of the approval was to demonstrate support for the measure in the face of massive clerical and conservative resistance. Although not a single voice was raised in defense of the rights of the Church, objections against the law were made by those who had hoped for a more sweeping bill in the European style, one that would automatically strip the Church of all its resources and in so doing replenish the government treasury. Ignacio Ramírez, a delegate from Jalisco, for example, argued that allowing the clergy to retain the proceeds from the sale of their property would only provide them with more ready cash "with which to start conspiracies." But most speakers stressed its politically neutral character. Like Comonfort, Guillermo Prieto, a *puro* delegate from Puebla, described the measure as "neither political nor religious, but altogether social and humanitarian." A resolution to approve the *Ley Lerdo* was approved, seventy-eight to fifteen. During the patriotic celebrations on September 28 later that same year, Prieto extolled the progress of the *Ley Lerdo* in his speech before the president. Such was his enthusiasm for the law that he proclaimed that a recent earthquake was a "heavenly and infallible announcement" that its goals would be achieved. He also declared that impoverishment of the Church should not be an important consideration, since "we can venerate a cross made of sticks as well as one made of gold."[31]

The formal debates over the actual articles of the constitution finally began on July 4, 1856.[32] Even without Arriaga's land reform program, the final document contained many elements that concerned conservative Catholics. For example, Article 3 declared that public education was to be free, but some feared this phrase might be construed to exclude religion from the classroom.[33] Article 9 legalized "associations for any legitimate purpose," which could be interpreted to include Protestant sects. Article 5 enshrined the government's official non-recognition of religious vows, and Articles 13 and 27 incorporated the *Ley Juárez* and the *Ley Lerdo*, respectively, into the constitution.[34] Articles 56 and 57 perpetuated the ban on priests holding political office but would restore their right to vote. More problematically, Article 123 gave the federal government the right to intervene in "matters of religious worship and external ecclesiastical discipline." Although all of these articles precipitated serious debate both inside and outside of the congress, the proposed Article 15, which promised freedom of worship to any and all religious creeds, created the greatest amount of controversy in the nation.[35]

Of the one hundred and twenty-six proposed articles, Article 15 was the only one to be excluded from the final document. In spite of its moderate language and strong liberal support, the majority of Mexicans completely rejected this innovation. The proposed text of the article read as follows:

> No law or official order shall be issued in the republic that prohibits or impedes the performance of public worship of any creed; but the Roman, Catholic, and Apostolic faith having been the exclusive religion of the Mexican people, the congress of the union will guard by means of just and prudent laws, protecting it in so far as it does not prejudice the interests of the people, nor the rights of national sovereignty.

For *puros*, eliminating the Catholic monopoly in public worship was considered an essential foundation for the entire reformation program.[36] In turn, this plan became the focal point of conservative resistance to the liberal project. Debate on the article engaged people from all walks of life and precipitated what has been called "the largest public debate in [Mexico's] history."[37] According to Zamacois: "Never had the national will been expressed in such a uniform and spontaneous manner as then. All the classes of society, the entire nation, manifested itself against freedom of worship."[38]

Officially, the Catholic Church opposed the notion of toleration because of the religious relativism it was supposed to breed. Pope Pius IX had already publicly condemned the main liberal arguments in favor of this position before 1856.[39] In Mexico, the bishops initiated formal opposition to religious toleration even before Article 15 was presented for debate. In fact, the July 4 session began with the reading of a letter from the Archbishop of Mexico City requesting that the religious status quo not be changed. He particularly objected to the suggestion that the Catholic faith "had been" that of the Mexican people, implying that this consensus lay in the past. "It is certain that the people of Mexico in general still love and profess the religion of our ancestors, as they loved and professed it," he announced, "notwithstanding that their sentiments and feelings have varied in other matters, for example, in the form of government."[40] Over the next few weeks, letters of protest were also presented to the congress from the bishops of Oaxaca, San Luis Potosí, Linares (now Nueva Leon), and Guadalajara, and from some of their respective cabildos.

Although the controversy over religious toleration raged for months outside the congress, Article 15 was debated on the floor of the chamber for only six days, from July 29 to August 5. Every day during this period the visitor's galleries were packed with spectators, including many women, who applauded, cheered, or booed the delegates depending on the position they adopted in their speeches. Cries of "Long live religion!" and "Long live the clergy!" alternated with shouts of "Down with the friars and the sacristans!" and "Long live liberty!" At times the delegates were showered with scraps of paper from above, on which were written threats like "Death to the heretics!" or encouraging statements like "Long live the reformation!"[41] Clearly emotions were running high over this issue. On the first day the bill was debated, for example, an elderly man was assaulted when he shouted, "Long live religion!" outside the presidential palace.[42]

The level of excitement surrounding this debate may also be judged by the controversy that surrounded the death of the *moderado* journalist Juan Bautista Morales. As it turned out, he died on the very day that public deliberations on Article 15 were to begin. Something of a celebrity because of his long-running newspaper polemic with *La Cruz*, his views on the inferiority of Catholic nations were an important weapon in the liberal pro-toleration arsenal. His death, at this precise moment, therefore appeared to some Catholics as a divine judgment on the bill itself. Subsequently, a rumor spread that Morales had retracted his anticlerical remarks and made peace with the Church before he died. Dismayed by the story, liberal delegates denied its veracity on the floor of the congress and denounced the cunning of priests who terrified innocent people on their deathbeds.[43] The tension created by the report was so great that the government was finally compelled to question the widow about her husband's last hours.[44] Likewise, the archbishop requested a signed statement from the attending priest, which was published in *La Cruz* on August 6, 1856.[45] Since these testimonies largely corroborated the original story, liberals had to content themselves with the fact that Morales had not actually signed a written retraction.

When formal debate on Article 15 finally began, supporters of religious toleration advanced a number of different arguments in its favor. Moderates, concerned as Morales had been over the relative underdevelopment of Mexico, in general supported the idea that increased immigration, especially of the

Protestant variety, was the solution to all of Mexico's economic problems.[46] José Antonio Gamboa, a deputy from Oaxaca, summed up this attitude when he declared that "colonization" by Europeans was a matter of life or death for Mexico. Mexico had already opened its doors to external commerce, he claimed, and now it wanted "its riches exploited, its countryside cultivated, and its immense territory populated." Already the country had everything to offer the immigrant, except freedom of worship. For this reason, he argued, European Protestants avoided Mexico and streamed into the United States, where their skills and ingenuity were put to good use.[47] Without increased population and development Mexico was also in danger of losing even more of its territory to its northern neighbor, he warned. Francisco Zarco contributed to the immigration argument by adding that "because of our [religious] intolerance we lost Texas, we lost California, we lost the Mesilla, and if we do not allow beneficial colonization, perhaps we will lose our nationality and our independence, saving what they call 'religious unity.'"[48]

Conservatives, for their part, always denied that religious exclusivity was the main reason that immigrants eschewed Mexico. For example, a petition against the bill submitted to the congress by the inhabitants of Tlalnepantla and Cuautenca (State of Mexico) offered a different explanation for Mexico's population problems: "When we consolidate the peace, have effective guarantees of personal security and respect for property, when our newspapers do not daily have to report stage robberies, then the natural advantages of our country and the elements of prosperity that abound in it will attract immigration."[49] Besides, the petition observed, Protestants were known to be very fickle about religious affiliation. According to observers, in the United States it was not uncommon for them to change denominations five or six times over a lifetime. For non-Catholics, the petition implied, religious considerations were not a serious obstacle when material considerations were involved.[50] But even some moderates recognized the weakness of the liberal case. Lafragua, who served as a representative for the State of Puebla, noted that if Catholic hegemony deterred Northern Europeans, it did not explain the lack of Spanish, French, Italian, and Irish colonists.[51] Furthermore, a petition from Querétaro also disagreed with the identification of population growth with national prosperity. "The most populated nations of the world are also the most miserable," it noted, suggesting that the critiques of Great Britain and the United States published earlier in response to Morales were well known.[52]

Material benefits were not the only argument used in favor of religious toleration during the debates. Some deputies sought to apply liberal economic principles to the question, stressing the moral benefits that would follow from competition in a free market of religious ideas. Zarco, for instance, admitted that he had never visited the United States, but claimed that Catholics he had met from there seemed more pious and devout than Mexicans.[53] José María Mata, the *puro* deputy from Veracruz, also agreed that US Catholics were superior to the Mexican variety. People there were Catholic because they wanted to be, he explained, and did not attend church "out of mere custom, to pass the time, or for fear of what might be said." While Catholics in the US were deemed virtuous, "in Mexico our worship is such that if Jesus returned to the world, he would have to repeat here the memorable scene that he enacted in the temple of Jerusalem."[54]

Ultimately, the existence of religious toleration in other countries was one of the most powerful arguments advanced in favor of Article 15. According to a petition from Veracruz in favor of the bill, freedom of religion was a "principle recognized, sanctioned, and currently put in practice in all the cultured nations of the globe."[55] Even the Turks tolerated other religions in their domain, liberals argued. The most powerful example, however, was that of the United States. "I contemplate the growing prosperity of that people that could not exist without religious liberty and therefore I do not fear the results of liberty of conscience in my own country," Zarco exclaimed.[56] Conservatives, however, pointed out that toleration in the US was not the result of choice, but of historical necessity. "Two hundred years ago a flood of pilgrims came to North America, to a land buried under the first snow of winter, and a nation was formed with outlaws and outcasts of all countries," explained Marcelino Castañeda, the only conservative in the congress. Because of the diversity of beliefs these settlers represented, "they raised altars for every creed" and established religious tolerance. But since Mexico had only one religion, there was no need to introduce toleration there.

Opponents of Article 15 also warned that the multiplicity of sects weakened religion wherever it existed. Castañeda claimed that countries with competing denominations were characterized by indifferentism and skepticism, along with "divisions in government, divisions in families, anguish in parents, children gone astray."[57] A petition signed by eight hundred and sixty-two citizens of Mexico City admitted that the United States was admired for its material prosperity. But because its government professed no religion, it claimed, "its inhabitants are divided into a thousand sects that multiply more every day." Public morality in that country had reached such a shameful state that the government authorized aggressive wars against its neighboring states, "and views coldly the devastation of entire provinces if it would result in the gain of one foot of territory." If prosperity demanded Protestant immigration, the signers of the petition insisted, they would "prefer without hesitation the unity of worship to population growth and all the advantages that this could produce among us."[58] Even one moderate was disturbed by the alleged moral consequences of religious diversity in the United States. Luis de la Rosa, the government's minister of foreign relations and a representative for Zacatecas, confessed that he had once been in favor of religious freedom, "but once I had seen the moral effect that it produces in the United States, I stopped desiring it for Mexico."[59]

Liberal admiration for the United States during these debates was also challenged in one other very significant area. The pronounced "fondness for foreigners" exhibited by some delegates caused Antonio Aguado, a deputy for Guanajuato, to point out that the constituent congress was charged with giving a constitution "not to the United States, nor to England, but to the Mexican people," and therefore it was their capacities and customs that had to be consulted.[60] He also felt that it was necessary to remind the members of one glaring anomaly in the much-praised American system. "Do we not see in the United States, in the midst of that pure democracy that is so admired, in that liberal constitution that is so celebrated, propounded the most atrocious, most cruel, most humiliating principle for the human race, that being slavery?" he asked.[61] Was not the persistence of slavery proof enough of the United States's moral bankruptcy?

On the other hand, while pragmatic arguments in favor of religious toleration were favored by *moderados, puro* deputies often adopted a more ideological stance. For Pablo Castellanos, a representative from Yucatán, Article 15 was still "a little timid" in its present form. The real question, he asserted, was whether Mexico was to have a theocratic or a civil government: "If we do not have the courage to resolve this issue, we abdicate in one moment the power of the people in favor of the clergy, and a bishop will come to be president of the republic."[62] Religious toleration, from this point of view, was necessary in order to break the power of the clergy over the people. "The moment the constitution refuses to enforce intolerance and an exclusive religion, the clergy will stop being powerful and the priest a public functionary," promised José María Castillo Velasco, a representative from the Federal District.[63]

Also central to the *puro* argument was the familiar anticlerical claim that "a great chasm" existed between authentic Christianity and the Roman Catholic clergy. In the congress, for example, the benevolent principles of the Gospel were frequently contrasted with the worst episodes of European history; the horrors of the Dark Ages, the Crusades, and the Spanish Inquisition were all ascribed to the perfidy of priests. Like Cruz-Aedo, delegates used this "Black Legend" to prove that the Catholic clergy in Mexico were not ministers of God, but self-serving imposters. Hence it fell to enlightened men like themselves to effect necessary changes in the religious structure of the nation. The clergy had always opposed change, it was charged, and they worked to prevent any social progress that would undermine their status or threaten their possessions. Perhaps the most striking example of the extreme anticlerical spirit was a speech by Prieto on July 30. Echoing the allegations leveled in "The Theocratic Power," he conjured up images of opulent canons lulled to sleep by crying beggars at their door and of priests seducing young virgins in the confessional and then hiding from responsibility behind the altar.[64]

Conservatives, of course, offered their own historical counterarguments in favor of the Catholic religion. Castañeda, for one, tried to demonstrate that Catholicism had always been in the vanguard of civilization. Only the arrival of the Catholic religion, he insisted, had been able to "break chains, condemn slavery and transform the ancient world composed of slaves and lords into a society of brothers."[65] Many of the petitions against toleration presented before the congress also celebrated the accomplishments of Catholic civilization. Some pointed to the conversion of the heathen in Mexico as evidence of the wonderful effects of Catholic doctrine. Others praised the universal elevation of women, the strengthening of families, and the development of gentle manners that they attributed to the influence of the Catholic faith. Some "manifestations" recalled the Church's triumph over pagan, Protestant, and philosophe persecution to demonstrate its divine and eternal character. In short, the entire array of historical and cultural arguments advanced in the pages of *La Cruz* had found their way into the popular petitions against Article 15.

Ideologically, another key element in the liberal arsenal in favor of toleration was insistence on "freedom of conscience."[66] "The question of tolerating worship is the non-interference of the public power in the acts that, without prejudice to others, men make to their God," Prieto proclaimed. Although a person might wish to enforce certain beliefs on himself, he argued, "we do not command the conscience of another, because we have no power over it."[67] In reply to Prieto's explanation, defenders of the status quo pointed out that, strictly speaking, freedom of conscience already existed in Mexico. No inquisition forced anyone to believe anything by force of pyre, whip, or other penalty. But authorizing public worship for non-Catholic sects was something entirely different than tolerating private beliefs, they argued. As Prisciliano Díaz González, deputy for the State of Mexico, explained, "the worship of the heart belongs to each man, but we also know that external worship belongs to society and to the whole people." "Everyone raises the temple that he likes and burns incense to the God he conceives in the secret of his heart, but he must also respect the external worship of society, for no single person is greater than the whole," he argued.[68]

As Díaz González's reply indicated, the central concern for many Mexicans was not freedom, but social unity. For years conservatives had argued that Catholicism was the only glue holding Mexican society together in the face of its many social divisions. Religious unity was also the most common theme advanced in the popular petitions against toleration. A "manifestation" signed by the women of León described the elements of that unity as "belief in the same truths, the participation in the same sacraments, the subjection to the same pastors according to the hierarchy established by our Lord Jesus Christ, his apostles and the sacrosanct laws of the Church." "Break that bond, destroy the only principle of union," they warned, "and then what will become of our beloved country?"[69] Likewise, a collective petition from seven small villages detailed the centrifugal forces that threatened the stability of the nation: "The variety of castes, the difference of interests, the inequality of fortunes, the lack of popular education, and above all the incarnation of political factions." The only thread that held together the hearts of all Mexicans was the Catholic faith, the petition claimed, "with only a few dishonorable exceptions."[70]

On July 29, a day distinguished by emotional speeches in favor of toleration, Castañeda made his most impassioned plea for the preservation of religious unity. Catholic worship, he explained, created a psychological unity that was a great consolation to the Mexican people. Above all, he insisted, this feeling was created by the public rituals surrounding the cult of the Blessed Sacrament. "The Mexican people want to live in Catholic unity," he declared:

> It loves with all its heart the solemn ceremonies and majesty of our worship, it finds its consolation, its hopes, and its joys within our temples. It takes pleasure in prostrating itself before God in the streets and plazas, in rendering public homage, in adoring God before the face of all.

Throughout the Catholic world, outdoor processions celebrated on the Feast of Corpus Christi were often experienced as intense moments of corporate unity and civic harmony.[71] Mexicans, Castañeda affirmed, did not want to destroy "these public solemnities in which all the faithful prostrate themselves before the Divine Majesty." Religious diversity would end this ritual bonding, he predicted, and "force God to remain hidden in the churches, and not adored in the streets and plazas."[72]

As might be expected, supporters of religious tolerance did not find such communalist arguments convincing. They argued on the floor of the congress that genuine unity did not need to be enforced by law.[73] Some insisted that religious unity in Mexico existed only in conservative dreams.[74] Mata, for example, claimed that Mexican society was already divided into three groups: idol worshipers, Catholics, and the indifferent. "What is there in common between the superstitious practices and remains of idolatry among our Indians," he asked, "and the practices of true Catholics?" The falloff in the numbers of people going to confession in the previous thirty years was further proof that many were no longer attached to the old religion. But he did not attribute this indifference to any decay in genuine religious sentiment; rather, he claimed, enlightenment had caused a decline in "fear and hypocrisy" and empowered people to display their true convictions.[75]

In spite of Mata's negative assessment of the state of religious faith in Mexico, it was clear that popular sentiment was almost uniformly in favor of maintaining the Catholic monopoly on public worship. Between June and September alone, laymen presented more than seventy anti-toleration petitions bearing thousands of signatures to the congress, not counting the numerous protestations submitted by clergy and the bishops. Some of the appeals originated in the primary cities of the country, others in rural towns and tiny villages. Some were signed by all the members of a community, from the mayor to common laborers. Others represented a homogenous group, like the one signed by members of the city council of Acámbaro (Guanajuato) or that presented by primary school teachers from Guadalajara. Copies of these petitions were also published in pamphlet form and circulated across the country, thus helping to spread the chief arguments in favor of the Catholic religion and against religious diversity throughout the population.

Of all the protests submitted to Congress against religious tolerance, the dozen or so signed exclusively by women seem to have made the biggest impression during the debates. Elite women in Mexico had always exerted political pressure in their families, but they did not often take part in public debate.[76] "There exists in Mexico a latent but certain influence that plays a great role in the interior politics of the country," the French ambassador reported in February 1856, "and that is the influence of women."[77] But this hidden power became manifest during the controversy surrounding Article 15. Although it is unknown who composed the petitions that the women presented, the sheer number of women who were willing to affix their signatures to the sentiments expressed therein is a powerful statement of popular sentiment. A single petition submitted by the women from Lagos contained 550 female signatures, while the total number of signatories reached into the thousands.[78]

Although women's petitions made many of the same arguments as those submitted by their male counterparts, they also had some unique features. Most began with some sort of disclaimer, recognizing the novelty of ladies appearing in the halls of government and admitting that this was not the not the usual arena for female activity. Like Castañeda, the women from San Luis Potosí emphasized the emotional consolations of the Catholic religion. Their petition made it clear that they preferred the "brilliance and splendor of [Catholic] religious ceremonies," to any of those "invented by men inspired by Satan." In one overly dramatic phrase, they exclaimed that any true Mexican woman would "prefer death to seeing Mexico overrun by non-Catholics."[79] On the other hand, the women of Mexico City argued that religion affected them more deeply than it did men because the formation of children was under their care. According to their petition, they were not willing to stand by and see "the children of our wombs disconnected from the holy and adorable religion in which we nourished them at our breasts."[80] In this case, it was precisely their role as mothers that empowered women to trespass into the male precincts of political power.[81]

The women of Morelia, meanwhile, appeared less concerned about their children than about their own fate in a future religious free-for-all. Here they argued that since society dictated that they always be under the dominance of men, women had a very personal interest in the fate of the country's religion. Men tended to abuse their power, they alleged, and only religion had the power to moderate social behavior. In the ancient world and under contemporary Islam, women were treated like chattel, the petition explained. Jews and Protestants, it was believed, could repudiate and abandon their wives at will. But historically women had been the most secure and their rights best protected under the Catholic religion. "The benefits of Catholicism would be enough to make it preferred to all known religions, even if we were not persuaded of its divinity," the petition proclaimed.[82]

La Cruz praised the courage of those females that had signed petitions and hoped that their example would inspire men into greater action in defense of the Church.[83] But many liberal delegates deeply resented participation by women in this most serious debate.[84] Some simply dismissed the women who had dared to sign petitions as misguided tools of the clergy. Priests were no longer able to find support among men, Mata sneered, and so had to go hunting among the women.[85] Zarco admitted that many well-known and virtuous ladies had signed the petitions, but argued that their confessors must have misled them, "either through surprise, condescension or vanity." No wonder they are afraid of Article 15, he explained, since they were convinced that the liberals were "raising a temple to Venus in the plaza and reestablishing human sacrifice to Huitzilopochtli, implementing polygamy, and dissolving marriage."[86] Prieto compared these "matrons" to Dido, "coming into the temple of the law to reclaim us from our alleged views."[87] The atheist, Ignacio Ramírez, took a different tack, dismissing the petitioners as a "phalanx of whores."[88]

Both the political mobilization of women and their chilly reception by liberals, however, reflected profound social changes occurring in Mexican society. As late as the 1840s, religion was still considered the domain of both sexes in Mexico. The process of secularization, however, had already begun the process of "feminizing" religious piety.[89] Part of this change was reflected in an insistence that a woman's primary role was to provide her children with a Christian education, a task previously overseen by fathers.[90] Liberalism in particular promoted an ideal of hyper-rational and skeptical masculinity that greatly contributed to the growth of anticlericalism among young males. Indeed, a large part of the appeal of Masonry for Mexican men was the fact that it was essentially a "masculine affair."[91] For liberals, the association of women with the Church and priests was a convenient strategy to disparage traditional religion. So the presence of female petitions in the constituent congress only confirmed their anticlerical and gender stereotypes.

In general, liberal deputies tried to dismiss the entire parade of petitioners as proof of the clerical power over the minds of the people. One orator claimed that all the petitions sounded so much alike that they must have all come from the same source. Others agreed, saying that the sophistication of the arguments proved that parish priests must have concocted the documents and then compelled the villagers to add their signatures.[92] But although a few of the documents advertised themselves as the work of the local curate, such as the one submitted by the Indians of Zalatitan, San

Gaspar, and Rosario (Jalisco), most contain no such evidence. In fact, some delegates, in contrast to those who saw in them the hands of the clergy, sought to undermine the petitions' force by depicting them as not clerical enough. They bragged that although the petitions defended the Catholic religion, this was usually done in pragmatic rather than theological terms, and none defended the clergy per se.[93] It seems unlikely then, that these petitions were all the work of a vast clerical conspiracy.[94]

Meanwhile, denying agency to those who signed petitions allowed some liberals to ignore the express wishes of the majority of the population while still upholding the fiction of popular sovereignty. Some delegates even argued that under the current, priest-ridden conditions of Mexico, petitions on such a sensitive topic could not truly represent the national will. Nevertheless, a number of more moderate delegates based their final opposition to Article 15 on their ideals of representative government. Díaz González, for instance, did not doubt that priests used their resources to influence the process, but he believed that the petitions still represented the thinking of the people. He explained that he had received many letters on the topic from his constituents and talked to concerned citizens from all over Mexico. "All tell me that the people, those who could never be called vulgar, ignorant, or fanatical, are alarmed," he reported. "The majority reject [toleration] because they see in the foundation of other sects an attack on their own religion and the germ of immorality." If the deputies could not discern the manifest "will of the people" in this obvious case, he maintained, one would have to wonder how they could claim to be their representatives in any other. Díaz González ended his speech with a reference to the Virgin of Guadalupe, whose image had graced the banner of Hidalgo. "Under her shadow I will fulfill the mission that the people of the State of Mexico gave me," he proclaimed, "I defend the cause of the people and with it the cause of God."[95] In reply, however, Zarco lashed out against the mention of supernatural events in the congress. "The history of our apparitions, the history of our miracles, the beliefs of our people in these matters, however pious they may be," he complained, "ought not to enter this debate, above all cheapened by those that defend Catholicism."[96]

Although priests undoubtedly railed against Article 15 from the pulpit, the Catholic press also played a major role in articulating and disseminating a unified discourse against religious toleration. *La Cruz* published numerous articles on the subject.[97] It also reprinted an essay against toleration written by the famous conservative legislator, Juan Rodríguez de San Miguel, in 1848.[98] In one article, Pesado directly attacked the vitriolic speech made by Mata on July 29, even challenging the philosophical basis of the liberal shibboleth, "freedom of conscience." Padre Ripaldo's catechism, he pointed out, defined conscience as "an internal judge that each man necessarily forms within himself, in order to do good and avoid evil." Its function, according to this definition, was to evaluate human actions in the light of immutable principles of natural and moral law. According to Pesado, claiming that the conscience was "free" under these conditions was a contradiction that called into question the very categories of right and wrong.[99]

La Cruz also frequently reported news items from around the world that challenged liberal claims about the benefits of toleration in other countries. One story concerned the case of forty Irish Catholic families who were living in Louisiana. On July 19, 1856, they directed a letter to President Comonfort via the counsel general in New Orleans, begging for religious asylum in Mexico. Although they had immigrated to the United States in the hopes of escaping persecution in Ireland, they claimed that things were even worse in their new country. "Rare is it that a day or night passes in which, without any provocation on our part, they do not deprive us of a relative or friend murdered in cold blood." At about the same time, the journal reported, the Mexican counsel in Washington was predicting that the rise of the "Know-Nothing Party" would definitely increase the number of Catholic emigrations from the United States. Such stories, *La Cruz* complained, were usually suppressed in the liberal media, giving a false impression of the reality of the religious situation in non-Catholic countries and Mexico's potential for attracting immigration.[100]

Ultimately, due to the defection of moderate liberals in the face of such a massive outpouring of popular sentiment, the cherished toleration bill died on the floor of the chamber. Perhaps most unexpectedly, President Comonfort and his cabinet eventually came out against toleration as well. The minister of foreign relations, Luis de la Rosa, first addressed the government's concerns about some of the proposed articles on July 8. Concerning Article 15, he proclaimed that the administration was opposed to this "dangerous innovation" for "great reasons of state and for serious political motives."[101] Lafragua, minister of the interior, appeared on August 1, claiming that the time was not right for such a move.[102] Even the minister of justice and ecclesiastical affairs, Ezequiel Montes, spoke on behalf of the government against it. In his speech on August 5, he acknowledged that the people of Mexico were illiterate and easily led but admitted that nevertheless the absolute majority of the population was opposed to the measure and so it should not be adopted.[103]

On August 5, the Congress voted 67 to 44 to table the controversial article.[104] When the final tally was announced in the chamber, the crowds in the balconies went wild. "The result produced an appalling confusion in the galleries," the minutes recorded: "whistles, applause, shouts of 'Long live religion!' 'Death to the heretics!' 'Death to the hypocrites!' 'Death to the cowards,' 'Long live the clergy!' etc. etc." The president of the congress tried to restore calm and resume business, but the excitement only increased, "with shouting every time more frenzied and intense." The bell was not able to restore order, and after some minutes the assembly was adjourned. The delegates then retreated to private quarters, where the bill was officially returned to commission. On January 26, 1857, without any further modifications or debate, the congress voted to "definitively retire" the issue of religious toleration.[105]

As Pesado later expressed it, the congress rejected Article 15 because of a "universal reprobation on the part of the public." All classes of society have risen against it," he pronounced, "because all saw in it a threat to the social order, the tranquility of the state, to the domestic peace, and to the happiness of individuals."[106] For conservatives, however, this was only a Pyrrhic victory. By concentrating all their energy on mobilization against this single issue, the anti-reformation forces had allowed other menacing articles to go virtually uncontested. Ultimately, the final document that resulted from this process was a recipe for social change that Catholics would still be unable to accept. In addition, by highlighting the chasm that existed between most Mexicans and the attitudes of the radical minority, the contest over religious toleration helped to undermine the legitimacy of the established government in the minds of many citizens. Combined with the hostility caused by the other contentious events of 1856, this alienation would lead to a final rupture in Mexican society when the constitution was implemented the following year.

CHAPTER 6

The Constitutional
Crisis of 1857

The constituent congress, having begun its work on February 18, 1856, approved the definitive draft of the new "Federal Constitution of the United States of Mexico" on January 31 of the following year. When the marathon final session adjourned at last, spectators in the galleries joined the delegates in a spontaneous round of applause and cheers of "Long live congress!" and "Long live the constitution!" In accordance with the transitional articles also approved at this time, the code would go into effect on September 16, a date intentionally chosen for its patriotic and revolutionary connotations. In the meantime, this delay would allow time for the selection of a new congress, which would also be installed on that date. A new president and judiciary would take office on December 1. Until then, the country would continue to be governed by the substitute-interim president in accord with the articles of the Plan of Ayutla. All that remained now was for the president and the members of the congress to swear an oath to uphold the new charter, after which it could be solemnly promulgated across the nation.[1]

Like the day chosen for its implementation, the date selected for the formal ratification of the constitution conveyed an important message about the nature of the new political order. It was José María Mata, a *puro* delegate from Veracruz, who proposed that the ceremony be scheduled for February 5, the feast day of Blessed Felipe de Jesús, the patron saint of Mexico City.[2] Since Blessed Felipe was the only Mexican to have been raised to the honor of the altar, the annual celebration of the "Holy Creole" was an important symbol of Mexico's religious identity and destiny. Typically, the patriotic character of this day was symbolized by the presence of the president and other civic dignitaries at a Solemn Pontifical Mass. This year, however, the religious celebration would be overshadowed by a display of secular political theater. At the same time, the Church's decision to continue the custom of an afternoon procession from the Metropolitan Cathedral to the Franciscan monastery, now closed, would be an unwelcome reminder of recent unhappy events in the city. Once this date was chosen, however, Comonfort tried to mitigate the divisiveness of this timing. As a conciliatory gesture, he decreed a general amnesty for political prisoners, mostly priests and conservative activists, in honor of the occasion.[3]

When the oath ceremony began on the morning of February 5, the galleries of the chamber of deputies were packed with spectators and invited guests. The carefully choreographed event began with a public reading of the text of the constitution by Mata, which secretaries then verified as the authentic version of the new charter. Following this ratification, León Guzmán, the acting vice-president of the congress, placed his right hand upon a copy of the Gospels and swore to uphold and defend the document just presented. Next, the honorary president of the convention, seventy-six-year-old Valentín Gómez Farías, was escorted to the front of the dais, where he took the oath kneeling before the crucifix that adorned the presidential table. For Francisco Zarco and other reformers of the new generation, "it was a moment of profound emotion, seeing this venerable old man, the patriarch of liberty in Mexico, giving the moral support of his name and his glory to the new political code." After this dramatic moment, the remaining deputies rose as a body and raised their right hands, eighty-eight voices responding in unison to the formula of the oath, "Yes, we swear."[4]

President Comonfort was not present when the ratification and oath ceremony began, having chosen to first attend the services in honor of Blessed Felipe at the cathedral across the Zocalo. At this point in the proceedings, however, he appeared at the door of the chamber and was led in to take the oath. "I, Ignacio Comonfort, substitute president of the republic," he intoned, "do swear before God, to recognize, defend and protect the political constitution of the Mexican Republic that the congress has issued today."[5] "God will reward you if you do," responded Guzmán, "and if not, you will have to answer for it before the country and before God." Although representatives of the clergy were conspicuously absent from these proceedings, the semi-official *El Estandarte Nacional* later commented with approval on the frequency with which the Divine Name was invoked during the course of this ostensibly civic ceremony.[6] In fact, not counting the formula of the oath itself, references to God, Divine Providence, the Supreme Being, the Creator, and the Supreme Lawgiver occurred a total of fourteen times in the official discourses.[7] In light of the actual goals of the constitution, some critics considered the use of religious language and Catholic symbolism hypocritical.[8] From the delegates' point of view, however, these elements were intended to demonstrate the compatibility of "true religion" with progressive ideals and to reflect the moral underpinnings of the liberal reforms that the document enshrined.

Unbeknownst to any of those present at this solemn event, however, a new and unexpected challenge to the Catholic credentials of the liberal program was at this very moment steaming its way across the Atlantic toward the port at Veracruz. This incendiary document, the so-called "Secret Allocution," was a discourse on the religious situation in Mexico delivered by Pope Pius IX in a closed consistory on December 15, 1856.[9] As it turned out, Bishop Labastida was responsible for much of the content of the address, having been summoned to Rome after his exile in the wake of the first Puebla uprising. Once in the Eternal City, the Mexican prelate became a frequent visitor to the Vatican, where he was repeatedly honored for his fidelity in the face of persecution back home. He also became a confidant of the pope, who relied on Labastida almost exclusively for information and insight on conditions in Mexico.[10] In this case, the strategy of deporting uncooperative clerics backfired badly, since the bishop's denunciation of liberal policies were now projected onto an international stage though the mouth of Christ's Vicar on earth. It was also Labastida who included the Latin text of the allocution in his sixth pastoral letter, issued in Rome on January 2, 1857, and it was in this form that the pontiff's bombshell landed on the shores of America five weeks later.[11]

According to the pope's own words, the purpose of his allocution was to "lament and deplore with great grief in our hearts the affliction and demolition of the Catholic Church in Mexico." Thanks to the specifics provided by his Mexican informant, Pius IX was able to describe the elements of this "cruel war" in meticulous detail, beginning with the *convocatoria* of October 16, 1855, which had stripped the clergy of the right to vote or hold political office. As might be expected, he emphatically denounced the *Ley Juárez* and the *Ley Lerdo*, as well as the punitive intervention in the Diocese of Puebla and the mistreatment of its worthy bishop. The pope also expressed his profound displeasure at the suppression of the Jesuit order and the destruction of the Franciscan community in Mexico City, inter alia, and praised those who had endured harassment, exile, or prison in defense of the Church. The "great majority" of Mexicans, the pontiff had been informed, remained firm in their Catholic faith and abhorred all these "evil deeds."[12]

Up to this point, the pope's jeremiad was not substantially different from the dozens of protests already lodged by the Mexican hierarchy. Much more troubling, however, was his repudiation of the newly minted Mexican Constitution, which, he had been informed, contained various articles opposed to the doctrine, institutions, and rights of the Catholic religion. In particular, he opposed the articles granting freedom of speech, a free press, and religious toleration, since he understood that these "rights" were chiefly designed "to more easily corrupt the souls and the customs of the people in order to extend the detestable pest of indifferentism and overthrow our most holy religion."[13] "Therefore," the pontiff proclaimed,

> in order that the faithful that live there may know and all the Catholic world recognize that we highly condemn all those things that the government of the Mexican Republic has done against the Catholic religion and its sacred ministers, pastors, laws, rights, properties and against the authority of this Holy See, we raise our voice with apostolic liberty . . . and we condemn, we reprove, we declare absolutely null and void all the above-mentioned laws.

Liberals immediately recognized that these comments constituted a serious threat to the legitimacy of their reforming regime. As Vigil recalled, "the allocution was a veritable revolutionary battering ram, because of the solemn approval given in it to disobedience and acts of insubordination to the established government."[14]

Taken completely off guard by the papal broadside, the Comonfort administration made a number of hasty gestures to limit its political fallout. At first, the government simply denied the authenticity of the document and tried, unsuccessfully, to impede its circulation.[15] At the same time, the cabinet lodged a protest with the papal nuncio in such threatening terms that Monsignor Clementi considered closing the apostolic mission and returning to Rome.[16] Obviously, the pope's condemnation placed the president and other moderates in a very awkward position. "I am a faithful and obedient son of the Roman Catholic Church, from which I will not be separated," Comonfort defiantly declared a few days later. As far as the pope's charges were concerned, however, he continued to insist that abolition of the clerical *fuero* and of mortmain did not constitute an attack on the Catholic religion itself. Nevertheless, for the first time he also offered to open a dialogue with the Mexican bishops on these and any other contentious points.[17]

Since the liberal administration was accustomed to issuing its anticlerical decrees without consulting the ecclesiastical authorities, Comonfort's gesture may have represented an important shift in the government's posture toward the Church.[18] For long-suffering Catholics, this abrupt change would also seem to have confirmed the wisdom of the ultramontane strategy, which always insisted on direct government negotiation with Rome. Shortly afterward, this impression was reinforced when Comonfort made two more concessions to Catholic sensibilities. First, he personally issued a warrant for the arrest of General Traconis, the much-maligned former Governor of Puebla, for notorious abuse and fraud committed during the controversial confiscation of ecclesiastical property in that diocese.[19] On the same day, he also signed a decree allowing the Franciscans to reoccupy a portion of their former convent in Mexico City. Although moderates praised this move as a demonstration of liberal clemency, conservatives, who had always defended the innocence of the friars, interpreted it as a belated act of reparation for the "demagogic barbarism" heretofore practiced by the liberal regime. The radicals, on the other hand, who wanted the rest of the monastery razed and the friars reassigned to "more useful" pastoral work, naturally denounced the move.[20]

In spite of Comonfort's overtures, the Catholic hierarchy was more determined than ever to resist the implementation of the new constitution. Encouraged by the pope's words and Comonfort's concessions, it opted instead for a campaign of passive resistance and noncompliance, which was inaugurated in Mexico City a few days later. While the rest of the capital celebrated the promulgation of the new charter on March 11 with artillery salvos and public illuminations, the city's numerous churches and convents remained dark and silent. According to one report, someone briefly managed to toll the bells of the Metropolitan Cathedral, but it was against the express wishes of the archbishop, who had forbidden any ecclesiastical participation in the festivities. Although the Governor of the Federal District, Juan José Baz, had specifically requested that all churches display the national flag and ring their bells to mark the occasion, Archbishop Garza cordially declined, reminding him that the bishops were opposed to some parts of the new code. "I hope that you will not take it badly that I did not give the orders you requested," he replied to the irate governor, "which might well have been interpreted as approval of the offending articles."[21]

For liberals, the non-participation of the clergy was a public provocation that dampened the public celebration of their recent legislative triumph. Even more importantly, church bells were a potent symbol of that religious legitimacy so coveted by the reformers. That is why efforts were made to prevent similar scenes from occurring in other parts of the country. In Guanajuato, for example, a cleric was exiled for refusing to ring the bells of his church when the constitution was promulgated there, and in Oaxaca an elderly priest was thrown into jail for the same reason.[22] In Morelia, on the other hand, supporters of the constitution broke down the doors to the bell towers of the Augustinian monastery and the cathedral and assaulted the official ringers in order to toll the bells. Liberals also seized the bell tower by force in San Luis Potosí, shouting defiantly, if somewhat enigmatically, "Long live the true religion!" In the town of Indaparapeo (Michoacán), where the priest had taken the added precaution of removing the clappers, some men nevertheless scaled the church tower and sounded the bells with hammers.[23] Apparently, six months later the memory of the Church's original snub still lingered, since this time the authorities threatened stiff fines for any ecclesiastical institution that refused to participate in the celebrations planned for September 16.[24]

The day after the ecclesiastical boycott of the celebrations in Mexico City, the archbishop announced the next phase of the Church's passive resistance campaign. This move, however, would have much more serious ramifications than the symbolic "battle of the bells." First, the chancery issued a statement to all priests of the archdiocese that clarified the reasons for the archbishop's negative response to the new constitution. Even more importantly, it also announced that because of the controversial articles it contained, no Roman Catholic could licitly swear to the new charter. The following Sunday, the archbishop himself repeated this prohibition in a sermon he preached in the *Sagrario* of the Metropolitan Cathedral.[25] The government's reaction to this new challenge was swift. On March 17 the minister of the interior, Ignacio de la Llave, issued a decree requiring government employees at every level, including members of the armed forces, to take an oath to uphold the new constitution.[26] Anyone who refused, the order stipulated, would be immediately deprived of his job. Since many government offices were still staffed with bureaucrats left over from previous regimes, some observers believed that the primary goal of this measure was to eliminate uncooperative conservatives from public service and open up new posts for liberal sympathizers.[27] But many Catholics suspected that the real motive was simply to force public employees to take a stand against the hierarchy, thereby increasing public support for reform.[28] Since civil service was the chief form of employment for the Mexican professional classes, everyone recognized that the threat of economic destitution created a powerful incentive for compliance.

Two days later, the mandatory oath was publicly administered to all civil officials of the Federal District in the main hall of the Palace of Ministers. In the presence of President Comonfort, the heads of each ministry, the military, and the courts each took the oath, which they in turn were to administer to the subalterns of their various departments. At this stage, however, some officials refused to swear and others qualified their oath to exclude those articles condemned by the Church. No statistics are available on the percentage of those who refused, but the French ambassador reported that their numbers were much higher than anyone had expected. In every office there were some who would not take the oath, not counting those who had already decided not to attend the mandatory proceedings at all. Twenty-seven superior military officers were among the nonjurors, including, ironically, General Florencio Villarreal, the original author of the Plan of Ayutla. Three superior court judges and many from the lower courts also failed to comply. It was said that two-thirds of the employees of the department of public works abstained, as well as a large number of individuals from the treasury. Although the majority of public employees did take the oath, either for pragmatic or ideological reasons, the number of nonjurors was still high enough to provoke a negative reaction from the liberal press.[29]

As the government may have intended, the enforcement of the compulsory oath created a serious dilemma for Mexican Catholics. It seems likely, however, that the administration did not anticipate the Church's devastating response. Having already determined that believers could not licitly swear to what they considered to be an anti-Catholic constitution, the hierarchy now raised the spiritual stakes for those who might choose to ignore its directives on this delicate point. On the day following the disastrous oath ceremony in Mexico City, Archbishop Garza issued a new set of guidelines for priests regarding those who had chosen to swear. Henceforth, anyone who had taken the oath would be required to make a public retraction before they could receive absolution in the sacrament of penance.[30] Since at this time the confession of sins and sacramental absolution were prerequisites for receiving Holy Communion, this decision would have serious consequences for practicing Catholics.

In desperation, government officials seized copies of the episcopal decrees that demanded retraction and, in some states, outlawed their circulation entirely. In Michoacán, Bishop Clemente de Jesús Munguía reported, the police entered churches to tear down his pastoral letters and fined priests who refused to display the federal laws in their place.[31] In many places the police also began to monitor sermons and to prosecute priests who made public references to the ban against the oath. On March 26, for instance, a priest in Puebla was charged with treason for preaching against the new code, and on April 18 a curate was expelled from his parish in Guerrero for reading his bishop's *bando* during mass.[32] Even the archbishop was not exempt from surveillance, and the interior minister, José María Lafragua, and the minister of justice, José María Iglesias, began to take turns sitting in front of his pulpit whenever he preached, in order to discourage any further anti-government remarks.[33]

In the weeks that followed the ceremonies in Mexico City, the constitution was promulgated and the oath administered in cities and towns across the republic, usually with similar mixed results. The quasi-religious ritual observed at Tlaltenango (Aguascalientes) was probably representative. There, the members of the municipal council and other local dignitaries processed around the town carrying a framed copy of the charter, stopping at four designated points to proclaim the text of the new code. When they finally arrived in the central plaza, the document was placed on a makeshift altar along with a copy of the Gospels and a crucifix, where the oath was formally administered. At one point, when shouts of "Death to the impious!" interrupted the proceedings, a political officer restored calm by explaining to the crowd that the constitution did not attack religion, but only eliminated inequalities created by monarchs in the past. In spite of these assurances, eight officials would only swear to a restricted form of the oath and seven others refused to take it altogether. Nevertheless, the celebration concluded peacefully with a military parade and three cheers for "Liberty, the constitution, and religion!"[34]

Although the constitution was installed in many places without serious incident, the proceedings did not always go as smoothly as planned. The ceremony at Naolinco (Veracruz), for example, was repeatedly delayed because the parish priest refused to lend the political officers the book of the Gospels and a crucifix with which to administer the oath.[35] And in Guadalajara troops had to be deployed to prevent anti-government demonstrations, with "disconsolate conservatives limited to yelling '*mueras*' (death to ____)" in one street while applause was heard in other places.[36] Tensions were also high in Puebla, where before the ceremony protesters flooded the streets with handbills that proclaimed, "GOD has said that anyone who swears to this constitution pledges his own damnation!"[37] In the town of Zamora, located in Munguía's diocese of Michoacán, the ceremony held on April 5 was actually followed by a riot in which crowds tore down and burned the document just posted and physically attacked those who had sworn to uphold it.[38] Other disturbances were also reported in La Piedad, Maravatío, and Pátzcuaro (Michoacán), Calvillo (Aguascalientes), and Tulancingo (México).[39]

To complicate matters even further, at this point some of those who had initially conformed also began making the public retractions required by the Church. As the long Lent of 1857 wore on, many officials retracted their oaths so that they could receive Holy Communion at Easter.[40] In some cases their retractions were also published in local newspapers, both to fulfill the requirement for public reparation and as an example for others to emulate.[41] While some retractors expressed their change of heart in their own words, ecclesiastical authorities also printed up a standard formula that could simply be signed by their less eloquent penitents. The standard formula for the retraction was as follows:

I, _____, wanting to live and die in the bosom of the Catholic, Apostolic, and Roman Church into which I have had the good fortune to be born, retract everything I voluntarily or involuntarily did or said against the truths and precepts of the Church, and especially I retract the solemn promise I made to uphold the constitution and the reform laws . . . and it is my desire from now on, as I do now, to do everything in my power to repair the scandal I have caused and to strive to my maximum effort and with absolute and complete submission to divine and ecclesiastical laws never to part again, either with words or actions, from the doctrines taught by the Church.[42]

For conservative commentators like Zamacois, the willingness of so many Mexicans to place their conscience above economic advantage "honors them exceedingly, reflecting a firmness of principles of which there are few examples in the world, and speaks very highly of virtues that Mexican society possessed at that time."[43] The French ambassador was also impressed by the numbers of nonjurors, but perhaps less flattering in his assessment of Mexican character. "The fact that such a great number of general officers and subalterns, higher functionaries and others have renounced (their employment) is very remarkable in a country where unselfishness is very rare, and where public employment is the only ambition of all the classes of society," he observed.[44]

Throughout the spring of 1857, the pattern of oath – resistance and oath – retraction further aggravated the already volatile political situation in Mexico. "On every side," recounted one local historian, the oath was "discussed, denounced, and defended." "The political question had been converted into a religious one!"[45] At the same time, because supporters of the constitution were being excluded from the sacraments of the Church, the religious question also became a highly political one. This was especially true as the country prepared for the solemn observances of Good Friday and Easter. Holy Week was always a period of particularly intense spiritual devotion in Mexico, and many people anticipated some sort of trouble during this year's celebration.[46] But the showdown, when it did occur, unfolded in a way that no one had anticipated or planned.

The symbolic confrontation of Holy Week 1857 actually began very quietly, with another exchange of letters between the archbishop and Governor Baz.[47] The issue at hand this time was an immemorial custom, according to which a representative of the secular authority, after receiving Holy Communion on Maundy Thursday, would enter the sanctuary of the Metropolitan Cathedral where the key to a special tabernacle was hung around his neck on a chain for safekeeping until the next day.[48] This year, however, everyone was aware that public functionaries were barred from receiving the sacraments on account of having taken the oath. That is why Baz wrote to the archbishop eight days in advance of the ceremony in order to clarify the awkward situation. In reply, Garza made it clear that the governor should not plan to attend the functions in his official capacity, as this would necessarily "give scandal to the faithful."[49] But despite President Comonfort's specific instructions not to press the matter any further, Baz was determined to force a confrontation with the Church. He therefore announced, clerical "threats" notwithstanding, that he had every intention of attending the ceremonies as the president's representative and that he would demand all the respect due him by virtue of his political office. The only possible scandal, he coldly instructed the archbishop, would occur if he did not show up as usual, since this would give the false impression that there existed "a separation between the civil authority and the Church."[50]

Thus it happened that at 8:45 on the morning of April 9, 1857, a messenger interrupted the divine service in the cathedral to announce that the governor and his retinue, bearing the mace and other emblems of his office, were waiting outside the main door.[51] At this point, a clerk was dispatched to inform the party that, on the specific orders of the archbishop, they were not to be formally received. The furious Baz stormed away but returned soon afterward on horseback and with a squadron of soldiers. When the troops proceeded to block off the exits to the temple, a rumor spread that all the worshippers were going to be arrested, creating pandemonium inside. Over the next few hours, witnesses reported, the screams of women and the shouts of men escalated into a full-scale demonstration against the liberal government and its godless minions. "Men and women without conscience shook the temple with cries of death and vengeance," Anselmo de la Portilla later insisted, chanting "Death to the government!" and "Death to the impious!" Meanwhile, a hostile crowd also formed in the plaza outside, and some soldiers, feeling threatened, fired two or three shots into the air to drive them away. Although the congregation was eventually allowed to leave unmolested, the cathedral canons and other ministers refused to abandon the safety of the choir until after nightfall, when the government troops were finally withdrawn. In recounting the details of this "disagreeable incident," Zamacois also recounted that after the troops were withdrawn, "an immense crowd" filled the cathedral for the evening devotions before the altar of repose. As a symbolic protest against the violation of the temple, more than ten thousand lights illuminated the cathedral on this occasion, which made a profound impression on everyone present.[52]

In the wake of this fiasco, officials initially feared a popular rebellion and dispatched troops around the city to maintain order. A few hours after the standoff ended, Governor Baz himself issued a proclamation in which he claimed that the clergy had committed this "outrage" in the hopes of provoking a full-scale revolt against the government. Perhaps, he speculated, their real goal was "to create victims among the people, whose blood would foment those profound and destructive hatreds that are so far from the religion of the Savior whose death Christianity recalls in these holy days." Nevertheless, he appealed to the inhabitants of the capital to remain calm and reassured them that the personal security of citizens and their private property would be respected and protected, except for that of those "who disturb the public order."[53]

Although the anticipated Catholic reaction in Mexico City never materialized, the unprecedented violation of the sacred precincts of the cathedral did send shock waves around the entire country. "The events that have occurred are almost the only object of conversation," *La Cruz* reported in the days that followed. Naturally, some reports were exaggerated, like one in Veracruz that claimed the canons had sought asylum in the French embassy.[54] There was also a widespread belief that Baz and his men had actually ridden into the cathedral on horseback and assaulted the priests.

This version of the story was in fact perpetuated by a satirical poem, "The Battle of Holy Thursday," that circulated widely in conservative circles. Written by Ignacio Aguilar y Marocho, the forty-seven stanzas of the poem depicted Comonfort as a despotic king and Baz as his pretentious dauphin, laying siege to the house of God and doing battle with the carved images of the saints in order to avenge his besmirched honor. "The pope's allocution encouraged everyone to stand firm," Baz declares in one verse. "But in spite of the archbishop, I am completely right!" "How dare they refuse the key to such an illustrious prince," he demands in another place. "I vow to the devil that this is a clear casus belli: Arise my subjects and give me aid in my war against the Sanhedrin!" And again: "The key was the booty that the arrogant clergy had hidden . . . but I swear I will have it next year, for I am the dauphin!"[55]

For their part, the authorities were determined to repay the defiant clergy for the "public insult" it had offered the secular government in not receiving Governor Baz. They also felt that a price had to be paid for the antigovernment demonstration that had erupted in the nave of the cathedral that day.[56] Above all, it was feared that any sign of weakness on the part of the government might encourage further outbreaks. As Iglesias put it, "the events that occurred in this capital on Maundy Thursday could easily have embroiled it in a great disaster, and that might still happen in the rest of the republic."[57] No action was taken on Good Friday, but the next day the minister of justice and ecclesiastical affairs announced the government's official response to this new clerical provocation: the "Law of Parish Perquisites." Obviously, the reformers had contemplated this decree, which automatically abolished stole fees, for some time. The issue of sacramental fees had been high on the radical agenda since the Ocampo controversy in Michoacán in 1855, and it had even resurfaced, without resolution, during the constituent congress.[58] Now, however, the alleged misbehavior of the archbishop and his cabildo provided the perfect opportunity for implementing a measure that demonstrated the hegemony of the state over ecclesiastical affairs.[59] In addition, for his act of lèse-majesté in denying an ecclesiastical reception to Governor Baz, the archbishop was placed under house arrest on Easter Monday. At the same time, a presidential order was issued for the incarceration of all the cathedral canons for their subversive and disrespectful behavior.[60]

Although Mexico City remained calm, news of these events increased tensions throughout the country and, as Iglesias had feared, more violent anti-government protests erupted in response. On Easter Sunday, for example, there were two serious outbreaks in Jalisco. According to official reports, a large crowd of peasants from the surrounding countryside was present in the main plaza in Lagos at 8:00 in the morning when the ceremony for promulgating the constitution began. When "some Indians" began shouting "Long live religion!" and "Death to the impious!" the military commander tried to restore calm by insisting that the new charter did not attack any dogmas of the Catholic faith. But this time official explanations were not effective. Instead, in the ensuing melee a nervous military patrol panicked and fired point-blank into the hostile crowd, leaving eight dead. Clashes between civilians and the military then broke out in various parts of the city and continued until the federal troops retreated from the city the next day. In the meantime, mobs looted the city hall, destroyed the municipal archives, and liberated prisoners from the local jail.[61] Also on April 12, eleven people were killed and many others wounded in a similar confrontation twenty-five miles away in San Juan de los Lagos.[62]

An even more serious disturbance occurred two days later at Mascota (Jalisco), where resistance to the oath escalated into a full-scale revolt against the national government. Here, when the citizens were assembled to receive the new constitution, some rebels took an oath to support the cause of God instead and seized control of the town. Federal troops attacked two weeks later, leaving thirteen of the insurgents dead. Meanwhile, resistance was also reported in other parts of the republic. In some places, like Zapotiltic, San Gabriel, and Tonila (Jalisco), citizens simply refused to participate in the promulgation ceremony. In Huamantla (Tlaxcala), the entire population of the town went into hiding when state officials arrived to administer the oath and there was a house-to-house search to find civilians who could certify the proceedings. Once a pair of witnesses was located, the constitution was proclaimed to the otherwise empty town. In Charcas (San Luis Potosí) the ceremony abruptly ended when the crowds began pelting the assembled dignitaries with stones. The homes of prominent liberals and the governor's carriage were also stoned in Aguascalientes (State of Aguascalientes) after the constitution was promulgated there, as a result of which two protesters were shot and killed by members of the national guard. When citizens refused to stage the required ceremonies in Armadillo (San Luis Potosí), fifty dragoons were dispatched to ensure compliance with the law. But riots broke out immediately after the soldiers were withdrawn and they had to be recalled the following day. The military commander reported that once the rebels had taken over the town, they committed "a thousand disorders" and celebrated their rampage with bell ringing and fireworks.

Troops were also deployed to put down disturbances in Santa María del Río (San Luis Potosí), Apan, Chiconquiaco and Tepetlan (Tlaxcala), Temoaya and Santiago Tianguistenco (State of Mexico) and San Juan de Río (Durango).[63]

From the conservative point of view, all these episodes served as proof that the liberal constitution did not reflect the will of the people and could never be enforced. Furthermore, some Catholics were already hailing those who lost their lives in these demonstrations as "victims of the demagogues and martyrs to their faith and patriotism."[64] Liberals, on the other hand, often attributed these disorders to "lower orders" or even "Indians." At the same time, by alleging that fanatical priests had incited these riots, they hoped to turn these demonstrations into a propaganda advantage for the liberal cause. The commander of the forces at Lagos, for instance, insisted that many of the protesters there were inspired by the "bad priests" who had ignored government warnings and read Bishop Espinosa's circular to their parishioners. The rest of the mob, he suggested, were just criminals, who "took part in the disorder for a chance to loot."[65] In a similar vein, General Juan Rocha, who personally put down the revolt at Mascota, was determined to blame the clergy for the bloodshed that resulted from his assault. To drive this point home, he personally deposited the bodies of dead protesters on the doorstep of the local priest, "telling him that he should see the outcome of his infamous machinations." The general hoped, he later wrote, that seeing the bodies of these "unfortunates who had been seduced and sacrificed," the priest would have to admit that the Church's anti-constitution campaign was the work of "a corrupted clergy that would go to any extreme to further their selfish goals."[66]

Although most liberals remained convinced that priests were the "principal movers" behind these outbreaks, in some places the clergy worked with civil leaders to pacify hostile populations and restore order. And in at least two cases priests even rescued liberal politicians from the angry crowds who were demanding their blood. In Zamora, a priest convinced those attacking the military barracks to withdraw. Two other priests were also part of the delegation that negotiated a peaceful withdrawal of the government troops. In San Juan de los Lagos, a number of priests and religious "occupied themselves in tranquilizing the people, convincing them that these actions were not productive." Toribio Esquivel, the political chief who filed this report, failed to mention that after he and his family were attacked, they sought refuge in the home of a priest, who got down on his knees before the mob and pleaded for their lives. A priest also helped to save the life of Col. Domingo Reyes, the political chief in Lagos.[67]

Whether or not an individual priest encouraged specific acts of violence in any particular town, resistance everywhere was obviously generated by the Church's official stand against the constitution. That is why for many liberals there was no significant difference between preaching the Church's position and inciting an anti-government riot. The prefect of Huamantla, for example, charged that the sermons of a certain Fr. Aguas against the constitution had "excited the people to such an extent that the look on every face strikes terror." And even though no rebellion had yet occurred, "in a thousand ways they manifest their opposition to [the constitution]." General Nicolas de la Portilla, on the other hand, discovered "no attempt at sedition, or at least not an armed revolt," when he occupied the town on April 19. What he did find was a population profoundly torn by conflicting loyalties. In his official report, he wrote that "they complained to me about the constitution and the supreme government, but they also spoke to me about their souls and consciences." "The affliction of these individuals is so great that it is not uncommon for them to break into tears," he added.[68] Another liberal observer, Captain Don Francisco Domingues, observed a similar crisis of conscience in Naolinco. "I encountered the people of this town submerged in the most profound discontent," he later reported, "and struggling with the agitation produced in their peaceful souls by their natural inclination to obey the government, on the one hand, and the dishonest suggestions [of their clergy] on the other."[69]

Throughout the country, the nonjuring crisis had serious ramifications at every level of society, even in areas where no physical violence occurred. In the State of Querétaro, the governor announced that anyone refusing the oath would automatically lose all their civil rights.[70] On the other hand, in places where no one was willing or able to replace the civil servants who were forced to resign, communities were often deprived of public services and local government for indefinite periods of time. And the families of those subject to the oath might be devastated no matter which decision an employee ultimately made. As the French ambassador observed, officials had to choose whether to "suffer the censure of the Church—and see themselves, consequently, at the margin of society and of their families— or lose their only means of existence."[71] As a result of this dilemma, many families were divided, and some were close to economic ruin. Certainly it was unfair, one petition to the president lamented, when the breadwinner of these families, "who in general pertains to the class of magistrates, judges, or other public employees," was suddenly "deprived of the salary acquired by many years of faithful service" because he could not in good conscience take an oath prohibited by the ecclesiastical authorities.[72] But in spite of these hardships, there were also many pressures within some Catholic families to refuse the oath. According to one dissenting priest, a wife had been persuaded to leave her husband because he had sworn to uphold the new constitution, "and there are many who seduce servants to leave the work of the field, the shop, or their place of employment" for the same reason. The bishops' ban on the oath, he charged, was the cause of "upsets and disturbances in families, in the towns, and even in the countryside."[73]

One story circulating in Mexico at this time epitomized the interpersonal complications caused by the oath. The anonymous priest who recorded this "amusing case" stated that he could not guarantee its accuracy, but given the circumstances of the day, he could vouch for its "probability or verisimilitude." Apparently, a certain military officer, betrothed to a virtuous young woman, had taken the oath as required. But when his fiancée discovered the fact, she peremptorily called off the engagement. Stunned, the officer immediately repented and, on his knees, promised that he would publicly retract the oath, which he did. But although this cost him his commission in the army, his beloved was not impressed. "What you have done with the constitution, you might do with me one day," she emphatically proclaimed. At that point, the soldier attempted to salvage his miliary career, offering to repeat the oath as many times as necessary to erase his folly. But his commanding officer rejoined that he could not accept someone who might betray his country in the same way that he had betrayed his own conscience. As he left the interview, one of his former comrades remarked sarcastically on the poor fellow's disappointment: "You didn't get to taste the sweetness and they have taken away the cup!"[74]

Although humorous, the story was also a warning to pious young women about the untrustworthy character of any man who willingly took the forbidden oath. At the same time, it reflected the problems created by those who made light of either swearing or retraction. Apparently, some people who had adjudicated ecclesiastical property or sworn the oath made insincere retractions when they subsequently found themselves gravely ill and desirous of receiving the sacraments of the Church. Their health being recovered, these same individuals might claim that their retractions were invalid in order to retain possession of their property or employment. Similar scenarios also occurred when someone who had taken the oath desired to get married, since only Catholic marriages were performed in Mexico at this time. For instance, there were a few reported cases in which the groom publicly invalidated his oath to get married and after the ceremony retracted his retraction.[75] Even worse, some couples did not even bother with the pretense of retracting the oath. In Zacatecas, Abraham González and his fiancée, in the presence of two witnesses, simply cornered their parish priest in his bed early one morning and announced their intention to be wed.[76] On the other hand, a story from Morelia claimed that a solider and a bureaucrat both threatened to cohabitate with their fiancées if they were denied the sacrament of matrimony due to their oaths. But liberal newspapers reported that the priests remained unmoved, "which indicates the inclinations of the clergy."[77]

The Comonfort administration was not insensible to the human cost of the oath requirement, but a capitulation to the clergy at this point, it felt, would set a dangerous precedent and might easily provoke a radical coup. Like many moderates, Comonfort hoped that the constitution might eventually be amended to eliminate its more controversial provisions. But in the meantime, the government had to find a way to neutralize Catholic opposition to the charter as it stood. The most promising of these strategies was initiated in the aftermath of the Easter disturbances, when Comonfort opted to bypass the recalcitrant bishops entirely and appeal the government's case directly to Rome.[78] Hoping to convince the pope of the benign intent and religious value of the Mexican reform program, Ezequiel Montes was designated "extraordinary envoy and minister plenipotentiary to the Holy See" and shipped off to Italy on May 1, 1857. Given his background in civil and canon law, Montes was the government's first choice to undertake this delicate mission. But thanks to his previous confrontations with the Mexican hierarchy, the new ambassador already had something of a negative reputation among the clergy, and the lurking presence in Rome of his old nemesis, Bishop Labastida, only aggravated the situation. "After two and a half hours of charges, explanations, replies and counter replies," reported Montes after one particularly grueling meeting with the secretary of state, Giacomo Antonelli, Montes left the Quirinal Palace "convinced that all was lost, because I found the terrain already horribly prepared against the Mexican government." But although Cardinal Antonelli received the emissary coolly, he did allow Montes to clarify the misrepresentations that had influenced the pope's negative assessment of the actual situation in Mexico.[79]

Meanwhile, both conservative and liberal newspapers in Mexico predicted that Montes' attempts would certainly fail, although for different reasons. Pessimistic commentary on the negotiations also appeared in the French and Italian Catholic press. Montes, however, persisted. Although he asked the Holy See to accept the disentailment of Church property, the end of the *fuero*, and the abolition of stole fees, he also offered to make the Mexican clergy paid employees of the state in return. The French ambassador, for one, believed that this would never be accepted, since it "put all the clergy at the mercy of the civil authorities," even though a similar scheme had been tried in France after the Concordat signed by Napoleon and Pope Pius VII in 1801.[80] The Mexican envoy even asked the pope to approve the suppression of the remaining religious orders in Mexico, with the exception of the Congregation of the Mission (Vincentians) and the Ministers of the Sick (Brothers of St. Camillus), small groups known for their work among the poor. To everyone's surprise, the Pope Pius IX tentatively agreed to all of the Mexican demands.[81] He did, however, request that the clergy be allowed to acquire property in the future, to which Cardinal Antonelli added the request that they also have their political rights restored. As it turned out, these two points were still in dispute—and the parties still awaiting the authorization of the new congress to conclude a final treaty—when the Comonfort government fell and the diplomatic mission was canceled at the beginning of 1858.[82]

From the beginning, the president's cabinet realized that its diplomatic initiative in Rome, even if successful, would take time to produce results. Meanwhile, the papal denunciation of the Mexican reforms would continue to inspire Catholic opposition to the constitution. That is why, along with its diplomatic initiative, the administration also launched a simultaneous attack on the troublesome "Secret Allocution." As planned, a government-sponsored publication, *Notes on Public Ecclesiastical Law*, was released in Mexico City on May 1, the same day that the Montes mission set sail for Rome.[83] Although it was published anonymously, it was not long before the author of the treatise was identified as Manuel Baranda, a well-known jurist and the former governor of Guanajuato.[84] His seventy-six-page booklet opened with the observation that the allocution had appeared during a time of political and social crisis in Mexico, and because of the partisan passions it aroused, threatened to provoke a "fratricidal war" in the nation. On one side of this struggle, wrote Baranda, were those who denounced the pope's discourse. On the opposite side were those who defended it, "exciting themselves with its doctrines." In such a volatile situation, what was needed was a "patriotic and religious voice" that could expose the truth about the controversial document and thereby "terminate the pretext for civil war, rekindle the true and heartfelt union between all Mexicans, and erase the symptoms of religious schism, whose consequences would be frightful."

According to Baranda, the incriminating "truth" about the allocution was that in spite of its imperious tone, its contents had absolutely no bearing on the real situation in Mexico. First of all, it was quite probable that the inopportune document was simply a forgery. Fake papal documents had appeared in the past, he pointed out, so there was good reason to be skeptical about this unlikely document as well. Even if the discourse was authentic, he continued, it contained so many factual errors that it could not be taken seriously. For example, the disentailment process enacted by the Lerdo Law liquidated ecclesiastical assets, but it was not an outright confiscation of Church property as the allocution charged. Such exaggerations suggested that "if the supreme pontiff did in fact write the allocution as it appears, it is clear that he has been deceived" and "made to believe the most scandalous lies." Furthermore, even if the outrageous charges had been true, the allocution would still have to be rejected, because it "trampled underfoot the prerogatives of the state." In particular, the "strong declamation that came from Rome against the constitution" should be ignored, because such pronouncements overstepped the boundaries of the papal office.

The key to Baranda's argument was his insistence on the absolute supremacy of the secular state. In the third and longest section of the treatise, he marshaled a wide array of historical examples to demonstrate the practical and theoretical limitations of papal power. He acknowledged that this question had been debated for centuries but believed that "the defenders of temporal authority have the advantage of being more numerous, more articulate, and superior in wisdom and dignity." In Mexico, however, the *patronato* question had confused the limits of the two powers, and the clergy had made matters worse by adopting ultramontane ideas, which "make a rational harmony with the civil power even more difficult."

In the end, although none of his arguments were new, Baranda did manage to articulate the government's position in a clear and compelling way. And apparently the administration was pleased with the result since it spent a great deal of money publishing and promoting the work. Iglesias even sent a copy, with special gilt binding, to the apostolic delegate, who was himself implicitly implicated in the alleged conspiracy to mislead the pope. The prelate promptly sent it back, unread, with "a very incendiary note," but the minister only had it redelivered, accompanied by a provocative letter of his own. This time Clementi appeared at the ministry of justice in person, where he exchanged heated words with Iglesias before tearing the booklet into pieces and throwing it into the trash. As the French ambassador observed, such unpleasant scenes would certainly not facilitate the reception of Montes in Rome.[85]

Although the liberal press had been attacking the allocution ever since it appeared, supporters of the Church recognized in the Baranda treatise a much more sophisticated threat to their papal-approved crusade against the unwelcome reforms. At a minimum, the editors of *La Cruz* observed, its appearance suggested that their enemies were abandoning the newspapers, where articles "are born and die in one day," in favor of more substantial works to disseminate their "shameless" and "unjust" ideas. In turn, this new threat provoked a flurry of anti-Baranda material from Catholic writers. The first stage of this counter-polemic began on May 28, when the editors of *La Cruz* published a twenty-eight-page tract entitled *Brief reflections on an anonymous booklet entitled "Points on Public Ecclesiastical Law."* [86] Its intent, the pamphlet's authors claimed, was not to address all the questions raised by the offending booklet, but to warn the public about some of the "absurdities" it contained. At the same time, they hoped to inspire future writers to provide a more conclusive refutation. In spite of these modest claims, *Ligeras reflexiones* provided a fairly comprehensive scriptural, canonical, and historical critique of Baranda's main arguments. In fact, the profound erudition of the response suggests that Munguía himself may have played a part in its formulation from his exile in Coyoacán. In the next few months, *La Cruz* published dozens of other articles dedicated to the rebuttal of Baranda's ideas, including the serialization of a scholarly work by José Julian Tornel y Mendivil that ran for over a year.[87]

José Joaquín Pesado himself entered the fray on July 2 with the first installment of six articles under his own name dedicated to refuting Baranda's work. The goal of this series, he asserted, was to expose the heretical principles that informed all of Baranda's ideas. Anti-Catholicism had three covert allies, he warned: Jansenism, Gallicanism, and regalism. And Baranda, it seems, had embraced the third option by advocating that the secular government usurp the spiritual authority of the Church. Furthermore, Pesado argued that the only way to combat this error, the real root of religious schism, was to recognize that the Church had its own government, totally independent from the civil power. Furthermore, while the power structures of civil governments were imperfect and always changing, that of the Church was "holy, perfect, unalterable, and perpetual."[88]

At the same time that *La Cruz* was churning out anti-Baranda articles, the ultramontane cause was given another boost by the work of the distinguished jurist Juan Rodríguez de San Miguel. Author of a number of important texts on legal theory and practice, Rodríguez was also responsible for the famous treatise, *Considerations on the true character and spirit of the declamations regarding the reform of the clergy, their corruption and riches*, first published in 1848. This pamphlet was so popular among Catholics that it was reissued in 1856, at the beginning of the anticlerical reforms, in at least two separate editions.[89] Now, following the success of his earlier work, Rodríguez published *Various observations against a work entitled "Points on Public Ecclesiastical Law"* in response to Baranda.[90] In his introduction, the author stated that he had wanted to read the controversial work ever since he heard that its goal was to "erase the symptoms of religious division" and restore unity among Mexicans. But he was gravely disappointed when he was finally able to borrow a copy from a friend, since he could not ignore "the contradictions in some of the assertions and the incidental and unsupported assertions" it contained. Rather than discuss all the controversial points it raised, however, he limited his observations to "a literary and scientific discussion of the facts, rights, authorities and rationales that have merit in this work." Like most of this debate, the result was tedious and legalistic in tone. But as one observer noted, "neither Baranda nor any newspaper ever challenged any of the points that [Rodríguez] raised, and afterward even liberals lost respect for [Baranda]."[91]

One month later, supporters of the Church scored an even bigger public relations victory with the publication of José Bernardo Couto's *Discourse on the constitution of the Church*.[92] Like Pesado, who was also his first cousin, Couto was in his youth a throughgoing liberal who had heartily approved of enlightened religious reforms. As a student and protégé of the archliberal, José María Luis Mora, in 1825 he won a prize of two hundred pesos for a dissertation on the limits of papal power.[93] A brilliant lawyer, he was frequently a delegate to the state legislature in Veracruz and had also served as a senator in the national congress. In 1845 he was appointed minister of justice by President José Joaquín Herrera and was a plenipotentiary to the peace negotiations with the United States after Mexico's defeat in 1847. After the triumph of the Ayutla Revolution, he was elected to the constituent congress as a representative from Aguascalientes but declined to serve on the grounds of other "public service" commitments. In fact, in December 1855 Comonfort had appointed both Couto and Rodríguez, two of the country's most eminent jurists, to a commission tasked with revision of the civil code. During this period Couto also began meeting daily with Pesado and Manuel Carpio to discuss the disturbing developments on the political scene. Influenced, no doubt, by these intellectual associations, at some point Couto also became a staunch supporter of the Church. "I thank Providence a thousand times over for offering me the occasion to address these issues at a mature age," he later wrote. "Of what use are the years, if not for correcting our judgments?"[94]

Couto's rebuttal to Baranda's work consisted of an elaborate analysis of historical and legal precedents, but his thesis was fairly straightforward. The Church and the state, he argued, were two complete societies, each totally independent in its own sphere. That is why the state had no right to interfere in the internal life of the Church and the Church should not meddle in purely secular affairs. As far as the Church was concerned, Jesus Christ founded it, "without the permission of any government," when he gave his own authority to Peter and the other apostles, who in turn passed on this authority to their legitimate successors. "This, in the language of today, is the constitutional charter of the Church, because the constitution of every moral body consists principally in the erection and organization of its leadership," Couto declared. Furthermore, if the Church had the right to exist, which no one denied, it must also have the power to pursue the goal of its existence. This implied that it was entitled to whatever social rights and material possessions it needed to fulfill its sacred mission. In fact, since the forms of secular government were different everywhere and constantly changing, this made the Catholic religion "the most grand and beautiful 'social contract' of all." Any plan that denied these obvious truths, Couto maintained, was a project for "subversion," not reform.

Couto, who had not gone on record in favor of the Church until now, suddenly found himself a Catholic hero. Hailed as a "Mexican Montalembert," his erudite and balanced response was especially appreciated by educated Catholics.[95] A "Vote of Thanks" signed by thirty-four leading citizens from Durango, for example, hailed him as "the brightest star on the Mexican bench." "Know that as Catholics we are grateful to see in your discourse such a definitive defense of our common mother [the Church]," their proclamation declared, "and as lovers of learning we heartily admire your luminous ideas, so perfectly developed."[96] The celebrated writer Alejandro Arango y Escandon even wrote a poem in Couto's honor, praising his piety and "magnanimous example" in this time of civil discord.[97] The liberal press also recognized the significance of Couto's argument, and took steps to diminish its impact. *El Monitor Republicano*, for example, reprinted, with editorial comments, the award-winning anti-papal treatise he had written thirty-two years before.[98]

In the end, the Comonfort administration made a serious tactical error when it opted to sponsor the anti-allocution campaign. Like its diplomatic mission to Rome, focusing on this particular target was itself another tacit admission of the important place held by the pope in the imagination of Mexican Catholics, a reality that most liberals would have preferred to ignore. In addition, the unexpected intervention by national figures like Rodríguez and Couto helped undermine the carefully cultivated illusion of a liberal monopoly on rational thinking. Finally, by provoking a clarification of Catholic political thought, the Baranda polemic only hardened conservative opposition to the liberal model of government-sponsored reform.

As it turned out, this hardening of ideological positions was also accelerated by another important debate that erupted at the same time. While the Baranda controversy focused on abstract questions of papal power and state sovereignty, this second polemic was rooted in more practical and immediate concerns. In fact, José Manuel Toribio Alvires, a supreme court justice from the State of Michoacán, instigated the debate in an attempt to resolve his own personal dilemma related to the constitution. Alvires, a moderate, had taken the oath without qualms when it was first offered to him on March 30. Only later, he claimed, did he come across a copy of Munguía's outlawed circular and realize that Catholics in his diocese were forbidden to swear. But having taken the oath in good conscience, he could see no reason why he should now make a public retraction. Instead, he began a crusade to convince his fellow Catholics of the unreasonableness of the bishops' position.

At first, Alvires expressed his ideas anonymously, in a series of articles published in *El Siglo Diez y Nueve* that he signed only with the initial "A."[99] But although he was "inclined by character and habits to keep silent and maintain an insignificant position on every issue," he eventually sacrificed his anonymity in order to resolve "the delicate issue of the oath" once and for all. Rather than appealing over the heads of the bishops to the pope, however, Alvires' plan was to undercut their authority from below. It was to that end that he addressed his *Reflections on the Episcopal Decrees that Forbid the Constitutional Oath* to "all good Catholics, and especially priests." First, he argued, since episcopal authority was limited to spiritual matters, the bishops had no competence to decide matters relating to civil law, much less to make judgments on the virtues of a national constitution. Furthermore, since the Bible commanded Christians to submit to the temporal power, the bishops' ban against taking the oath was "null and void." At the same time, the canonical penalties they imposed were illicit because they punished an "artificial sin" not listed in the Decalogue.[100] From this point it followed that the absolution given by priests to those who did not retract the oath was still valid. And as far as Alvires was concerned, "this is the principal point of all the canonical and moral questions." Finally, since the constitution contained nothing "opposed to the institution, doctrines, or rights of the Catholic Church," he called upon the bishops to reverse their "uncharitable" position. Failing that, he suggested, good priests should simply ignore them.

Alvires later insisted that he had only taken up the pen in order to prevent a religious war. "I hope to heaven that these reflections, dictated by the purest faith, the most wholesome intention and the spirit of peace, order and charity, reunite the feelings of all Mexicans, terminating the schismatic divergence of opinions," he wrote. But his comments could not help but provoke a spirited response. Aguilar y Marocho, for example, referred to Alvires as the "madman from Morelia" for claiming that the bishops had no authority to forbid the oath.[101] Then there was the inevitable reaction by *La Cruz*, which took the lead in questioning the judge's competence to pontificate on religious questions. "Although the writer is only a layman, he tries to instruct the sheep over whom he has no jurisdiction, as well as the pastors, to whom he ought to be subjected," insisted Pesado.[102] A cathedral canon from Guadalajara, Agustín de la Rosa, also weighed in with a scholarly response to the canonical questions Alvires raised.[103] Perhaps the most memorable reply was the biting *Doubts of a Student Regarding the Reflections of Sr. Alvires on the Episcopal Degrees that Prohibit the Constitutional Oath*, whose sarcastic questions implied that Alvires just might be a heretic, an apostate, or worse.[104] Another important and heated exchange occurred between Alvires and two priests from Morelia, his own hometown.[105]

Faced with this barrage of criticism, Alvires, against his pacific inclinations, was induced to add two more installments to his original treatise.[106] Central to these additions was an attack on a circular that Munguía issued on May 16, permitting Catholics in his diocese to swear a restricted form of the oath. Such inconsistencies and changes in policy only highlighted the bishops' fallibility, Alvires charged. He also attacked the "Secret Allocution," arguing that not even the pope had a right to interfere in political issues of a purely temporal nature. As far as he was concerned, only a complete separation between spiritual and secular authority could dissipate the "black clouds of idiotic and exaggerated ultramontanism," a movement that he considered retrograde "even by Mexican standards."[107] In the end, however, frustrated with the relentless opposition his ideas generated, Alvires abandoned the thankless job of national reconciliation and left to the government "the cause of defending my religious honor." On July 28, the state congress in Michoacán obliged when it officially declared him "*benemérito*" (meritorious) for his efforts to resolve the religious impasse.[108]

In spite of this liberal recognition, Alvires's reflections did little to diminish the "schismatic divergence of opinions" and "reunite the feelings of all Mexicans." On the contrary, by the summer of 1857 the battle lines were more clearly drawn than ever. On one side were those who held that the ideas embodied in the new constitution were not incompatible with the Catholic faith. Included in this group were many who believed that religion in Mexico might actually benefit, in one way or another, from this kind of reform. For example, *El Monitor Republicano* declared that the "eminently religious" progressives had never persecuted the Church. Even their desire to limit the influence of priests, it explained, was intended for "the good of the Church, for the good of the people, and for the greater brilliance of religion."[109] Conversely, other Mexicans were convinced that the new charter, in both its spirit and letter, constituted a real threat to religion. In this company were also those who held that it was the job of the bishops, and only the bishops, to formulate the appropriate Catholic response to this threat. "Once the verdict had been pronounced by the authority of the Church, in a matter which pertains to its exclusive jurisdiction," *La Cruz* insisted, "the ordinary layman ought to submit himself to it, without getting involved in the deeper questions."[110]

As the summer wore on, the religious dimension of the oath crisis assumed an even greater importance, as both sides attempted to use this controversy to define the contours of the future Mexican Church. Those who had taken the oath were still required to make a retraction in order to receive the sacraments of the Church, but this was something that convinced liberals like Alvires were determined never to do. It was said that to prevent false or temporary deathbed retractions at the hour of death, some priests now brought a notary and two witnesses along when they came to administer the last rites. There were also complaints that some clergymen interrogated family members and servants when the true dispositions of the dying were unknown.[111] "It is a true scandal what is happening today," Munguía observed, "the anguish and disturbance of the dying, these domestic schisms, all these sudden retractions, and the ruined reputations of those who fail to retract."[112] Now that unrepentant liberals were dying without the consolations of their religion, however, the anticlerical press began to demand that the government intervene. Local officials agreed, and on June 15 a priest in Puruándiro (Michoacán) was indicted for withholding the sacraments from a dying man. Twelve days later another priest was exiled for refusing the last rites to the mayor of Zochila (Oaxaca).[113] In an even more famous case, a priest in Mexico City who had denied the sacraments to Comonfort's nephew was arrested at 4 o'clock on the morning of July 15.[114] In each of these instances, however, as the editors of *La Cruz* pointed out, priests were being punished simply for following the directives of their ecclesiastical superiors.

At the same time, some clergy also attempted creative solutions to the dilemma caused by the conflicting demands of Church and State. Liberals, however, were outraged when a priest performed a post-mortem penance for the first governor of the State of Colima. General José Manuel Dolores Álvarez Zamora had been killed on August 26 in a shoot-out with local rebels. Since it was theoretically possible that the deceased might have repented of his oath had he known he was going to die that day, the priest decided to perform a penance on behalf of the popular leader in order to justify his interment in consecrated ground, reciting the *Miserere* while chastising the corpse with a wand. Rather than a practical solution to an intractable problem, however, for liberals such actions were clearly a misuse of religious rituals for political gain. One newspaper even described the post-mortem ritual as "an act of barbarism worthy of the Comanches" rather than an act of charity.[115] Another incident occurred in Puebla on August 31, when Paulino María Pérez, an officer in the national guard, died without retracting the oath. Although he had in fact received the last rites from a sympathetic military chaplain, the local curate still refused him a Christian burial because of the un-retracted oath. When the family protested to the authorities, the new governor, Miguel Cástulo Alatriste, demanded that the diocesan administrator allow the burial in consecrated ground. But although Canon Reyero y Lugo felt duty-bound to uphold the curate's decision, he did offer a compromise. Since the chaplain was unable to verify Pérez's retraction, the colonel's widow would be allowed to abjure the oath on his behalf. This suggestion, however, was rejected, and Reyero was exiled to Orizaba (Veracruz) for his impudence. To add insult to injury, the governor himself marched at the head of the funeral cortege and with a large number of his supporters forced open the gate to the cemetery at the Carmelite monastery, where the cadaver was finally interred.[116]

Pesado, who professed to be shocked more by the profanation of a sacred place than by the arrest of another diocesan official, wondered why liberals did not simply build their own graveyards where those who chose to spend their lives outside the fellowship of the Church could enjoy that same privilege after death. "The liberal party in Mexico demands a rare, or rather an incomprehensible, thing," he said. They desire "to be indifferent to religion, or schismatic, while living, and impenitent at the hour of death, but want to pass as a good Catholic afterward."[117] For liberals, however, the events surrounding the illicit Pérez burial only highlighted the folly of allowing the hierarchy to determine who was and who was not a member of the Church. On September 5, the legislature in Puebla responded by passing a new law that criminalized the Church's position on the matter. Henceforth, a penalty of two to five years in prison was automatically levied on anyone "demanding, prescribing, or in any way obliging" for any reason whatsoever a retraction of the oath.[118]

At this point, as government intervention in the administration of the sacraments made clear, some secular officials were simply no longer willing to recognize any religious authority higher than their own. As in Puebla, by and large it was the *puro* state governors and other local officials who took the most radical stand against the official leaders of the Church. In reality, the oath controversy had all but eliminated orthodox Catholics from political life, leaving only fervent anticlericals in charge of developing local religious policy. In Guerrero, priests were now made subject to the oath and those who refused to take it were expelled from the state. Similarly, the Congress of Zacatecas voted to seize the ecclesiastical tithe, already voluntary, in retribution for clerical resistance to the implementation of the ban on stole fees. Many governors were also awarded extraordinary powers to arrest, imprison, and exile dissidents without trial, a faculty that Manuel Doblado in Guanajuato used to exile twenty-five uncooperative clerics.[119]

The fundamental social schism that now existed in Mexico is also reflected in the confrontation that took place between Governor Santiago Vidaurri of Nueva León and the Bishop of Linares-Monterrey, Francisco de Paula Verea y González, in early September 1857. On the surface, the causes of the conflict resembled those responsible for the clash that marred the Holy Week observances in Mexico City. But whereas in Mexico City most ordinary citizens were vocally supportive of the clergy, in the Bajío region opinion was much more divided. As in Mexico City, the conflict in Monterrey also began with an exchange of letters between the governor and the local bishop over an issue of liturgical protocol. The celebration of the Nativity of the Blessed Virgin Mary on September 8 was also the patronal feast of the State of Nuevo León, and the mayor and the city council of Monterrey were accustomed to attend the divine services as a body on that day. Bishop Verea, however, informed the governor that due to the ongoing persecution of the Church by secular authorities, they would not be allowed to process into the cathedral in their official capacity as in previous years. Although Governor Vidaurri responded to this decision with various charges and threats, the bishop remained firm in his decision.

Rumors of this exchange contributed to the immense crowd that gathered in and around the cathedral when the day of the festival arrived. At the same time, some citizens congregated at the city hall to demonstrate their support for the governor's stand. As expected, when the mayor and other officials arrived at the cathedral, they found the main door locked, and so had to enter through smaller doors on the side of the vestibule. Although they were not prevented from attending the liturgy, there was no official reception nor were any places of honor reserved for them in front of the high altar. As they had been instructed, therefore, when the service ended, members of the mayor's party blocked the exits, and the mayor himself entered the sacristy to inform the canons that they were under arrest. The immense crowd in the atrium outside the cathedral was silent as the priests were led away, but according to the liberal press, government supporters cheered when the prisoners reached city hall. The mayor and two aldermen then returned to the episcopal residence to apprehend the bishop, who was considered the chief instigator of the affair. When Bishop Verea was brought out, the multitude in the square knelt on the ground and the men uncovered their heads to receive his blessing. In contrast, the spectators at city hall again raised cheers for the governor, President Comonfort, national sovereignty, and the city council when the new prisoner arrived. Among these cheers, as one commentor noted, "perhaps for the very first time in the nation," was "Respect for the law!"

Once the bishop and canons were in custody, Governor Vidaurri offered to release the entire party if only Verea would make a public submission to the constitution, the *Ley Lerdo* and the *Ley Iglesias*, the three points on which the bishops had most egregiously and persistently defied the secular power. When the prelate refused, he was summarily sentenced to exile from his diocese and two days later was escorted out of the state by a force of twenty-five men. *La Cruz* reported that the people of Nuevo León went into mourning over the loss of their bishop, although the liberal press insinuated that he had only gotten what he deserved. Vidaurri, for one, suggested that the removal of Verea, a native of Guadalajara, would restore "the sweet harmony that ought to exist between the secular and religious authorities," since the character of local clergy was supposedly milder than that of the stubborn outsider. Later, when other priests abandoned their curacies in the wake of the deportation, government officials stepped in and took over the parishes themselves. In place of Mass, some local magistrates personally led the recitation of the rosary or preached extemporaneous sermons to the bewildered congregations. According to Vidaurri, "the temporal power can and even must intervene in all those ecclesiastical acts that affect the social order." This duty, he added, extended "even to the spiritual order when, unfortunately, morals are corrupted and ideas are introduced that are repugnant to our holy religion."[120]

On the surface, the drawn-out conflict over the 1857 Constitution may seem to have been little more than a naked power struggle between liberals and the Church, with an enlightened government bent on modernization and reform facing an entrenched clergy unwilling to relinquish the commanding heights of moral and cultural control. In this war of attrition, liberals understood that even without Article 15, the other legislation granting freedom of speech, freedom of association, freedom of the press, and free schools had already laid the groundwork for an ideologically diverse society. Even more importantly, the new constitution had also incorporated the earlier reform acts that would inevitably diminish the power and influence of the clergy over time. In February 1857, therefore, liberals seemed to be on the verge of achieving the Church and society they had always desired. From this perspective, the clergy and its supporters were fighting a rearguard action against modernity and progress, in the end only discrediting themselves and the ideals they claimed to serve.

But at a deeper level, the nonjuring crisis was a religious struggle for the nation's soul and a battle to define the identity, and therefore the future, of Mexico. As the earnest discourses of both sides made clear, behind the political conflict was the issue of religious authority, an intangible reality that nevertheless would determine the content and expression of the faith of the Mexican people. By consistently emphasizing their religious credentials and insisting on recognition from the Church, liberal reformers implicitly acknowledged the essential place held by the Catholic religion in the collective psyche of all Mexicans. But as the events of 1857 made clear, the religious unity trumpeted by conservatives throughout 1856 had already disappeared. Ironically, it was Catholic spokesmen like Pesado, Couto, and Rodríguez who recognized the dangerous implications of this fact and began to insist on absolute independence of the Church from entangling alliances with the heterodox secular state. The religious schism that everyone feared had already occurred, but it would take a religious civil war to make the depth of that final rupture unmistakably clear.

CHAPTER 7

The War of the Reforma
(1858–1860)

By the end of 1857, Mexico was in the final stage of its culture war, a conflict between opposing interpretations of Mexico's past and alternative visions for its future. Because Mexico was still a Catholic country, these clashing worldviews necessarily included competing ideas about faith and religion. Simmering since the trauma of Mexico's defeat in the war with the United States, the issues at stake had become much clearer since liberals seized power in 1855. Increasingly, their materialistic agenda generated new legislation that promised to fundamentally transform the nation. The rhetoric, pro and con, surrounding these changes, and especially the constitutional debates in 1856, hardened the already deep divisions in Mexican society. But the imposition of the completed constitution in 1857 finally forced citizens at every level to choose sides. Now, the newspaper contests, liturgical standoffs, and periodic revolts exploded into an actual civil war. During the next three years of conflict, each side would continue to cherish its own worldview, nourished by signs of God's favor in victory or the proof of the perfidy of the enemy in defeat. In this context, the images generated by playwrights, poets, and preachers continued to play a role as vital as that of the armies in the outcome of the war. Propaganda is a crucial element in every modern war. But when national identity and cultural meaning is at stake, only total annihilation of the opposing side, both militarily and morally, can bring peace.[1]

When war finally began, it originated in an unexpected quarter. The *moderado* president Ignacio Comonfort took office on December 1, 1857, and the newly elected congress sat for the first time on December 14. But on December 17, following consultations with Comonfort, Brigadier General Félix María Zuloaga declared the Plan of Tacubaya.[2] This latest *pronunciamiento* immediately suspended the constitution and declared that a new convention would be convened to write a better one, which this time would be subject to a plebiscite. As planned, Comonfort assumed leadership of the interim government and issued his own manifesto to the nation on December 19. First, he noted that the recent constitution had been repudiated by large sections of the Mexican population. The country was in a crisis, he asserted, because that charter, intended to create stability, did not represent the national will. He promised to continue to follow the path of liberal reform, but this time "no measure will be dictated that attacks the conscience or beliefs of the citizens; because I judge that true liberty, rightly understood, is not incompatible with the respect that ought to be given to the customs and traditions of the people."[3]

As it turned out the Plan of Tacubaya was the beginning of three years of civil war, also known as the "War of the Reforma." Surprisingly, no conservatives or clergymen were involved in the *pronunciamento*, which began as a coup by moderates against their own government.[4] That is because, as Will Fowler has noted, the underlying political struggle was "not simply a bipolar war between conservatives and liberals, but a war in which two antagonistic liberal visions brutally confronted each other: that of the *moderados* and the *puros*."[5] In this case, the moderate Comonfort planned to unseat the radical congress and modify their unpopular constitution. After the coup, he sent telegrams to the state governors, liberals all, and initially most supported Comonfort's plan.[6] But the states of the central lowlands (the Bajío)—Guanajuato, Aguascalientes, Queretaro and Jalisco—resisted. Here, the more radical governors formed a "coalition" to maintain the 1857 Constitution that liberals had worked so hard to create. Neither were conservatives convinced by the promises of the moderates, and on January 11 a second military coup was launched in Mexico City by General José de la Parra. The standoff between garrisons loyal to the three factions—*moderados*, *puros*, and conservatives—lasted until January 21, 1858, when conservative troops under colonels Luis Gonzalez Osollo and Miguel Miramón arrived and defeated Comonfort's supporters.[7] Comonfort then left the city in peace, having already released Benito Juaréz, imprisoned earlier for opposing the original Tacubaya Plan.[8] By this action, Comonfort not only conferred his constitutional power on Juaréz, but handed over the entire Reforma movement into the hands of the radicals. In accord with the provisions of the suspended 1857 Constitution, Juárez, as chief justice of the supreme court, would be the temporary head of state in the absence of an elected president. He was recognized as such when he reached Guanajuato, where he created his own cabinet and alternative government. Unsurprisingly, members of his cabinet included the *puro* stalwarts Melchor Ocampo, Santos Degollado, and Guillermo Prieto.

Meanwhile, in Mexico City a solemn Te Deum was intoned in the Metropolitan Cathedral to celebrate the end of liberal rule, with General Zuloaga and his entourage in attendance. Afterward, a hastily assembled *junta de notables* (committee of notables) convened to create a truly conservative government. Zuloaga was elected "interim president" and a new governing council was formed. Among its members were staunch Catholic activists such as José Joaquín Pesado, Bernardo Couto, Juan Rodríguez de San Miguel, and even the irrepressible Father Francis Miranda.[9] The following day, Zuloaga issued his "Five Laws," nullifying all the Reforma legislation. A few days later a delegation representing seven hundred women of the capital presented a heartfelt vote of thanks to Zuloaga for this action.[10] As he later explained in an official letter to Pope Pius IX, the previous regime had "attacked the Church, ignored customs, and sanctioned principles dissolvent to the family and property." Furthermore, since the "supreme chief" of the Plan of Tacubaya would not take the necessary steps to solve these problems, "a second appeal to arms" was required. But, with the pope's blessing, the new government in Mexico City would bring an end to the bitter persecution that the Church had recently endured.[11]

A feeling of religious euphoria was evident in Mexico City during these early months of the new conservative regime. After the fall of Comonfort, one observer noted the "indescribable joy" on the faces of all the people, "caused by the pure and grand triumph of our holy cause, precursor of our well-being and happiness."[12] Religious ceremonies also abounded. As might be expected, the festival of Blessed Felipe de Jesús was celebrated on February 5 with all its former splendor, with military and political officials in conspicuous attendance.[13] A few weeks later, a Requiem Mass was celebrated in the *Sagrario* of the Metropolitan Cathedral in Mexico City for the soldiers that perished in the recent coup "defending sound principles." In connection with the religious observance, the flags on government buildings were flown at half-staff that day and there were artillery salvos every quarter hour until evening.[14] At the end of February, the image of *Nuestra Señora de los Remedios* was brought into the city from its shrine in Naucalpan, eight miles away. Over the centuries, this statue, the oldest

Marian icon in Mexico, was only processed to the capital during time of drought, plague, or other natural disasters. This time, President Zuloaga and his troops marched behind the statue through decorated streets, accompanied by "the most decent of the population, being particularly considerable the presence of ladies." When the procession arrived at the cathedral, prayers were offered throughout the night, asking that Divine Providence, "through the intercession of the most holy Virgin, establish peace in our republic and free it in the future from the enemies of Catholic civilization, who are the enemies of society."[15]

The ceremonies for Holy Week in April 1858 were likewise particularly intense, since they were intended to repair the insult given to God by the previous year's "sacrilegious scandal." As one citizen exclaimed, "Now you will see such services, such displays, such splendors of worship! Now we are going to make amendment to God for all the horrors of the last Holy Week, with which that cursed Baz tempted heaven."[16] The civil authorities were again welcomed into the cathedral, and "instead of the cries of anger and terror that had then resonated in the sanctuary, there arose the prayers of the men that Providence had placed in charge of the destinies of the republic." According to *La Cruz*, this was "proof of the harmony that now happily reigns between Church and State."[17] A week later, an image of the Immaculate Conception was processed from the reopened church of San Franciso to the National and Pontifical University, also recently reopened by the conservative government.[18]

In Puebla, the city that had endured two conservative revolts, two liberal sieges, and harsh collective punishments, the joy of liberation was tempered by the memory of past suffering. This collective grief was expressed on February 13, 1858, in an elaborate public funeral for "victims of the demagogic tyranny." In the Church of St. Francis, a catafalque was erected and decorated with poems and Latin inscriptions in honor of sixteen "illustrious" heroes who had died at the hands of the liberals. The list included the name of an officer, found unarmed and shot after the second capitulation of Puebla.[19] There were also the names of five "respectable" youths who had been executed without trial on November 11, 1857, for participation in another conspiracy against the government.[20] Most surprising in this list were the names of José María Benitez and Carlos Castillero, since they were actually victims of conservative violence rather than liberal retribution. Benitez, a courier, had been mistaken for a liberal deserter and was killed by gunfire from a house where a group of men, including the mayor, the local priest, and his brother, were gathered. When Castillero arrived on the scene a few minutes later, he was apprehended and placed in the local jail. But fearful that their initial crime would be reported, the perpetrators convinced the local villagers to kill the prisoner and hide the body. Later, when his battered corpse was discovered, an official inquiry was launched, leading to the arrest of the priest. Along with the mayor, witnesses claimed that he had encouraged the murder by claiming that God would punish the village if it spared the unbeliever.[21] Nevertheless, the preacher, Carmelite Father Pablo Antonio del Niño Jesus, declared that all sixteen had died "like the Maccabees, in defense of religion, law and traditional customs."[22] His sermon, which also recalled the other recent sufferings of the city and its people, was interrupted by the frequent sobs of "men, women and even soldiers" that filled the temple. After the service, as the bells of all the city's churches tolled, the political, religious, and military leaders processed together to the governor's palace. As a sign of communal mourning, black crepe hung from all the balconies of the houses along the route taken by the cortège.[23]

Since a large portion of the professional military supported the new regime, the conservatives would have the advantage of better trained troops and more experienced leaders throughout the three years of war that followed the coups.[24] These included thirty-seven-year-old General Leonardo Márquez Araujo, who had fought in Texas and was distinguished for his actions during the US invasion. He was also the man who led the military coup to install Santa Anna as dictator in 1852.[25] Another key figure was Tomás Mejía Camacho, a full-blooded Otomi, also thirty-seven-years old and likewise distinguished for service during the previous war. He had pronounced for "religion and *fueros*" in October 1856, maintaining one of the numerous regional revolts never completely quelled by the Comonfort administration.[26] However, the most important military figures on the conservative side were the two dashing young officers that had ousted Comonfort from the presidential palace. Twenty-nine-year-old Luis Gonzaga Osollo had entered the *Colegio Militar* at the tender age of eleven and fought the American invaders at the age of eighteen.[27] In 1856 he participated in both failed conservative revolts in Puebla. Undaunted, he lost his right arm to a cannon ball during another revolt after the constitution was promulgated in February 1857.[28] Similarly, Miguel Miramón entered the *Colegio Militar* in 1846 at the age of fifteen, in time to be wounded in the cadets' defense of Chapultepec Castle against the American assault on September 13, 1847. He later fought for Santa Anna against the Ayutla rebels and participated in the Puebla revolts after the dictator's fall. He was only twenty-six-years old when he and Osollo were promoted to the rank of brigadier general for their role in the coup against Comonfort.[29] The new army they commanded was named the "Regenerated Army of the Three Guarantees," recalling the alliance that won Mexico's independence in 1821 with its promise of support for the Catholic faith.

Despite such promising signs of collaboration, however, the Catholic agenda and religious sensibilities were not always identical to those of the conservative military and political leadership. For example, at the Battle of Salamanca, one of General Osollo's former comrades, Colonel José María Calderon, was killed on the opposing side. After the conservative victory, Osollo ordered a military funeral for the fallen officer, but the local priest refused to officiate at a funeral for an unrepentant liberal. He only complied after Osollo threatened to shoot him and bury his corpse in the same grave with Calderon.[30] More surprising, the most important Catholic journal in the country, *La Cruz*, suddenly ceased publication just seven months after the beginning of the new regime. In its last issue, the editors merely announced that this unexpected development was due to "circumstances beyond our control."[31] Ironically, the journal had survived the years of liberal rule but was finally silenced under a "Catholic" government, probably for criticizing the forced loans being demanded from the Church to pay for the war.[32]

Funding the new government and army would be the conservatives' most pressing problem throughout the conflict. Initially, the government asked the Church to guarantee a loan of a million and a half pesos, which the archbishop refused. However, in spite of his reluctance to mortgage church funds, on January 28 he approved a loan of just one hundred and fifty thousand pesos to meet the administration's immediate needs.[33] Two more requests for emergency funds were made in July. Archbishop Gaza refused the second request at around the same time that *La Cruz* disappeared. The government then turned to forced loans from its wealthier citizens, and even foreigners in conservative territory.[34] The loans requested from the Diocese of Puebla, also in conservative hands, were likewise denied. From abroad, Bishop Labastida had instructed his cabildo to follow the same course with the Zuloaga government that he had adopted in response to President Comonfort's earlier demands. In fact, while in Rome he had considered various ways that Church assets might licitly be used to help in the conservative cause, but all of these had been overruled by Pope Pius IX.[35] Liberal propaganda always insisted that the clergy was funding the conservative side, which was true. But the actual aid provided by the Church was never as much as liberals imagined or as much as the conservative government required.[36]

Despite its financial shortfalls, the conservative army won a string of victories during the first year of the war that made its two young generals seem almost invincible. The States of Mexico and Puebla remained conservative strongholds throughout the war, while liberals retained control of the major ports. But other large cities in and around the Bajío, including Guanajuato, Zacatecas, Morelia (Michoacán), Querétaro, San Luis Potosí, and Guadalajara (Jalisco) changed hands numerous times.[37] In January, Osollo's troops occupied the city of Querétaro, forcing the Juárez government to flee to Guadalajara. He also defeated liberal forces at the Battles of Celaya and Salamanca (Guanajuato) in March, opening the way for an assault on Guadalajara. Ultimately, this city changed hands four times during the war and endured five liberal sieges. The sufferings of its population during the conflict in many ways epitomized the vicissitudes of the entire national struggle.

Although the liberal government of Benito Juárez was temporarily located in Guadalajara, there was also substantial conservative and Catholic opposition in the city. "The society was profoundly divided in its opinions and in its sentiments," one *tapatío* recalled, "and a hitherto unknown excitement dominated." "Whether in the streets or the salons, politics, religion and philosophy were discussed, always with passion if not with good judgment."[38] Even female fashion became a sign of the ideological polarization when some women began to appear at social functions in green dresses, the color associated with the conservatives, while others made a point of wearing red, the international color of the left. In response, some conservatives wore red slippers at balls and dances to show that they stomped on the ideals of liberalism, "while those of the opposite opinion shod themselves in green."[39] One fervent liberal even pasted pictures of General Miramón to the soles of her shoes, which provoked a shouting match with another young woman one Sunday after Mass, a showdown that culminated in a physical assault.[40] Likewise, when some pious ladies began to wear crosses around their neck to show their support for the Church, those in the liberal camp proudly adorned their chests with little hatchets made of gold, an ironic symbol for their own party.[41] In Guadalajara, conservative women also helped circulate an underground Catholic newspaper, *La Tarántula*, surreptitiously stuffing copies in mailboxes and under doors across the city. Liberals complained that the clergy encouraged Catholic families to read it aloud after the evening rosary, and to pray "for the extermination of the heretics and impious, that is to say, of the liberals."[42] In particular, the clandestine paper "contained writings inciting Catholics to enlist in a crusade against the constitutional government." In response, one liberal club allegedly called for the death of Bishop Espinosa and all conservative activists in the city.[43]

In this atmosphere, it was not surprising that when news of the conservative victories reached the city, a revolt began with the cry, "¡Viva la religión!"[44] Some federal soldiers under Colonel Antonio Landa mutinied, combating the national guard troops commanded by Miguel Cruz-Aedo. On March 13, the insurgents occupied the state capital, capturing Juárez and his cabinet. Some of the rebels wanted to shoot Juárez and the other prisoners but Landa himself intervened and they were spared. Instead, in the courtyard they made a large bonfire of the government printing press and incinerated thousands of copies of the hated 1857 Constitution. The revolt collapsed, however, when liberal reinforcements arrived. At this point, the French consulate brokered a cease-fire, Juárez and company were released, and the rebels were allowed to withdraw from the city.[45] Afterward, Juárez issued a statement describing his harrowing experience as just one "phase in the struggle of humanity between those who tyrannize and those who liberate." Furthermore, despite the recent setbacks, he promised, "with God's help" the ultimate victory "of the people" would be achieved.[46] A few days later, as the conservative army approached, Juárez and his fugitive government escaped west to the Pacific coast to begin their long journey, via Panama, Cuba, and New Orleans, back to Veracruz.

General Osollo's army entered Guadalajara without opposition on March 23, and a council of notables was appointed to elect a new governor. In his proclamation after being chosen, Governor Urbano Tovar described the previous regime as "a period of atheistic politics, collapsed morals, antisocial and dissolvent politics, and foolish, absurd legislation."[47] The Catholic population seemed to agree, and staged elaborate liturgies in all the major churches of the city to celebrate their new freedom. On April 10, Bishop Espinosa himself officiated at the local sanctuary of Our Lady of Guadalupe to fulfill a vow he had made to the Virgin, once the Church was "free from persecutions." There was also a massive procession through the city a few days later, the streets brilliantly illuminated and decked with flowers. The numerous religious orders, brotherhoods, and parishes, along with students, soldiers, officials, and even the city's orphans, marched in companies carrying images of their heavenly patrons. Along the route, a statue of a woman in flowing robes was erected, representing the Church, holding aloft a cross and a chalice; an angel kneeling at her feet displayed the olive branch of peace. When the extravagant spectacle ended, the ecstatic crowd unhitched the bishop's horses and joyfully pulled his carriage back to the episcopal palace themselves.[48]

More darkly, however, along with notable conservative victories, the spring of 1858 saw the beginning of the cycle of violence for which the Three Years War became infamous. This bloodletting started when a liberal force under Colonel Juan Zuazua was halted by Miramón's army outside San Luis Potosí on April 17. In response, Zuazua withdrew and defeated the conservatives at Zacatecas on April 27 instead. There, General Antonio Manero was captured, along with sixty of his officers and four hundred and twenty soldiers, after their ammunition ran out.[49] Zuazua's decision to shoot the general and four others, including Col. Antonio Landa, who had spared the life of Juárez in Guadalajara, sent a shock wave across the country. As the historian Alfonso Trueba put it, thus was revealed "the face of Huichilobos" in the conflict.[50] Conservatives reciprocated on May 21 by executing the retired governor of Jalisco, Ignacio Herrera y Cairo, who was accused of stockpiling weapons for the liberals on his hacienda.[51] After the fact, the conservative government in Mexico City issued a statement denouncing this action, stating that "nothing can tarnish the luster of the arms [of the Restoration Army] and the flag that it carries as much as imitating the barbaric conduct of its enemy."[52] Nevertheless, the following month, General Miguel María de Echeagaray ordered the execution of sixteen men from the garrison in Xalapa (Veracruz) that had revolted in favor of the liberal government. "I ordered the execution of the mutineers," he confessed, "but I rest easy in my military conscience. . . . The blood of my brother General Manero still seethes on the fatherland's altar, and more blood is required so that [the blood] of that brave and ill-fated soldier does not dry out."[53]

This surge in violence and reprisals was also accompanied by increased attacks against the Catholic Church and its symbols. Naturally, the clergy were especially targeted since the anticlerical newspapers constantly blamed them for fomenting and prolonging the war. Thus, after taking (and sacking) Zacatecas, Zuazua exiled Bishop Verea, who had taken refuge there after his expulsion from Monterrey in September of the previous year. When he occupied San Luis Potosí a few months later, Zuazua likewise exiled Bishop Pedro Barajas and twenty-six of his priests from the city. Throughout constitutional territory, many priests were expelled from their parishes, deported, imprisoned, or held for ransom. Those who wore distinctive habits were sometimes afraid to even venture outside.[54] At the hands of radicals, or their bandit allies, the clergy might be publicly humiliated, physically assaulted, and even killed.[55] For example, Pragedis García, the priest of Jilotlán de los Dolores (Jalisco), was arrested and forced to march fifteen leagues barefoot. When his bloody feet could no longer support him, he was dragged to death behind a horse.[56] The priest of Telolapan (Guerrero) was beaten when constitutionalists sacked the town and was left tied to the whipping post overnight.[57] The most famous case was that of Francisco Ortega y García, the priest implicated in the rebellion in Zacapoaxtla in 1855. He was arrested in his rectory at Coscomatepec (Veracruz) on April 1, 1859. General Ignacio de la Llave condemned him to death because, he reportedly explained, "this weakling is the hero, the defender of religion." He was then savagely beaten, his ears cut off and eyes gouged out, before he was placed before a firing squad, after which his body was drawn and quartered. According to conservative reports, although Father Ortega endured tortures "like those the first martyrs suffered," he also offered forgiveness to his persecutors before he died. This happened not in some heathen country, it was noted, "but in the midst of a society that calls itself civilized and Christian, and at the hands of men who say they are reformers of clerical abuse and preachers of universal brotherhood." Even if the "demagogues" ultimately triumph in Mexico with the help of the "foreign foe," one editor predicted, "they will never be able to wash away the stain of this cold-blooded, cowardly and sacrilegious murder."[58]

At this stage, church buildings also became a more frequent target, both as symbols of clerical power and because their wealth could be used to finance the liberal army. For example, on May 27, 1858, Colonel Miguel Blanco looted the famous shrine of Our Lady of San Juan de los Lagos (Jalisco) and seized 100,000 pesos that had been buried beneath the floor in a side chapel.[59] Blanco was also involved in an even more notorious action in Morelia (Michoacán) in September of that same year. When the ecclesiastical cabildo denied him a loan of 90,000 pesos, Governor Epitacio Huerta sent two hundred men under Blanco and Porfirio García de León to plunder the cathedral of its riches. After breaking down the doors, the team spent five days sacking the building. All the church plate, along with all the other gold and silver objects and jewels, were taken. Even the cadavers of deceased bishops were disinterred to get at their episcopal rings. The biggest prize of all was the solid silver balustrades (the *crujía*) connecting the sanctuary to the choir.[60] In the end, Blanco and company removed around five hundred kilos of silver, thirteen kilos of gold, and a great quantity of jewels from the church. Later he had most of the silver melted into bars and delivered to the US legation in Mexico City to be smuggled to the liberal forces in

Veracruz. Although this was not the first time that silver had been appropriated from the cathedral for military purposes, many Mexicans on both sides of the struggle condemned the blatantly anti-Catholic tone of this confiscation.[61] Naturally, much damage was done to the art and fabric of the cathedral by the violent removal of its valuables; the sense of sacrilege being compounded by the vulgar shouts and raucous songs that were said to have accompanied the plunder.[62] Predictably, Bishop Clemente de Jesús Munguía, from his exile in Coyoacán, lamented the desecration of his cathedral and excommunicated everyone involved.[63] But even Manuel Toribio Alvires, the *moderado* who had so adamantly defended his constitutional oath in April 1857, resigned as chief justice of the supreme court of Michoacán in protest.

An anonymous conservative writer also made the sack of the cathedral the subject of a "historical comedy in three acts and in verse" printed in Mexico City at the end of the year. *Porfirio, or The Hero of the Silver Aisle* depicted the dishonesty and greed of Huerta, Blanco and Porfirio García de León, the main protagonist of the piece, as they conspire to "shock the world" with their audacious "anticlerical project."[64] In the play, Porfirio reflects that if this plan is accomplished, he will be excoriated by everyone and die outside the Church, buried "like a dog."[65] But for the plotters, the silver *crujía* had become an obsession, a veritable "Potosí," "a river of silver" that would solve all their military and personal problems.[66] Their fictitious conversations include the inevitable praise for the United States ("if you want to have reform / the United States must be the norm") and for the religious wreckage of the French Revolution ("smashing altars will bring us glory / as we know from France's story").[67] In one scene, an Italian officer even toasts Porfirio as a "disciple of Mazzini," thus associating Mexican liberals with the radicals of the 1848 revolutions in Europe.[68] The deed accomplished, the officers celebrate the melting down of chalices and the *crujía*, looking forward to the day when all the clergy, along with Munguía, will be burned alive in a similar fashion.[69] In the denouement of the play, however, Porfirio's mistress discovers the sacrilegious source of the jewels he has brought home. So instead of becoming a wealthy society lady as she had been promised, she abandons him with the words, "Get away from me you cursed one, your atrocious crime fills me with horror!"[70]

In the meantime, the war continued on various fronts with increasing rancor. Before leaving Mexico on April 7, 1858, Juárez had named Santos Degollado as military commander of the liberal armies of the north and west. In this capacity, Degollado and his subalterns, including Cruz-Aedo, launched the first campaign to retake Guadalajara on May 21, 1858. After weeks of inconclusive fighting, liberal troops penetrated the city center and occupied the massive Hospicio Cabañas complex.[71] One day, Colonels Cruz-Aedo and Refugio González, along with an American, Joseph Chessman, decked themselves out in pilfered priestly vestments and put on an anticlerical show from the top of one of the buildings. After some "savage howls" to draw a crowd, they shouted down that they were "ministers of God, preaching the true religion and defending the constitution." With "obscene, hateful, and shocking words" they attacked the Catholic religion, telling the people and soldiers below that Catholic bishops and priests were just "low-life fanatics" that should be ignored.[72] Later, after looting the Church of Santo Domingo, Cruz-Aedo and his friends taunted their enemies on the other side of the barricade by playing "Cangrejos" (March of the crabs) on the church organ. Guillermo Prieto had composed the poem in 1854 and once put to music it became immensely popular among liberals. Its verses compared the conservatives to crabs because they were said to walk backward (into the past) rather than forward (into the future) like the progressives.[73] In spite of these provocations, however, the liberals could advance no further and the siege was lifted on June 13 when Miramón marched to relieve the city.[74]

Conservative rejoicing over Degollado's defeat, however, was cut short by news of the sudden death of General Osollo in San Luis Potosí. The chief of the conservative Army of the North died of a fever on the afternoon of June 18, one day before his thirtieth birthday.[75] He had received the last rites from Bishop Barajas, who reported that at the end the young general had turned to an image of the Immaculate Conception, praying to the Holy Virgin in these words: "My Mother, with no self-interest or aspiration I have defended the rights of my country and those of your Son; now it is up to you to ask Him to take me to His kingdom."[76] Miramón declared a period of eight days of mourning for his fallen comrade and Requiem Masses for the repose of his soul were celebrated across conservative-held territory. One of the most elaborate of these ceremonies was in Guadalajara, "liberated" by Osollo only three months before. There, crowds packed the cathedral for the wake and funeral services while all the church bells of the city tolled in recognition of this "irreparable loss."[77] Tributes to the hero were also published in conservative newspapers and poems were written in his honor. In Mexico City, his image "printed on China paper" was soon available for sale, and it was even possible to purchase a song, "A Memory of the Charming General Luis G. Osollo," with musical accompaniment for piano or guitar for only four bits.[78]

The death of Osollo was indeed a massive blow to the conservative cause, and Zuazua took advantage of this loss to launch a new attack on San Luis Postosí on June 29. His troops occupied and looted the city on June 30, which they held until fleeing before Miramón's forces on September 10. Inspired by this success, liberals laid siege to Guadalajara again on July 3, 1858, but withdrew once more on July 21 when Miramón's army reappeared. The third siege began on September 27. This time, with Chessman's help, liberals detonated mines beneath conservative positions at 10:00 p.m. on October 27 and stormed the city. The carnage was terrible, but General José María Blancarte and his men held out in the San Franciso monastery until 10:45 the next morning. The terms of their capitulation, brokered by the Prussian consulate, included a guarantee of the officers' safety, but this promise was never honored, to the consternation of military men on both sides of the conflict.

In fact, liberal reprisals began in earnest as soon as they had secured control of the city. In his diary, Malo recorded that the victors behaved "with the fury of savages and the Jacobins of the French Revolution."[79] In particular, Lieutenant Colonels Monayo and Piélago, both connected to the execution of ex-Governor Herrera y Cairo five months earlier, were hunted down by Lieutenant Colonel Antonio Rojas and hanged from the balcony of the bishop's palace. Piélago, mortally wounded in the recent fighting, was dragged from the bed where he already lay dying. His clothing was pulled down when he was hanged and when the rope broke his naked body landed on the pavement below. Still alive, he was strung up before a crowd of onlookers a second time. The two corpses were later thrown down and their heads set on fire, the posthumous torture accompanied by music from a military band. Then, when a passerby criticized the macabre proceedings, he was shot to death by someone in the mob. These executions were followed by the assassination of Felipe Rodríguez, an important conservative journalist, found hiding in a rebozo factory. At 7:00 a.m. on October 30, Rojas finished his work by shooting General Blancarte point blank when he answered the door of the house where he was staying. "We can't break their pride by being nice," Rojas reportedly explained.[80] Although many liberals blamed these murders on Rojas's bandit background, the choice of victims might also have reflected a more complicated Masonic vendetta.[81]

Church buildings and the clergy were also prime targets of liberal vengeance during these days of looting and riot. Priests were hunted down and abused, sometimes beaten, and often held for ransom.[82] All the churches and convents of the city were pillaged, and great quantities of gold, silver, and jewels were taken away.[83] Unfortunately, many citizens had left their valuables at the Convent of Jesus and Mary for safekeeping, counting on the traditional respect shown in Christian countries for the sanctity of the cloister. However, they were to be sadly disappointed, as were the terrified nuns who were handled roughly by the intruders.[84]

Another measure against the clergy was a decree against "traitors" that Degollado issued on November 4. The new law made any action to replace or modify the 1857 Constitution a capital crime. Anyone who even criticized the constitution in speech or writing was now deemed a "conspirator" and would be subject to fines, prison, or deportation. The clergy, the main targets of the laws, could also be punished for denying the sacraments to any liberal or for requiring a retraction of any oath.[85] These measures were probably inspired by the recent case of General Juan Nepomuceno Rocha's uncle, who died during the Guadalajara campaign. In spite of threats and blows, the local priest delayed administering the last rites to the unrepentant general, who therefore died unabsolved. In his rage at this insult, the general was said to have knocked the priest to the ground and kicked him. Nevertheless, he later threw some gold in the priest's face and demanded that his relative be buried in consecrated ground. The priest was beaten again after refusing, and Rocha himself forced open the cemetery gates and buried his uncle.[86]

Under the influence of his secretary, Ignacio Vallarta, Degollado also began to order the destruction of religious buildings in Guadalajara. Vallarta, another former member of the Student Phalanx, shared that group's enthusiasm for modernity and dislike for symbols of Mexico's Catholic past. In a speech that he had delivered at the recent September 16 celebrations, he lamented that in his country the "most advanced ideas of social progress are still confronted with the most detestable fanaticism." To illustrate his point, he contrasted the sight of "a magnificent factory" and the "leaning and worm-eaten tower of a monastery;" "the hum of activity in the former contrasting with the silence of idleness in the other."[87] His dream of removing these eyesores began to be realized when Degollado ordered the destruction of part of the Dominican monastery and church in order to "straighten a street" and create a new plaza.[88] He also tore down the Carmelite monastery and church in order to extend another road, which was renamed for Benito Júarez.[89] New streets were also opened through the Conciliar Seminary, the College of San Diego, and the Dominican Convent of Santa María de Gracia, dividing it into four parts. Obviously, the symbolic value of these civic improvements was more important than new traffic patterns. Although some of the buildings in Guadalajara were already badly damaged by cannonballs, these demolitions were still expensive and could not otherwise be justified in the midst of a war.[90] Furthermore, such renovations also took place in Morelia, where liberals knocked down part of the bishop's residence and of the Carmelite convent to open new streets. In the following year, new public plazas were built in Morelia on the properties of the San Francisco and San Agustín monasteries and the Santa Catalina de Sena convent.[91] In conservative circles, this phenomenon was already known as the "street-opening-mania."[92] Catholics also complained when officials melted down the church bells in Morelia, although conservatives had resorted to the same exigency in previous wars.[93]

Miramón's forces launched a new attack on Guadalajara on December 12, always an auspicious day for Mexicans, and after a few days of fighting the liberals were again driven from the city.[94] Conservatives in the city now had an opportunity to revenge their six weeks of suffering, and Miramón ordered the execution of captured liberal officers in reprisal for the deaths of Blancarte and the other conservative officers. However, the city received another major shock when an ammunition dump abandoned at the state capitol exploded at 10:45 a.m. on January 10, 1859. Most of the capital building and surrounding houses were destroyed and hundreds of military personnel and civilians were killed. Miraculously, Generals Miramón and Márquez were inside but escaped unharmed.[95] Soon after, Miramón departed for Mexico City, where a military coup had temporarily unseated President Zuloaga. General Márquez, who had been named governor and military commander of Jalisco, was left in control of the city. On January 31 he ordered the first of many ceremonies in honor of the murdered General Blancarte and his companions.[96]

In the beginning of 1859, only two major Mexican cities, Morelia and Veracruz, still remained in liberal hands.[97] Veracruz, as Mexico's principal seaport, was the most crucial.[98] Along with easy access to military supplies from the United States, its customs house provided the main source of government revenue, which probably explains why Juárez established his government there on May 4, 1858. Conservatives recognized this strategic advantage, and in late 1858 General Miguel María Echeagaray was ordered to march from Xalapa against the city. However, on December 20 he mutinied against the conservative government and issued the Plan of Ayotla (Veracruz) instead.[99] The revolt spread to Mexico City, where the modified Plan of Navidad was proclaimed. This *pronunciamiento* recognized that Mexico was in desperate straits after a year of civil war, and that neither the current [conservative] government, "nor the one called constitutional, possesses the financial or moral capital needed to bring peace to the republic."[100] It therefore deposed Zuloaga and created a junta to elect a new supreme leader. Initially, Echeagaray had hoped to gain the support of liberals to end the war and create a new constitution that would be acceptable to both sides. But this door closed when the emergency junta simply chose the popular Miramón to replace Zuloaga as president.

When the victorious general arrived from Guadalajara on January 21, however, he refused the new position and reinstalled Zuloaga to his former post on January 24. But Zuloaga, in turn, named Miramón "substitute president" on January 31. This time Miramón accepted the new appointment, making him de facto political and military leader of the conservatives, and he was sworn in on February 2, 1859. In his diary, Malo recorded the great sadness he felt following these political machinations. His hopes for Mexico, previously inspired by the "generous and chivalrous deeds" of Miramón, were dashed now that "bad advisors" had misled the general. "Poor republic," he lamented, "only meteors appear in it, and no long-lasting stars."[101]

In spite of his string of victories, Miramón knew that the future of the conservative cause depended on control of the vital port of Veracruz. As president, he attended the Solemn Mass at the Metropolitan Cathedral on February 5 in honor of Blessed Felipe de Jesús. The following day, in preparation for a new campaign, he joined his troops at the Basilica of Our Lady of Guadalupe to pray for divine protection.[102] Ten days later a salvo of cannons announced that he was leaving the capital to personally direct the attack on Veracruz.[103] In the State of Veracruz, the liberals, with the help of an American artilleryman, blew up all the bridges along the route to the city.[104] Although the conservatives fought their way to the outskirts of the city on March 18, the siege was lifted eleven days later when Miramón realized he could not succeed as long as the liberals could be resupplied from the sea. Also, to draw conservatives away from the port, Degollado's army had attacked Mexico City on March 14. So Miramón and his army left Veracruz on March 29 to rush back to the conservative capital.[105]

An earlier liberal attack on Mexico City, in October 1858, had been easily repulsed.[106] This second attempt would also fail, but events following this defeat would nevertheless provide an important propaganda victory for the liberal cause. This time, liberal forces penetrated further into the city, occupying the castle at Chapultepec on March 19. On March 23, they cut off the water supply to the city, the same tactic used by Cortés against the

Aztecs in 1521.[107] The first major assault took place on April 2, with fighting around the San Antonio de las Huertas monastery. There, after fierce fighting, liberals were finally repulsed with massive losses: around a thousand men missing, wounded, or killed. After the battle, the bodies of five Americans were also found among their dead, including that of a Captain Green, under whose jacket was discovered a paten and chalice stolen from the monastery chapel.[108] Meanwhile, General Tomás Mejía and his troops arrived to relieve the city, followed by General Márquez and his forces from Guadalajara. The most important battle occurred in the western suburb of Tacubaya on April 10–11.[109] During the fighting, citizens crowded the highest points in Mexico City to view the distant battle with telescopes.[110] The spectators included the new first lady, "Concha" Miramón, who joined some clergyman stationed in the towers of the cathedral.[111] As they watched, Márquez's troops routed the liberals, capturing a large quantity of equipment and supplies and taking two hundred prisoners. Even Degollado's ceremonial sash and uniform were found and later prominently displayed on the gate of the presidential palace.[112]

General Miramón arrived soon after the fighting and, as was now customary, ordered the execution of captured officers. But what actually happened next remains unclear.[113] The *puro* Franciso Zarco, still living in the capital and understandably enraged by exuberant victory celebrations there, immediately dashed off a highly detailed account of the executions. He claimed that on Márquez's orders fifty-three innocent people were murdered in cold blood after the battle.[114] According to Zarco, the victims included heroic physicians, "martyrs of science and duty," the helpless wounded, some unfortunate foreigners, hapless civilians, and even two teenagers, killed just because "they were blonde."[115] His anonymous pamphlet, *The Murders of Tacubaya*, included many heartrending scenes, inspiring examples of spotless liberal character, and some heroic last words. The demonic and merciless conservatives, on the other hand, were said to have denied the last sacraments to the condemned and left their naked bodies to rot on the ground. Zarco's narrative was also frequently interrupted by rants against the Catholic clergy, whom he blamed for this tragedy. The civil war, he insisted, was "started, stirred up and supported" by the hierarchy, "whose treasures have paid for every reactionary movement."[116]

As might be expected, a conservative response to this broadside soon appeared.[117] The anonymous author of *The Demagogues and their Writings* refuted Zarco's claims point by point, arguing that only sixteen had been executed, all of whom had taken up arms. He also insisted that they had been given access to a priest, which some had rejected, and that their bodies had already been buried. In contrast to the horrors related by Zarco, this alternative version focused primarily on the previous atrocities committed by liberals.[118] Conservatives already knew the emotional impact of such grisly stories, and commemorations of the "victims of the demagogues" had been an important part of their political propaganda from the beginning of the war.[119] Now the liberals would have their own victims to remember. Curiously, in some places Zarco's account seems to have borrowed specific details from the earlier conservative narratives, as if competing with the martyrology of the other side. For example, the unlikely report of fifty-three nude corpses may have reflected the fact that Colonel Piélago was left naked when hanged. Likewise, the five conservative officers executed in Zacatecas were supposed to have been denied access to a priest, a trope that also appears in Zarco's story. Conservative reports had claimed that Father Ortega had forgiven his tormentors; Zarco also wrote that the twenty-one-year-old lawyer, Manuel Mateos, like Christ, forgave his killers "because they know not what they do."[120] Above all, from a liberal point of view, the tragic fate of the medical doctors, as men of science, would certainly overshadow any clerical deaths attributed to their side.

Despite any implausible or unverifiable details in Zarco's account, his version spread quickly, reinvigorating the flagging liberal cause. In fact, when the story reached Veracruz, Melchor Ocampo, now minister of the interior, increased the number of victims to over a hundred.[121] The story was further embellished by other liberal writers and reached its apogee in the play that debuted in Guadalajara later that same year.[122] Along with Zarco's details, *The Martyrs of Tacubaya* by Aurelio Luis Gallardo included other fictitious elements and characters, like the distraught mother of the murdered teenagers and a romantic scene between a Daughter of Charity tending the wounded and one of the doomed doctors. There was also a conscientious friar whose appeals for mercy are rejected by Márquez. "I desire blood in my burning frenzy," the general admits to himself, "it seems that I was nursed at the breast of a panther."[123] The impact of these scenes was so powerful that the actor playing General Márquez often had to remove his costume immediately after the performance to keep from being attacked by the audience.[124] But whether based on historical facts, raw emotion, or political calculation, the tragic story of the "Tacubaya Martyrs" would henceforth symbolize the ultimate goodness of the liberal cause. Likewise, General Márquez, now known as the "Tiger of Tacubaya," would epitomize the hypocrisy and brutality of the conservatives.[125] In the future, even the harshest liberal policies could be justified by comparison with these al-leged conservative atrocities. Inspired by Zarco's pamphlet, for example, the Governor of Zacatecas, General Jesús González Ortega, nationalized all church property in his state on June 14. Two days he later decreed that any priest who refused the sacraments to anyone or requested, or even ac-cepted, the retraction of an oath, would be shot.[126]

The story of the Tacubaya martyrs would eventually even reach the United States, where President James Buchanan was informed that three American physicians assisting the wounded had been among those executed. This shocking news was included in his "State of the Union Address" on December 19, 1859, part of his pitch for a pending treaty that would advance US interests and "restore peace and order" in Mexico. "As a good neighbor," President Buchanan implored the Congress, "shall we not extend a helping hand to save her?"[127] Ironically, the United States had initially recognized the legitimacy of the conservative government in Mexico City because the ambassador at the time, John Forsyth, believed that, in desperate need of funds, it could be pressured into selling more Mexican territory.[128] At the same time, Forsyth, who disliked the "church party," had allowed the US legation in Tacubaya to be used to hide liberal loot and as a haven by fugitives like Miguel Lerdo.[129] But when the Zuloaga government balked at Forsyth's schemes, the United States broke off diplomatic relations and the ambassa-dor was recalled.[130] Then on March 7, 1859, Robert Milligan McLane was appointed as Envoy Extraordinary and Minister Plenipotentiary to the lib-eral regime, reaching Veracruz just after the end of Miramón's first siege. On April 6, McLane officially recognized the Juárez government as "the only existing government of the republic." This shift in policy reflected President Buchanan's new conviction that the liberals, desperate for US recognition and loans, would be the most amenable to territorial concessions.[131]

Thanks to the promise of US help and the Tacubaya propaganda coup, the Juárez government finally seemed to have the "financial and moral capi-tal" it needed to prosecute the war. It was also time to unveil the ulti-mate liberal plan for the nation, laid out in a manifesto signed by Juárez, Ocampo, Lerdo, and Manuel Ruiz on July 7, 1859.[132] This roadmap to national progress and prosperity included all the changes that liberals had demanded since 1848.[133] Mexico's future, it declared, depended primarily on economic modernization. But this would require reforms in public edu-cation, taxes, pensions, and the modernization of trade regulations. There were also plans for improving highways, building railroads, and increasing mining exports. To make all this possible, it added, "the immigration of active and industrious people from other countries" was indispensable.[134] But above all, this modernization plan required the end of Mexico as a Catholic confessional state.

To justify the stunning anti-Catholic measures to come, the manifesto blamed the clergy for the "bloody and fratricidal" war that Mexico was experiencing. Echoing the charges in Zarco's tract, it claimed, falsely, that the Tacubaya coup of 1857 had been orchestrated by the Catholic hierarchy "and the bayonets at its disposal."[135] The clergy, it claimed, were even now sustaining the conflict to protect their own interests, "inherited from the colonial system."[136] Only by stripping the Church of its resources could the war be ended. Furthermore, this drastic measure would prevent similar abuses of clerical power and wealth in the future. Although not mentioned, the nationalization of all ecclesiastical property would also provide more than enough collateral for anticipated American loans.[137] In place of the forced liquidation of real estate holdings as in the previous *Ley Lerdo*, the new law issued on July 12 simply confiscated all ecclesiastical financial assets of any kind, this time with no compensation.[138] Juárez, for example, wasted no time in selling off the Franciscan monastery in Veracruz to an American for 75,000 pesos.[139] Under the new law, only diocesan church buildings used for actual worship and the residences of secular priests were spared.

The manifesto also called for the suppression of religious orders and all other Catholic organizations in the country, a measure long desired by the secularists. When the new law appeared, all religious communities of men were to be immediately closed and the wearing of habits forbidden. As compensation, regular priests who left their monasteries and joined the secular clergy were entitled to a one-time payment of five hundred pesos. Elderly and infirm religious would also be allowed a pension. Like the cash bonus, these allowances were easily funded from the confiscation of their orders' assets. Monastic libraries and works of art, along with all monastic land and buildings, also became the property of the state. Any friar or monk who resisted their new identity would be expelled from the country. Nuns, on the other hand, presented a different problem. They could not be absorbed into the diocesan clergy, and many were now past marriageable age. So instead of immediate extinction, their communities would be allowed to die more slowly. Any woman not already in final vows was required to leave the convent, with her original dowry in hand. But others who chose to do so could remain, and a small maintenance would be calculated from their community resources. However, no new novices could be admitted, and once the last of the old sisters died, the convent would cease to exist.[140]

All other lay confraternities, brotherhoods, charitable foundations, and lay organizations were closed immediately and their resources, sometimes substantial, were confiscated.[141]

Additional legislation was decreed in the following months, progressively secularizing every aspect of civil society. On July 23, marriage was redefined as a civil contract rather than a sacrament.[142] Church weddings were not forbidden, but Catholics would also be required to submit to secular ceremonies presided over by civil functionaries. As in the 1857 Law of Civil Registry, failure to secure a civil marriage would mean that the spouses had no legal standing, and their children would be considered illegitimate by the state.[143] Another law on July 28 further modified the 1857 regulations "in order to end the compulsory and exclusive intrusion of the clergy at the important moments of an individual's life."[144] The registration of births, deaths and marriages, formally sacred events recorded in parish registers, became "vital statistics" and therefore the property of the state.[145] Then, on July 31 all cemeteries and other places of interment were placed under government control.[146] Clergy might still officiate at the burial of a Catholic, but only without cost and with the permission of the civil authorities. Thanks to this law, there would be no more of those ugly scenes in which public dissenters had been refused burial in consecrated ground.

On August 3, Juárez's envoy to Rome was recalled and all official relations between liberal Mexico and the Holy See came to an end.[147] Then, on August 11, the number of state-recognized holidays was reduced.[148] New Year's Day and Independence Day (September 16), as well as the most popular Christian holy days (Christmas, Holy Thursday, Good Friday, and Corpus Christi) remained civic holidays on the new calendar. The feasts of San Felipe de Jesús (February 5) and the other saints were gone, but the indispensable *Día de los Muertos* (celebrated on November 1 and 2) was retained. Of the various feasts associated with the Virgin Mary, only Our Lady of Guadalupe (December 12) survived, although Ocampo objected vehemently to its inclusion in the list.[149] In any event, also reflecting the uncomfortable events of the past two years, this decree forbade the attendance of civic authorities at any public religious function.

As minister of the interior, Ocampo issued an order that the promulgation of these initial reforms should be commemorated with the greatest pomp and ceremony. It seems that exuberant celebrations were held with gusto in all the liberal strongholds, although conservative reports focused only on their negative aspects. For example, it was said that in San Luis Potosí fines had to be levied to force the inhabitants to decorate their houses for the occasion.

There a banquet was also held, where blasphemous toasts and anti-Catholic speeches were made. In Morelia, the homes of known conservatives were stoned during the celebrations, and in Aguascalientes many Catholic families left town to escape the drunken revelry. In Zacatecas, Governor González Ortega renamed the main thoroughfares of the city "Reforma Road," "Exclaustration Avenue" and "Religious Toleration Street."[150] He also sponsored a bull fight to commemorate the new laws. According to reports, he opened the *corrida* himself with a passionate discourse against religion. He also insisted that all the bulls to be killed be given the names of famous popes, along with lewd adjectives, first.[151]

As might be expected, there was also a rush to close all the male religious houses in liberal-held territory. Given their animosity toward these orders, it is also not surprising that the expulsion of the friars and monks was not a delicate affair. For example, in Zacatecas three hundred soldiers arrived at the massive complex of the Apostolic College of Our Lady of Guadalupe at 10:00 o'clock on the night of August 1 with four pieces of artillery.[152] After surrounding the residence of the religious, they demanded that the inhabitants leave immediately, without retrieving any personal belongings. When some concerned civilians tried to intervene, soldiers fired into the crowd, killing some of the protesters.[153] The religious were also expelled from the other monasteries in the city and their buildings handed over to profane uses.[154] Soldiers also beat civilians who attempted to assist the Carmelites who were ejected from their monastery in San Luis Potosí.[155] In Morelia, the Franciscans were evicted at midnight, also forbidden to take anything with them on their exile. As an afterthought, they were also forced to remove their habits before being escorted from the city, in order to fulfil the letter of the exclaustration decree.[156] Constitutional troops from Morelia also closed a local monastery and seized its inmates when they occupied Acámbaro (Guanajuato). But this time more than a thousand women occupied the main square of the town and issued their own *pronunciamiento* in the name of religion. They then declared the city in a state of siege and placed some leading liberals under arrest, guarding them in shifts and forcing them to sign a petition for the release of the monks.[157]

Catholic protests against these first Reforma laws were not slow in coming. Starting on July 29, the Archbishop of Mexico City issued an unprecedented five pastoral letters to the faithful of Mexico condemning the liberal legislation.[158] In these he pronounced the Juárez government illegitimate and the decrees from Veracruz null and void. In contradiction to the claims of the Juárez administration, he insisted that the hierarchy had no part in the Tacubaya coup or the events of January 11, 1858. He also denied that the clergy engaged in partisan politics, even though, as the horrific murder of Father Ortega revealed, they were often the direct target of liberal spite.[159] He also spoke out in defense of sacramental marriage, religious orders, and the right of the Church to own property. Archbishop Garza also contributed to the joint episcopal statement, the first ever issued in Mexico, on August 30.[160] In their *Manifestación* to the nation, the united bishops present in Mexico City categorically denied that the Church had instigated the war to enthrone a political party that supported its own interests, or that the clergy was in any way responsible for the nation's suffering. "The Church only defends itself with spiritual weapons," they explained. Instead, the recent decrees had unmasked the real object of the anticlerical campaign: the total destruction of the Catholic religion in Mexico.[161] Bishop Espinosa of Guadalajara and his cabildo also issued their own individual protests, the bishop in particular railing against imposition of civil marriage, known in some circles as the "civil cohabitation law."[162] Likewise, in his extensive treatise defending Christian matrimony, Agustín de la Rosa predicted that civil marriage would inaugurate "an epoch of degradation, immorality and misfortune in the domestic sphere."[163]

Even lay groups published formal denunciations of the Reforma laws, including one by the government employees in Toluca and another by representatives of all the barrios of Mexico City. There were also protests by women in Mexico City and Guadalajara.[164] The latter, signed by seven hundred and sixty-two women, expressed the "repugnance" with which they had read the decrees "against the Catholic Church, our mother." This document also accused liberals of planning "to hand over our country, whole or in part, to the power of the North American nation, so opposed to ours in religion, in custom, and traditions of race and belief."[165] The officers of the 1st Corp of the conservative army in Guadalajara also issued their own protest against "the traitor Don Benito Juárez" for his blatant attacks on the Catholic Church, his "communistic ideas," and his alliance with the United States.[166]

American support for the liberal cause was also a central theme of the Independence Day address on September 16, 1859, in Toluca (State of Mexico). In his speech, the orator Francisco Zúñiga recalled that Mexico's sovereignty was originally based on adherence to the Three Guarantees of 1821: Religion, Independence, and Unity. However, this foundation was now being undermined by "the cunning and treacherous hand of the North Americans." Their divisive doctrines were the reason for Mexico's humiliating defeat in 1848, and only by returning to the Catholic faith could Mexico be saved from total annihilation. But "scorn and reform of the Catholic religion" had been "preached by the Yankee and adopted by the demagogues." Liberals—"mere Yankee henchmen"—were now threatened by conservative victories, and so were appealing to their "boss" for help. But "no one who is not a traitor would fight at the side of the Yankee," Zúñiga proclaimed.[167]

As everyone knew, many Americans were already fighting for the liberal cause. American mercenaries had been active in almost every battle, including at Ahualulco de los Pinos, where an American, Col. Edward H. Jordan, had actually been given command of the liberal forces.[168] The United States was also providing the constitutionalists a steady stream of military supplies. Writing of the battles in Zacatecas and San Luis Potosí, Luis Gonzaga Cuevas recalled that "no one doubted that this territory received weapons and every kind of resource from the United States."[169] According to *La Sociedad*, the Juárez government had also contracted for thirty officers and four thousand men from the US.[170] However Lerdo's scheme to hire an additional ten thousand American mercenaries was rejected by the Juárez cabinet because of the shadow it would cast on his regime.[171] Nevertheless, American gunners were present at many other battles, including the Battle of Estancia de las Vacas on November 13, 1859. Although conservative troops there were outnumbered by more than two to one, this clash resulted in another major victory for Miramón.[172]

Throughout the summer of 1859 the Juárez government was negotiating a new treaty with the United States, offering substantial concessions to its northern neighbor in exchange for much-needed cash. The conservatives in Mexico City, also seeking foreign aid, had concluded their own treaty with Spain on September 26. The goal of the Mon-Almonte Treaty was to obtain Spanish loans and support for the conservative cause. In return for acceding to Spanish financial demands, the conservative government in Mexico City was recognized as the only legitimate government of Mexico.[173] The United States had already recognized the liberal government in Veracruz, but further negotiations had stalled due to American designs on Baja California. To resolve this impasse, Ocampo took over as Juárez's minister of foreign affairs on December 1, and the McLane-Ocampo Treaty was officially signed on December 14, 1859. But instead of handing over more Mexican territory, the treaty only gave the US perpetual transit rights over the Tehuantepec Peninsula, the possible location of a future railroad connecting the Atlantic and Pacific Oceans. Americans were also granted free passage along specific duty-free routes from the US border to Mexican ports on the Pacific. Most surprising, under certain conditions American troops would be allowed to intervene in Mexico itself to restore order or protect US interests. Furthermore, the US would be allowed to unilaterally determine duties for goods traded along the common border, and its citizens were to be exempt from forced loans and granted religious protections in all Mexican territory. In return for all these advantages, the liberal government was promised four million dollars. Although the Juárez administration "expected great results from the treaties," they were ultimately rejected by the US Senate and the windfall never arrived.[174] Nevertheless, by that time another US intervention had already ensured the final liberal victory.

Despite the increased American support for the Juárez government, conservatives were still optimistic about their chances for victory as 1859 drew to a close, in large measure because of the aura that surrounded the now twenty-eight-year-old Miramón.[175] Following his victory at the Battle of Estancia de las Vacas in November, the general had hurried back to Guadalajara, where he was greeted by a twenty-one-gun salute and the ringing of church bells. General Márquez, on the other hand, had failed to send requested reinforcements to the recent battle, perhaps anticipating a conservative defeat in the face of such terrible odds. Miramón therefore removed him as governor and sent him a prisoner to Mexico City.[176] But the fall of this recent hero did little to dampen enthusiasm for Miramón, who won another victory at Tonila (Jalisco) on December 24.[177] On December 29, Mexico City erupted with artillery salvos, bellringing, and fireworks to celebrate the president's latest triumph.[178] That same day, the "Young Macabee" and his officers assisted at a Te Deum sung in his honor in the cathedral of Guadalajara.[179] Some observers were struck by the significance of the date, which on the liturgical calendar also commemorated the Old Testament King David. In this context, the chants that accompanied the formal entrance of the president seemed especially appropriate: "I have found David my servant: with my holy oil I have anointed him." Some liberals, however, were troubled by the premature apotheosis of the young general and mocked the solemn sentiments exhibited at the service.[180]

Miramón returned to Mexico City on January 7, 1860, and attended yet another Te Deum at the Basilica of Guadalupe. This was followed by a parade through the streets of the capital, Miramón in an open carriage. In the evening there was a fireworks display and a musical performance at the

National Theater. The program included a new hymn in Miramón's honor written by Francisco González Bocanegra, the author of Mexico's national anthem. The song celebrated the recent victories at Colima and Estancia de las Vacas and included the chorus: "Glory! Glory" to the undefeated warrior / of the fatherland's defense and honor."[181] Miramón seemed invincible, and it seemed that only the "heroic city" of Veracruz now stood in the way of a final conservative victory.[182]

The previous siege of Veracruz failed because the liberals could be constantly resupplied though the port. But to blockade the enemy from the sea, conservatives would need ships of their own, so Miramón dispatched Rear Admiral Tomás Marin to Havana to purchase them. Eventually a small fleet was acquired, consisting of two steamers christened the *General Miramón* and the *Marquis de la Havana*. On January 9, 1860, the American ex-consul in Mexico City, John Black, alerted McLane that the conservatives were planning to attack Veracruz again, this time with four thousand men. He also thought that the port might be blockaded by French and Spanish naval forces during the siege. But on January 14 he updated his warning, noting that the conservatives had acquired ships in Cuba. McLane immediately informed the liberal government, and on February 24 Juárez declared that any conservative ships in the sea were to be regarded as "pirates." At this point, McLane hastened to Washington to get authorization for US naval involvement in the protection of the liberal regime.

As planned, Miramón laid siege to Veracruz by land again on February 29, 1860.[183] At this time there were four American ships operating near the port. The steamships *Indianaola* and the *Wave* had been contracted to transport munitions for the liberals and had troops on board but no cannons. The armed frigate, *USS Savannah*, and the sloop-of-war, *USS Saratoga*, were also in the area.[184] In the absence of McLane, the US charge d'affaires, Charles LeDoux Elgee, arranged conferences between US naval authorities and the liberal government on February 28. At this meeting, liberals appealed for military assistance, but the senior commander, Captain Jarvis of the *Savannah*, hesitated. Although he hoped that the liberals would win the war, he explained, without direct orders from Washington he could not intervene directly unless Marin's ships actually "interfered with free trade."[185]

On March 6, the *General Miramón* and the *Maquis de la Havana* sailed past the port of Veracruz and anchored off the point known as Anton Lizardo. The Mexicans immediately alerted the *Savannah*, and Commander Jarvis, perhaps pressured by Elgee, ordered the *Saratoga*, the *Wave*, and the *Indianaola* to intercept the ships and arrest Rear Admiral Marin. The American fleet reached Anton Lizardo just before midnight and began firing on the Mexican ships when they attempted to flee. The Americans later claimed that these were warning shots, but when the *General Miramón* returned fire, the *Saratoga* began firing in earnest. Soldiers on the two American steamers also added their musket fire to the melee. One shot blew a hole in the wooden hull of the *Marquis de la Havana* and it surrendered. The US ships then drove the *Miramón* upon the shoals, one of the cannon shots having disabled its tiller. American troops then boarded the ship and thirty Mexican sailors were wounded in the fight before the captain surrendered. In the end, one American was killed and three wounded. The Mexican officers and crew were then taken prisoner and sent to New Orleans along with the captured ships. Turner also confiscated the four thousand rifles and one thousand artillery shells onboard, which were intended to resupply Miramón's troops.[186]

Although the Buchanan administration endorsed the action after the fact and declared that it "was proper and fully justified by the circumstances," a US admiralty court later ruled that the capture of the ships and their crews in Mexican waters was illegal.[187] But that was too late to help the conservative campaign, for having run out of ammunition and without support from the sea, Miramón lifted the hopeless siege on March 21. Although the liberals had heretofore been unable to defeat their enemy on the battlefield, retaining control of Veracruz meant that the conservatives could be slowly strangled for want of supplies. The brief Battle of Anton Lizardo was the only official US military intervention in the War of the Reforma, but nevertheless it was decisive for the final outcome of the war.

As it turned out, the failure of the second siege of Veracruz signaled the beginning of the end of the conservative cause, although this was not clear at the time. In the spring of 1860 the liberal armies in the interior of the country were reorganized and new campaigns were launched in the Bajío, funded in part by the 180,000 pesos worth of silver recently seized from the Cathedral of Durango.[188] On April 24, 1860, liberal forces under General José López Uraga won a major victory at the Battle of Loma Alta (Zacatecas), capturing almost the entire army of General Rómulo Diaz de la Vega in the process.[189] His troops went on to occupy the city of San Luis Potosí and joined a new liberal assault on Guadalajara in May. In the face of these setbacks, the retired "interim president" of the conservative government, General Zuloaga, revoked the position of "substitute president" and attempted to resume power on May 9, 1860. Miramón, however, ignored his demotion. Instead, he made Zuloaga a prisoner and took him along on his march to relieve Guadalajara.[190] Although Miramón was able to drive the combined liberal forces away from the city, their numbers remained formidable. He encountered them again at the Battle of Silao (Guanajuato) on August 10, 1860.[191] Badly outnumbered, Miramón still expected another miraculous victory, which this time did not materialize. His eighteen guns were simply no match for the thirty-eight artillery pieces on the opposing side. Miramón, having narrowly escaped after the defeat, complained that "the liberal artillery, served by North American gunners, won the battle."[192] The now-desperate Miramón returned to Mexico City, where he reorganized his cabinet after the *junta de notables* officially named him the new "interim president." At this point, General Márquez was released after nine months of confinement and restored to army command. Later, the rehabilitated general was sent to relieve the garrison trapped at Guadalajara.[193]

The final liberal siege of Guadalajara was the most devastating of all. It started on September 26, 1860, and lasted thirty-three days. This time, five thousand conservative defenders were faced with twenty thousand liberal troops outside the city.[194] Liberals also commanded one hundred and twenty-five fieldpieces, which reduced some sections of the city to rubble.[195] This destruction, along with weeks of street-to-street fighting, produced a "hell of killing," in the words of one survivor.[196] Once again, the American Chessman was in charge of digging mines under the city, but this time he contracted pneumonia while working underground and died.[197] In these dire straits, the conservative commander, General Severo del Castillo, had demanded that the cathedral hand over its gold and silver sacred vessels "in the interest of order and the triumph of the cause of the Church," an irony not lost on liberal commentators.[198] By October the population was starving and the hospitals filling up with those suffering from an unnamed fever.[199] When no relief arrived from Mexico City, Castillo surrendered to General Ignacio Zaragoza on October 29 and the starving civilians were allowed to evacuate the city.[200] Márquez, en route to Guadalajara, was defeated at the Tepetates Ranch (near Zapotlanejo, Jalisco) on November 1, and the liberal forces occupied the ruined city on November 3.[201]

After the fall of Guadalajara, both sides recognized that the end of the war was clearly in sight. On November 13, President Miramón declared that Mexico City was under siege. After that, his wife recorded, "terror and despair reigned" in the city.[202] In his manifesto to the nation on November 19, Miramón lamented the "great disasters in the war have replaced the splendid triumphs previously obtained by our arms." He also acknowledged that of all the territory that the conservatives once controlled, only Mexico City and Puebla remained "free of enemy rule."[203] For his part, Juárez finally fulfilled the *puro*, if not Yankee expectations, by declaring religious toleration in Mexico. Religious liberty had been described in the liberal manifesto of July 7, 1859, as "necessary for Mexico's prosperity and growth, as well as being a requirement of contemporary civilization."[204] But considering the universal opposition to the measure displayed during the constitutional debates in 1856, the radicals hesitated to impose it on the nation until their final victory was assured. That day had now arrived, and Juárez issued the "Law on the Freedom of Worship" on December 4, 1860.[205] With this decree, all the historic rights and privileges of the Catholic Church were dissolved and civil law would henceforth prevail in every venue. Freedom of worship, rather than freedom of religion, meant that all denominations and religions would be on equal footing in Mexico. But this liberty existed only within the walls of the church buildings and no rites might be celebrated outside. Religious processions and public manifestations of piety, traditionally an important feature of Catholic life, were henceforth banned.[206]

General Miramón won his last victory at the Battle of Toluca on December 9. Among the prisoners taken after the battle were General Felipe Berriozábal and his subordinates, including Santos Degollado and Benito Gómez Farias.[207] Although the captive officers might have expected summary execution, they were transported to Mexico City and there treated well, another sign of the shifting political climate. The final battle of the war occurred just thirteen days later at San Miguel Calpulalpan, about sixty miles north of Mexico City. On the morning of December 22, the conservative force of eight thousand men was defeated by a liberal army of around eleven thousand.[208] After the battle, the shocked Miramón rode back to the capital, which he reached after midnight. After consulting with other conservative leaders, he sent General Berriozábal to negotiate a surrender with the victorious General González Ortega. When no terms were offered, Miramón, Zuloaga, and the other conservative generals handed over the city to their former prisoner and fled the city around 9:00 p.m. on Christmas eve.

Liberal troops began to appear in the streets on Christmas morning, and by evening around ten thousand were in the capital. Throughout the day the cathedral and most of the churches remained locked, although Christmas Masses were offered in a few chapels. Shops were also closed, and some houses flew foreign flags to announce that citizens of other countries were inside, hoping that this would provide some protection from the expected looting. In fact, this did not occur, since General Zaragoza had decreed the death penalty for military or civilian looters.[209] However, those associated with the conservative regime were already being hunted down and taken into custody, and those who could went into hiding. For example, the owner and editor of the *Diario de Avisos* and José Joaquín Pesado's son-in-law, Vicente Segura, was denounced by a servant in the home of relatives and was shot by the official who came to arrest him. He was wounded but managed to escape the house, only to be gunned down shortly afterward in the street.[210]

On January 1, 1861, the victors staged a triumphal entry of 28,000 troops into the city. The parade route was decorated with draperies, flags, and flowers, and triumphal arches covered the main streets, including one with large letters proclaiming "Constitution of 1857." At one stop, when General González Ortega was given a wreath of flowers, he magnanimously placed it on the head of the demoted and oft-defeated Santos Degollado instead. Florencio María del Castillo, an outspoken liberal who had suffered under the recent conservative administration, considered the euphoria of the crowd on this day to be the ultimate victory. For him, this meant that the conservatives had lost the most important battle of all, the one for public opinion. In particular, he noted the large numbers of women on the balconies showing their appreciation for the liberal troops. Surely, he opined, this disproved the myth that most women had conservative sympathies. Instead, the celebrations on this day proved that Mexicans of both sexes "loved liberty, desired the reforms, and wanted to march on the road of progress." Significantly, after the national anthem was sung, the French "La Marseillaise" was intoned and the jubilant crowd joined in on the chorus.[211] A more thoughtful observer, however, noted that the population still remained divided:

> What is certain is that in the midst of this great celebration, signs of grief were not lacking. Among the faces animated with the rosy blush of joy, there were others, not a few, distorted by shock and discouragement: the glances of love and of joy were met with flashes of anger or clouds of scorn. That is because among our brothers of the victorious party passed our brothers of the defeated one.[212]

Not all the conservatives, however, were willing to admit final defeat. On January 4, news was received that Puebla had surrendered, meaning that there were no longer any cities in conservative hands. But Generals

Márquez, Zuloaga, Tomas Mejía, and others continued an ever more vicious guerilla warfare in the countryside. Miramón, for his part, eventually sailed out of Veracruz disguised as a French sailor to return to the fight another day. But for most Mexicans, the liberal occupation of Mexico City meant that the Reforma was now a fait accompli. Or as one supporter of the clergy explained it, all the consequences of liberal victory were the "consummation of the decree of Calpulalpan." As he recognized, a culture war is a zero-sum game, and the conservatives had already lost the final battle.[213]

CHAPTER 8

The End of
Catholic Mexico

Since its independence in 1821, Mexico had existed as a Catholic confessional state.[1] Mexicans were baptized, married, and buried by the Catholic Church, which also provided the nation's social services and most of its education. Catholic Mexicans were entirely free in the practice of their religion, which was protected by the state, and public expressions of faith were encouraged. Christian ideals permeated the laws and customs of the country, and religious institutions flourished. Protestant visitors or immigrants, on the other hand, did not enjoy the same liberty. But many liberals, especially since the defeat of 1848, longed for Mexico to become a secular state that would attract non-Catholic immigrants. Over time, they believed, this demographic shift would replace traditional Catholic culture and values with more energetic habits and fashionable attitudes.

As a result of their victory in the War of the Reforma, liberals controlled the entire country. The brutality of the war had polarized opinion on both sides of the political divide, and now the most radical liberal faction was in power. At this point, there were also scores to be settled with the clergy, as well as with members of the laity who had supported the defeated conservative regime. So instead of a program for the gradual secularization of Mexican society, liberals now opted for an immediate purging of all signs of the previous religious culture from all public spaces. This scorched earth policy explains the harshness with which the Veracruz Reforma program was finally implemented in the rest of Mexico.

The Reforma laws came into effect in Mexico City on December 28, 1860, just a few days after the conservative government fled and General González Ortega assumed control of the capital. When the new policies were announced, the Archbishop of Mexico City advised the faithful to ignore them as much as possible. However, he added, Catholics should not resist if they were imposed by force, and violence should be avoided.[2] Even more punitive actions began immediately after Juárez was installed in the presidential palace, a dignity he had been so long denied. The liberal president and his entourage formally entered the capital on January 11, 1861, and the next day he ordered the expulsion of all foreign ambassadors previously accredited to the conservative regime.[3] Naturally, this included the apostolic delegate, Bishop Luigi Clementi. Then, on January 16, Juárez issued a decree expelling most of the Mexican episcopate from the country.[4]

On January 21, the banished bishops, Archbishop José Lázaro de la Garza and his auxiliary, Bishop Joaquín Fernández de Madrid (Mexico City), along with Bishops Pedro Espinosa (Guadalajara), Clemente de Jesús Munguía (Michoacán), Franciso de Paula Verea (Linares/Nueva León), and Pedro Barajas (San Luis Potosí), left Mexico City in the company of the ejected foreign diplomats.[5] The prelates were kept under armed guard overnight in Puebla, and the next day, weeping crowds followed their carriages for miles when they left the city. But one of the coaches had a serious accident along the way, leaving Bishop Espinosa with a wound to the head and Bishop Verea with his arm in a splint. These two therefore had to remain for a few more days in Córdoba (Veracruz) with Bishop Barajas, who was the most badly injured of all and in critical condition.[6] As it turned out, however, they were the lucky ones.

When the other three stagecoaches reached Veracruz on the afternoon of January 27, they were met by a howling mob of "ferocious beasts."[7] The occupants of the first coach, including the Spanish ambassador, were able to disembark and duck inside a building before the other two coaches were surrounded. But the coach containing the archbishop and Bishops Mungia and Madrid was stoned by a mob screaming "Death to the clergy! Death to the friars! Death to the bishops!" Although they managed to escape into the house of a Spanish businessman, the archbishop was injured in the chest and head. The crowd then attempted to overturn the third carriage, containing Monsignor Clementi and his secretary. Fleeing the coach, they were saved by a young man who braved the shower of stones to rescue them, although one of the coachmen was killed in the melee. The apostolic delegate sustained a broken hand and was wounded in the back and knee, but once inside a house was able to cross the roof to the French consulate. Still demanding that the bishops be hanged, the rioters broke into various buildings looking for them but without success. At midnight on March 30, Governor Zamora had them secretly transported to the fortress at San Juan Ulúa, from whence they eventually embarked on British ships. Although radical newspapers like *El Heraldo* tried to justify the attack, most Mexicans were upset by the assault on the elderly, unarmed and defenseless prisoners. According to the conservative daily, *The Green Parrot*, this was not only an attack on the Catholic religion, but on civilization itself.[8]

At the same time, the Metropolitan Cathedral, the symbol of episcopal power, and the Basilica of Our Lady of Guadalupe, the most important shrine in Mexico, were also targets of liberal revenge. In fact, throughout 1861 Governor Baz agitated to have the cathedral itself, site of his humiliation in 1856, razed in order to erect a new school on the site.[9] He also planned to have the Sagrario, the parish church attached to the cathedral, torn down and replaced by a new federal building.[10] Confiscation of archdiocesan assets had already begun on December 29, 1860, but reformers also had their eyes on the rich liturgical accoutrements inside it temples. So on the night of January 16, 1861, the same date that the archbishop's exile was decreed, government commissioners appeared at his cathedral demanding that the clergy hand over its treasures. Among the many precious objects confiscated that night was a massive monstrance, decorated with 5,872 diamonds, 2,643 emeralds, 544 rubies, 106 amethysts, and 28 sapphires.[11] Although this sacred object was eventually redeemed by a wealthy woman and restored to the cathedral, the shrine of Our Lady of Guadalupe was not so fortunate.[12] Here, on March 5, along with a gold frame that once held the miraculous image, officials also carried away a monstrance with the sacred Host still inside. "What horror!" exclaimed Malo when he reported the sacrilege. The plunder of holy objects from this shrine, "for three centuries the focus of the love and hope of the Mexicans," was so shocking to Catholics that Juárez disavowed any knowledge of the crime and ordered an investigation. A few days later the police located the remains of the monstrance, already melted down.[13] However, the shrine was plundered again on April 29, this time with official approval.[14]

Liberals also wasted no time in suppressing the male religious orders in the capital in accord with the law of July 27, 1859. On December 27, just two days after the fall of the conservative regime, all monks and friars in the city were expelled from their monasteries and their buildings confiscated. This included the final suppression of the Monastery of San

Francisco, which had first been closed by President Comonfort in 1856. Afterward, even more of the historic complex was demolished to open additional new streets and the remaining buildings were sold off to the highest bidders.[15] The rest of the men's communities suffered a similar fate, and new streets were cut through the property of Santo Domingo and San Fernando, among others.[16] The Carmelite monastery was sold for 20,000 pesos and became a paper factory.[17] The destruction of these historic buildings also resulted in the loss of their massive libraries containing thousands of volumes and some irreplaceable manuscripts.[18] Church plate and other valuables were also confiscated by state officials, and priceless works of art by famous masters were often sold off at low prices.[19] Antique wood carvings, meanwhile, were sometimes simply burned for fuel and carved marble sculptures broken up for other uses.[20] These losses were itemized in an anonymous booklet published in 1864. This *Report on the Ecclesiastical Property and Public Wealth Destroyed and the Victims of the Demagogues between 1858 and June 1863* claimed that "the work of our ancestors," which had required centuries to develop, had been attacked in the name of "liberty, reform and progress." The past was being erased, he lamented: "The monuments that show the marks of civilization, in the triple order of religion, knowledge and the law, and that link the history of the current generation with its forebears, once disconnected, can now be destroyed without society restoring them."[21] Indeed, the transformation of the cultural landscape of the past by the destruction of religious buildings and art was clearly the aim of the iconoclasts.[22]

Monastic orders, which had emerged in the first Christian centuries, have always been an important presence in any Catholic society. Furthermore, active religious orders like the Franciscans and the Dominicans had evangelized New Spain after the conquest and they had always been at the center of the spiritual life of the nation. Now that they were suddenly gone, an official justification was provided in the Constitutional Political Catechism, published by Nicolás Pizarro in March 1861. This text was created as a patriotic alternative for the indoctrination of youth, replacing the catechism of Padre Ripalda previously used for the teaching of religion.[23] Here, in response to the question, "Why has the suppression of the regular ecclesiastical orders been mandated?" students memorized the old Masonic canard: "Because far from serving the benefit of society and the improvement of religion, they were a cause of scandal and corruption."[24] Similar sentiments were echoed in all the liberal newspapers. For example, after the suppression of the monasteries in Guadalajara, *La Reforma* boasted that "our society has been purged of a useless and harmful class that has too long weighed upon it."[25] One alleged proof of the perfidy of the friars was actually uncovered during the looting of the Dominican monastery in Mexico City in February. The discovery of thirteen mummified cadavers there excited the liberal press, although the former superior of the community identified the remains as merely those of deceased members of the community. Liberals, however, were unconvinced and put the mummies on public display as "victims of the Inquisition."[26]

Along with the suppression of the orders, the other Reforma laws were implemented quickly in Mexico City as well. For example, the Pontifical University of Mexico, founded in 1551, was closed again on January 25.[27] The nationalization of all Church-owned real estate, including that returned during the conservative interregnum, was also a top priority. In addition to the property and assets seized, on February 2 Juárez issued a decree that secularized the hospitals and other charitable foundations throughout the nation.[28] Once inspired and funded by Christian charity, the new government-controlled institutions would now reflect a more modern social welfare model.[29] But new sources of funding also had to be developed, and not all the previous establishments survived the transition.[30] On the other hand, faced with a shortage of trained personnel, on February 19 Juárez specifically exempted the institutions run by the Daughters of Charity from his decree.[31] However, on May 28 the government issued a clarification, insisting that the sisters could no longer be considered a religious community and could only continue their charitable work as private individuals.[32]

Although the original Reforma regulations had outlined a more gradual path for the extinction of the cloistered female religious orders, the Juárez administration now modified the original plan. On the evening of February 13, detachments of soldiers appeared suddenly at all twenty-two convents in Mexico City, terrifying the inhabitants within. In the weeks prior to this action, government agents had already forcibly entered the convents to inventory their possessions and seize important legal and financial documents. Now, the goal was to concentrate all the city's nuns in just nine convents, irrespective of their order.[33] At midnight all the women, regardless of their age or state of health, were forcibly removed from the thirteen doomed religious houses and crammed into dirty carriages recently used to transport the corpses of typhus victims.[34] According to one report, the commissioners also insisted on calling the nuns "señorita," instead of "sister" or "reverend mother," throughout the ordeal.[35] An identical action was taken against the thirteen convents in Puebla during the night on February 23.[36] The remaining convents in Guadalajara were merged in the wee hours of the morning on April 9. To celebrate this accomplishment, liberals there sponsored a dance later the same day, decorating the ballroom with plundered religious paraphernalia.[37] In Mexico City, the destruction of the deserted convents followed soon after, with new streets being opened through the properties of the Concepción, San Bernardino and Capuchina convents.[38] Other buildings were sold off or appropriated by the state. For example, the church of the Convent of Santa Isabel became a yarn factory and buildings of the Convent of the Encarnación was repurposed as a school of arts and crafts.[39] Although many Catholics were opposed to the removal of the nuns, the midnight mergers had been a surprise and no protests were recorded.[40] However, crowds surrounded the remaining convents in Mexico City in October when a rumor spread of another exclaustration decree. The government immediately sent troops to break up the crowds, but when the group around San José de Gracia refused to disperse, shots were fired, leaving two of the protesters dead.[41]

The new cultural dispensation profoundly affected not only the lives of the clergy and religious, but also those of ordinary Catholics.[42] Staring on January 5, 1861, for example, the implications of the 1860 religious toleration decree were first felt in Mexico City. On that day new regulations were issued that restricted the ringing of church bells, radically transforming the acoustic environment of the city.[43] The new rules also forbade the usual public ceremonies associated with taking viaticum to the dying.[44] In the past, foreigners were often astounded by the sight of people of all ranks kneeling in the streets when the Blessed Sacrament passed by, and sometimes the irreverence shown by visiting Protestants had resulted in altercations with local Catholics.[45] But although this expression of Eucharistic devotion was precious to many believers, such public demonstrations of faith would no longer be allowed. In fact, the pastor of Santa Veracruz parish was arrested on February 1 because some women of his parish had followed him singing hymns when he had gone to administer the last rites.[46] Nevertheless, on February 8, one hundred and seventy women from the parish of San Miguel signed an appeal to the government asking that they be allowed to accompany the sacred viaticum when it was taken to the dying during the night.[47] As the government feared, when such permission was granted in Toluca on March 26, six hundred people showed up in a massive demonstration of faith. Some men even unhitched the mules to pull the carriage of the priest transporting the holy sacrament. But this behavior upset the local authorities and resulted in the arrest of seventeen participants.[48] Clearly, in Mexico "freedom of worship" was not the same thing as religious liberty. In a religiously diverse society, it was argued, any public expression of one faith was potentially detrimental to all the others and therefore had to be suppressed.[49] In 1862, the same logic would be used to justify a ban on the wearing of any clerical or religious garb in public, another blow to Catholic sensibilities.[50]

Catholic devotional life in Mexico also suffered in other ways under the new regime. Most dramatically, the ban on religious brotherhoods and confraternities abruptly eliminated the primary space for religious and charitable activities of the laity.[51] For a time, some of the chapels associated with the suppressed convents and monasteries remained open for public worship. Historically, many of these sanctuaries were the focal points of popular local devotions related to specific holy images. However, the governor of the Federal District, Juan José Baz, ordered the closure of twenty-nine of these chapels on October 24, 1861.[52] Furthermore, Juárez also cancelled all the annual outdoor religious celebrations dear to specific neighborhoods and institutions in Mexico City. Then on May 1, the national lottery instituted in 1774 to fund the shrine of the Virgin of Guadalupe was banned.[53] This was also the first year since the Spanish Conquest that there was no public procession to honor the Blessed Sacrament on the Feast of Corpus Christi.[54]

Equally disheartening to the faithful was the official disrespect demonstrated toward Catholicism itself on an almost daily basis. A small but telling example of this new attitude occurred in Puebla on May 10. A few days earlier the temporary administrator of the diocese, Canon Franciso Irigoyen, had issued a pastoral letter addressing the current religious situation in Mexico. Although Malo described the document as "energetic and wise," the liberal press claimed that it reflected the "rebellious spirit of the clergy" and showed that the "intrigues of the sacristy" had not yet disappeared. According to one report, the priest who attempted to read it publicly in the Church of San Francisco in Puebla was pulled bodily from the pulpit by a government official who stormed into the building. However, the arrest of the priest and the subsequent exile of Monsignor Irigoyen for having published the letter were nothing new and therefore not surprising. But what witnesses noted most was that the official had not removed his hat inside the church, even though at that time the Blessed Sacrament was exposed (in a monstrance) on the altar for veneration.[55] Since the agent had doubtless been raised as a Catholic, this disrespect could only be interpreted as another calculated insult rather than an inadvertent offense.

In contrast to the hostility shown to the Catholic faith, the Juárez administration was eager to sponsor alternative religious denominations in Mexico. For example, on February 27, 1861, he gave the chapel of the Hospital of the Divine Savior to some German Protestants who had requested a site for public worship. "This is something new," opined Malo, "that the government suppresses Catholic Churches and gives them to the Protestants, when those who want to have a temple should build it themselves."[56] The government also gave four closed churches to a group of schismatic priests attempting to found a new "patriotic" church in Mexico.[57] During the nonjuring crisis of 1857, some liberal priests had rejected the intransigence of their bishops and supported the liberal constitution instead. A handful of these "constitutional padres" organized themselves in 1859 to continue the cause of ecclesiastical reform. In February 1861 they were contacted by Melchor Ocampo, who encouraged them to form an independent "Church of Mexico" without ties to Rome. This movement maintained the outward forms of Catholicism, with the exception of clerical celibacy, while endorsing all the laws of the Reforma.[58] Over time, the "Mexican Apostolic Catholic Society" attracted more disaffected clergymen as well as other liberal supporters, although clerical broadsides insisted that its priests were "schismatics, Protestants and excommunicated." Not only were the sacraments that they celebrated invalid, the warnings declared, but just to attend one of their services was a sin.[59] In Guanajuato, the dissident priests were even allowed to hold a procession during Holy Week in 1861, but some of the public threw stones at them.[60]

Due to widespread popular suspicion, the Mexican Church movement struggled in its initial years. The unexpected death of Ocampo, its main supporter, was also a major setback to the new denomination.[61] It flourished, however, for a few years after the period of the French Intervention, at which point it was rebranded as the "Mexican Church of Jesus." In 1867 Juárez donated the church of San José de Gracia and the main chapel of the former Franciscan monastery in Mexico City to the group, which at its peak boasted more than twenty-three congregations. But over time its membership split between those who adopted the Episcopalian liturgy and those who embraced more Masonic services, which also excluded women. The former had also hoped to obtain ordination for a bishop from the American Protestant Episcopal Church, but this never transpired. Eventually, in an effort to draw more Mexicans away from the Roman Catholic Church, Juárez shifted his support to foreign Protestant missionary societies and the "Iglesia de Jesús" disappeared.[62]

In spite of conservative hopes, the antebellum religious union of Church and State was not restored during the brief Second Mexican Empire. Following their defeat in 1860, Mexican conservatives, including General Miramón, had appealed to Emperor Napoleon III of France for intervention in Mexico. Only the protection of another Catholic power, preferably a dynastic connection, they believed, could preserve Mexico from further Yankee incursions. This dream became a possibility when a financially straitened Juárez decreed a suspension of debt payments to European powers in July 1861. When diplomatic relations with Great Britain and France fractured, Spain joined them in a "Triple Alliance" that occupied Veracruz on December 17 to collect the outstanding debts. But British and Spanish forces withdrew in February 1862 when they realized the nature of Napoleon III's plan. More French troops landed the following month and marched toward Mexico City. In spite of a military defeat at Puebla on May 5, 1862, French forces, joined by the still-active conservative guerilla armies, reached Mexico City on May 31, 1863. At this point the Juárez government was forced to flee the capital again, this time accompanied by streams of refugees. French troops formally entered the city on June 10 "amidst great rejoicing" by conservatives, and a Te Deum was sung in the cathedral to celebrate the end of another anti-Catholic regime.[63] The French then installed a three-man Mexican regency—which included the former Bishop of Puebla and new Archbishop of Mexico City, Pelagio Antonio de Labastida y Dávalos—to rule the country until the newly designated Emperor of Mexico, Ferdinand Maximilian of Hapsburg, arrived.[64]

Under this temporary triumvirate, the restrictions on Catholic practice imposed by Juárez were quickly removed. Clerical attire was permitted in public, secular marriage ceremonies were no longer mandatory, and the Blessed Sacrament could again be carried openly in the streets. Some convents were reoccupied and even some male religious orders were restored.[65] However, the archbishop was removed from his position in the government on November 17 for opposing the French plans for a Napoleonic-style solution to the Church property question. Although Catholics and conservatives remained optimistic, Maximilian, imbued with French sensibilities and also a Mason, refused to repeal the Reforma laws when he assumed power on June 12, 1864.[66] Although he did agree to declare Mexico an officially Catholic country, he insisted on religious toleration and continued to encourage Protestant immigration and expansion in his realm.[67] This policy was rejected by the Mexican bishops, who continued to deny the sacraments to anyone still holding church property. In the end, the emperor and his wife were simply unable to understand the inflexibility of the Catholic hierarchy, and their disdain for the Mexican clergy was eventually reciprocated.[68] In spite of the frequent liturgies celebrated in honor of the monarchy, for which the bishops would later be excoriated by liberals, the Catholic restoration was over even before the ephemeral empire's fall. With renewed US support after its own civil war ended, Juárez defeated the supporters of Maximilian at Querétaro on May 15, 1867. The defeated emperor was executed by firing squad, along with Generals Miramón and Tomás Mejía, on June 19.[69]

With the return of Juárez, the religious restrictions of 1861 also returned in force. The bishops left the country again, and the revived religious orders were re-suppressed. This time, however, there was no hope of a future reversal since no conservative armies remained in the field to threaten liberal rule. Furthermore, those who had accepted the French intervention were now considered traitors to the nation, a charge that also extended to anyone showing sympathy for the old order. During the War of the Reforma, the reputation of the liberals had been blemished by their dependence on the United States. But now the tables were turned and the conservative cause would hereafter always be reviled as anti-patriotic.

In the decades that followed, the laws restricting Catholic practice were often ignored, particularly in out-of-the-way places. Even some clandestine convents managed to survive and thinly disguised Catholic schools periodically appeared.[70] Sometimes, a sentimental attachment to the old faith also resurfaced among liberals. Juárez's own wife, Margarita Maza de Juárez, called for a priest on her deathbed and made her husband promise to allow their daughters to marry in the church, as they wished to do.[71] This tendency could even affect radicals like Ignacio Altamirano, who became nostalgic about the Catholic traditions of his childhood later in life.[72] But folk customs and underground nuns notwithstanding, the nation itself was no longer Catholic in any meaningful way.

The culture war in Mexico was won by the liberals, and society would henceforth be organized based on the materialistic and anticlerical ideology of the Enlightenment. This creed would later be modified by Positivism, then Marxism, and even post-Modernism, but the marginalization of religion was now a permanent feature of Mexican life. On the other hand, periodic revolts showed that the Catholic religion still played an essential role in the personal lives of many Mexicans.[73] For example, there was a popular revolt in Michoacán from 1873 to 1877, after President Sebastián Lerdo de Tejada incorporated the Reforma decrees into the 1857 Constitution.[74] A peasant revolt in the State of Chihuahua in 1891 was triggered, at least in part, by the continuing ban on outdoor religious processions.[75] Most famously, the anti-Catholic persecutions that followed the Mexican Revolution (1910–1920) triggered the widespread Cristero Rebellion (1926–1929), which resulted in the death of perhaps 100,000 Mexicans.[76] Unlike the conservative resistance during the War of the Reforma, these grassroots revolts were not fought by professional armies nor led by political elites with an alternative vision for Mexico's future. But although all these movements ultimately failed, they did at least highlight the enduring gap between the official national ideology and the enduring faith of a large proportion of the population.

The anti-religious laws of the Reforma, reinforced and expanded in the 1917 Constitution, were eventually repealed, but not as a response to pressure from the still-majority Catholic population. In fact, when Pope John Paul II made his historic visits to Mexico in 1979 and 1990, his religious vestments and the massive outdoor liturgies he celebrated were still technically illegal. President Carlos Salinas Gotari (president 1988–1994), however, argued that such religious restrictions were incompatible with modern ideas of personal liberty. At his urging the constitution was amended to remove these restrictions in 1992. But by this time, numerous Protestant denominations and sects, along with other contemporary "spiritual" movements and non-religious ideologies, were well established across the country. Modernization and migration had also weakened local cultural identities. In the end, the liberation of the Church could only occur at a time when it was no longer in any position to challenge the power of the state or threaten the dominant secular culture.

The Reform through
the Church.

Notes

INTRODUCTION

1. An Austrian engineer, Allois Bollon Kuhmackl, designed the boulevard in 1865. It achieved its modern appearance, including the addition of numerous monuments, during the *Porfiriato*, the work of a beautification commission chaired by José Ives Limantour. Today, the street extends far west and northeast of its original boundaries. Alfonso Vásquez Mellado, *La Ciudad de los Palacios: Imágenes de cinco siglos* (Mexico City: Editorial Diana, 1990), 194, 221.

2. Degollodo Avenue was named in honor of General Santos Degollado (1811–1861).

3. For instance, the *Encyclopedia of Latin America* describes the Reforma as "the period in Mexican history from the revolution of Ayutla in late 1855 to the end of the War of the Reform in late 1860, in its narrower limits, or to mid-1867 and the defeat of Maximilian in its broader application." Helen Delpar, *Encyclopedia of Latin America* (New York: McGraw-Hill, 1974), 524. However, significant anticlerical legislation continued to appear after 1867. That is why in other reference works the Reforma is defined as the period from 1855 to 1876. See Ernest E. Rossi and Jack C. Plano, *Latin America: A Political Dictionary* (Santa Barbara, CA: ABC-CLIO, 1992), 34; and Michael S. Werner, ed., *Encyclopedia of Mexico: History, Society and Culture* (Chicago: Fitzroy Dearborn Publisher, 1997), 2:1239.

4. Patricia Galeana de Valadés, "Los liberales y la iglesia," in *The Mexican and Mexican American Experience in the 19th Century*, ed. Jaime E. Rodríguez O. (Tempe, AZ: Bilingual Press, 1989), 52.

5. Benjamin T. Smith, *The Roots of Conservatism in Mexico: Catholicism, Society, and Politics in the Mixteca Baja, 1750–1962* (Albuquerque: University of New Mexico Press, 2012), 149.

6. Enrique Krause, *La historia cuenta* (Mexico City: Tusquets Editores, 1998), 123. Krause also complains that religious conflict is one of the national realities that are conventionally denied in official Mexican historiography.

7. "This was not a war between Catholics and non-Catholics, but a war between and within the soul of Catholics." Brian Connaughton, "1856–1857: Conciencia religiosa y controversia ciudadana," in *Prácticas populares, cultura política y poder en México, siglo xix*, ed. Brian Connaughton (Mexico City: Universidad Autónoma Metropolitana,

2008), 459. Austin Ivereigh characterizes it as a "hot family feud" in his introduction to *The Politics of Religion in an Age of Revival: Studies in Nineteenth-Century Europe and Latin America*, ed. Austen Ivereigh (London: Institute of Latin American Studies, 2000), 18.

8. José María Vigil, *La Reforma*, vol. 5 of *México a través de los siglos*, ed. Vicente Riva Palacio (Barcelona: Espasa y Compañía, 1888). Vigil's version also became a model for many subsequent treatments of the Reforma. According to Edmundo O'Gorman, Justo Sierra relied almost entirely on *México a través de los siglos* for his history of Mexico first published 1900–02. Justo Sierra, *Evolución política del pueblo mexicano*, 2nd ed., ed. Edmundo O'Gorman (Mexico City: Universidad Nacional Autónoma de México, 1957), 3. Mexican historians like Daniel Cosío Villegas and Jesús Reyes Heroles perpetuated variations of the official version across the twentieth century. David Bushnell argues that this phenomenon has been true of historical writing on Latin America in general. "The principal historians of the Latin American countries themselves tended to be liberals, and most of the foreign historians studying the region were instinctively drawn to share the view that liberal reformers of the past century . . . had been standard-bearers of progress committed to enlarging the sphere of human freedom in opposition to the massed corporate interests of church, army, and great landowners." David Bushnell, "Assessing the Legacy of Liberalism," in *Liberals, Politics, and Power: State Formation in Nineteenth-Century Latin America*, ed. Barbara Tenenbaum and Vincent Peloso (Athens: University of Georgia Press, 1996), 278.

9. Barbara A. Tennenbaum, "Development and Sovereignty: Intellectuals and the Second Empire," in *Los intelectuales y el poder en México*, eds. Roderic A. Camp, Charles A. Hale, and Josefina Zoraida Vázquez (Los Angeles: UCLA Latin American Center Publications, 1991), 77. Ironically, large landowners often benefited from the laws of the Reforma and the military still remained powerful after the conservative defeat.

10. Callcott's book, a revision of his doctoral dissertation at Columbia University, appeared at the height of the persecutions of the Church in Mexico under the Calles regime. It was therefore, at least in part, an endorsement of that president's anti-religious stand. Wilfrid Hardy Callcott, *Church and State in Mexico: 1822–1857* (Durham, NC: Duke University Press, 1926).

11. According to Bushnell, "As is well known, much of the literature in question is imbued with a Mexican official mythology that treats the conflict between liberals and conservatives as one between the forces of freedom and enlightenment on one side, obscurantism, and oppression on the other . . . Indeed, the same basic interpretation won the allegiance of the early generations of U.S. historians studying Latin America, who often projected it uncritically onto other Latin American nations." Bushnell, "Assessing the Legacy of Liberalism," 284.

12. For example, Sinkin, *Mexican Reforma, 1855–1876: A Study in Liberal Nation-Building* (Austin: University of Texas Press, 1979); and Walter V. Scholes, *Mexican Politics during the Juárez Regime, 1855–72* (Columbia: University of Missouri Press, 1957). A more recent analysis of the political challenges faced by Mexico from the Texas Revolt to the end of the War of the Reform is found in Brian Hamnett, *Reform, Rebellion and Party in Mexico, 1836–1861* (Cardiff, UK: University of Wales Press, 2022). This work

explores "the struggle for representative government" in Mexico, culminating in the Reforma. Hamnett suggest that this latter conflict, which "finished off any possibility of a Catholic State in Mexico," might be seen as liberalism's final attempt to "*rebuild the State*" (italics in the original 2, 7, 247).

13. Again from Bushnell, "Among Mexicanists especially, there is a highly developed sub-genre of church-state studies dealing with the liberals' attack on church property and income" (289). See Robert W. Matson, "Church Wealth in Nineteenth-Century Mexico: A Review of the Literature," *Catholic Historical Review* 64, no. 4 (October 1979), 600–609. See also Michael P. Costeloe, *Church Wealth in Mexico: A Study of the 'Juzgado de Capellanías' in the Archbishopric of Mexico, 1800–1856* (Cambridge: Cambridge University Press, 1967); Jan Bazant, *Alienation of Church Wealth in Mexico: Social and Economic Aspects of the Liberal Revolution, 1856–1875* (Cambridge: Cambridge University Press, 1971); Robert J. Knowlton, *Church Property and the Mexican Reform, 1856–1910* (DeKalb, IL: Northern Illinois University Press, 1976). Edward Wright-Rios has summarized this historiography as follows: The social historians "revealed that the church had not been as wealthy as liberals claimed, and generally managed its assets well while providing easy credit." In addition, "the speculators were the chief bene-ficiaries of expropriation," which did not "improve state finances significantly or produce a nation of small property holders." Edward Wright-Rios, *Revolutions in Mexican Catholicism: Reform and Revelation in Oaxaca, 1887–1934* (Durham, NC: Duke University Press, 2009), 17.

14. For example, see Florencia Mallon, *Peasant and Nation: The Making of Postcolonial Mexico and Peru* (Berkeley: University of California Press, 1994), 91–98.

15. For a description of the conflict in Guerrero, see Peter F. Guardino, *Peasants, Politics, and the Formation of Mexico's National State: Guerrero, 1800–1857* (Stanford, CA: Stanford University Press, 1996), 178–210. For peasant activity in support of the liberal cause in the Sierra del Norte region, see Guy P. C. Thomson, "Popular Aspects of Liberalism in Mexico, 1848–1888," *Bulletin of Latin American Research* 10, no. 3 (1991): 265–92. The conflict in Oaxaca is described in Charles R. Berry, *La Reforma in Oaxaca, 1856–57* (Lincoln: University of Nebraska Press, 1981), 27–80; and Francie Chassen-López, "Guerra, nación y género: Las oaxaqueños en la Guerra de Tres Años," in *México durante la Guerra de Reforma*, vol. 2, *Contextos, prácticas culturales, imaginarios y representaciones*, ed. Celia del Palacio Montiel (Xalapa, MX: Universidad Veracruzana, 2011), 97–137. For analysis of popular support for the conservative side in Jalisco and Nayarit, see Zachary Brittsan, *Popular Politics and Rebellion in Mexico: Manuel Lozada and La Reforma, 1855–1876* (Nashville, TN: Vanderbilt University Press, 2015). Peasant op-position to the Reforma is also analyzed in Smith, *Roots of Conservatism*, 120–58.

16. Will Fowler, *La Guerra de Tres Años, 1857–1861: El conflicto del que nació el estado laico mexicano* (Mexico City: Crítica, 2020). Fowler notes that this book is the first study to be published on the civil war of the Reforma since 1953, which was also in Span-ish. Will Fowler, *The Grammar of Civil War: A Mexican Case Study, 1857–61* (Lincoln: University of Nebraska Press, 2022), 208.

17. Fowler, *Grammar of Civil War*, 24, 108, 129, 214–16. He identifies the typical elements causing civil wars as structural, social, and cultural factors along with economic

disparity. These factors come together during an "activation period" to provoke the actual war.

18. Fowler notes that in spite of the other social tensions present in Mexico, "it was the unresolved clash of Church-State interests that proved the most contested and divisive . . . it was the 'religious question' that proved the most polarizing," "adding a poisonous religious dimension to the impending crisis." Fowler, *Grammar of Civil War*, 109, 217.

19. Fowler, 93, 217.

20. Fowler, 73, 126, 218.

21. Fowler acknowledges the scholarship that denies that members of the clergy were a completely homogeneous group but argues that their "conservative tendencies" became "all the more pronounced and widespread" over time. Fowler, 138–39.

22. For example, when referring to the 1859 decree implementing the Reforma, Fowler reduces the entire issue to the question of the clerical *fuero* although this decree also justified the confiscation of Church property, the suppression of religious orders, and the abolition of all other Catholic institutions in Mexico. "Unlike the progressive values that were so eloquently defended by Melchor Ocampo in Juárez's cabinet's compelling manifesto of 7 July 1859," he writes, "the defense of the colonial *fueros* became as anachronistic, regressive, stigmatic, and ultimately indefensible as that of human trafficking and slavery in the Confederate States north of the border during the ensuing U.S. Civil War (1861–65)." Fowler, 182.

23. Jeffrey Cox, "Secularization and Other Master Narratives of Religion in Modern Europe," *Kirchliche Zeitgeschichte* 14, no. 1 (2001), 24.

24. Cox, 27.

25. For example, David Hempton notes that "secularization theories have largely been abandoned by most of their erstwhile inventors as being inapplicable to most parts of the world except western Europe." David Hempton, "Established Churches and the Growth of Religious Pluralism: A Case Study of Christianisation and Secularisation in England since 1700," in *The Decline of Christendom in Western Europe, 1700–2000*, ed. Hugh McLeod and Werner Ustorf (Cambridge: Cambridge University Press, 2003), 81. For a summary of other criticisms of the secularization theory, see the introduction by Hugh McLeod, 13–19.

26. See Jaime del Arenal Fenochio, "La historiografía conservadora mexicana del siglo xix," *Metapolítica* 6, no. 22 (March–April 2002), 47–55.

27. The Reforma was covered in volumes 14 and 15 of Niceto de Zamacois, *Historia de Méjico, desde sus tiempos mas remotos hasta nuestros dias* (Mexico City: J. F. Parres, 1880). 22 vols. Because of the conservative sympathies of the author, the publication of Zamacios's twenty-two volume history of Mexico in 1880 may have helped inspire the liberal version of Mexico's national history produced by Riva Palacio. Like Vigil, Zamacois was an eyewitness and participant in many of the events of the Reforma. During the 1850s he was editor of the conservative newspaper, *La Espada*. Another conservative journalist, Ignacio Álvarez, also published his history of Mexico with a similarly negative view of the reform process. Ignacio Álvarez, *Revolucion de la Reforma*, vol. 6 of *Estudios sobre la historia general de Mexico* (Zacatecas, MX: Timoteo Macias, 1877).

28. Bushnell characterizes this genre thus: "Among the older treatments [of religious controversy in Latin America] are those by proclerical authors detailing all the injuries done to the church by its adversaries." Bushnell, "Assessing the Legacy of Liberalism," 289. See volume 5 of Mariano Cuevas, *Historia de la iglesia en México* (El Paso, TX: Editorial "Revista Católica," 1928), 5 vols. Because of the religious persecution in Mexico during this period, Cuevas, a Mexican Jesuit, wrote and published in Texas.

29. This two-volume work covers the period from 1821 to 1878. The nature of the contest between Church and State is reflected in her title, "Political and Religious Power." Marta Eugenia García Ugarte, *Poder político y religioso: México Siglo XIX* (Mexico City: Universidad Nacional Autónoma de México, 2010.)

30. For examples of this tendency in the hierarchy, see Pablo Mijangos y González, "Clemente de Jesús Munguía y el fracaso de los liberalismos católicos en México (1846–1861)" and Alicia Tecuanhuey Sandoval, "Antes del conflicto general: Puebla, 1855–1860" in *México durante la Guerra de Reforma*, vol. 1, *Iglesia, religión y Leyes de Reforma*, ed. Brian Connaughton (Xalapa, MX: Universidad Veracruzana, 2011), 167–98, 199–244.

31. Brian Connaughton, introduction to *México durante la Guerra de Reforma*, vol. 1, *Iglesia, religión y Leyes de la Reforma*, ed. Brian Connaughton (Xalapa, MX: Universidad Veracruzana, 2011), 19.

32. By holding the liberals blameless, Connaughton concludes by agreeing with nineteenth-century polemicists that "fanatical" clergy were to blame for the religious consequences of the Reforma. Brian Connaughton, *La mancuerna discordante: La república católica liberal en México hasta La Reforma* (Mexico City: Universidad Autónoma Metropolitana, Unidad Iztapalapa, 2019), 215–16.

33. During the Reforma, Krause argues, "Catholic liberalism, tolerant and moderate, that had predominated in the congress [of 1857], was submerged in history." Enrique Krause, "La Reforma: 'Tiempo-eje' de México," in *Las Leyes de Reforma y el Estado laico: importancia histórica y validez contemporánea*, ed. Roberto Blancarte (Mexico City: El Colegio de México, 2013), 22.

34. Basilo José Arrillaga, SJ (1791–1867), held various academic and political positions during his life and edited Catholic newspapers during the 1840s. He was also the Jesuit provincial (superior) before the suppression of the order in Mexico in 1856. His massive collection of documents, reflecting the turbulent period in which he lived, has been incorporated into the special collections of the Biblioteca Eusebio F. Kino. The library also holds the important Mariano Cuevas collection relating to Mexican Church history. It is part of the Instituto Libre de Filosofía y Ciencias belonging to the Mexican province of the Society of Jesus.

35. Will Fowler notes that *The Grammar of Civil War*, although in English, "is not a narrative history of the War of the Reforma, although chapter 2 provides a succinct account of what happened when" (xi).

36. As Hunter explains, during a culture war, the ideological conflict is primarily among "different kinds of intellectuals and knowledge workers – who may very well have identical educational and class backgrounds." They are the ones who "create the concepts, supply the language, and explicate the logic of public discussion." James

Davison Hunter, *Culture Wars: The Struggle to Define America* (New York: Basic Books, 1991), 59, 64.

37. Emphasis in the original. Hunter, *Culture Wars*, 118, 131.
38. James Davison Hunter, "Response to Davis and Robinson: Remembering Durkheim," *Journal for the Scientific Study of Religion* 35, no. 3 (September 1996): 247; "Reflections on the Culture War Hypothesis," in *America at War with Itself: Cultural Conflict in Contemporary Society*, ed. James L. Nolan, Jr. (Greenwich, CT: JAI Press, 1995), 247; Hunter, *Culture Wars*, 143.
39. Enrique Krause, "La Reforma," 22. Ramón López Velarde (1888–1921) was a popular Mexican poet. Peter the Hermit was a medieval ascetic. According to legend, he helped initiate the First Crusade.
40. James Davison Hunter, *Before the Shooting Begins: Searching for Democracy in America's Culture War* (New York: The Free Press, 1994), vii–viii.
41. For the application of Hunter's paradigm to nineteenth-century Europe, where the term "culture war" originated (including the relationship between the current term and Bismarck's *Kulturkamphf*), see Christopher Clark and Wolfram Kaiser, introduction to *Culture Wars: Secular-Catholic Conflict in Nineteenth-Century Europe*, ed. Christopher Clark and Wolfram Kaiser (Cambridge: Cambridge University Press, 2009), 8.
42. Clark and Kaiser, *Culture Wars*, 5.
43. Ivereigh suggests that the Mexican case was extreme "because of the great wealth of property that was at stake." Ivereigh, *The Politics of Religion*, 6. But the economic question was mainly acute because Church wealth provided resources and prestige to the clergy in their battle with liberal reformers. By divesting the clergy of all visible means of support, the reforming politicians hoped to level the playing field, if not gain a tactical advantage, in the even more important culture war.
44. Charles A. Hale, "The War with the United States and the Crisis in Mexican Thought," *The Americas* 14, no. 1 (October 1957): 173.
45. Sinkin, *The Mexican Reforma*, 24.
46. Wolfgang Schivelbusch, *The Culture of Defeat: On National Trauma, Mourning, and Recovery* (New York: Metropolitan Books, 2003), 15–19.
47. Gastón García Cantú notes, "The Mexican reaction almost always manifested its opposition to the United States. An anti-Yankee sentiment defined its political ideal." Gastón García Cantú, ed., *El pensamiento de la reacción mexicana: Historia documental, 1810–1962* (Mexico City: Empresas Editoriales, 1965), 363.
48. For example, the conservative leader Lucas Alamán enthusiastically celebrated Mexico's Catholic and Hispanic heritage in his voluminous national history, published between 1849 and 1852. For an example of the renewed commitment to religion in Guadalajara, see Brian Connaughton, *Clerical Ideology in a Revolutionary Age: The Guadalajara Church and the Idea of the Mexican Nation, 1788–1853* (Calgary, AB: University of Calgary Press, 2003), 124–26.
49. Schivelbusch, *The Culture of Defeat*, 33.
50. Donathon C. Olliff, *Reforma Mexico and the United States: A Search for Alternatives to Annexation, 1854–1861* (Tuscaloosa: University of Alabama Press, 1981), 23. "Some young liberals," he adds, "appear to have blamed their conservative compatriots

rather than the expansive greed of their northern neighbor for the war and its disastrous consequences." 12.

51. Schivelbusch, *The Culture of Defeat*, 26. For a comparison of the post-war liberal plan to "abolish" Mexico's past and the conservative embrace of it, see Sinkin, *The Mexican Reforma*, 24–29.

52. As an exemplar of righteousness, Rodríguez examines the post-war poetry of Guillermo Prieto; he uses Nicolás Pizarro Suárez's 1861 utopian novel, *El Monedero*, to explore the theme of agony. Jaime Javier Rodríguez, *The Literature of the U.S.-Mexican War: Narrative, Time, and Identity* (Austin: University of Texas Press, 2010), 153–206.

53. See Erika Pani, preface to *La Reforma: Herramientas para la Historia*, by Pablo Mijangos y González (Mexico City: Fondo de Cultura Económica, 2018), 11. This book, part of a series (Tools for History), provides a comprehensive bibliography of historical scholarship on the Reforma.

54. Celia del Palacio, preface to *Iglesia, religión y Leyes de la Reforma*, vol. 1 of *México durante la Guerra de Reforma*, ed. Brian Connaughton (Xalapa, MX: Universidad Veracruzana, 2011), 7.

CHAPTER ONE

1. See D. A. Brading, *Church and State in Bourbon Mexico: The Diocese of Michoacán, 1749–1810* (Cambridge: Cambridge University Press, 1994), 62.

2. For a study of the social and political impact of the Jesuit expulsion, see Magnus Mörner, ed., *The Expulsion of the Jesuits from Latin America* (New York: Alfred A Knopf, 1965).

3. See N. M. Farriss, *Crown and Clergy in Colonial Mexico, 1759–1821: The Crisis of Ecclesiastical Privilege* (London: The Athlone Press, 1968), 237.

4. See Eric Van Young, "Popular Religion and the Politics of Insurgency in Mexico, 1810–1821" in *The Politics of Religion in an Age of Revival: Studies in Nineteenth-Century Europe and Latin America*, ed. Austen Ivereigh (London: Institute of Latin American Studies, 2000), 82–83.

5. Along with the preservation of clerical privileges and a Catholic monopoly in public worship, the "three guarantees" of the *Plan de Iguala* also promised independence from Spain with a constitutional monarchy (under a suitable European prince if available) and civil equality between *criollos* (native-born Mexicans) and *peninsulares* (those born in Spain). When no willing European prince could be found, Iturbide had himself crowned emperor. His empire, which lasted only ten months, was replaced by a republic in 1823.

6. Brading points out that the clerics promoted by Spain during the Bourbon period tended to be "of a Jansenizing bent," recruited from "a broad middle party in the church." D. A. Brading, "Tridentine Catholicism and Enlightened Despotism in Bourbon Mexico," *Journal of Latin American Studies* 15, no. 1 (May 1983): 5–6. Jean Meyer adds that the Mexican reaction against the Bourbons never came from the *peninsular* bishops because they were "progressive reformers and representatives of the Enlightenment." Jean Meyer, *The Cristero Rebellion: The Mexican People Between*

Church and State, 1926–1929, trans. by Richard Southern (Cambridge: Cambridge University Press, 1976), 2.

7. Farriss, *Crown and Clergy in Colonial Mexico*, 252.

8. Section I, article 3 of the Constitution of 1824. José M. Gamboa, *Leyes constitucionales de México durante el siglo xix* (Mexico City: Oficina Tipografía de la Secretaría de Fomento, 1901), 313–14.

9. See D. A. Brading, *The Origins of Mexican Nationalism* (Cambridge: Cambridge University Press, 1985).

10. See D. A. Brading, *Mexican Phoenix: Our Lady of Guadalupe: Image and Tradition Across Five Centuries* (Cambridge: Cambridge University Press, 2001), 228–30.

11. See Anne Staples, "Clerics as Politicians: Church, State, and Political Power in Independent Mexico," in *Mexico in the Age of Democratic Revolutions, 1750–1850*, ed. Jaime E. Rodríguez O. (Boulder, CO: Lynne Rienner Publishers, 1994), 236. For an example of this political/religious rhetoric in Guadalajara, see Brian Connaughton, *Clerical Ideology in a Revolutionary Age*, 13–19. For an analysis of the role that religious rhetoric played in the creation of national identity in Guatemala, another "chosen nation," see Douglass Sullivan-González, *Piety, Power, and Politics: Religion and Nation Formation in Guatemala, 1821–1871* (Pittsburgh, PA: University of Pittsburgh Press, 1998).

12. At the same time, it must also be recognized that the "inclusive community of Christian subjects" in Mexico was also still fundamentally divided by race and class, according to Matthew O'Hara. Because these divisions were reflected in ecclesiastical institutions (e.g., parish boundaries), he writes that Catholicism "served as both an integrative and divisive social force" in Spanish America. Matthew D. O'Hara, *A Flock Divided: Race, Religion and Politics in Mexico, 1749–1857* (Durham, NC: Duke University Press, 2010), 3–4.

13. Previous popes had hesitated to offend Ferdinand VII while he was working to restore the Church in Spain after the chaos of the Napoleonic Wars. At no point, however, was the Holy See disinterested or indifferent to the Mexican situation, pace Will Fowler, who suggests that the Mexican clergy probably worried that they were "serving God in a country God did not accept existed (as purported by the Pope)." Will Fowler, *The Grammar of Civil War*, 93. But a liberal regime came to power after Ferdinand's death in 1833 and Spain broke off its relations with Rome in 1836. This allowed the Holy See to establish formal diplomatic ties with Mexico in November, 1836, one month before its independence was recognized by the Spanish crown.

14. Michael P. Costeloe, *Church and State in Independent Mexico: A Study of the Patronage Debate, 1821–1857* (London: Royal Historical Society, 1978); Luis Medina Ascensio, SJ, *La iglesia y el estado liberal: 1836–1867*, vol. 2 of *México y el Vaticano* (Mexico City: Editorial Jus, 1984), 56–123.

15. For a description of the shared values of the political elites, the *gente de bien*, see Michael P. Costeloe, "*Hombres de bien* in the Age of Santa Anna," in *Mexico in the Age of Democratic Revolutions, 1750–1850*, ed. Jaime E. Rodriguez O. (Boulder, CO: Lynne Reinner Publishers, 1994), 243–57. According to Will Fowler, "the class/social values of the Creole oligarchy were more significant than the liberal–conservative dialectic," and many of the elites changed political sides over time. Will Fowler, "Dreams of

Stability: Mexican Political Thought during the 'Forgotten Years': An Analysis of the Beliefs of the Creole Intelligentsia (1821–1853)," *Bulletin of Latin American Research* 14, no. 3 (September 1995): 292.

16. Huberto Morales and William Fowler, introduction to *El conservadurismo mexicano en el siglo XIX (1810-1910)*, ed. Huberto Morales and William Fowler (Puebla: Benemérita Universidad Autónoma de Puebla, 1999), 13.

17. In Protestant countries "a dissenter was free to join another sect or to practice no religion at all." In Latin America, on the other hand, "he had to protest within the framework of the predominant religious institution; to have done otherwise would have exposed him to social ostracism and civil danger." José Sánchez, *Anticlericalism: A Brief History* (South Bend, IN: University of Notre Dame Press, 1972), ix.

18. See Fanny Calderón de la Barca, *Life in Mexico*, ed. by Howard T. Fisher and Marion Hall Fisher (New York: Doubleday, 1966).

19. Fanny Calderón de la Barca to William Prescott (June 1840). Roger Wolcott, *The Correspondence of William Hickling Prescott, 1833–1847* (Boston: Houghton Mifflin, 1925), 130. Calderón herself was highly critical of Catholicism until her own conversion in 1847. See David A. Gilbert, "Finding Faith in the Nineteenth Century: Fanny Calderón de la Barca's Journey to the Catholic Church (via Mexico)," *The Catholic Social Science Review* 23 (2018): 141–55.

20. See Pamela Voekel, *Alone Before God: The Religious Origins of Modernity in Mexico* (Durham, NC: Duke University Press, 2002). In her work, Voekel describes the liberal religious project as "Reform Catholicism," an "enlightened" rejection of the mediation of the Church (especially a corrupted clergy) in favor of a more direct and individualist approach to God. Although her narrative ends in the 1830s, the attitudes she describes were still embraced by many liberals during the Reforma, after which their plan to transform the Church was abandoned. But Brian Larkin describes the religious reform movement during the Bourbon period as a clerical effort that was also more orthodox than Voekel suggests. See Brian Larkin, *The Very Nature of God: Baroque Catholicism and Religious Reform in Bourbon Mexico City* (Albuquerque, NM: University of New Mexico Press, 2010). Matthew O'Hara argues that the main real target of the Bourbon religious reforms was popular religion, especially in its Indian manifestations. O'Hara, *A Flock Divided*, 64–69, 125–27, 141–43. Ironically, the creation of a unique indigenous expression of Catholicism had been one of the primary goals of the early missionaries. See Jaime Lara, *Christian Texts for Aztecs: Art and Liturgy in Colonial Mexico* (Notre Dame, IN: University of Notre Dame Press, 2008).

21. A decline in religious observance during this period is reflected in the clerical complaints found in the archives of the Archdiocese of Mexico. See Gabriela Díaz Patiño, *Católicos, liberales y protestantes: El debate por las imágenes religiosas en la formación de una cultura nacional (1848–1908)* (Mexico City: El Colegio de México: 2016), 162–64.

22. "El Cristianismo del porvenir," *El Monitor Republicano* (Mexico City), December 13, 1855. Catholic liberals insisted that reason and liberty, by their definition, were the essence of true Christianity. See Iñigo Fernández Fernández, "El liberalismo católico en la prensa mexicana de la primera mitad del siglo XIX (1833–1857)," *Historia 396* (Pontificia Universidad Católica de Valparaiso, Chile) 4, no. 1 (2014): 63–68. See also

Erika Pani, "Iglesia, Estado y Reforma: Las complejidades de una ruptura," in *Iglesia, religión y Leyes de la Reforma*, vol. 1 of *México durante la Guerra de Reforma*, ed. Brian Connaughton (Xalapa, MX: Universidad Veracruzana, 2011), 45–51.

23. The term *puro* seems to have derived from a slogan adopted by one of the early federalists: "¡pura federación y nada de cola!" (pure federalism and nothing else!). See José Cornejo Franco, *De la independencia a la reforma* (Guadalajara: Ediciones del Gobierno del Estado, 1959), 18.

24. Anne Staples, "Clerics as Politicians," 227.

25. Miguel Lerdo de Tejada, *Cuadro Sinóptico de la República Mexicana en 1856* (Mexico City: Ignacio Cumplido, 1856), 80. In 1856, the male religious orders included 763 Friars Minor (Franciscans), 133 Mercedarians, 199 Augustinians, 79 Carmelites and 141 Dominicans (not counting the province of Oaxaca). Francisco Morales, OFM, "Mexican Society and the Franciscan Order in a Period of Transition," in *The Americas* 54, no. 3 (January 1998): 354n94. Although some members of these orders were lay brothers rather than priests, they were also considered clergymen, along with any diocesan seminarians having already received the first tonsure.

26. For example, in 1811 the Bishop of Michoacán had complained of the excess number or priests in his diocese, indicating that the geographic density of priests was uneven. Brading, "Tridentine Catholicism," 21.

27. Pablo Mijangos y González, *The Lawyer of the Church: Bishop Clemente de Jesús Munguía and the Clerical Response to the Mexican Liberal Reforma* (Lincoln: University of Nebraska Press, 2015), 29–64. One disgruntled former student was the revolutionary, Miguel Cruz-Aedo. He once wrote a pamphlet in which he denounced the traditional character of the teaching in the seminary and claimed that some unspecified immorality took place behind its walls. Miguel Cruz-Aedo, *Los pobrecitos estudiantes del seminario de Guadalajara* (Mexico City: R. Rafael, 1852), 19 pages. These charges were then refuted in writing by other students and faculty. See Dennis Paul Ricker, "The Lower Secular Clergy of Central Mexico: 1821–1857" (PhD diss., University of Texas at Austin, 1982), 102.

28. See Raymond Patrick Harrington, "The Secular Clergy in the Diocese of Merida de Yucatán: 1780–1850" (PhD diss., The Catholic University of America, 1983). Although the power of priests was once unchallenged in rural Mexico, the power of the Catholic clergy was already diminished by the end of the colonial period as a result of Bourbon policies. See William B. Taylor, *Magistrates of the Sacred: Priests and Parishioners in Eighteenth-Century Mexico* (Stanford, CA: Stanford University Press, 1996), 449–51.

29. On the other hand, Florencia Mallon uncovered the will of a priest in Zapotitlán (Puebla) who recognized eleven illegitimate children in his will. Florencia E. Mallon, *Peasant and Nation*, 93.

30. Ricker, "The Lower Secular Clergy," vii, 212, 330–331. The goal of Ricker's project was to explain the rise of anticlericalism in Mexico. His evidence ruled out deficits in seminary training or the racial-ethnic origin of the clergy as a factor. Although he found Mexican clergy to be highly nationalistic, his final explanation for the liberal animus toward them was their lack of "patriotism" for not accepting beneficial reforms.

31. The goals of the Spanish version of Jansenism are spelled out in Brading, *Church and State in Bourbon Mexico*, 11–12.

32. James F. McMillan, "Religion and Politics in Nineteenth-Century France: Further Reflections on Why Catholics and Republicans Couldn't Stand Each Other," in *The Politics of Religion in an Age of Revival: Studies in Nineteenth-Century Europe and Latin America*, ed. Austen Ivereigh (London: Institute of Latin American Studies, 2000), 46. See also Sánchez, *Anticlericalism*, 200–205 and Joseph N. Moody, *The Church as Enemy: Anticlericalism in Nineteenth Century French Literature* (Washington, DC: Corpus Books, 1968), 2–4.

33. Sánchez, *Anticlericalism*, 3. At times, anticlericalism could also function as a conspiracy theory, in which "Catholicism appeared as a machine of clerical command and laical obedience." See Manuel Borutta, "Anti-Catholicism and the Culture War in Risorgimento Italy," in *The Risorgimento Revisited: Nationalism and Culture in Nineteenth Century Italy*, eds. Silvana Patriarca and Lucy Riall (New York: Palgrave Macmillan, 2012), 207.

34. A good example is the rise of militant anticlericalism in Spain after its disastrous war with the United States in 1898 as taken up by Frances Lannon, "1898 and the Politics of Catholic Identity in Spain," in *The Politics of Religion in an Age of Revival: Studies in Nineteenth-Century Europe and Latin America*, ed. by Austen Ivereigh (London: Institute of Latin American Studies, 2000), 72–73.

35. "Masonry, through its lodges and the debates they generated around them, had a key role in the definition of the canon of secular thought at this time that was vital for the creation of a liberal and lay state." Lodges also promoted "foundational myths and a literary canon that would have a great impact on the imaginations of their members." Guillermo de Los Reyes, "El impacto de la masonería en los orígenes del discurso secular, laico y anticlerical en México" in *Secularización del Estado y la Sociedad*, ed. Patricia Galeana (Mexico City, Siglo XXI Editores, 2010), 102, 120.

36. Luis J. Zalce y Rodríguez, *Apuntes para la historia de la masonería en México* (Mexico City: Talleres Tipográficos de la Penitenciaría del Distrito Federal, 1950), 105–6. According to Anne Staples, the Church's monopoly on education was a myth created by José María Luis Mora, "something that in fact never existed." Staples, "Clerics as Politicians," 234.

37. See Jean-Pierre Bastian, "Una ausencia notoria: la francmasonería en la historiografía mexicanista," *Historia Mexicana* 44, no. 3 (January-March 1995): 449.

38. Charles A. Hale, *Mexican Liberalism in the Age of Mora, 1821–1853* (New Haven, CT: Yale University Press, 1968), 35.

39. D. A. Brading, "Liberal Patriotism and the Mexican Reforma," *Journal of Latin American Studies* 20, no. 1 (May 1988): 31.

40. Peter Steinfels, "The Failed Encounter: The Catholic Church and Liberalism in the Nineteenth Century," in *Catholicism and Liberalism: Contributions to American Public Policy*, ed. R. Bruce Douglass and David Hollenbach (Cambridge: Cambridge University Press, 1994), 25, 30.

41. Both Gómez Farías and Mora were leading members of the National Rite Masonic lodge. Zalce y Rodríguz, *Apuntes para la historia*, 104.

42. See Hale, *Mexican Liberalism*, 144–45.

43. Anne Staples also argues that secularization continued at the local level throughout this period, in spite of the negative reaction to the Gómez Farías reforms. For instance, regulations on the ringing of church bells, the banning of intramural burials (inside churches), the suppression of popular fiestas or religious customs, etc. were all signs of displacement of religious activity from civic life. Anne Staples, "Secularización: Estado e iglesia en tiempos de Gómez Farías," *Estudios de historia moderna y contemporánea de México* 10, no. 10 (1986):109–23.

44. See Michael P. Costeloe, "The Administration, Collection and Distribution of Tithes in the Archbishopric of Mexico, 1800-1860," *Americas* 23, no. 1 (July 1966): 20–23. Although voluntary, the minister of finance reported in 1856 many people still continued to pay the tithe "for reasons of conscience, or other motives." Lerdo, *Cuadro Sinóptico*, 81.

45. Callcott, *Church and State in Mexico*, 173.

46. Anne Staples, "La educación como instrumento ideológico del estado. El conservadurismo educativo en el México decimonónico," in Huberto Morales and William Fowler, *El conservadurismo mexicano en el siglo XIX (1810–1910)* (Puebla: Benemérita Universidad Autónoma de Puebla, 1999), 103–14.

47. Even Mora noted that the religious orders lost status and prestige when their Spanish members were replaced with men from less elite families with "poorer cultural backgrounds." See Staples, "Clerics as Politicians," 234.

48. Morales, "Mexican Society and the Franciscan Order," 351–56. See also Francisco Morales, OFM, "Procesos internos de reforma en las órdenes religiosas: Propuestas y obstáculos," in *Historia de la Iglesia en el Siglo XIX*, ed. Manuel Ramos Medina (Mexico City: Centro de Estudios de Historia de México Condumex, 1998), 149–77.

49. See García Ugarte, *Poder político y religioso*, 1:486–88, 501.

50. The revolt was triggered by the *Siete Leyes* (Seven Laws) implemented by Santa Anna. These abolished the federal system created by the 1824 Constitution and centralized power in Mexico City, leaving the new citizens of Texas with little local political power. Although Santa Anna had been compelled, while a prisoner of war, to sign a treaty accepting the independence of Texas, the Mexican Congress never ratified this treaty nor was it recognized by subsequent Mexican presidents.

51. Lorenzo de Zavala was the former Mexican ambassador to France. For the liberal inspiration of Zavala's efforts, see Hale, *Mexican Liberalism*, 202–4.

52. Although President Polk and his supporters had designs on Texas and other Mexican territories, they believed that Mexico, being threatened, would capitulate without a fight. But although the Mexican army was weak, patriotism among its political class was not. Amy S. Greenberg, *A Wicked War: Polk, Clay, Lincoln, and the 1846 U.S. Invasion of Mexico* (New York: Alfred A. Knopf, 2012), 75–77.

53. Since Gómez Farías had launched earlier attacks on Church property, it was easy to imagine that this "emergency" measure was not entirely patriotic. The "Polka Revolt" on February 26, 1847, included both conservative and *moderado* military officers who opposed the legislation.

54. Letter of Robert E. Lee to John Mackay, October 2, 1847. Quoted in Emory M. Thomas, *Robert E. Lee: A Biography* (New York: Norton, 1995), 137. Anti-Catholicism

permeated US rhetoric about Mexico during this period. See John C. Pinheiro, *Missionaries of Republicanism: A Religious History of the Mexican-American War* (New York: Oxford University Press, 2014).

55. For a description of the anticlerical culture of the port city, see Voekel, *Alone Before God*, 128–33.

56. See Mijangos y González, *The Lawyer of the Church*, 137–45; José Bravo Ugarte, SJ, *Munguía: Obispo y arzobispo de Michoacán (1810–1868), su vida y su obra* (Mexico City: Editorial Jus, 1967), 51–55; D.A. Brading, "Ultramontane Intransigence and the Mexican Reform: Clemente de Jesús Munguía," in *The Politics of Religion in an Age of Revival: Studies in Nineteenth-Century Europe and Latin America*, ed. Austen Ivereigh (London: Institute of Latin American Studies, 2000), 115–17.

57. Margaret Chowning, *Wealth and Power in Provincial Mexico: Michoacán from the Late Colony to the Revolution* (Stanford, CA: Stanford University Press, 1999), 233. According to Taylor, "the most common and persistent source of friction between parish priests and Indian parishioners in the late colonial period was the fees for spiritual services that the *curas* treated as an indispensable part of their living." See "Arancel Disputes" in Taylor, *Magistrates of the Sacred*, 424–47. Ocampo became governor of Michoacán in May 1852 and initiated other campaigns against Munguía before his resignation in 1853. See Mijangos y González, *The Lawyer of the Church*, 147–53.

58. For a summary of the nine-month debate, which lasted from March to November 1851, see Martín Quirarte, *El problema religioso en México* (Mexico City: Institutio Nacional de Antropología, 1967), 213–25. Quirate identifies the "cura de Michoacán" as either Agustín Dueñas, the priest of Maravatío, José María Gutiérrez, priest of Uruapan, or as Bishop Munguía himself. In any event, he feels that Munguía was involved behind the scenes. The complete texts of the debate may be found in Melchor Ocampo, *Obras Completas*, vol. 1 (Mexico City: F. Vázqeuz, 1900).

59. Letter of Lucas Alamán to Antonio López de Santa Anna, March 23, 1853. This letter was included in an anonymous pamphlet on conservative principles published in September 1855, in the wake of the triumph of the Ayutla Revolution. *El partido conservador en México* (Mexico City: J.M. Andrade y F. Escalante, 1855), 40–44.

60. Lucas Alamán, *Disertaciones sobre la Historia de la República Mexicana*, 3 vols. (Mexico City, Lara: 1844–1849) and *Historia de México, desde los primeros movimientos que prepararon su independencia en el año de 1808, hasta la época presente*, 5 vols. (Mexico City, Lara, 1849–1852).

61. See José C. Valadés, *Alamán: Estadista e Historiador* (Mexico City: Universidad Nacional Autónoma de México, 1987).

62. Hale, *Mexican Liberalism*, 262.

63. In *Partido conservador*, 41–42.

64. From a facsimile of the 1591 edition of the catechism included in José M. Sánchez, *Doctrina cristiana del Jerónimo de Ripalda é intento bibliográfico de la misma. Años 1591–1900* (Madrid: Imprenta Alemana, 1909), 21.

65. According to Hale, utilitarianism, "based on a secular view of human nature," was the main philosophical foundation of Mexican liberalism. Hale, *Mexican Liberalism*, 148.

66. "El Porvenir de México. La idea anexionista y la idea conservador," *El Universal*, October 13, 16, 18, 1850. For the contradictions in liberal attitudes toward the US, especially after the invasion of 1847, see Hale, *Mexican Liberalism*, chap. 6.

67. This was the second restoration of the Jesuits since their expulsion in 1767. The Spanish crown allowed the order to return to Mexico in 1816 but had expelled it again in 1821. Santa Anna attempted to restore the order without success in 1843. José Gutiérrez Casillas, SJ, *Jesuitas en México durante el siglo XIX* (Mexico City: Editorial Porrúa, 1972), 27–63, 105–7.

68. See García Ugarte, *Poder político y religioso*, 1:464–65. A history of the restored college is found in Gerardo Decorme, SJ, *Historia de la Compañia de Jesús en la Republica Mexicana durante el siglo XIX* (Guadalajara: J.M. Yguiniz, 1921), 2:56–94.

69. See Will Fowler, *Tornel and Santa Anna: The Writer and the Caudillo, Mexico 1795–1853* (Westport, CT: Greenwood Press, 2000), 262–66 and Will Fowler, *Mexico in the Age of Proposals, 1821–1853* (Westport, CT: Greenwood Press, 1998), 248–53. Liberals particularly resented the *Ley Lares*, which limited the freedom of the press, and the "Law of Conspirators" that expedited the execution of anti-government plotters.

70. For the sum of ten million dollars, Santa Anna alienated 30,000 square miles of national territory. In US history this transaction is known as the "Gadsden Purchase."

71. The original plan was slightly modified on March 11, 1854. See Thomas B. Davis and Amando Ricon Virulegio, *The Political Plans of Mexico* (Lanham, MD: University Press of America, 1987), 500–9.

72. "Plan demagógico," *El Universal*, April 19, 22, 1854.

73. His Plan of San Luis Potosí was issued on August 13, 1855. The revolt led by Haro y Tamariz was joined to the broader Ayutla movement during the Lagos accords on Sept. 16. Jan Bazant, *Antonio Haro y Tamariz y sus aventuras políticas, 1811–1869* (Mexico City: El Colegio de México, 1985), 75–103.

74. *Partido conservador*, 25.

75. In particular, the outspoken Bishop Munguía and Father Mucio Valdovinos, a former counselor to the dictator, publicly criticized some of his harsher policies. Álvarez, *Revolucion de la Reforma*, 98.

76. According to Ivereigh, new research challenges six primary "presuppositions" of the standard view of nineteenth-century religious conflict: that society was becoming less religious in the nineteenth century, that liberal forces were popular and clerical forces defended only privileged sectors, that anticlericalism was a reaction against the defense of privilege, that the church was anti-modern, and that the church, by resisting the liberal-democratic state, retarded the transition to democracy. Ivereigh, *The Politics of Religion*, 4, 6.

77. Christopher Clark, "The New Catholicism and the European Culture Wars" in *Culture Wars: Secular-Catholic Conflict in Nineteenth-Century Europe*, ed. Christopher Clark and Wolfram Kaiser (Cambridge; Cambridge University Press, 2009), 13.

78. Mijangos y González, *The Lawyer of the Church*, xix.

79. Raymond Grew, "Liberty and the Catholic Church in Nineteenth-Century Europe," in *Freedom and Religion in the Nineteenth Century*, ed. by Richard Helmstadter (Stanford, CA: Stanford University Press, 1977), 199.

80. Although Giovanni Maria Mastai-Ferretti began his pontificate as something of a progressive, political events in Italy turned him into an uncompromising opponent of liberalism after 1848. See Frank J. Coppa, "The Holy See in a turbulent decade: 1846-1856" and "Papal intransigence and infallibility in an age of liberalism and nationalism" in *The Modern Papacy since 1789* (New York: Longman, 1998), 84–99, 100–116.

81. According to Grew, Catholics mastered the techniques of mass mobilization, and thus helped spread democratic practices into sectors of society neglected by liberal elites. At the same time, "Catholics were also as effective as Marxists in unmasking the liberal state's claims to neutrality, claims essential to its legitimacy." Grew, "Liberty and the Catholic Church," 229–32. See also Clark, "The New Catholicism," 45–46 and Margaret Lavinia Anderson, "The Divisions of the Pope: The Catholic Revival and Europe's Transition to Democracy" in *The Politics of Religion in an Age of Revival: Studies in Nineteenth-Century Europe and Latin America*, ed. Austen Ivereigh (London: Institute of Latin American Studies, 2000), 22–42.

82. Marta Eugenia García Ugarte claims that until 1855 the Mexican hierarchy avoided the "intransigent ultramontanism" of Europe and maintained a "relative autonomy" from Rome, allowing the church to participate more effectively in the process of national construction. She argues that only the official separation of Church and State in 1859 forced Mexican bishops to repudiate the more conciliatory policies of their predecessors. Nevertheless, ultramontane ideas were clearly sweeping the country even before the Reforma crisis. Marta Eugenia García Ugarte, *Liberalismo e iglesia católica en México, 1824–1855.* (Mexico City: Instituto Mexicano de Doctrina Social Cristiana, 1999), 80–81.

83. Fausto Zerón-Medina, *Felicidad de México* (Mexico City: Editorial Clío, 1995), 115–16. In 1749 a Mexican Jesuit had even prophesied that in the last days the pope would move his residence from Rome to the shrine of Our Lady of Guadalupe at Tepeyac. See Brading, *Mexican Phoenix*, 163–64.

84. *El Nuncio Apostólico en México: Monseñor Luis Clementi, arzobispo impartibus di Damsco* (Mexico: n.p., 1854), 32.

85. *Decreto concediendo el pase al breve en que se nombre Delegado Apostolico á Monseñor Luis Clementi; Dictamen sobre la admisión del misma breve* (Mexico City: Ignacio Cumplido, 1853).

86. This dogma asserted that the Virgin Mary was preserved free from the effects of original sin from the first moment of her conception. Pius IX solemnly declared the doctrine, the subject of Scholastic debate since the twelfth century, to be an article of Catholic faith in the bull *Ineffabilis Deus* on December 8, 1854. For the impact of this decree in Mexico, see Díaz Patiño, *Cátolicos, liberals y protestantes*, 261–75.

87. Elias Amador, *Bosquejo histórico de Zacatecas* (Zacatecas: Tipografía de Hospicio de Niños en Guadalupe, 1912), 2:528–29.

88. Juan Real Ledezma, ed., *Historia: La confrontación de la Universidad de Guadalajara y el Instituto de Ciencias del Estado de Jalisco, 1821–1861* (October 2013), https://www.udg.mx/es/nuestra/presentacion/historia/periodos/periodo-ii.

89. The preacher, Gil Alamán, was the son of the conservative writer and politician, Lucas Alamán. *Sermon predicado por el padre Don Gil Alamán, presbítero de la congregación del*

Oratorio de San Felipe Neri de México, el día 17 de junio de 1855, primero de los tres días en que celebró solemnemente la misma congregación en su iglesia la declaración dogmática de la Inmaculada Concepción de la Santísima Virgen María, Madre de Dios (Mexico City: Andrade y Escalante, 1856), 40–41. Another Mexican churchman considered this unprecedented declaration an almost miraculous sign of divine intervention: "the most happy omen for the glory of God our Lord and for the peace and happiness of men on earth." Diego de Aranda y Carpinterio, *Carta pastoral en la que se hace saber a todo el venerable clero secular y regular de la diócesis de Guadalajara la encíclica de N.S.P. el Sr. Pio IX sobre el interesante asunto de la Inmaculada Concepción de María Sma.* (Guadalajara: Rodríguez, 1849), 2.

90. *Sermón que en el aniversario de la definición dogmática sobre la Inmaculada Concepción de María Santísima predicó en la santa iglesia catedral de Durango, el Dr. José Real Águila . . . el día 8 de diciembre de 1855* (Durango: Imprenta del Gobierno á cargo de M. González, 1855), 12 pages.

91. The number of members exploded after conferences for women were introduced in 1863. Silvia Marina Arrom, "Catholic Philanthropy and Civil Society: The Lay Volunteers of Saint Vincent de Paul in Nineteenth-Century Mexico," in *Philanthropy and Social Change in Latin America*, ed. Cynthia Sanborn and Felipe Portocarrero (Cambridge, MA: Harvard University Press, 2005), 31–62. See also Margaret Chowning, *Catholic Women and Mexican Politics* (Princeton, NJ: Princeton University Press, 2023), 78–80.

92. The vigil was always conducted in a parish church or chapel before a monstrance containing the consecrated Host. Unlike the Vincentian associations, women dominated most of the local chapters of the *Vela*. Chowning, *Catholic Women*, 81–92.

93. *Pedro Espinosa y Dávalos, A N. M. I. V. S. Dean y Cabildo, al V. Clero secular y regular y á todos los fieles de esta Diócesis* (Guadalajara: 1854), 10 pages.

94. For a description of the flourishing, and changing, religious environment in the decades before the Reforma, see William B. Taylor, *Shrines and Miraculous Images: Religious Life in Mexico Before the Reforma* (Albuquerque: University of New Mexico Press, 2019), 165–205.

CHAPTER TWO

1. For the anticlerical culture in Guadalajara, see Sinkin, *The Mexican Reforma*, 37–38.

2. These factions were represented by Manuel Doblado (Guanajuato), Santiago Vidaurri (Nuevo León), and Antonio de Haro y Tamariz (San Luis Potosí). The states of Guerrero, Jalisco and Michoacán and the Mexico City garrison had already accepted the Plan of Ayutla. At the conference held on September 16, all the remaining rebel leaders except Vidaurri agreed to accept the plan and the interim presidency of Juan Álvarez. See José Roberto Juárez, "La lucha por el poder a la caída de Santa Anna," *Historia Mexicana* 10, no. 1 (July–September 1960): 72–77.

3. The "Organic Statute of Jalisco" promulgated by Comonfort on August 29 guaranteed freedom of thought and expression, with the restriction that this speech did not "offend religion, morality, and private conduct." Luis Pérez Verdía, *Historia particular*

del Estado de Jalisco desde los primeros tiempos de que hay noticia, hasta nuestros días (Guadalajara: Tipografía de la Escuela de Artes y Oficios del Estado, 1910), 2:399.

4. Martín Carrera, the provisional president since August 14, resigned on September 11. Accepted as temporary chief by the signatories of the Lagos agreement, General Juan Álvarez was elected interim president by the Convention of Cuernavaca on October 4.

5. See Javier Rodríguez Piña, "Conservatives Contest the Meaning of Independence, 1846–1855," in *¡Viva Mexico! ¡Viva la Independencia! Celebrations of September 16,* eds. William H. Beezley and David E. Lorey (Wilmington, DE: SR Books, 2001), 101–29.

6. Vigil later wrote: "In Guadalajara, as in the rest of the country, discourses were delivered during the mentioned festivals in which the most vehement radicalism and the most bitter censures against the conservative party and clergy dominated." In fact, Vigil himself delivered a public discourse in Guadalajara on the evening of September 15, the opening of the patriotic holidays. Vigil, *La Reforma,* 71.

7. Guillermo Prieto, *Oración cívica pronunciada por el ciudadano Guillermo Prieto en la Alameda de México, el día 16 de septiembre de 1855, aniversario del glorioso grito de "¡Independencia!" dado por el cura de Dolores en 1810* (Mexico City: Ignacio Cumplido, 1855), 14 pages.

8. Ignacio L. Vallarta, *Discurso que en el solemne aniversario del día 16 de septiembre de 1810, leyó en la plaza principal de Guadalajara el C. Ignacio L. Vallarta, miembro de la sociedad literaria "La Esperanza"* (Guadalajara: Tipografía del Gobierno, 1855), 24 pages. Also see the description of this speech in Enrique Plasencia de la Parra, *Independencia y nacionalismo a la luz del discurso conmemorativo. 1825–1867* (Mexico City: Consejo Nacional para la Cultura y las Artes, 1991), 97–99, 102–3.

9. "Repuesta a las doctrines impías, o examen crítico del discurso que pronunció el 17 de Setiembre de 1855 en el salón principal del Instituto del Estado de Jalisco, el ciudadano Miguel Cruz Aedo, académico de la Esperanza," *La Cruz* 1, no. 8 (December 20, 1855): 233–43.

10. Plasencia de la Parra, *Independencia y nacionalismo,* 14.

11. Agustín Rivera, *Anales Mexicanos: La Reforma y el Segundo Imperio* (1891; repr., Mexico City: Universidad Nacional Autónoma de México, 1994), 56–57n16. Agustín Rivera y Sanromán (1824–1916) was a priest, a lawyer, and author. He had attended the Morelia Seminary and took classes under Munguía in the 1830s but nevertheless inclined toward liberal opinions later in life. He was a prolific writer, and his *Anales Mexicanos* provides an indispensable chronology of events in Mexico from 1854 to 1898, along with valuable eyewitness commentary. See also "Miguel Cruz-Aedo y Ortega" in Juan Real Ledezma, ed., *Enciclopedia histórica y biografía de la Universidad de Guadalajara: Los universitarios entre el Instituo y la Universidad* (June 2017), http://enciclopedia. udg.mx/capitulos/los-universitarios-entre-el-instituto-y-la-universidad.

12. For a history of the latter group, see Celia del Palacio, *La Primera Generación Romántica en Guadalajara: El Falange de Estudio* (Guadalajara: Editorial Universidad de Guadalajara, 1993).

13. Cornejo Franco, *De la independencia a la reforma,* 28.

14. *La Revolución* advertised itself as a "democratic, independent newspaper." Its motto was: "To be or not to be; that is the question." According to an Italian treatise on the Masons, this was also the motto of numerous secret anticlerical societies in Europe. See Tomás S. Gardida, trans., "Ligera ojeada sobre la demagogia y las sociedades secretas en nuestros días," *La Cruz* 3, no.4 (August 28, 1856): 119. The paper only existed between August 19 and December 7, 1855. Maria del Carmen Ruiz Catañeda, *Periodismo Politico de la Refoma en la Ciudad de Mexico: 1854–1861* (Mexico City: Instituto de Investigaciones Sociales, 1954), 139–40.

15. "Nuestra proposición," *La Revolución* (Guadalajara, Mexico), August 28, 1855.

16. According to a contemporary critique of the Degollado administration, this speech was the start of the liberal anti-Catholic crusade. "These fatal passions, enemies of faith and authority, began to be exposed in a solemn mode by Cruz Aedo, on the 17th of September, in the discourse that he pronounced in memory of the victims of independence, with Santos Degollado presiding. In [the governor's] presence, he depreciated the Supreme Pontiff of the Church, censorship, indulgences, the sacrament of penance; he proclaimed universal tolerance, contrary to what we read in the Holy Scriptures." [Germán Ascensión Villalvazo y Rodríguez], *D. Santos Degollado considerado como gobernador de Jalisco, y como general en jefe de las fuerzas que sitiaron* (Guadalajara: Tipografía del Gobierno, 1859), 6. Although published anonymously, this work has been attributed to Germán A. Villalvazo, the secretary of the Bishop of Guadalajara. Rivera, *Anales Mexicanos*, 45n21.

17. Miguel Cruz-Aedo, *Discurso pronunciado en el salón principal del instituto del estado, el 17 de Setiembre de 1855, aniversario de las víctimas de la patria, por el C. Miguel Cruz-Aedo, miembro de la sociedad literaria, "La Esperanza"* (Guadalajara: 1855, Tipografía del Gobierno), 19 pages. In effect, this speech was a reworking of a series of articles on the conservative party that appeared in *La Revolución* between August 31 and September 4. The Dominican Tomás de Torquemada (1420–1498) was Spain's first Grand Inquisitor. The Franciscan, Juan de Zumárraga y Arrazola (1468–1548), was the first Bishop of Mexico (1530–1548).

18. According to *La Cruz*, blaming the clergy for the present evils of Mexico was only a trick used by "pseudo-liberals" in order to "get their claws into the ecclesiastical coffers." "Repuesta a las doctrines impías," *La Cruz* 1, no. 8 (December 20, 1855): 233–43.

19. Cruz-Aedo, *Discurso pronunciado*, 11. Indulgences were token good works that could replace the extensive penances that accompanied confession and absolution in the early Church. By the late Middle Ages these alternative acts took many forms, including monetary donations. But financial incentives led to abuses, famously criticized by Martin Luther, and the substitution of donations for other penances was abolished by the Council of Trent on December 4, 1563.

20. Cruz-Aedo, 16. The confessional was a frequent target of Protestant and liberal attacks everywhere. In the nineteenth century, the common charge was that the practice undermined the absolute authority of the father in the family.

21. Cruz-Aedo, 8, 12. This biblical imagery is taken form the book of Revelation, chapter 17.

22. Cruz-Aedo, 8, 15.

23. *Diálogo entre Martin y Juan Diego* (Mexico City: V. Segura Argüelles, 1855), 13 pages. This publication contains the first two dialogues. The third and fourth appeared in *Diálogo entre Martin y Juan Diego* (Mexico City: Tomás S. Gardida, 1855), 22 pages. By the time the final dialogues were printed, they were already banned in Guadalajara under a new censorship law issued by Degollado on September 20, 1855. Around the same time, another sarcastic dialogue, falsely attributed to Cruz-Aedo and dated September 25, 1855, also appeared. *Intervalo lucido de Miguel Cruz-Aedo* (Mexico City: Segura Arguelles, 1855), 6 pages. Cruz-Aedo later complained of "the insulting satires that have constantly appeared on the streets of the city." Miguel Cruz-Aedo, et al, "Primera carta." *La Revolución*, October 10, 1855.

24. Jacqueline Covo claims the name Juan Diego by itself "represents tradition and Mexican prudence." Jacqueline Covo, *Las ideas de la Reforma en México (1855–1861)* (Mexico City: Universidad Nacional Autónoma de México, 1983), 220n280. As the name of the converted Indian who received the vision of the Virgin of Guadalupe in 1531, it also carried important religious and patriotic connotations. The name Martin also connected the liberal sympathizer with the Protestant Martin Luther.

25. The catechism in question was that of Padre Ripalda. Santa Anna approved a version revised by Bishop Mungía for use in all public schools on January 25, 1854. See advertisement, "Catecismo de la doctrina por el Padre Ripalda," in Mariano Galván Rivera, *Guía de forasteros en la ciudad de México para el año de 1854* (Mexico City: Santiago Perez, 1854), 352. See also Staples, "La educación como instrumento," 103–4.

26. [Villalvazo], *D. Santos Degollado*, 6.

27. The bishop's letter (October 1, 1855) and the governor's reply (October 4, 1855) were reprinted in "El Obispo de Guadalajara y el Gobernador de Jalisco," *El Siglo Diez y Nueve*, October 21, 1855.

28. For a description of Espinosa's pastoral initiatives among rural peasants, see Brittsan, *Popular Politics*, 21–22.

29. Emphasis in the original. [Villalvazo], *D. Santos Degollado*, 11.

30. "El Cura de Zapotlán," *El Siglo Diez y Nueve*, October 18, 1855.

31. "Caridad," *El Siglo Diez y Nueve*, October 24, 1855. The article was copied from *El Monitor Republicano*.

32. "Abusos," *El Monitor Republicano*, October 30, 1855.

33. "Sigue el pulpito convertido en tribuna," *El Siglo Diez y Nueve*, November 21, 1855. This article related a story from Sahuayo (Michaocán), first published in *La Revolución*.

34. [Villalvazo], *D. Santos Degollado*, 25.

35. Vicente Fuentes Díaz, *Santos Degollado, La Victoria de la República* (Mexico City: Secretaría de Educación Pública, 1967), 1–13; and Angel Pola, "Santos Degollado" *in El Libro Rojo: 1520–1867* (Mexico City: A. Pola, 1906), 2:360–96.

36. Hélène Rivière d'Arc, *Guadalajara y su región: Influencias y dificultades de una metrópolis mexicana*, trans. Carlos Montemayor and Josefina Anaya (Mexico City: SepSetentris, 1973), 47–48.

37. Vigil, who reprinted Degollado's complete response, was impressed by "the energy of the concepts and the very significant allusions" in the governor's letter, "expressed in a courteous and respectful format." Vigil, *La Reforma*, 71.

38. Victoriano Salado Álvarez, *Episodios Nacionales: Santa Anna, la reforma, la intervención, el Imperio* (1904; repr., Mexico City: Editorial Porrúa, 1984), 229; Cornejo Franco, *De la independencia a la reforma*, 33.

39. Salado Álvarez reports that in their speeches Cruz-Aedo and his friends "spoke of things that had never been heard: the abuses of the clergy, the need to reform what exists and to restrain those who exploited the credibility of the masses." Salado Álvarez, *Episodios Nacionales*, 177.

40. The Institute of Sciences of the State of Jalisco had been created as a progressive alternative to the University of Guadalajara in 1826 but Santa Anna had closed this "nest of impiety" in 1834. It was revived in 1846 and absorbed into the university in 1853. Later, Degollado suppressed the university and re-established the Institute. Pola, "Santos Degollado," 2:371. See Real Ledezma, *Historia: La confrontación de la Universidad de Guadalajara y el Instituto de Ciencias del Estado de Jalisco, 1821–1861*, October 2013. https://www.udg.mx/es/nuestra/presentacion/historia/periodos/periodo-ii.

41. See "El gobernador y el obispo," *La Revolución*, October 10, 1855. The governor reprimanded them for "this *slightest* offense" according to "El Exmo. Sr. Gobernador y el Illmo. Sr. Obispo," *El Monitor Republicanó*, October 21, 1855.

42. These events are described in [Villalvazo], *D. Santos Degollado*, 7, 25.

43. At the same time, liberals were outraged by these "seditious and alarming words" on the signs "fixed on doors and windows of homes," according to a manifesto signed by members of a Republican Battalion on October 5, 1855. "Remitidos," *La Revolución*, October 10, 1855; reprinted in "Guadalajara," *El Monitor Republicano*, October 21, 1855.

44. Pedro Espinosa y Dávalos, *Quinta carta pastoral que el Illmo. Señor obispo de Guadalajara, dirige a sus diocesanos* (Guadalajara: Rodríguez, 1855), 10 pages.

45. Matthew 26:31.

46. This term is taken from Revelation 2:9.

47. The paper also claimed that the bishop's "Catholic inspiration" was mostly copied from a reply to Guillermo Prieto's Independence Day discourse printed in the conservative newspaper, *La Verdad*. "Cronica," *La Revolución*, October 5, 1855.

48. Miguel Cruz-Aedo et al., "Primera carta." The editors of *La Revolución* often denied the charges that they were heretics, impious, or libertines. Here, the writers professed "a profound respect for the Catholic religion, Roman and apostolic, and a complete submission to the dogmas and moral teachings of the holy books, an absolute assent to the common opinion of the Church." Although they stated that they "could not be more explicit," their carefully crafted formula is still ambiguous. However, in a separate article the editors stated that "we are Catholic, apostolic, and Roman and we believe all that our holy mother the Church believes." "¡Protesta!" *La Revolución*, October 10, 1855.

49. [Villalvazo], *D. Santos Degollado*, 9.

50. Quoted in [Villalvazo], 9.

51. "Revista Religiosa de Europa y America: Del Pais," *La Cruz* 1, no. 10 (January 3, 1856): 325–26.

52. [Manuel Álvarez, SJ], *El fanal de la juventud, ó sean breves avisos á las personas que por su sencillez ó falta de instrucción, se hallan mas espuestas á padecer naufragio* (The Lighthouse

of Youth: Or brief advice to persons who because of their simplicity or lack of instruction find themselves more exposed to suffer shipwreck) (Mexico City: Imprenta de Abadiano, 1860), 204 pages. The accompanying frontispiece shows a youth kneeling upon the shore, while a raging sea casts wreckage from a ship upon the rocks at his feet. A light streams toward his face from the heart of the Virgin Mary, who is shown sitting upon a cloud above the ocean, holding the infant Christ. The caption reads: "*Ave Maris Stella*" (Hail, Star of the Sea).

53. In his introduction, the author states these dialogues were based on actual events, although the names are changed. Published anonymously, Basilio Arriaga's inventory lists Manuel Álvarez, an ex-Jesuit brother (temporal coadjutor) as the author. At the time it was written, probably around 1859, the Jesuit order was again suppressed in Mexico.

54. [Álvarez], *El final de la juventud*, 102–3.

55. See Juárez, "La lucha por el poder," 78–85.

56. The president of the conference was Valentín Gómez Farías and the vice president was Melchor Ocampo. Benito Juárez was appointed as one of the secretaries. All three were active Masons of the National Rite. Zalce y Rodriguez, *Apuntes para la historia*, 180.

57. Letter for November 17, 1855, in William R. Manning, ed., *Diplomatic Correspondence of the United States: Inter-American Affairs, 1831–1860*, vol. 9 of *Mexico: 1848 (Mid-Year)–1860* (Washington, DC: Carnegie Endowment for International Peace, 1937), 796. Scholes interpreted Gadsden's remarks as evidence that the aging Álvarez did not make preparations to ensure his own election. Scholes, *Mexican Politics*, 4n5. Ultimately, Álvarez received thirteen votes out of twenty. Comonfort and Ocampo each received three votes, and Vidaurri received one. Vigil, *La Reforma*, 76.

58. The ministers were: Melchor Ocampo (foreign relations), Benito Juárez (justice and ecclesiastical affairs), Guillermo Prieto (finance), Ponciano Arriaga (interior) and Santos Degollado (public works). Because of the ideological tensions between Ocampo and Comonfort, after two weeks Ocampo resigned his position.

59. Vigil, *La Reforma*, 77.

60. "El poder teocrático," *La Revolución*, October 8 to 28, 1855.

61. "¡Alerta, Pueblos!" *El Monitor Republicano*, October 17, 1855; "Motin Clerical," *El Siglo Diez y Nueve*, October 17, 1855; "El Pueblo," *El Monitor Republicano*, October 18, 1855; "El Exmo. Sr. Goberador y Illmo. Sr. Obispo," and "¡¡Viva la Religion!!" *El Monitor Republicano*, October 21, 1855; and "Guadalajara," *El Siglo Diez y Nueve*, October 24, 1855.

62. The newspaper claimed that this sacrilegious and seditious "disorder" was witnessed by thousands of people. It also demanded arrests and punishment for the instigators. "¡¡Viva la Religion!!" *La Revolución*, October 10, 1855. However, this characterization of the event was later attacked in an anonymous pamphlet as an example of the dissimulation of the liberal press. "O people of Guadalajara!" it said, "you see what happened on the night of October 8, and nevertheless, read in number 13 of *La Revolución* the report of this event and you will marvel at the shamelessness with which the editors lie and claim that you witnessed what did not exist." *Tolerancia* (s.d., s.p.), 15

pages. Three decades later, Vigil admitted that although the crowd shouted anti-liberal slogans, "nothing occurred against the public order." Vigil, *La Reforma*, 72.

63. The details of this "serious riot" were recorded by the French ambassador. Lilia Díaz López, trans. and ed., *Versión francesa de México: Informes diplomáticos (1853–1858)*, (Mexico City: El Colegio de México, 1963), 1:218. Jean Alexis, Viscount de Gabriac (1830–1903), was the French "Extraordinary Envoy and Minister Plenipotentiary" to Mexico from June 1854 to July 1860. Because his position gave him access to high-level government officials and politicians of both parties, his dispatches are a rich source of detailed information and insider gossip about events in Mexico. A monarchist and advocate for increased French involvement in the country, he secretly supported the conservative cause. Yet at the same time, he was unsympathetic to what he regarded as excessive Mexican religiosity and highly critical of the clerical domination of society and politics. His dispatches thus provide a unique perspective on the Reforma period. See Nancy Nichols Barker, *The French Experience in Mexico, 1821–1861* (Chapel Hill: University of North Carolina Press, 1979), 148–66.

64. José Ramón Malo y Ortíz was born in Valladolid (later Morelia, Michoacán) in 1799 and died in Mexico City in 1879. He was a nephew of General Agustín de Iturbide, and later wrote an important book about the former emperor's exile and death. His personal diary from 1832 to 1864 was published in 1948 as *Diario de sucesos notables*. Malo was also a priest, and his diary entries provide a valuable chronology of contemporary events from the Catholic point of view. José Ramón Malo, *Diario de sucesos notables*, ed. Mariano Cuevas, SJ (Mexico City: Editorial Patria, 1948), 2:436–7.

65. "El Clero—La Religion," *El Monitor Republicano*, October 18, 1855; and "Pasquines," *El Monitor Republicano*, October 21, 1855. Scholes minimizes the provocative nature of radical journalism by claiming that newspapers like *La Revolución* were "a small part of the press" and that they "never lasted long and never assumed the stature of *Siglo*." Scholes, *Mexican Politics*, 6. But he does not consider the fact that inflammatory articles like "El poder teocrático" were often republished in the more influential papers.

66. Along with reprinting the agenda from *La Revolución*, *El Monitor Republicano* also published a reform plan of its own. This included, among other provisions, the disentailment of Church lands and reinvestment of its wealth, abolition of the *fuero*, secularization of male religious orders and the concentration of all existing nuns in a single convent, the cancellation of stole fees, religious toleration, and severe punishment for any priest who preached against the government. There was also a demand for an "absolute prohibition on the sale of indulgences and relics," practices unknown since their abolition by the Council of Trent in the sixteenth century. "Reformas necesarias," *El Monitor Republicano*, October 17, 1855, and October 21, 1855. This series also included demands for reforms of the military and of the national economy.

67. The installment of "The Theocratic Power" for October 25, 1855, was devoted exclusively to an attack on the Jesuits. For a summary of this campaign, see Decorme, *Historia de la Compañía de Jesús*, 73–75.

68. According to Article 5 of the revised plan, the interim president was to convoke an extraordinary congress within two weeks of taking office. The plan also stipulated that the *convocatoria* of December 10, 1841, be used as a basis for the election law.

69. For examples, see Anne Staples, "Clerics as Politicians," 231–41.

70. Female suffrage was not introduced into Mexico until 1953.

71. Díaz López, *Versión francesa de México*, 1:216.

72. "Esclusiones," *El Monitor Republicano*, October 12, 1855.

73. "¡Un cargador vale mas que el arzobispo!" *El Siglo Diez y Nueve*, October 30 and November 4, 8, 1855.

74. "Contradicciones de los que atacan al clero," *La Cruz* 1, no. 4 (November 22, 1855): 105–9.

75. Vigil, *La Reforma*, 81.

76. Miranda was also a former editor of *La Universal* and an occasional contributor to *La Cruz*. The liberal press called him a "professional reactionary, enemy of liberty, and plotter against the current order of things." "Reaccionarios," *El Siglo Diez y Nueve*, November 23, 1855.

77. Letters from Bishop Pelagio Antonio Labastida to the governor dated November 21 and 27, 1855, are contained in Zamacois, *Historia de Méjico*, 14:841–49. Vigil claimed that the lack of due process in such cases was necessary because of the government's precarious position at the time. Vigil, *La Reforma*, 88.

78. The regulation of the *fuero* was only a small part of the comprehensive "Law on the Administration of Justice." Article 42 suppressed all special courts, except those belonging to the army and the Church. It removed military and ecclesiastical jurisdiction in civil cases, allowing common crimes to be heard in Church courts only "while a law is drawn up to regulate this point." Article 44 declared that even this limited *fuero* could be renounced. Article 4 transferred all civil cases already in progress to secular judges.

79. For a summary of liberal articles suggesting that there were scandalous reasons why the clergy wanted to retain the *fuero*, see Covo, *Las ideas de la Reforma*, 202n210. In fact, some conservatives complained that the goal of the law was to expose the human frailty of the clergy to the public in order to erode its prestige. See Zamacois, *Historia de Méjico*, 14:127.

80. *Contestaciones habidas entre el Illmo. Señor Arzobispo y el Ministerio de Justicia con motivo de la ley sobre administración de ese ramo.* (Mexico City: 1855, José Mariano Fernandez de Lara). Similar protests were later lodged by Bishop Munguía of Michoacán and Bishop Labastida of Puebla. In his survey of pamphlets published in Mexico during the *Reforma*, Javier Rodríguez Piña describes the *Ley Juárez* as the first of the "five moments" that produced the bulk of ecclesiastical protests. See Javier Rodríguez Piña, "La defensa de la Iglesia ante la legislación liberal en el periodo 1855–1861," *Sequencia*, No. 39 (September/December 1997): 73–82. For a summary of these objections and Juárez' response, see Robert J. Knowlton, "Clerical Response to the Mexican *Reforma*, 1855–1875," *Catholic Historical Review* 50, no. 4 (January 1965): 510–11.

81. Díaz López, *Versión francesa de México*, 1:234. *El Siglo Diez y Nueve* reported that rumors of the archbishop's imminent exile were entirely false and were only spread to disparage the government. "Falsos Rumores," *El Siglo Diez y Nueve*, December 1, 1855.

82. Francisco Sosa, *Biografías de mexicanos distinguidos* (Mexico City: Oficina Tipográfica de la Secretaría de Fomento, 1884), 404–11.

83. The most significant examples were those signed between Pope Pius VII and Napoleon in 1801 and between Pope Pius IX and Spain (1851), Costa Rica (1853), and Guatemala (1854). The concordat with Austria was signed in 1855. It was described (as a warning to the bishops) in "A los obispos," *El Siglo Diez y Nueve*, December 6, 1855. Its details were also published in José Joaquín Pesado, "Concordato de Austria con Roma," *La Cruz* 2, no. 2 (March 27, 1856): 55–57.

84. "Ataques e inconsecuencias de los enemigos del clero," *La Cruz* 1, no. 7 (December 13, 1855): 212. Emphasis in the original.

85. "Independencia de la iglesia," *La Cruz* 1, no. 8 (December 20, 1855): 243-246. A number of articles were also dedicated to demonstrating that the *fuero* was an inalienable right of the Church, and not a privilege granted by the state. See "El clero y el ejercito en la cuestion del fuero," *La Cruz* 1, no. 5 (November 29, 1855): 158–64 and the long series entitled "Sobre el fuero eclesiastico," *La Cruz* 2, nos. 4, 5, 6 (April 10, 17, 24, 1856): 115–19, 143–46, 175–79.

86. "Ataques e inconsecuencias," 212–13.

87. Zamacois, *Historia de Méjico*, 14:128. At this time Zamacois was the editor of *La Espada* (The Sword).

88. Zamacois, *Historia de Méjico*, 14:128.

89. The failure of elections to dislodge the party or faction in power led to the frequent coups known as *pronunciamientos* in Mexico. See Will Fowler, *Independent Mexico: The Pronunciamiento in the Age of Santa Anna, 1821–1858* (Lincoln: University of Nebraska Press, 2016).

90. This and subsequent quotations come from *Protesta que hacen los poblanos, en favor del fuero eclesiástico* (Puebla: José María Rivera, 1855), 12 pages.

91. Apparently, this demonstration was in response to the government's negative reply to the archbishop's letter, which was released on December 2. Malo, *Diario de sucesos notables*, 2:440.

92. Quoted in Zamacois, *Historia de Méjico*, 14:130–31. Bazant also sees in Dobado's fears the effect of conservative propaganda claiming that Álvarez had accepted a US protectorate over Mexico. Bazant, *Antonio Haro y Tamariz*, 101.

93. The many contradictions in Doblado's position are examined in Silvestre Villegas Revueltas, "El doblez de Doblado, ¿personalidad o táctica?" chap. in *El liberalismo moderado en México: 1852–1864* (Mexico City: Universidad Nacional Autónoma de México, 1997), 81–97.

94. Munguía wrote letters to Doblado on November 24 and December 5 and sent him a copy of his protest against the *Ley Juárez*. Bazant, *Antonio Haro y Tamariz*, 100.

95. Quoted in [Villalvazo], *D. Santos Degollado*, 19–21.

CHAPTER THREE

1. For a description of the unprecedented role of the laity in the ultramontane press, see Christopher Clark, "The New Catholicism and the European Culture Wars," 25–26.

2. Pope Pius IX, *Inter Multiplices* (March 21, 1853) in *The Papal Encyclicals: 1740–1878*, vol. 1, ed. Claudia Carlen (McGrath, NH: McGrath Publishing Co., 1981), 317.

3. In Italy, *La Civiltá Cattolica* (1850) also reflected the ideal of serious religious apologetics, but it was a Jesuit rather than a lay initiative.

4. The editor of *El Observador Católico* (The Catholic observer; 1848–50) was the famous scholar Basilio Arriaga, a priest and superior of the Jesuit order in Mexico, between its various suppressions. The editors of *La Voz de la Religión* (1848–1851) were Juan Bautista Morales, a moderate liberal, and Anselmo de la Portilla, a Spaniard. José Bravo Ugarte claims that Morales was always "indecisive in his Catholic ideas." Portilla, on the other hand, was the future panegyrist of Comonfort. Because of the political tendencies of its editors, the paper, published from 1848 to 1851, cannot be considered conservative. See José Bravo Ugarte, SJ, *Periodistas y periodicos mexicanos hasta 1935* (Mexico City: Editorial Jus, 1966), 55.

5. Created on the presses of Rafael y Rafael, its editor was Manuel Díez de Bonilla. Contributors included Lucas Alamán, Anselmo de la Portilla, the Carmelite priest Juan Crisótomo Nájera, and Ignacio Aguilar y Marocho. It was replaced by *La Sociedad* on December 1, 1855.

6. For descriptions of liberal and conservative newspapers of the period, see Gerald McGowan, *Prensa y poder, 1854–1857* (Mexico City: El Colegio de Mexico, 1978), 349–64; and Celia del Palacio Montiel, "La prensa de la Reforma" in *México durante la Guerra de Reforma*, vol. 2, *Contextos, prácticas culturales, imaginarios y representaciones*, ed. Celia del Palacio Montiel (Xalapa, MX: Universidad Veracruzana, 2011), 155–206.

7. However, the audience for newspapers was still only a small, educated elite rather than "the public." Palacio Montiel, 160–66.

8. Doralicia Carmona Dávila, "Juárez lamenta la suspensión del periódico 'Siglo XIX,'" *Memoria política de México*, March 3, 2021, https://memoriapoliticademexico.org/Efemerides/9/20091858.html.

9. Yolanda Argudín, *Historia del periodismo en México desde el virreinato hasta nuestros días* (Mexico City: Panorama, 1987), 66.

10. "The Revised Plan of Ayutla" (March 11, 1854) in Davis and Virulegio, *The Political Plans of Mexico*, 506. The original version of the plan (March 1, 1854) had spoken only of "arbitrary restriction." In some places, however, freedom of the press was very short lived under the new regime. For instance, Governor Degollado issued a new censorship law for the State of Jalisco on September 20, 1855.

11. This discrepancy has been attributed to the concentration of conservatives in the capital and other major cities in the center of the country, while liberals were more numerous in the capitals of the states. Maria del Carmen Ruiz Castañeda, *La prensa periodica en torno a la Constitucion de 1857* (Mexico City: Imprenta Universitaria, 1959), 34.

12. Two of the most important liberal newspapers were also published in Mexico City. *El Siglo Diez y Nueve* (The nineteenth century), published from 1841 to 1896, was led by Francisco Zarco from 1848 to 1856. *El Monitor Republicano* (The republican monitor), published from 1846 to 1895, was founded and directed by Vicente García Torres. See Ruiz Castañeda, *Periodismo politico*, 60–77.

13. A cross on a shield, held aloft by two angels, was pictured above the title in the masthead of the journal. The motto, "Faith, Faithfulness," appeared beneath the shield.

Reacting to the prospectus of the new journal, one liberal newspaper exclaimed" Watch out Mexicans! Behind the Cross is the devil, and behind the devil the conservatives!" "La Cruz," *El Monitor Republicano*, October 18, 1855.

14. Along with running his diocese, Munguía wrote numerous pastoral letters and other treatises on the issues of the day. He was finally exiled from his diocese for his writings on April 22, 1856. Although he subsequently came to live in Coyoacán, a suburb of Mexico City, there is no evidence that he remained directly involved with *La Cruz*. Bravo Ugarte, *Munguía*, 66. For the activities of Munguía during this phase of the Reforma, see Mijangos y González, *The Lawyer of the Church*, 154–87.

15. José María Roa Bárcena, *Biografía de D. José Joaquín Pesado* (Mexico City: Editorial Jus, 1962), 9–16, 24–29.

16. The paper ceased to be published when the co-editor, Francisco Modesto de Olaguíbel, was arrested and placed in prison for his views.

17. For a discussion of the importance of the Academia de San Juan de Letrán, see Alicia Perales Ojeda, *Las asociaciones literarias mexicanas*, 2nd ed., rev. (Mexico City: Universidad Nacional Autónoma de México, 2000), 74–81.

18. Pesado served as minister of the interior from March 22 to September 25, and from October 18 to December 12, 1838. He also served as minister of foreign relations from November 14 until early December of that year, during the conflict with France known as "The Pastry War."

19. Quoted in Roa Bárcena, *Biografía*, 53.

20. Carpio was also a man of science and on the forefront of the modernization of medicine in Mexico. See Voekel, *Alone before God*, 182, 204.

21. Guillermo Prieto, *Memorias de mis tiempos*, (Mexico City: Editorial Patria, 1948), 1:126–33.

22. Segura Argüelles published *El Omnibus* (1854–56) and *El Diario de Avisos* (1856–60). Juan Nepomuceno Rodríguez de San Miguel, *Reforma del clero, o sean declamaciones sobre su corrupcion y sus riquezas* (1848; repr. Morelia: I. Arango, 1856), 10 pages.

23. Members of this group were also responsible for the creation of the Mexican edition of the *Diccionario Universal de Historia y Geografía*, published in 1853. Pesado contributed a number of articles to this work, including an important study on the conservative hero, the ex-Emperor Agustín Iturbide. Roa Bárcena, *Biografía*, 86–88; and Perales Ojeda, *Las asociaciones literarias mexicanas*, 46–48. Segura was a literary disciple of Pesado, as well as his son-in-law.

24. A journalist, novelist, and historian as well as a poet, Roa Bárcena was still an active man of letters when he died in 1908. He wrote his biography of Pesado in 1873. See John Hays Hammond, "José María Roa Bárcena: Mexican Writer and Champion of Catholicism," *The Americas* 6, no. 1 (July 1949): 45–55.

25. Barbara Tennenbaum suggests that the contributors to *La Cruz* read "like a 'who's who' of the Conservative Party." Barbara A. Tennenbaum, "Development and Sovereignty," 79n9.

26. Ricardo Couto, *José Bernardo Couto* (Veracruz: Editorial Citlaltepetl, 1961), 18. Other writers have also commented on the friendship between Pesado, Couto, and Carpio. In 1849, Pesado published a collection of Carpio's poems. After his death in 1860, Couto wrote Carpio's biography.

27. For an analysis of the relationship between Couto and Pesado, see Andrea Acle Aguirre, "Amigos y Alliados: José Bernardo Couto (1803-1862) y José Joaquín Pesado (1801–1861)," *Historia Mexicana* 61, no. 1 (2011): 163–230.

28. Acle Aguirre, "Amigos y Alliados," 192–95.

29. Roa Bárcena, *Biografía*, 92.

30. "A nuestros suscritores," *La Cruz* 1, no. 20 (March 13, 1856): 643.

31. Roa Bárcena, *Biografía*, 93.

32. José María Roa Bárcena, trans., "Influencia de las órdenes religiosas en las sociedades y necesidad de su restablecimiento en Francia, por el abate Clemente Grandcour," *La Cruz* 1, no. 2 (November 8, 1855): 49 to 3, no. 8 (September 25, 1856): 237 passim.

33. For a literary analysis of the aesthetic strategy employed in this section, see Sergio Gutiérrez Negrón, "Estética, polémica y Dios: aestesis teológica en el semanario mexicano *La Cruz (1855–1858)*," in *Sensibilidades conservadores: el debate cultural sobre la civilización en América Latina y España durante el Siglo XIX*, ed. Kari Soriano Salkjelsvik (Madrid: Iberoamericana, 2021), 353–72.

34. José Maria Roa Bárcena, *La Quinta Modelo* (Mexico City: Instituto Nacional de Bellas Artes, 1984).

35. "[*La Quinta Modelo*] is a story of good (those who defend tradition) and evil (those who accept new ideas), in an open critique of the liberals that took part in the Constitution of 1857." Begoña Arteta, "José María Roa Bárcena," in *En busca de un discurso integrado de la nación, 1848–1884*, ed. Antonia Pi-Suñer Llorens (Mexico City: Universidad Nacional Autónoma de México, 1996), 242. See also Rafael Olea Franco, "*La Quinta Modelo* de Roa Bárcena en el debate cultural," in *México durante la Guerra de Reforma*, vol. 2, *Contextos, prácticas culturales, imaginarios y representaciones*, ed. Celia del Palacio Montiel (Xalapa, MX: Universidad Veracruzana, 2011), 289–309.

36. In the novel, Gaspar also displays a borrowed copy of the works of the French socialist, Henri-François-Alphonse Esquiros, whose *L'évangile du peuple* (1840) depicted Jesus as a social reformer.

37. Because of its comedic depictions, "the novel may be justly termed the *Don Quijote* of liberalism." Hammond, "José María Roa Bárcena," 51.

38. Since Roa Bárcena's novel was republished in its entirety in 1870, it has been misidentified as a reaction to the pro-Reforma novel *El Monedero* (The counterfeiter), which also includes a utopian experiment, published by Nicolás Pizarro in 1861. However, since *La Quinta Modelo* was already serialized by *La Cruz* in 1857, *El Monedero* was probably influenced by Roa Bárcena's novel instead. See Maria Eugenia García Ugarte, *Poder político y religioso*, 1:633n1786. For an analysis of *El Monedero* and its utopian community ("New Philadelphia"), see Jaime Javier Rodríguez, *The Literatures of the U.S.-Mexican War*, 182–206.

39. *Diccionario Porrúa: Historia, biografía, y geografía de México*, 6th ed., s.v. "Cruz (La)."

40. Most newspapers in Mexico provided weekly liturgical calendars and schedules of important religious services at this time.

41. According to Brading, the neo-classical taste and reaction against baroque extravagance was not unique to liberal reformers. "In the nineteenth-century, when the ultramontane clergy sought to revive the Catholic Church, they retained many of the attitudes toward popular religion already manifest among the so-called Jansenists." This

included denunciation of "miracle-mongering, the pilgrimages and the alms-giving associated with the popular cult of holy images." Brading, *Mexican Phoenix*, 218.

42. This is not to suggest that there was a conscious chasm between elite and popular Catholicism in Mexico. In his monumental work on the English Reformation, Eamon Duffy has warned against the use of the term "popular religion," "a term laden with questionable assumptions about the nature of *non-popular* religion and the gap between the two." He prefers the word "traditional" to denote "the general character of a religious culture which was rooted in a repertoire of inherited and shared beliefs and symbols, while remaining capable of enormous flexibility and variety." Eamon Duffy, *The Stripping of the Altars: Traditional Religion in England 1400–1580* (New Haven, CT: Yale University Press, 1992), 3. Similarly, David Cahill questions the utility of an "official verses informal, popular versus elite" dichotomy. His description of Corpus Christi processions in colonial Peru shows that "elites and underclasses mimicked one another" in religious activity. David Cahill, "Popular Religion and Appropriation: The Example of Corpus Christi in Eighteenth-Century Cuzco," *Latin American Research Review* 31, no. 2 (1996): 100. Likewise, William Taylor doubts that a "radical separation between rural and urban or popular and elite" religious mentalities played a role in Mexico before the Reforma. Taylor, *Shrines and Miraculous Images*, 205. Edward Wright-Rios's study of Oaxaca in the later nineteenth century also does not show "a perpetual standoff" between popular religion and the institutional church. Rather, "it reveals ongoing processes of interaction and negotiation *within* the church." Wright-Rios, *Revolutions in Mexican Catholicism*, 7.

43. In addition, at times its articles were reprinted in other conservative journals such as *La Verdad* or *El Omnibus*.

44. "A nuestros suscritores," *La Cruz* 2, no. 20 (July 31, 1856): 652.

45. Vigil, *La Reforma*, 72, 88, 106. The reference to "long articles" suggests that Vigil was thinking in particular of *La Cruz*.

46. Justo Sierra, *Evolución política*, 280.

47. This play presented very unflattering portraits of thirteen characters that its author considered the most influential members of the conservative party. *La Sociedad de los trece; ó, los conservadores por dentro: juguete cómico en un acto* [The society of the thirteen; or, the conservatives from the inside: comic play in one act] (Mexico City, 1859), 24 pages. As part of its satire, the play was falsely attributed to Mucio Valdovinos, a priest and sometime contributor to *La Cruz*, and pretended to have been published on the presses of Vicente Segura Argüelles, the conservative publisher. Both men appeared, along with Pesado, Munguía, and Alexis de Gabriac, as members of the "conservative lodge."

48. *Reglamento de la sociedad conservadora de las garantías sociales* (n.p: 1859), 24 pages. This document was alleged to have been written by Manuel Bonilla. It was reprinted, along with annotations and commentary, by liberals who claimed to have "discovered" it.

49. Many twentieth-century writers have also identified the newspaper with the conservative political party. According to Scholes, "*La Cruz* was undoubtedly the most intelligent conservative publication of the period and Pesado, who did a great deal of writing for it, took extremely intelligent positions." Scholes, *Mexican Politics*, 18n36.

According to Ruiz Castañeda, "In spite of its subtitle ["Exclusively Religious Periodical"], *La Cruz* can and ought to be studied as a political publication, given that it took part in the most heated debates and counts among its editors political writers as effective as Munguía and Pesado. *La Cruz* was the periodical of the conservatives and had as its program the defense of the Catholic religion from assaults of liberalism and impiety, which they connected; since reforming politics assumed such a highly religious color, there is nothing strange that the articles of this weekly, wanting to direct themselves only to religion, should also take on a political shade." Ruiz Castañeda, *Periodismo político*, 91–92. On the other hand, Covo suggests that the journal managed to avoid most political issues. "*La Cruz* cleverly situated itself in the theological terrain, where polemics could only occur with difficulty, given that its chief editor, the irascible Bishop Munguía, rejected the ideological presuppositions that constitute the basis of liberalism, the primacy of reason over authority." Covo, *Las ideas de la Reforma*, 178.

50. "Prospecto," *La Cruz* 1, no. 1 (November 1, 1856): 1–3.

51. "Errores de la filosofía sobre la existencia de Dios y su divina naturaleza," *La Cruz* 2, no. 3 (April 3, 1856): 80.

52. "Errores dominantes," *La Cruz* 1, no. 1 (November 1, 1855): 11.

53. Roa Bárcena, *Biografía*, 93. Similar charges were leveled against other conservative newspapers as well. Liberals claimed that the articles of *La Verdad* must have been written by "some of those false ministers of Christ." "Clero farisaico," *El Monitor Republicano*, October 12, 1855. The editors of *La Patria* were called "whitened sepulchers" and it was said that their newspaper "every day reveals more of the cassock that it wears under its clothes." "La Patria," *El Monitor Republicano*, October 30, 1855.

54. This was the *Ley Lafragua*, that took effect on January 1, 1856. Previously, most articles and pamphlets were published anonymously, which probably contributed to the lack of civility in the partisan press.

55. "A nuestros suscritores," *La Cruz* 2, no. 20 (July 31, 1856): 652.

56. "Esposición," *La Cruz* 1, no. 1 (November 1, 1856): 3–11.

57. "Errores dominantes," *La Cruz* 1, no. 1 (November 1, 1855): 11–15. In the next issue of the magazine, clerical shortcomings were again blamed on the corruption of the wider society. How, it asked, could the head possibly be healthy when the social body was eaten by worms? "How the people are, so are the priests." "El poder teocratico," *La Cruz* 1, no. 2 (November 8, 1855): 46.

58. "El poder teocratico," *La Cruz* 1, no. 2 (November 8, 1855): 41–48.

59. *La Cruz* also explained the offending articles as fulfillment of Jesus's prophecy that, like himself, his disciples would be persecuted. Among other texts, they quoted John 15:21: "But all these things they will do to you because of and for HATRED of my name, *because they do not know him who sent me.*" The word "hatred" was also placed between two manicules (pointing fingers) for emphasis.

60. "El poder teocratico," *La Cruz* 1, no. 4 (November 22, 1855): 109–16. The French Revolution had also been praised by Guillermo Prieto in his speech in Mexico City the day before Cruz-Aedo's discourse.

61. The followers of Donatus were North African Christians who separated from the Catholic Church in 312. The Donatist controversy first arose over the question of the

readmission of church members who had committed apostasy during the Roman persecutions. (The Donatists required re-baptism in these cases.) Later, the Donatists denied the validity of any sacraments celebrated by priests in a state of sin. This position was rejected by Catholics, who held that "the unworthiness of Christ's ministers does not hinder the effect of the sacraments." In the fifth century, St. Augustine wrote prolifically against the Donatist sect. In the sixteenth century, the Council of Trent declared, "If anyone says, that a minister, being in mortal sin . . . neither effects, nor confers the sacraments; let him be anathema." Canon 12 of the "Decree on the Sacraments" (March 3, 1547) in J. Waterworth, trans., *The Canons and Decrees of the Sacred and Oecumenical Council of Trent* (London: C. Dolman, 1848), 55.

62. "El poder teocratico," *La Cruz* 1, no. 2 (November 8, 1855): 48.

63. For Morales as the consummate liberal Catholic, see Rubén Ruiz Guerra, "Los dilemas de la conciencia: Juan Bautista Morales y su defensa liberal de la iglesia," in *Historia de la Iglesia en el Siglo XIX*, ed. Manuel Ramos Medina (Mexico City: Centro de Estudios de Historia de México Condumex, 1998), 411–22.

64. Ruiz Castañeda states that because of interest in the debate, all the contemporary periodicals grouped themselves around either Morales or Pesado, "by which the polemic was prolonged a long time, absorbing the interest of society." Although she dates the beginning of the polemic from the first response by *La Cruz*, this occurred on November 29, 1855, not 1856 as she indicates. Ruiz Castañeda, *Periodismo politico,* 94.

65. Vincente Rocafuerte, *Ensayo sobre tolerancia religiosa por el ciudadano,* 2nd ed. (México City: Martin Rivera, 1831), 15–16, 80. Morales's refutation was printed as J. B. M., *Disertacion contra la tolerancia religioso* (Mexico City: Galvan, 1831), 59 pages.

66. Juan Batista Morales, "Estado de la República," *El Siglo Diez y Nueve,* October 6, 1855. Ignacio Cumplido published this newspaper under various incarnations from 1841–45. When it resumed publication in 1848 after the war with the US, it was directed by the eighteen-year-old Fransisco Zarco, who attacked, "with the zeal of a missionary, the fundamental problem of forming a public opinion favorable to liberalism." It soon became the most important liberal periodical in Mexico, and Zarco one of the foremost champions of liberalism during the Reforma. Raymond C. Wheat, *Francisco Zarco: El portavoz liberal de la Reforma* (Mexico City: Editorial Porrúa, 1957), 63.

67. Thomas Babington Macaulay, *The History of England from the Accession of James II,* 5 vols. (London: Longman, Brown, Green, and Longmans, 1848).

68. "Inseparable from the liberal admiration of the economic institutions of the United States was the prospect of a protectorate of that country over Mexico." Olliff, *Reforma Mexico,* 24. As Vigil recalled, in the fall of 1855 there was a rumor that "the leaders of the revolution had signed a treaty with the United States, in virtue of which Mexico would be established as an American protectorate." See Vigil, *La Reforma,* 72. One liberal newspaper called this "gross calumny used by conservatives and agitators to spread alarm." "Otra calumnia," *El Siglo Diez y Nueve,* September 20, 1855.

69. Olliff notes that liberal newspapers regularly praised the economic progress of England, Belgium, and the United States. But developments in the United States were usually seen as "more plausible models for Mexico." Olliff, *Reforma Mexico,* 23.

70. Charles de Montalembert, *Du Devoir des Catholiques dans la Question de la Liberté d'Enseignement* (Paris: Au bureau de l'Univers, 1843).

71. In a reply to *La Cruz*, Morales explained that he was referring to Italy, Spain, and Mexico, but not France, in his original criticism of "Catholic countries."

72. "El catolicsmo y los sacerdotes: un articulo de Sr. D. J. B. M.," *La Cruz* 1, no. 5 (November 29, 1855): 129–44.

73. Jaime Luciano Balmes, *El protestantismo comparado con el catolicismo en sus relaciones con la civilización europea*, 4 vols. (Barcelona, Antonio Brusi: 1844). An edition of this book was also published in Mexico City on the presses of Rafael y Rafael in 1846. Pope Leo XIII described Balmes as "the foremost political talent of the nineteenth century and one of the greatest in the history of political writers." This work, in particular, constitutes both a philosophy of history and a basic sociology of Catholic influence on society. See G. Fraile, "Balmes, Jaime Luciano," in *The New Catholic Encyclopedia*, 2nd ed. (Detroit: Gale Group, 2003), 2:32–33. Balmes was even quoted in the *Diálogo entre Martin y Juan Diego*, published in 1855 in response to Cruz-Aedo's speech.

74. "Los paises catolicos y los paises protestantes," *La Cruz*, 1, no. 10 (January 3, 1856): 307–13.

75. "Tres proposiciones del Señor Don Juan Bautista Morales," *La Cruz* 1, 15 (February 7, 1856); 457–69.

76. Pesado took this material from Giovanni Perrone, SJ, *Il Protestantsimo e la regola di fede* (Turin, Italy: Giacinto Marietti, 1854).

77. "This Protestantism, the religion of the 'I,' has produced in England the most monstrous egoism. But of the egoism of the rich has been born the misery and stupidity of the poor; in that classic country of culture, the story of the impoverished family should be written with tears of blood." Pesado quoted this material from Jean Guame, *Histoire de la societé domestique chez tous les peoples anciens et modernes, ou influence du Christianisme sur la famille*, 2 vols. (Paris: Guame freres, 1844).

78. José Joaquin Pesado, "Tres proposiciones del Señor Don Juan Bautista Morales," *La Cruz* 1, no. 17 (February 21, 1856): 521–31.

79. "Attacks on religion" was interpreted to mean only assaults on defined dogmas, but ecclesiastical structures, personnel, or practices were still fair game. Conservatives frequently complained that the law was selectively applied against them and that attacks on the Church were never punished. See Zamacois, *Historia de Méjico*, 14:150–52, 224.

CHAPTER FOUR

1. The most significant of these was a revolt in Querétaro lead by Tomás Mejía and two other generals. They issued the Plan of Toliman on December 2, 1855. Davis and Virulegio, *The Political Plans of Mexico*, 518–20.

2. Vigil, *La Reforma*, 91.

3. Prieto, *Memorias de mis tiempos*, 2:243–45.

4. Alexis de Gabriac's entry for December 11, 1855. Díaz López, *Versión francesa de México*, 1:237.

5. "Desordenes," *El Siglo Diez y Nueve*, December 11, 1855; "La Situación" and "Los Sucesos de Lunes," *El Omnibus*, December 12 and 13, 1855. See also Zamacois, *Historia de Méjico*, 14:133.

6. Recorded by Ignacio Aguilar y Marocho on December 12, 1855. Aguilar y Marocho (1813–1884) was an important conservative lawyer, journalist, and politician. He was also a former classmate and close friend of Bishop Munguía and held very strong Catholic opinions. In the 1840s and 1850s he held a number of political posts in Michoacán and San Luis Potosí and served as interior minister in Santa Anna's final cabinet. After the triumph of the Ayutla Revolution he was involved in conservative conspiracies and was persecuted by the liberal government. He also wrote a number of famous satires mocking the liberal regime. His *Primer calendario de la familia enferma para el año bisiesto de 1860* was published under a pseudonym in 1860. It contained a "diary of the sickness" of the Mexican family as well as humorous "recommended remedies." Most importantly, the diary contained a meticulous record of daily events in the republic from 1854 to 1859. Although the entries were often sarcastic, their accuracy has been confirmed by comparison with alternative sources. This work, therefore, provides an important, if highly partisan, alternative chronology of this period. Ignacio Aguilar y Marocho, *La familia enferma*, (1860; repr., Mexico City: Editorial Jus, 1960), 36. Also see José Roberto Juárez, review of *La famila enferma*, by Ignacio Aguilar y Marocho, *Hispanic American Historical Review* 51, no. 2 (May 1971): 367–68. For the origin and use of the term "sick family" as a metaphor for the liberal state in Mexico, see Ty West, "La familia enferma: el liberalismo como enfermedad (México, 1857–1864)," in *Sensibilidades conservadores: el debate cultural sobre la civilización en América Latina y España durante el Siglo XIX*, ed. Kari Soriano Salkjelsvik (Madrid: Iberoamericana, 2021), 189–213.

7. "Falsedades," *El Monitor Republicano*, December 13, 1855.

8. The National Rite Freemasons "did not look on favorably" on the lack of *puros* in the new administration. Zalce y Rodriguez, *Apuntes para la historia*, 181. Comonfort's cabinet consisted of: Luis de la Rosa (foreign relations), Ezequiel Montes (justice, ecclesiastical affairs and public education), Manuel Silicio (public works), José María Lafragua (interior), Manuel Payno (treasury), and José María Yáñez (war).

9. "El motin en Puebla" and "El motin de Puebla," *El Siglo Diez y Nueve*, December 14 and 19, 1855; and "Criminal asonada en Puebla," *El Monitor Republicano*, December 15, 1855.

10. Bishop Labastida's statement was published on flyers "in giant letters" on December 13 and circulated around the city. See Bazant, *Antonio Haro y Tamariz*, 103. It read: "Notice to the People: I assure you that the supreme governor of this state does not intend nor has tried anything against my person. On the contrary, I am presently in the greatest harmony with him and I am very confident that he desires nothing *against me or against the Church*, of which he has given all manner of guarantees. Therefore, there is no motive for alarm nor for these disturbances." Reprinted in "Aviso al Pueblo," *El Siglo Diez y Nueve*, December 15, 1855.

11. Vigil recorded "some losses." Vigil, *La Reforma*, 99. In his diary entry for December 20, 1855, Malo claimed that more than one hundred people were killed before order was

restored. Malo, *Diario de sucesos notables*, 2:442. Liberal newspaper reports also mentioned that Güitián's force had been diminished by the melee.

12. Perhaps Father Ortega fell under the influence of Francisco Javier Miranda during the former's temporary assignment to the *Sagrario* in Puebla. This association might explain his radical action in Zacapoaxtla. However, the actual motives for the Zacapoaxtla rebellion are obscure and its composition complex. It was connected to and later co-opted by non-clerical political interest groups, which raises important questions about its ultimate religious character. However, the liberal press always blamed Ortega for the revolt. For example, see "El clero y las revoluciones de Mexico," *El Tribuno del Pueblo*, September 23, 1856. Here, the "patricidal hand" of the priest of Zacapoaxtla was said to have been armed to start the revolution and "drench with blood the people of the countryside of Montero and the streets of Puebla."

13. The start of revolt is usually dated December 12, when the manifesto was signed, but it was already being reported in Mexico City on December 10. "Zacapoastla" [*sic*], *El Siglo Diez y Nueve*, December 10, 1855.

14. The congregation of representatives from across the district and the simultaneous pronouncements in neighboring villages suggest that the rebellion was planned well in advance. Clearly, the elevation of Comonfort had no effect on the decision to rebel. See Bazant, *Antonio Haro y Tamariz*, 107; Guy P. C. Thomson, "La contrareforma en Puebla, 1854–1886," in *El conservadurismo mexicano en el siglo XIX (1810–1910)*, ed. Humberto Morales and William Fowler (Puebla: Benemérita Universidad Autónoma de Puebla, 1999), 249–51.

15. "El General Güitián," *El Siglo Diez y Nueve*, December 20, 1855.

16. Florencia Mallon interprets the Plan of Zacapoaxtla as "an attempt by conservative regional notables to put together a counterdiscourse tying land issues to an anti-liberal agenda." For the multitude of peasant participants, she believes, "religion was simply an entry point to an entire articulation that connected political independence and participation to control of land, labor, and revenue and finally to general questions of conflict over power." Since religious issues disappeared from subsequent modifications of the plan, and all versions were focused entirely on national issues, however, it is not entirely clear how this particular discourse served as "an entry point" to local power struggles and land disputes. In any event, the *perceived* significance of the revolt for both liberals and conservatives is its most important aspect. Basing her conclusion on liberal interpretations of the revolt, Mallon concludes that, "the clergy's clear conspiratorial role made it difficult for liberals in positions of power to be sympathetic regarding any aspect of religion." The basic non-religious motives of the "subaltern" participants would not have been obvious to liberal commentators, she explains, since they confused the mundane function of ritual in "local political culture" with an intellectual adherence to the Catholic faith. Mallon, *Peasant and Nation*, 91–98.

17. Labastida alluded to this fear in a letter to the government written on February 3, 1856. See "Contestación del obispo del Puebla" in Zamacois, *Historia de Méjico*, 14:929–37. If this was actually the intention of Father Ortega y García, he might have fancied himself another Hidalgo. See Bazant, *Antonio Haro y Tamariz*, 120–21.

18. The letters are reproduced in Vigil, *La Reforma*, 101. See also García Ugarte, *Poder político y religioso*, 1:525–26.

19. [Maximilian of Hapsburg], *Los traidores pintados por si mismos. Libro secreto de Maximiliano, en que aparece la idea que tenía de sus servidores* (Mexico City: Imprenta del Gobierno, 1867), 22.

20. Anselmo de la Portilla, *Méjico en 1856 y 1857: Gobierno de General Comonfort* (New York: S. Hallet, 1858), 33. Speaking of Labastida, another contemporary also wrote, "although young, enlightenment, modesty, love of neighbor, and a benevolence without limits was recognized in him; he was a well-beloved father to members of his diocese, a true pastor of the flock of Jesus Christ." From the papers of Juan de la Portilla, quoted in Antonio Carrion, *Historia de la Ciudad de Puebla de los Angeles* (Puebla: Colegio Salesiano, 1897), 2:439.

21. Davis and Virulegio, *The Political Plans of Mexico*, 524–26. The plan presented by Father Ortega y García on December 12 mistakenly called for a return to the centralist Constitution of 1836. This historical slippage was corrected in the amplified and reformed version of the plan issued by the generals on December 17. Bazant, *Antonio Haro y Tamariz*, 102–7.

22. Besides General Güitián, Generals Luis Osollo and Juan Olloqui also revolted in the Zacapoaxtla district. Lt. Col. Miguel Miramón revolted with his battalion in Tlatalu-quitepec. Apparently, Güitan suggested adding the motto "For religion and *fueros*" to the plan and Olloqui agreed. But Miramón and Osollo objected and it was omitted. See Ramón Sánchez Flores, *Zacapoaxtla: República de indios y villa de españoles*, 2nd ed. (Zacapoaxtla, MX: Edición del XIV Distrito Local Electoral, 1984), 130.

23. Vigil, *La Reforma*, 101.

24. General Ignacio de la Llave y Segura Zevallos (1818–1863) was a veteran of the US-Mexican War. His older sister, Luz María de la Llave (1804–1840), married Pesado in 1822. After her death, Pesado married Juana Segura Argüelles in 1842. The thirty-six-year-old general was a dedicated liberal from his youth and declared for the Revolution of Ayutla on July 7, 1855. He later became the governor of the State of Veracruz and was killed near Guanajuato in 1863. His biography is contained in a special commemorative issue of the Veracruz journal *Revista Jarocha*. Leonardo Pasquel, "Numero dedicado al General Ignacio de la Llave en el primer Centenario de su muerte: 1863–1963," *Revista Jarocha*, 5, no. 25 (June 1963): 3–27.

25. "La reaccion," *El Siglo Diez y Nueve*, December 29, 1855. The newspaper called this "a criminal defection" and rejoiced that at least the deserters were not able to carry away the cannons.

26. On January 4 Aguilar y Marocho recorded the deportation of eighteen persons and the imprisonment "of many others as a precaution." Aguilar y Marocho, *La familia enferma*, 37.

27. At first the liberal press denied that he had defected and characterized the rumor as an insult to the "disciplined and loyal troops" under his command. Once the "scandalous defection" was confirmed, it condemned the general as a perverse, disloyal traitor who "sold his honor and military reputation for thirty pieces of silver." This "criminal act," one writer argued, also demonstrated that the unreformed part of the

military, a "gangrenous limb," still needed to be amputated. "Falsos Rumores" and "Escandalosa Defeccion," *El Siglo Diez y Nueve,* January 14 and 16, 1856.

28. Zamacois, *Historia de Méjico,* 14:166. Vigil was familiar with this charge, which he deemed "a puerile pretext." Vigil, *La Reforma,* 105. For Mallon, religion served not only as "the point of articulation downward, toward processes of hegemonic politics," but also as "a point of articulation that led sideways to the military institution," since both the Church and the military were targets of liberal attacks. The first Plan of Zacapoaxtla had denounced the "persecution of the two most respected classes of society, the clergy and the military." According to Mallon, "this helps to explain why during the two months between the original Zacapoaxtla declaration and the formation of a special national army, four different military expeditions sent to the Sierra to repress the rebels all joined them instead, ultimately taking Puebla city." Mallon, *Peasant and Nation,* 96. The absence of explicit language from all subsequent plans devised by the generals, however, suggests that the army did not need religious explanations for its alienation from the government or religious rationales for its actions.

29. Bazant, *Antonio Haro y Tamariz,* 116–17.

30. "Manifiesto del Gral. Luis Osollo, al tomar posesión de Puebla al mando del Ejército Restaurador de la Libertad y el Orden," Puebla, January 23, 1856. Excerpt quoted in Mallon, *Peasant and Nation,* 93.

31. Some historians speculate that had Haro y Tamariz pressed on, the capital and the entire country could have fallen under his control. Bazant, *Antonio Haro y Tamariz,* 115–16. Vigil, however, dismissed this possibility. Vigil, *La Reforma,* 106.

32. Díaz López, *Versión Francesa de México,* 1:248-49.

33. Although recruitment was officially voluntary, Zamacois claims that the levy was coercive and highly unpopular. Zamacois, *Historia de Méjico,* 14:168. A large part of the new force was created by a recall of the national guard mustered out after the fall of Santa Anna. Mallon, who sees in the national guard a kind of liberal "communitarian" alternative to conservative populism, states, "When the Liberal government was finally able to repress the Conservative Puebla revolution in March 1856, it was only with an army formed expressly for that purpose and composed mainly of national guard rather than regular army soldiers." Mallon, *Peasant and Nation,* 96.

34. The editor of Malo's diary, Mariano Cuevas, suggests that the archbishop made a mistake in accepting this invitation, since "he supported the Catholic party." Rather, this incident suggests that the divisions between the Church and the government were not yet fixed at this stage. Malo, *Diario de sucesos notables,* 2:445. Alternatively, Marta Eugenia García Ugarte argues that the archbishop's behavior reflects a generational divide. At 70 years of age, Archbishop Lázaro Garza y Ballesteros was the oldest member of the Mexican hierarchy, while Bishop Labastida was the youngest. She holds that the difference in outlook and tensions between the two prelates were reflected in their responses to the revolt as well as the religious rites celebrated for Comonfort's troops in Mexico City. García Ugarte, *Poder político y religioso,* 1:450–52, 540.

35. Francisco Zarco, *Historia del congreso extraordinario constituyente (1856–1857)* (Mexico City: El Colegio de México, 1956), 30–32.

36. See "Ocotlán, Battle of (1856)," in David F. Marley, *Mexico at War: From the Struggle for Independence to the 21st-Century Drug Wars* (Santa Barbara, CA: ABC-CLIO, 2014), 267–69. Comonfort personally commanded the 10,000 troops that marched on Puebla on March 23. The government forces at the final siege are estimated to have contained 14,000 to 16,000 men. The rebel army numbered about 4,000.

37. The French ambassador wrote: "News arrived yesterday of the surrender of Puebla. We cannot believe it. All the world was saying that the rumors of victory, spread by the government, were completely false." Díaz López, *Versión francesa de México*, 1:259.

38. The terms of the capitulation appear in Vigil, *La Reforma*, 117–18n2.

39. "La capitulacion," *El Siglo Diez y Nueve*, March 24, 1856.

40. Díaz López, *Versión francesa de México*, 1:264.

41. Decree of Comonfort (March 25, 1856) in Zamacois, *Historia de Méjico*, 14:195–96n1.

42. Among the escaped generals were Luis Osollo and Leonardo Márquez.

43. One famous case involved a federal general who had two brothers in the condemned band. In response to his public appeal for clemency, he was deported from the country. See "Representación del General D. Rómulo de la Vega, respecto de los oficiales hechos prisioneros en Puebla," (April 10, 1856) in Zamacois, *Historia de Méjico*, 14:949–52.

44. Aguilar y Marocho, *La familia enferma*, 40.

45. Although the original sentences were lifted, the officers were still required to leave the country within a specified period of time.

46. Mariano Cuevas interprets this "public opinion" to mean the liberal press. Mariano Cuevas, SJ, *Historia de la Iglesia en Mexico*, 6th ed. (Mexico City: Editorial Porrúa, 1992), 5:286.

47. Decree of Comonfort of March 31, 1856. In Zamacois, *Historia de Méjico*, 14:198–99n1; and Vigil, *La Reforma*, 123–24n1.

48. Guy P. C. Thomson and David LaFrance, *Patriotism, Politics, and Popular Liberalism in Nineteenth-Century Mexico* (Wilmington, DE: Scholarly Resources, 1999), 49.

49. Díaz López, *Versión francesa de México*, 265, 269.

50. This discourse is quoted in Vigil, *La Reforma*, 121–22.

51. "Reparacion! Justicia!" and "Pueblo y su Obispo," *El Siglo Diez y Nueve*. April 2, 1856. Apparently, however, even liberals were surprised by Comonfort's decree, since just the day before the same paper had reprinted an article from Veracruz insisting that rumors of the confiscation of clerical property were conservative lies intended to enflame fanaticism. "Manejos de los Reaccionarios," *El Signo Diez y Nueve*, April 1, 1856.

52. Díaz López, *Versión francesa de México*, 271.

53. Reported by Gabriac on April 11, 1856. Díaz López, *Versión francesa de México*, 272.

54. From the papers of Juan de la Portilla, quoted in Carrion, *Historia de la Ciudad*, 2:439–40. On April 10, 1856, Labastida lodged a formal complaint with the governor about the behavior of Duque Estrada and his men. His letter, and the governor's reply, can be found in Zamacois, *Historia de Méjico*, 14:939–43. The non-cooperation of the bishop and the use of troops to maintain order was also reported in the liberal press. "Puebla," *El Heraldo*, April 5, 1856. Reprinted in *El Siglo Diez y Nueve*, April 10, 1856.

55. Aguilar y Marocho defined the intervention decree as a license for officials "to stick in their hands up to the elbow and take whatever they could." Aguilar y Marocho, *La familia enferma*, 39.

56. Letter of Pelagio Antonio de Labastida y Dávilos to Ignacio Comonfort (April 1, 1856) in Zamacois, *Historia de Méjico*, 14:945–47. In this letter, Labastida also referred to the president's previous attempt to extort 70,000 pesos from the diocese "to avoid scandal." Apparently, the bishop had offered the government a loan of 10,000 instead, but this was rejected. He therefore recognized the new punitive decree as the result of these failed negotiations.

57. Gabriac entry for April 11, 1856. Díaz López, *Versión francesa de México*. 272. According to reports by Juan de la Portilla, Comonfort replaced the moderate Ibarra y Ramos on April 11 because he was not aggressive enough to enforce the decree. Carrion, *Historia de la Ciudad*, 2:428–29.

58. See "Contestacion del obispo de Puebla al gobierno," (February 3, 1856) and "Esposicion del obispo de Puebla," (April 5, 1856) in Zamacois, *Historia de Méjico*, 14:911–37.

59. Quoted in Zamacois, 14:207. In spite of liberal accusations, history has exonerated Bishop Labastida from any part in the revolt.

60. Vigil, *La Reforma*, 134.

61. The bishop had already admitted that "some Capuchin nuns gave crosses to soldiers that asked for them."

62. As evidence supporting Montes's claim, Vigil's history includes two notices, published during the government siege of Puebla, for public novenas to the Virgin of Guadalupe, asking for peace for the nation and "divine assistance in the public calamities that surround and threaten us." Vigil, *La Reforma*, 126n1. These same novenas were first published in the liberal press in 1856. "Devocion de los reaccionarios," *El Siglo Diez y Nueve*, April 1, 1856. If these events had included explicit prayers for a conservative victory, they were at least not advertised.

63. Letter of Ezequiel Montes to the Bishop of Puebla, (April 16, 1856), in Zamacois, *Historia de Méjico*, 14:881–96. This treatise was based on a collection of texts from Church history and law that had been compiled by José María Luis Mora to justify confiscations in the 1830s. Labastida recognized the document's origin and easily refuted its claims. *La Cruz* also published an exposé of the mistranslated fragments and deletions that it contained. Alejandro Ortega, "Testos del los Santos Padres," *La Cruz* 2, no. 11 (May 29, 1856): 357–60.

64. Zamacois, *Historia de Méjico*, 14:921.

65. Vigil, *La Reforma*, 125.

66. Comment by Gabriac on May 18, 1856. Díaz López, *Versión francesa de México*, 1:281.

67. Aguilar y Marocho, *La familia enferma*, 42.

68. On other hand, Comonfort exempted La Soledad Convent from confiscations because the sisters had nursed federal soldiers in their hospital after the siege of Puebla. García Ugarte, *Poder político y religioso*, 1:553–54, 595. However, the nuns later renounced their exemption in solidarity with the other religious communities that suffered the full force of the government's punitive measures. See "Puebla," *La Cruz* 2, no. 12 (June 5, 1856): 392.

69. "Documentos relativos a la intervencion de los bienes eclesiásticos en el obispado de Puebla," *La Cruz* 2, no. 8 (May 10, 1856): 3.

70. On April 14, 1856, Malo recorded the closure in his diary: "The newspaper *La Patria* was suspended for having published the answer of the Bishop of Puebla to the government about the intervention of clerical property. Under the rule of 'liberty' there is more tyranny than in the time of General Santa Anna." Malo, *Diario de sucesos notables*, 2:455.

71. Zamacois, *Historia de Méjico*, 14:216–17.

72. In his dispatch for May 1, 1856, Gabriac reported, "The periodicals have published part of the correspondence between the minister of justice, Ezequiel Montes, a young rhetorician gifted with more philosophical pretensions than true wisdom, and Mons. Labastida, whose logic, from the point of view of ecclesiastical law, has overcome without difficulty the arguments of the *puro* government." Díaz López, *Versión francesa de México*, 275–6. On the other hand, Francisco Zarco wrote that "Sr. Montes defended the authority of the secular power in a brilliant and incontestable manner and justified the intervention measures with reasons taken from the same councils and the support of the opinions of the holy fathers." Francisco Zarco, "La intervencion de los bienes del clero del Puebla," *El Siglo Diez y Nueve*, April 27, 1856.

73. The remark was reported by *El Heraldo*, which claimed that the bishop was trying to provoke another civil war. This article was then reprinted by other liberal newspapers. For example: "Noticias de Puebla," *El Monitor Republicano*, May 13, 1856. There were even rumors that the bishop had ordered his clergy to preach open rebellion against the government. See Vigil, *La Reforma*, 136. Ignacio Álvarez, another contemporary historian, claimed that what the bishop really said was that "Catholic priests are the guardians of the treasure of the Faith; and that in order to preserve it they ought to be willing to shed the last drop of their blood." Álvarez, *Revolucion de la Reforma*, 135.

74. According to Aguilar y Marocho, "Many ecclesiastics who lamented this occurrence were imprisoned, for whoever manifested sentiments against the departure of their prelate was judged to be a conspirator." Aguilar y Marocho, *La familia enferma*, 40.

75. José J. Gonzalez, "Mas sobre el destierro del Senor Obisop de Puebla," *El Monitor Republicano*, May 16, 1856.

76. Reprinted in Zamacois, *Historia de Méjico*, 14:965–78. García Ugarte argues that the showdown between Comonfort and Labastida was a primarily a personal affair, and that the bishop's arrest and exile was merely because "he was on obstacle on Comonfort's road." García Ugarte, *Poder político y religioso*, 1:538–39, 563.

77. The petition also expressed *poblano* opposition to the introduction of religious tolerance in Mexico, an issue being debated in the constituent congress at this time. "Representacion que muchos vecinos de Puebla elevaron al presidente de la república, pidiendo que se revocara la órden de destierro contra el obispo." (n.d., n.p.) Reproduced (without signatures) in Zamacois, *Historia de Méjico*, 14:979–84. Juan de la Portilla also described the city as "presenting an aspect of grief" after Labastida's arrest. Quoted in Carrion, *Historia de la Ciudad*, 2:439. For an accounting of the financial impact of the interventions, see García Ugarte, *Poder político y religioso*, 1:569–79.

78. This comment was made by Anselmo de la Portilla, Comonfort's friend and biographer, who added, "[Labastida] believed that he fulfilled his duty; but the government undoubtedly fulfilled its duty as well." Portilla, *Méjico en 1856 and 1857.* 34.

79. Vigil, *La Reforma*, 138.

80. The work, rediscovered only in 1678, was translated into Spanish for *La Cruz* by a woman identified only as "la señorita Doña C.P.," probably Pesado's daughter. Lactancio, "Tratado de la muerte de los perseguidores de la Iglesia," *La Cruz* 2, no. 10 (May 22, 1856): 322 to 2, no. 20 (July 31, 1856: 648 passim. The serialization continued in the following eight issues. For a Latin-English parallel of the complete text, see J. L. Creed, ed. and trans., *Lactantius: De Mortibus Persecutorum* (Oxford: Oxford University Press, 1984).

81. According to the law, all properties held or administered by civil or ecclesiastical corporations would be transferred to those who had rented them, for a value corresponding to the rent that they paid in the present, calculated as interest at 6 percent per year. If the renters were unwilling or unable to buy, the properties would be sold at public auction. Other communal properties, like the *ejidos* held by Indian villages, were also affected by this decree. Because of the difficulty that the government had enforcing the confiscation decree in Puebla, Article 29 of the new law provided for fines and imprisonment for officials who failed to cooperate.

82. The decree can be found in Vigil, *La Reforma*, 150–51n1. Paradoxically, recent scholarship indicates that the liberal economic program was "largely misdirected." Rather than a cause of stagnation, the Church "acted like a modern development bank" and was the main economic engine in nineteenth-century Mexico. The destruction of its economic power therefore resulted in an unforeseen decline in manufacturing and the concentration of land in fewer hands. See Juan Carlos Moreno and Jaime Ros, "Mexico's Market Reforms in Historical Perspective," CEPAL Review 84 (December 2004), 39–40, https://doi.org/10.18356/2ef4odb4-en.

83. Aguilar y Marocho, *La familia enferma*, 41.

84. *Contestacions habidas entre el illmo. Sr. arzobispo de México, Dr. D. Lázaro de la Garza y Ballesteros, y el Exmo. Sr. ministro de justicia, negocios eclesiásticos e instrucción pública, Lic. D. Ezequiel Montes, con motivo de la ley espedida en 25 de junio de 1856, sobre la desamortización de los bienes de la corporaciones civiles y eclesiásticas de la República* (Mexico City: Jose A. Godoy, 1856), 54 pages. For Montes's arguments, see Vigil, *La Reforma*, 159 and García Ugarte, *Poder político y religioso*, 1:593–94.

85. Block letters in the original. This petition was directed to the constituent congress in protest of Article 15, which proposed religious toleration in Mexico. This emphatic statement against the *Ley Lerdo* at the beginning of the document was a response to an article in *Monitor Republicano* that had erroneously boasted that the citizens of this state supported the forced sale. *Representación que hace el vecindario de Querétaro al soberano congreso, para que no sea admitida la tolerancia de cultos propuesta en el proyecto de Constitución.* (Querétaro: Mariano Rodriguez Velazquez, July 1856), 12 pages.

86. See "Desamortizacion eclesiastica," *La Cruz* 3. No. 5 (September 4, 1856): 158.

87. Only the Bishop of Oaxaca, José Agustín Domínguez, did not contribute to the flurry of protests. Brian Connaughton argues that this was the first occasion when Mexican

bishops united to overcome "diocesan regionalism and its differing and disparate reactions to liberalism." Brian Connaughton, "La larga cuesta del conservadurismo mexicano, del disgusto resentido a la propuesta partidaria, 1789–1854," in *El conservadurismo mexicano en el siglo XIX (1810-1910)*, ed. Huberto Morales and William Fowler (Puebla: Benemérita Universidad Autónoma de Puebla, 1999), 180. See also García Ugarte, *Poder político y religioso*, 1:591–601.

88. Munguía would never return to his diocese. See Mijangos y González, *The Lawyer of the Church*, 162–64.

89. Pedro Espinosa y Dávalos, *Protesta del Illmo. Sr. obispo de Guadalajara contra la ley de 25 de junio de 1856* (Guadalajara: n.p., 1856), 16 pages. See also *Comunicaciones cambiadas entre el Excmo. Sr. ministro de Justicia y Negocios Eclesiásticos, y el illmo. Sr. obispo de Guadalajara, con motivo de la Ley de desamortización sancionada en 25 de junio de 1856* (Guadalajara: Rodríguez, 1857), 48 pages.

90. "Protesta del Obispo D. Pelagio Antonio de Labastida sobre un decreto sobre bienes de la Iglesia," in Zamacois, *Historia de Méjico*, 14:1007–23.

91. "Buen Sentido," *El Monitor Republicano*, August 23, 1856. See also García Ugarte, *Poder político y religioso*, 1:598, 602.

92. Because of the large number of pamphlets published by the upper clergy in defense of the Church's position, this period has been identified as the "second moment" in the Church-State conflict described by Rodríguez Piña. He also finds a "relative radicalization of the religious discourse" in this second phase of the conflict. Rodríguez Piña, "La defensa de la iglesia," 77.

93. The injunction issued by the Governor of Chiapas and the reply of Bishop Cárlos M. Colina appeared in "Dos comunicaciones del gobierno de Chiapas," *La Cruz* 3, no. 18 (December 4, 1856): 574–76.

94. Bazant, *Alienation of Church Wealth*, 114.

95. "Ajudicacions de fincas conforme á la ley de desamortizacion," *El Monitor Republicano*, August 23, 1856.

96. At times, buyers obtained Church property for pennies on the peso. See García Ugarte, *Poder político y religioso*, 1:613.

97. Pérez Verdía, *Historia particular*, 2:416. See also Bazant, *Alienation of Church Wealth*, 114.

98. For instance, see "Desamortizacion eclesiastica," *La Cruz* 3, no. 5 (September 4, 1856): 158–59. After the conservative coup in January 1858, the paper also published lists of the names of those who wished to renounce their purchases and restore their reputations now that the religious and political stakes were higher.

99. García Ugarte, *Poder político y religioso*, 1:605, 622, 630.

100. Decorme, *Historia de la Compañia de Jesús*, 2:113–14.

101. García Ugarte, *Poder político y religioso*, 1:603–7.

102. For example, *El Siglo Diez y Nueve* reported a "riot" in Maravatío (Michoacán), which it blamed on the local priest who had dared to read Munguía's pastoral letter the pulpit. "La Reaccion," *El Siglo Diez y Nueve*, September 6, 1856.

103. From a government circular dated October 22, 1856, and quoted in "Nueva circular del gobierno," *La Cruz* 3, no. 14 (November 6, 1856): 446–48. On October 7, 1856,

Ezequiel Montes issued a letter to the nation's bishops, denouncing the "unspeakable conduct of some ecclesiastics, that with their words and their example excite rebellion against the supreme government." Quoted in "Una circular," *La Cruz* 3, no. 11 (October 16, 1856): 351–52. In reply, the Archbishop of Mexico City assured Montes that in person and in writing he had formally charged all the ecclesiastics of his diocese "to stick exclusively to the exercise of their sacred ministry and neither directly nor indirectly to take part or get involved in political matters." Other prelates responded in similar tones, and in some cases recalled parish priests who were known to be politically involved. See Vigil, *La Reforma*, 107.

104. Robert J. Knowlton, *Church Property*, 35–45.

105. For the participation of priests, actual or alleged, in the numerous regional revolts in this period, see García Ugarte, *Poder político y religioso*, 1:617–37.

106. Rivera, *Anales Mexicanos*, 15.

107. Apparently Pantiga had written a letter to the head of the diplomatic corps in order to dissuade foreign nationals from acquiring Church property, since "all the alienation that had been made of Church land was held [by the Church] as null and of no value." Malo, *Diario de sucesos notables*, 2:465.

108. Zamacois, *Historia de Méjico*, 14:304; Aguilar y Marocho, *La familia enferma*, 42–43.

109. Díaz Lopez, *Versión francesa de México*, 1:311.

110. Malo reports that the four Dominicans were placed in a chapel with two other priests and two military men to be shot, but the execution was stayed by a presidential telegram at the last moment. Malo, *Diario de sucesos notables*, 2:467–8. Aguilar y Marocho also reports that the four were joined by two other priests and some other "honorable residents," all of whom were "scandalously abused." Aguilar y Marocho, *La familia enferma*, 44.

111. Comonfort named the new street "Independence Road." The liberal priest, Agustín Rivera, noted that there was no attempt to commemorate "Fray Pedro de Gante, Fray Benardino de Sahagún, Fray Antonio Margil de Jesús [the patron saint of Texas] and the other very illustrious missionaries to whom Mexico owes a debt of eternal gratitude, whose bodies were buried in said convent." Rivera, *Anales Mexicanos*, 16–17.

112. Religious objects belonging to the monastery were to be handed over to the archbishop. The official decree was published in "El convento de San Francisco de Mexico," *La Cruz* 3, no. 8 (September 25, 1856): 253–54.

113. For the history of the complex, see Manuel Ramirez Aparicio, *Los conventos suprimidos en México* (Mexico City: J.M. Aguilar, 1861), 189–390.

114. José María Roa Bárcena, "Monasterio de San Francisco," *La Cruz* 2, no. 7 (May 1, 1856): 226–31. According to Morales, above all the other religious houses in Mexico City, St. Francis was still "closely associated with a civic and religious environment which was about to disappear from Mexican society." Morales, "Mexican Society," 352.

115. This sentiment was expressed in a small book published during the conservative restoration that vehemently denied any illegal political activities by the Franciscans. *Los religiosos de San Francisco y su convento de México* (Mexico City: 1858). A fragment of this book exists in the Lafragua collection, pages 44–56 only, with illustrations.

116. This poster was transcribed by Vigil as an example of the hysteria of the "reaction," which he attributed to the "incessant preaching of the clergy." Vigil, *La Reforma*, 187n1.

117. For instance, see the proclamations published in Querétaro on October 14, 1856, during the occupation by rebel forces under Tomás Mejía. Quoted in Vigil, *La Reforma*, 188n1.

118. Aguilar y Marocho, *La familia enferma*, 45.

119. This program has been called a "liberal offensive against the social and cultural space of devotional images." See Díaz Patiño, *Católicos, liberales y protestantes*, 119–27.

120. Baz claimed that this measure was necessary to extend an important street. His project would have also required the destruction of a convent belonging to the Poor Clares. The documents pertaining to this debate are found in *Ayuntamiento, á quien se ha pasado de preferencia y con recomendación del Supremo Gobierno, para que informe lo conveniente* (Mexico City: Imprenta del Catolico, 1846), 7 pages.

121. Carrion, *Historia de la Ciudad*, 2:449.

122. Aguilar y Marocho, *La familia enferma*, 46.

123. José María Brito, "El clero y las revoluciones de México," *El Tribuno del Pueblo*, September 18, 1856.

124. See Vigil, *La Reforma*, 184.

125. Carrion, *Historia de la Ciudad*, 2:452–77; "Puebla, Conservative Revolt and Liberal Sieges of (1856)" in Marley, *Mexico at War*, 306. Orihuela was captured after the capitulation and shot in violation of the terms of surrender. Aguilar y Marocho, *La familia enferma*, 47; and Rivera, *Anales Mexicanos*, 18.

126. It was reported that the priest also caused a disturbance in the hospital when he announced that the soldiers were excommunicated. See Brian Connaughton, "1856–1857," 424–28.

127. Malo, *Diario de sucesos notables*, 2:479.

128. At the same time, the growing tensions between the liberal factions were exacerbated by Lerdo's resignation from the administration on December 19, 1856. Comonfort's hasty formation of a new cabinet on January 3 prevented a major political catastrophe but could not erase the growing distrust and resentments between the *moderado* President and *puros* who still dominated the constituent congress. Lafragua retained control of the ministry of the interior, but Montes was placed over the office of foreign relations. The subsequent appointment of José María Iglesias as minister of justice and ecclesiastical affairs seems to have pacified the radicals for the time being.

129. On February 4, Lafragua left as minister plenipotentiary for Spain. At that time Gen. Ignacio de la Llave, Pesado's former brother-in-law, was appointed minister of the interior.

130. For a discussion of the long liberal campaign for control of burials, see "The Battle for Church Burials," chap. 4 in Pamela Voekel, *Alone before God*, 106–22.

131. García Ugarte, *Poder político y religioso*, 1:638.

132. "Monjas," *El Monitor Republicano*, October 12, 1855.

133. See "On Regulars and Nuns" (December 3–4, 1563) in Waterworth, *Canons and Decrees*, 246.

134. On June 18, 1857, the new law was utilized to prevent the profession of a nun in Guadalajara. Aguilar y Marocho, *La familia enferma*, 52.

135. "Un Jalisciense" [pseud.], *Tendencias de la demagogia mejicana, manifestadas por sus propios hechos* (Guadalajara: Rodríguez, 1857), 24. See also "El Registro Civil" in *La Cruz* 5, no. 10 (February 26, 1857): 322–25; and Pedro Espinosa y Dávalos, *El Illmo. Señor Obispo de Guadalajara en union con su cabildo, representa al supreme gobierno pidiendo la modificación o derogación de algunos artículos de la ley sobre Registro Civil* (Guadalajara: Rodríguez, 1857), 21 pages.

CHAPTER FIVE

1. In his diary entry for December 29, 1855, the French ambassador reported that "the preliminary elections here provoked scandalous scenes and the ballot box favored a radical majority." Díaz López, *Versión francesa de México*, 1:243.

2. Jacqueline Covo states that the political clubs disappeared after the elections, their primary mission having been accomplished. Jacqueline Covo, "Los clubes políticos en la revolución de Ayutla," *Historia Mexicana* 26, no. 3 (January–March 1977): 455.

3. These exceptions to the liberal monopoly were Bernardo Couto for Aguascalientes and Marcelino Castañeda for Durango. Couto, however, claimed that he had too many other responsibilities and renounced his seat in the congress. The fifty-year-old Castañeda, once governor of Durango, was also a former chief justice of the Supreme Court.

4. "[In the congress] there were something like forty youths, deputies that wanted to introduce the most advanced liberal ideas into the constitution. Degollado always voted with them." Pola, "Santos Degollado," 2:372–73. Degollado was replaced as governor of Jalisco on May 30, 1856, so that he could act as a delegate from Michoacán. His first appearance in the congress on July 1, 1856, was greeted with applause "by almost all of the chamber." Francisco Zarco, *Historia del congreso*, 436.

5. Díaz López, *Versión francesa de México*, 1:233–34.

6. See Jan Bazant, "Tres revoluciones mexicanas," *Historia Mexicana* 10, no. 2 (October–December 1960): 231; and Lloyd J. Mecham, *Church and State in Latin America: A history of politico-ecclesiastical relations*, rev. ed. (Chapel Hill: University of North Carolina Press, 1966), 361.

7. "El gobierno de Comonfort pide a las autoridades eclesiasticas se hagan oraciones publicas por el feliz exito de los trabajos del congreso" (February 20, 1856), in Rogelio Orozco Farias, *Fuentes históricas: México 1821–1867*, 2nd ed. (Mexico City: Editorial Progreso, 1965), 147. The delegates cited rules that forbade their corporate attendance at any public functions, although the president noted that there were precedents for participation in religious ceremonies. See Vigil, *La Reforma*, 131. Other signs also pointed to a basic hostility toward religion among some of the delegates. For instance, two months later delegates decreed that the cross used in military decorations was not a Christian symbol and therefore had no religious significance. This incident was significant enough to be entered in Malo's diary on April 14, 1856. Malo, *Diario de sucesos notables*, 2:455. Later, once debate on the proposed constitution

began, some radicals even tried, unsuccessfully, to have the name of God removed from the preamble.

8. Marcelino Castañeda cast the one negative vote. Since the law was already in effect, he argued, ratification by the congress would only be antagonistic.

9. Malo, *Diario de sucesos notables*, 2:456.

10. Zarco was a Mason and one of the delegates from the State of Durango. He was also the founder and director of the important liberal newspaper *El Siglo Diez y Nueve*, which published daily summaries of the events in the constituent congress. These columns formed the basis for the chronicle of the congress, *Historia del congreso extra-dordinario constituyente*, which he published between 1857 and 1861. The material later published in the *Actas oficiales y minutario de decretos del congreso extraordinario constituyente de 1856–1857* was initially recorded in *El Siglo Diez y Nueve*, *El Diario Oficial*, and *El Estandarte Nacional*. Zarco, *Historia del congreso*, 128.

11. Lafragua, the minister of the interior, issued these provisional statues on May 15. The entire text is contained in Zarco, 209–14. Again, critics pointed out that this approval was only symbolic, being unnecessary for the implementation of the statutes and not required by the mandate of the congress.

12. According to Article 5 of the Plan of Ayutla, the deputies could not pass new legislation of their own, but they could revise laws made during the final Santa Anna administration.

13. A law passed on November 5, 1833, had removed legal recognition of religious vows in Mexico, but Santa Anna suspended this law on July 26, 1854. In 1856, Miguel Lerdo de Tejada reported that there were 1,484 nuns in Mexico. There were also 533 young women and 1,266 servants living in various convents at the time. In addition, the Daughters of Charity had 37 professed members and 41 novices. Miguel Lerdo de Tejada, *Cuadro Sinóptico*, 80.

14. "Monjas," *La Revolución*, October 20, 1855.

15. "Las esposas de Jesuscristo," *La Cruz* 2, no. 12 (June 5, 1856): 391.

16. The Jesuits had been allowed to return to Mexico by a decree issued by Santa Anna on September 19, 1853. At that time the *Colegio de San Gregorio*, secularized during the 1767 expulsion, was also returned to the order.

17. In commenting on the debate, Malo reflected: "Sad and disheartening is the occupation of the fathers of the country who spend their time revoking beneficial laws while external enemies threaten us on all sides and the republic is threatened with total internal dissolution." Malo, *Diario de sucesos notables*, 2:461; See also Francisco Vera, "La Compañia de Jesus," *La Cruz* 2, no. 13 (June 12, 1856): 424.

18. "Jesuitas," *El Monitor Republicano*, June 5, 1856.

19. Two delegates from Puebla, Francisco Lazo Estrada and Alejandro Ruiz, presented the commission's recommendation. Zarco, *Historia del congreso*, 267–69.

20. "We must be very dwarfish to see these religious as giants, some very old and infirm, others young, and without relations or knowledge of the country." Speech on June 6, 1856. Zarco, 279.

21. Speech on June 6, 1856. Zarco, 284. Closer to home, Joaquín García Granados also pointed out the role the Jesuits were playing in the conservative government in Gua-

temala. Speech on June 6, 1856. Zarco, 288. According to Moody, the "image of the Jesuit as alien to the spirit of the age and an obstacle to progress" became a central theme of anticlericalism after the eighteenth century. "The Jesuit became the focus of all the unfavorable attitudes toward religion and Catholicism . . . he was the symbol of all that was to be eradicated if the best hopes of man were to be fulfilled." Moody, *The Church as Enemy*, 10–11.

22. In order that the students enrolled in San Gregorio might be able to complete their current program of studies, the government gave the Jesuits until November 15 to dissolve the order and vacate the college. Basilio Arrillaga, the superior of the Jesuits in Mexico, closed the school on October 26. The fate of the fathers and brothers, and of the buildings they left behind, are described in Decorme, *Historia de la Compañia de Jesús*, 2:105–10.

23. Aguilar y Marocho, *La familia enferma*, 41.

24. Zamacois, *Historia de Méjico*, 14:299.

25. Malo also repeated a complaint from the 1855 petition in his diary: "[A] hundred heads of families will have to send their sons abroad in order to be educated in Jesuit establishments, a goal which could be achieved without separating them from their families when the Jesuits existed here." Malo, *Diario de sucesos notables*, 2:461–2.

26. José Mariano Dávila, "Observaciones al dictámen de la mayoría de la comision de negocios eclesiásticos del congreso constituyente acerca del decreto que restableció en la república la Compañía de Jesus," *La Cruz* 2, no. 17 (July 10, 1856): 527 to 3, no. 4 (August 28, 1856): 108 passim. See also, Un mexicano católico [pseud.], "Breves observaciones sobre la authoridad de la iglesia y sobre la Compañía de Jesus," *La Cruz* 2, no. 14 (June 19, 1856): 441–45.

27. Zarco, *Historia del congreso*, 329–65.

28. Speech on June 23, 1856. Zarco, 387–404.

29. These petitions used biblical arguments, among others, to demonstrate the divine institution of private property. *Representación que hacen al congreso constituyente various dueños de propiedades territoriales, conta algunos articulos de los proyectos de leyes fundamentals que se discuten actualmente* (Mexico City: Ignacio Cumplido, 1856) 18 pages; and *Representación que hacen al congreso constituyente various dueños de finacas rusticas y urbanas en Michoacán, Guanajato y Guerrero* (Morelia: I. Arango, 1856), 10 pages.

30. Zarco, *Historia del congreso*, 423–35.

31. These remarks were reported with sarcasm in "Dichos Celebres," *La Cruz* 3, no. 10 (October 9, 1856): 317–18.

32. The significance of this date was not lost on the delegates and observers, although the two parties interpreted the coincidence in different ways.

33. This fear became a reality on December 2, 1867. See "Ley orgánico de la Instruccion pública en el Distrito Federal," in Manuel Dublan and José María Lozano, eds., *Legislación Mexicana ó colección completa de las disposiciones legislativas expendidas desde la Independencia de la República* (Mexico City: Imprenta del Comercio, 1876), 10:193–205.

34. The article numbers refer to the final draft of the constitution, which are different from those in the original draft. See Zarco, *Historia del congreso*, 1345–61.

35. See Walter Scholes, "Church and State at the Mexican Constitutional Convention, 1856–1857," *The Americas* 4, no. 2 (October 1947): 164.

36. The first bill for toleration was presented in 1833. For a brief history of liberal agitation on this issue, see Fernández Fernández, "El liberalismo católico," 66–68.

37. Antonio Martinez Báez, ed., *Representaciones sobre la Tolerancia Religiosa* (Mexico City: Colección "El Siglo XIX," 1959), 5.

38. Zamacois, *Historia de Méjico*, 14:323.

39. Among the propositions explicitly denounced were the following, later included in *The Syllabus of Errors* (1864):

    "In the present day it is no longer expedient that the Catholic religion should be held as the only religion of the state, to the exclusion of other forms of worship." [Allocution *Nemo Vestrum*, July 26, 1855]

    "Hence it has been wisely decided by law, in some Catholic countries, that persons coming to reside therein shall enjoy the public exercise of their own peculiar worship." [Allocution *Acerbissimum*, September 27, 1852]

40. The archbishop's letter was copied in "Tolerancia de cultos," *La Cruz* 2, no. 17 (July 10, 1856): 542–45.

41. For instance, in the minutes for July 30, Zarco recorded: "The crowd that filled the galleries was greater than the day before; not lacking agents of the reactionaries. They were unable to disrupt the proceedings, in spite of repeatedly throwing down into the hall with the strongest arm printed papers on which were read the words, "Long live the Roman pontiff and the clergy!" "The people do not want tolerance!" and "Death to the enemies of the Catholic Religion!" Zarco, *Historia del congreso*, 577. It is interesting to note that three months before, *La Cruz* had published an account from a Spanish newspaper about a similar debate in the *cortes* of Madrid. The women's galleries there were full every day, it was reported, and they dropped flowers on the heads of those deputies who opposed toleration. Those who supported it were showered with alfalfa and called "Franco-masons" and "brutes" by the ladies. "Revista religiosa de Europa," *La Cruz* 2, no. 6 (April 24, 1856): 198.

42. Aguilar y Marocho, *La familia enferma*, 43.

43. For example, see the speeches of José Antonio Gamboa and Francisco Zarco on August 4, 1856. Zarco, *Historia del congreso*, 663, 675.

44. Vigil, *La Reforma*, 173–74.

45. "Una declaración del Doctor Cano" in *La Cruz* 3, no. 3 (August 21, 1856): 92–96. In his final agony Morales had indeed called for a young priest, who was also his godson and a friend of the family, to administer the last rites of the Church. As an integral part of his deathbed ministry, the priest encouraged the dying man to be reconciled with all his enemies. In reply to the question about his earlier anticlerical remarks, Morales stated: "Although I wrote with conviction, I never had the intention of offending the clergy nor attacking the religion that I profess; but as error might have adhered to my discourse, I subject my writings to the final judgment of the Holy Church." In the end he asked to be taken to the shrine of Our Lady of Guadalupe, for whom he had a special devotion, where he died. It was noted that he also had an image of the Virgin of Guadalupe by his bedside at home.

46. According to Olliff, "Emphasis on foreign immigration as essential to the future of Mexico reflected a liberal rejection of both the Spanish and Amerindian heritage. It implied that without the infusion of northern European blood, the Indian, Spanish, and mestizo populations of Mexico were incapable of acquiring the technological skills, social habits, and philosophical outlook essential for a prosperous modern economy." Olliff, *Reforma Mexico*, 17.

47. Speech on July 29, 1856. Zarco, *Historia del congreso*, 561–68.

48. Speech on July 29, 1856. Zarco, 574.

49. Castañeda argued the same idea in Congress on July 28: "But it is said that without religious tolerance there cannot be immigration, without it there will be no population, without population no railroads, and without this no agriculture, nor industry . . . When we have peace, justice, and good government, when we can guarantee order and security to the nation, then we will have prosperity, industry will come, capital will come." Zarco, 552. Gamboa disagreed, claiming that settlers would not be moving into the US West, where Indians attacks were common and Lynch law was in force, if law and order was a requirement for immigration. (564). Rafael Gonzalez Páez argued that populating the countryside would actually help decrease the crimes committed there. (579.)

50. *Representacion que al soberano congreso constituyente hacen los vecinos del pueblo de Tlalne-pantla Cuautenca* (Mexico City: L. Inclan, 1856), 8 pages. It was signed on April 30, 1856.

51. Speech on May 1, 1856. Quoted in Zamacois, *Historia de Méjico*, 14:327–30.

52. *Representacion que hace el vecindario de Queretaro al soberano congreso* (Querétaro: Mariano Rodriguez Velazquez, 1856), 5. Presented to Congress on August 4, 1856.

53. Speech on July 29, 1856, Zarco, *Historia del congreso*, 575.

54. Speech on July 29, 1856. Zarco, 559.

55. This petition, dated August 15, 1856, was one of only three petitions that were submitted in favor of Article 15. Martinez Báez, *Representaciones*, 42–44.

56. Speech on July 29, 1856. Zarco, *Historia del congreso*, 575.

57. Speech on July 28, 1856. Zarco, 551.

58. Among the important signatories of this petition were José Joaquín Pesado, Bernardo Couto, Manuel Carpio, Luis Gonzaga Cuevas, Basilio Arriaga, Mauricio Castañeda and José Ramón Malo. The petition itself states that "innumerable persons" were unable to sign because of the rush to present the document to the Congress. *Representacion al soberano congreso contra el art. 15 del proyecto de constitución sobre la tolerancia religiosa* (Mexico City: Andrade y Escalante, 1856), 15 pages. Presented to Congress on June 29, 1856.

59. Speech on July 8, 1856. Zarco, *Historia del congreso*, 478.

60. In response, Pedro Ampudia argued that it just as honorable to study any people "that has resolved great problems." Speech on August 5, 1856. Zarco, *Historia del congreso*, 682.

61. Speech on August 4, 1856. Zarco, *Historia del congreso*, 667. Slavery was abolished in Mexico in 1829.

62. Speech on July 8, 1856. Zarco, 476.

63. Speech on July 29, 1856. Zarco, 570.

64. Speech on July 30, 1856. Zarco, 582.

65. Speech on July 29, 1856. Zarco, 550.

66. See the speech by Rafael Jacquez, delegate from Guerrero, on July 30, 1856. Zarco, 593–97.

67. Speech on July 30, 1856. Zarco, 581.

68. Speech on July 30, 1856. Zarco, 598.

69. Petition dated July 21, 1856. In Martinez Báez, *Representaciones,* 35–39.

70. *Representacion que eleven al soberano congreso, los vecinos de las municipalidades de Cuautitlan, Tepotzolan, Huehuetoca, San Miguel, Tultepec, Tultitlan, y Teoloyucan, pidiendo se repruebe el art. 15 del proyecto de constitucion sobre tolerancia de cultos* (Mexico City: Vicente Segura, 1857), 6. Presented to Congress on August 4, 1856.

71. Fanny Calderón de la Barca was particularly struck by the public devotion to the Blessed Sacrament during her time in Mexico. Calderón de la Barca, *Life in Mexico,* 117, 201–202, 275, 471, 477.

72. Speech on July 29, 1856. Zarco, *Historia del congreso,* 548–52.

73. In his speech on July 29, Zarco stated: "As a Catholic, I reject the protection that is offered to the religion I profess. Catholicism, revelation, and the eternal truth do not need the protection of the powers of the earth, do not need the force of kings, nor of republics; on the contrary, Catholic truth is what protects the human race." Zarco, *Historia del congreso,* 572.

74. Pedro de Ampudia, a delegate from Yucatán, said: "The Catholic unity, that is so much vaunted, is a lie. In the ports and in the frontiers, there is no worship, or priest, or administration of the sacraments; in the del Monte mines a Protestant chapel already exists." Speech on August 5, 1856. Zarco, *Historia del congreso,* 683.

75. Speech on July 29, 1856. Zarco, 558. The Bishop of Oaxaca also admitted to his concern over the actual religious beliefs of the indigenous people in his diocese. In his protest against Article 15 dated July 15, 1856, he warned of the risk of these people returning to idolatry "if the legislature opened the door" by introducing religious tolerance. Liberal deputies, however, chose to interpret this argument as an admission of the Church's failure to adequately evangelize the Indians. Martinez Báez, *Representaciones,* 40–41.

76. According to Silvia Arrom, during the nineteenth century "women's principal political weapon was the petition." Although individual women occasionally made personal appeals to colonial authorities, after independence women also began to take more collective action on specific issues. "Although they did so only rarely and may have been organized by men, women did nonetheless lobby as a feminine pressure group for the first time, taking a highly visible stance on public issues." For example, fifty women signed a petition to oppose the expulsion of the Spanish from Mexico in 1829. See Silvia Marina Arrom, *The Women of Mexico City, 1790–1857* (Stanford, CA: Stanford University Press, 1985), 42–43.

77. "I would not have believed it myself," he wrote, "but have had to give in to the evidence. Family relations are of an intimacy and intensity similar only to that of the Spaniards. In the bosom of the family, the *puro* gives in to the constant sermons of his mother, of his wife, of his daughter or his sister. This forces him to sacrifice his convictions and social doctrine." Díaz López, *Versión francesa de México,* 1:250.

78. The women's petitions are discussed in Martinez Báez, *Representaciones*, 14–19. For a more detailed study of women's petitions, see Margaret Chowning, "Throwing Themselves upon the Political Barricades: Catholic Women Enter National Politics in the Midcentury Petition Campaign," chap. 4 in *Catholic Women and Mexican Politics*.

79. Petition of the Women of San Luis Potosí, presented on July 31, 1856. Martinez Báez, *Representaciones*, 23–25.

80. Petition by the Women of Mexico City, presented on July 8, 1856. Martinez Báez, 21–22.

81. Actually, although women's petitions were admitted into the congress, these were always delivered and read before the delegates by males. Women were confined to the visitor's galleries during these proceedings.

82. Petition by the women of Morelia, presented July 28, 1856. Martinez Báez, *Representaciones*, 26–30.

83. "The gentle sex has given on this occasion a brilliant example of its piety with numerous expositions, so that if they appeared to be viewed by some with demonstrations of disrespect, in reality they caused a great sensation. The ladies have been treated at times in an indecorous manner; but it is necessary to confess that the majority of the congress, and the numerous spectators that attended in the galleries, manifested in an unequivocal manner its displeasure at this misbehavior." José Joaquín Pesado, "Controversia," in *La Cruz* 3, no. 2 (August 14, 1856): 48.

84. Some delegates tried to have these petitions excluded on technical grounds. It was argued that female petitions could not be presented to the congress because their signers were not citizens or because a woman required her husband's permission to autograph a legal document. Although the officers decided to accept the women's petitions, they were often greeted by groans and laughter when they were read.

85. Speech on July 29, 1856. Zarco, *Historia del congreso*, 558.

86. Speech on July 29, 1856. Zarco, 574.

87. Speech on July 30, 1856. Zarco, 582. Queen Dido, in Roman legend, was the founder of Carthage.

88. Speech on July 7, 1856. Zarco, 468.

89. On the other hand, Edward Wright-Rios notes that while the "feminization of piety" is often taken for granted when speaking of the nineteenth century, "the mechanics of this transformation remain murky." Edward Wright-Rios, *Revolutions in Mexican Catholicism*, 285–86. See also Chowning, *Catholic Women and Mexican Politics*, 7–9.

90. These attitudes toward the roles of women seem to have been shared by both liberals and conservatives of the newer generation. The idealization of female qualities, which made them alone suitable for the moral training of children, was a characteristic of the Romantic Movement that was entering Mexico at this time. Conservatives, however, integrated these sentiments into a positive vision of the Church, which was presented as the guarantor of female virtue. For instance, see José María Roa Bárcena, "Educación del hombre," *La Cruz* 2, nos. 3, 19 (April 3 and July 24, 1856): 92–94, 617–20. Although the "moral authority of the wife and mother" was "a theme dear to the nineteenth-century bourgeoisie," the Church also responded in creative ways

to the changing roles of women. Raymond Grew, "Liberty and the Catholic Church in Nineteenth-Century Europe," 121–22.

91. See Meyer, *The Cristero Rebellion*, 28.

92. This charge was made by Francisco Zarco on July 29, 1856. Zarco, *Historia del congreso*, 573.

93. Vigil, *La Reforma*, 163.

94. After consulting four petitions presented on July 25, Martinez Báez concludes that only in one case had the parish priest been involved by inviting the town council and inhabitants to draw up a petition. Martinez Báez, *Representaciones*, 17.

95. Speech on July 30, 1856. Zarco, *Historia del congreso*, 599–602.

96. Speech on August 4, 1856. Zarco, 672–73.

97. In particular, see José Joaquín Pesado, "Breves observaciones sobre la tolerancia religiosa," *La Cruz* 2, no. 16 (July 3, 1856): 489–96; "Dos palabras mas sobre la tolerancia religiosa en México," *La Cruz* 2, no. 17 (July 10, 1856): 525–26; and "Sobre la tolerancia civil de cultos en México," *La Cruz* 2, no. 19 (July 24, 1856): 593–99.

98. Juan Rodríguez de San Miguel, "Disertación sobre la libertad de cultos en la Republica Mexicana," *La Cruz* 2, nos. 10, 13,16 (May 22, June 12, July 3, 1856): 312–21; 403–11; 496–506.

99. José Joaquín Pesado, "Breve refutation de las principales razones con que se ha sostenido la libertad de cultos en el congreso general," in *La Cruz* 3, no. 2 (August 14, 1856): 42–48.

100. The government replied in the affirmative to the refugees' request on September 9. Roa Bárcena remarked that, "the indifference with which the liberal press has viewed the exposition of the Irish to whom we referred seems to demonstrate that, raising the party spirit to an extreme, the immigration of Catholics is accepted with disgust. . . . Protestant foreigners are preferred." José María Roa Bárcena, "Controversia" in *La Cruz* 3, no. 10 (October 9, 1856): 294–98.

101. Zarco, *Historia del congreso*, 477-79.

102. Zarco, 625–34.

103. Zarco, 684-86.

104. Twenty-two deputies were absent during the voting. Although some were reported sick or were occupied elsewhere, it was noted that some simply walked out of the chamber before the voting took place. Although the labels *puro* and *moderado* are often difficult to apply with any certainty, the breakdown of this vote along factional lines might be the best indication of the predominant leanings of individual deputies. The record of each delegate's vote is recorded in Francisco Zarco, *Actas oficiales y minutario de decretos del congreso extraordinario constituyente de 1856–1857* (Mexico City: El Colegio de Mexico, 1957), 308. It is interesting to note that Santos Degollado voted against retiring the bill, while his son, Joaquín María Degollado, a deputy for Jalisco, voted for it.

105. Zarco, *Historia del congreso*, 689, 1220. The vote on January 26, 1857, was 57 to 22.

106. Pesado, "Breve refutation," 48.

CHAPTER SIX

1. Francisco Zarco, *Historia del congreso*, 1268–73.
2. Mata made this proposal on February 3, 1857. Zarco, 1273.
3. Felipe de Jesús (née Felipe de las Casas Martínez) was a Franciscan friar born in Mexico City in 1575 and martyred at Nagasaki, Japan on February 5, 1592. He was beatified by Pope Urban VIII on September 14, 1627, and proclaimed the patron of Mexico City in 1629. Pope Pius IX canonized him on June 8, 1862, making him the first native-born saint from anywhere in North America. As it turned out, most of the Mexican bishops were present in Rome for this celebration, the entire hierarchy having been exiled from Mexico by the liberals in 1861. For a study of the important role played by Blessed Felipe in the creation of criollo consciousness in Mexico, see Ronald J. Morgan, "Birth Pangs of a Criollo Saint: Defending the Mexican Origins of St. Felipe de Jesús," in *Spanish American Saints and the Rhetoric of Identity, 1600–1810* (Tucson: University of Arizona Press, 2002), 143–69. The notice of the numerous activities published in *La Cruz* for the feast of "The Glorious Martyr of Japan, Illustrious Mexican Saint Felipe de Jesus, patron of Mexico" indicates that in 1857 the traditional procession was held as usual. "Santos y festividades religiosas de la semana," *La Cruz* 4, no. 7 (February 5, 1857): 219. After the Reforma, the sanctoral celebration had to compete with the civic calendar, which now designates February 5 as "Constitution Day."
4. Gómez Farías was elected to replace Guzmán as president during the last session of the congress on January 31 precisely so that he could preside over the culmination of the reformers' work. For a description of the ratification ceremony, including the discourses by Zarco, Comonfort, and Guzmán, see Zarco, *Historia del congreso*, 1289–95.
5. Because Comonfort suspended the constitution seven months later, there has been much discussion about his sincerity at the time he took the oath. The French ambassador stated that the president expressed his misgivings very soon after the event. Díaz López, *Versión francesa de México*, 1:393. Based on his own later confession, it seems that Comonfort mainly took the oath because this was required by the commitments that he had made to the Plan of Ayutla. At the same time, his comments on this occasion reflected his lingering hope that the document might eventually be amended to eliminate its more controversial provisions. Only intervening events made it clear that no compromise was possible. See Vigil, *La Reforma*, 219–22; Zamacois, *Historia de Méjico*, 14:474–78; and Brian Hamnett, "The Comonfort Presidency, 1855–1857," *Bulletin of Latin American Research* 15, no. 1 (January 1996): 91–95.
6. The editors of *La Cruz* found it amusing that *El Estandarte Nacional* should devote so much attention to the constant references to God. See "La nueva constitucion," *La Cruz* 4, no. 8 (February 12, 1857): 251–52.
7. In the United States, it is widely recognized that public invocations of God are only religious vestiges used for "solemnizing public occasions." As Justice William Brennan explained in his opinion in *Lynch v. Donnelly* (1984), such "ceremonial deism" has lost, through rote repetition "any significant religious content." This, however, was not yet the case in nineteenth-century Mexico. According to Vigil, "the defenders of the

constitution and the other reformist measures began by making a profession of religious faith in an effort to prove that such dispositions were in no way opposed to the fundamental principles of the Catholic faith." Vigil, *La Reforma*, 229.

8. The Jesuit historian Jesús García Gutiérrez reflected a common Catholic view of this event when he wrote: "I believe that these invocations to the Supreme Being and to Divine Providence were not sincere, but a cloak of hypocrisy in order to deceive the people." Jesús García Gutiérrez, SJ, *Apuntamientos de historia eclesiástica Mejicana* (Mexico City: Victoria, 1922), 146. Similarly, the Jesuit historian Mariano Cuevas described Gómez Farías's religious display as a "sacrilege" and an "intrinsic impiety." Cuevas, *Historia de la iglesia en México*, 5:310.

9. A consistory is a ceremonial meeting of the pope and the sacred college of cardinals for the promulgation of certain official acts. These gatherings may be private, semi-public, or public, depending on the nature of the business at hand. There was therefore nothing unusual about the setting for this allocution, nor the subsequent release and publication of the papal text.

10. Labastida received the summons to Rome, dated August 23, when he arrived in England on August 25, 1856. Ignacio Montes de Oca, who visited him in Rome, later recalled that the bishop was appointed "domestic prelate" and "assistant to the pontifical throne," honorary posts traditionally granted by popes "to those prelates most dear to their heart or those whose conduct they wish to approve before the eyes of the world." *Honras Fúnebres* quoted in Itzel Magaña Ocaña, "Pelagio Antonio de Labastida y Davalos, Obispo y Arzobispo de México frente a la Reforma y el Segundo Imperio" (Thesis, Universidad Nacional Autonoma de México, 1993), 37–39. In January 1857 *La Cruz* reported that Labastida was a frequent guest at the pope's table and that he had been awarded a medal commemorating the dogmatic decree on the Immaculate Conception as a sign of special favor. "El Illmo. Sr. Labastida," *La Cruz* 4, no. 3 (January 8, 1857): 93. In his dispatch on February 9, 1957, Gabriac wrote: "The president also believes that the Holy Father is influenced in Rome by Monsignor Labastida, the exiled Bishop of Puebla, as well as by Señors Gutiérrez, Larrainzar, and Haro." Díaz López, *Versión francesa de México*, 1:395. But while the refugee politicians may have been feeding additional information to the bishop, only Labastida had frequent access to the pope. Vigil also blames Labastida for the content and tone of the papal discourse. Vigil, *La Reforma*, 225–27.

11. It is not clear on which date the allocution actually arrived in Mexico. On February 12, *La Cruz* reported that its arrival had been discussed in the Mexico City press "for the past few days." "Alocucion de S.S. Pio IX," *La Cruz* 4, no. 8 (February 12, 1857): 256. On February 18 Gabriac wrote that it had arrived in "the last mail." Díaz López, *Versión francesa de México*, 1:402. The document must have arrived at about the same time in the United States, for it was published in *The Catholic Mirror* (Baltimore and Richmond) on February 7. "La alocucion de S.S. Pio IX," *La Cruz* 4, no. 15 (April 2, 1857): 502. In any event, the text was circulating in Mexico within a few days of the official signing of the constitution.

12. The central focus of the allocution was on Mexico, but the pope also placed events there in a global context by his references to similar problems occurring in other parts

of Latin America and in Switzerland. The complete text of the allocution may be found in J. Pérez Lugo [Joaquín Ramírez Cabañas], *La cuestión religiosa de México* (Mexico City: Publicaciones del Centro Cultural "Cuauhtemoc," 1926), 318–21.

13. Although Article 15, which would have granted freedom of worship in the Mexican Republic, was tabled on August 5, 1856, it was not definitely retired until January 26, 1857, six weeks after the papal allocution was pronounced. In spite of popular opposition to the article, in December 1856 Labastida must have still expected the controversial article to appear in the finished constitution.

14. Vigil, *La Reforma*, 227.

15. According to Covo, "This allocution was first considered apocryphal by the liberals who did not believe, or pretended not to believe, that the pope would confront the civil power and independence of the nation head-on." Covo, *Las ideas de la Reforma*, 481–82n16. José María Lafragua, the minister of the interior, issued a statement on February 10, 1857, claiming that the papal allocution was a fake and on February 14, a priest in Chila (Puebla) was exiled for "for demonstrating the authenticity of the pontifical allocution." Aguilar y Marocho, *La familia enferma*, 48–49. In spite of government efforts, Gabriac reported that the discourse was "translated and widely distributed," although the president threatened to charge with treason any priest who read it from the pulpit. Díaz López, *Versión francesa de México*, 1:402–3. On February 14, 1857, Malo also recorded that it was widely published on clandestine presses "because of government opposition." Malo, *Diario de sucesos notables*, 2:482. We also know that on May 27 Ignacio Arango, a publisher in Morelia, was fined 300 pesos for printing the document. Juan N. Salinas, *Dudas de un estudiante con motivo de las reflexiones del Sr. Alvires sobre los decretos episcopales que prohiben el juramento constitucional* (Morelia: Ignacio Arango, 1857), 8. In January 1858, soon after the overthrow of the liberal regime, the Bishop of Guadalajara published it openly for the first time, along with a short commentary. See Pedro Espinosa, *Carta pastoral del Illmo. Sr. Obispo de Guadalajara en que se inserta la alocución de Su Santidad* (Guadalajara: Tipografía de Rodriguez, 1858), 22 pages.

16. The French ambassador claimed to have dissuaded him from this course of action by pointing out that such a gesture would actually constitute a victory for the diplomatic machinations of the US delegation. Díaz López, *Versión francesa de México*, 1:402–3.

17. The text of Comonfort's speech is recorded in Zarco, *Historia del congreso*, 1342–44.

18. Although Comonfort's comments and his tentative overtures to the Church may reflect a personal religious dilemma in the face of the papal condemnation, they also suggest the temporary ascendancy of a more moderate political strategy. Since his conciliatory remarks were delivered at the official closing of the constituent congress, they may be seen as a reassertion of executive and *moderado* power in the political vacuum created by the termination of that assembly.

19. In his diary, Malo only reported that Traconis was charged with "misuse of funds." Malo, *Diario de sucesos notables*, 2:482. Aguilar y Marocho claimed that "so many and so great were the abuses of Traconis and his secretary that public indignation, even that of the liberals, could not be calmed." Aguilar y Marocho, *La familia enferma*, 49. According to the most popular rumor, the general's actual arrest was occasioned by

his illegal confiscation of the jewels that wealthy families had loaned to a certain convent to adorn its sacred images for a religious festival. When Traconis tried to sell these items for cash, the injured parties approached Comonfort directly and demanded an investigation, which accidentally uncovered evidence of more widespread abuse and fraud relating to the confiscation of ecclesiastical property in the Puebla diocese. Díaz López, *Versión francesa de México*, 404.

20. "El Convento de San Francisco," *La Cruz* 4, no. 10 (February 26, 1857): 321–22. See also Zamacois, *Historia de Méjico*, 14:501–4 and Vigil, *La Reforma*, 223.

21. Garza's reply to Baz was included in a circular issued on March 12 entitled "La nueva constitucion y la iglesia Mexicana." In his diary entry for March 11, Malo wrote that the cathedral bells were rung "without the permission of the archbishop, who is opposed to making any favorable demonstration." Malo, *Diario de sucesos notables*, 2:482–83. However, the French ambassador reported that "the bells remained quiet and there was not a single flicker in the towers of the numerous religious buildings of the capital." Díaz López, *Versión francesa de México*, 1:406.

22. "El Sr. Cura Santaella," *Diario de Aviso*, April 14, 1857. Here the priest was labeled a "sexagenarian," although Aguilar y Marocho reported that he was "an old man of seventy." Aguilar y Marocho, *La familia enferma*, 50. The harsh conditions under which the priest was held are described in "Oajaca," *Diario de Aviso*, April 20, 1857.

23. "In order to celebrate the promulgation of the code, in many cities it has been necessary to storm the bell towers to toll the bells." Everywhere, *La Cruz* reported, "the authorities have tried in vain to get the inhabitants to illuminate their houses and make a show of celebration." "La nueva constitucion," *La Cruz* 4, no. 18 (April 23, 1857): 615–16. Álvarez also stated, "in almost every place in the country the bell towers were forced to ring the bells to solemnize the fact that the country had been given a constitution." Álvarez, *Revolucion de la Reforma*, 143. Aguilar y Marocho recorded other bell-ringing incidents on March 20, 23, 27, April 25 and May 16. Aguilar y Marocho, *La familia enferma*, 49–51. Covo provides a list of similar episodes drawn from reports in the liberal press. Covo, *Las ideas de la Reforma*, 480n11. See also Vigil, *La Reforma*, 232. On the other hand, liberal newspapers boasted when a cathedral prebend in Oaxaca celebrated a Te Deum as proof that the local bishop supported the constitution. In response, the conservative press published documents to disprove this interpretation. "La constitution en Oajaca," and "El tiempo todo lo aclara," *Diario de Avisos*, April 4 and May 23, 1857.

24. At 7:00 p.m. on August 21, 1857, the secretary of the Federal District held a meeting with pastors, college rectors, and the majordomos of the city's convents to insist on an "extraordinary illumination" of their buildings on September 16. Three days prior to the official celebration, the cabildo was threatened with a thousand-peso fine if the Metropolitan Cathedral refused to comply, which, Malo noted, "was a little stronger than that levied when Santa Anna was dictator." Malo, *Diario de sucesos notables*, 2:494–95; and Aguilar y Marocho, *La familia enferma*, 55. Later, a parish priest in Guanajuato was fined 100 pesos when he refused to ring his church bells to celebrate Comonfort's election, and books from his library were confiscated when he refused to pay. See David Brading, "Ultramontane Intransigence," 133.

25. The Sagrario is the chapel that serves as the parish church for the Cathedral of Mexico City. The archbishop also announced that he would refuse to take the oath, even if it was required. His circular was signed by J. Primo de Rivera ("on behalf of the ecclesiastical government of the Archdiocese of Mexico City") on March 12, 1857. A second circular to the same effect was issued on March 18. See "Oposición del clero al juramento de la constitución de 1857," in Pérez Lugo, *La cuestión religiosa*, 323–24. On March 25 Malo wrote in his diary, "The archbishop preached in the Sagrario against the Law of June 25 and demonstrated that Catholics cannot swear to the constitution." Malo, *Diario de sucesos notables*, 2:483. This sermon and the archiepiscopal circular are also mentioned in "El juramento de la constitución," *La Cruz* 4, no. 15 (April 2, 1857): 500–501. Ultimately, the government decided that the clergy, not being actual employees of the state, would not be asked to take the oath (although this position was later reversed in the State of Guerrero).

26. It was already customary for higher officials to take a public oath to the prevailing constitution. Such civic oaths, and their associated religious symbolism, had their roots in the colonial period. See O'Hara, *A Flock Divided*, 175–76.

27. Covo, *Las ideas de la Reforma*, 479. Portilla speculated that de la Llave intended to "remove from all public posts anyone who did not see in the new code the symbol of progressive ideas." Portilla, *Mejico en 1856 y 1857*, 192. Rather than a ploy to provide new positions for liberals, however, Gabriac remarked that because of its financial difficulties, the government seemed glad to have inadvertently reduced the number of public employees on the payroll. Díaz López, *Versión francesa de México*, 1:406.

28. Zamacois, for one, argued that the oath requirement was calculated to drive a wedge between the people and the clergy. Zamacois, *Historia de Méjico*, 14:527–28.

29. Gabriac reported that, "a large number of general officials and their subordinates, as well as upper-level functionaries and others have refused." Díaz López, *Versión francesa de México*, 406–7. Malo wrote that "many were missing in the ministries and offices that presented themselves to swear." Malo, *Diario de sucesos notables*, 2:484. Rivera also recorded that "many employees did not want to swear and left their posts." Rivera, *Anales Mexicanos*, 20. The most thorough description of the event is provided by Zamacois, who included an article from *Diario de Avisos* that lists the names of many of the more prominent nonjurors in Mexico City and other localities. Zamacois, *Historia de Méjico*, 14:512–23.

30. See Malo, *Diario de sucesos notables*, 2:484. This order was simultaneously issued by Garza in Mexico City and Múnguia, the Bishop of Michoacán. The following day a similar order was issued by Bishop Espinosa in Guadalajara.

31. Munguía made this charge in his circular dated September 10, 1857. See Brading, "Ultramontane Intransigence," 133. On June 15, 1857, *La Cruz* reported that the bishops of Sonora, Durango, and Monterrey had issued formal warnings against taking the oath. The editor also commented at that time that the rest of the Mexican bishops had already published similar circulars. After a confrontation with state officials in Nueva Leon, however, the bishop agreed that his circular would not be read during Sunday Mass. At the same time, the official newspaper defended the government's use of "a firm hand" against any ecclesiastics who would "disturb the peace" by

publicly reading or referring to the controversial document, since the state had a duty to prevent "disturbances and riots." See "Cuestion del juramento," *La Cruz* 5, no.7 (June 25, 1857): 229. For a second time, the publisher Ignacio Arango was fined 300 pesos for printing Munguía's ban. Salinas, *Dudas de un estudiante*, 8.

32. See Aguilar y Marocho, *La familia enferma*. 50.

33. "The police tightly control the sermons of the clergy during these final days of Lent," the French ambassador reported. Díaz López, *Versión francesa de México*, 1:407. In his catalog of the alleged abuses committed by the liberal government during this period, an anonymous priest in Jalisco wrote that "It is prohibited to publish the protests and pastorals of the bishops and to send circulars to the pastors and priests . . . effectively, they have circulated an order to the governors of the states encouraging them to prevent such publications and circulars and their reading in the churches . . . after that they named commissioners, who were certainly not models of virtue and piety, to attend the temples, with the object of hearing what is said or preached from the pulpit, and to go afterward and denounce the sermon as subversive; and these commissioners were zealous to the point of demanding that they be advised beforehand when there would be preaching so that they would not be late!" Un Jalisciense [pseud.], *Tendencias de la demagogia Mejicana, manifestados por sus propios hechos* (Guadalajara: Rodríguez, 1857), 9.

34. The details of this ceremony were recorded a local newspaper, *La Sombra de Gracia*, April 24, 1857. Quoted in Covo, *Las ideas de la Reforma*. 480.

35. Ultimately, the priest was arrested and punished for this act of insubordination and the required religious objects were seized. Details of this episode were reported in a military dispatch from Naolinco dated April 21, 1857. Antonio Pompa y Pompa, ed., *Colección de documentos inéditos o muy raros relativos a la Reforma en México*, Vol. 1 (Mexico City: Institutio Nacional de Antropología y Historia, 1957), 67–69.

36. Pérez Verdía, *Historia particular*, 2:419.

37. Quoted in Covo, *Las ideas de la Reforma*, 481.

38. According to official reports, the disturbance in Zamora was encouraged by the local prefect, Mariano Villaseñor, one of the prominent nonjurors of the town. A number of confrontations between the population and government troops occurred there throughout the night of April 5, with mobs roaming the streets and "yelling 'vivas' to the padres and 'death' to the constitution." The next day the garrison was disarmed and the national guard expelled from the city. Pompa y Pompa, *Coleccción de documentos*, 39–41.

39. Military dispatches from Michoacán claimed that in the towns "in which the clerical party has great influence" it was impossible to publish the constitution "because the inhabitants are revolting." From Tulancingo it was reported that "all the reactionaries of this town have refused to swear to the constitution and have left the public posts or employments they occupied." The local governor also suspected that the conservatives and the clergy were planning to create a major disturbance during Holy Week. Pompa y Pompa, *Coleccción de documentos*, 33–34, 38.

40. Zamacois, *Historia de Méjico*, 14:525. Since the Fourth Lateran Council (1215), Roman Catholics have been obliged to confess their sins and to receive Holy Communion at

least once a year, and that during the Easter season, which is the period between the first Sunday of Lent and Trinity Sunday. This obligation is known as the "Easter Duty."

41. Here is an example of the genre, written by a repentant artillery officer: "Prostrate on my sickbed and gravely ill, my soul suffered great recriminations on considering that having professed the Roman Catholic and Apostolic religion, I found myself separated from the communion of the faithful, for having, as a second lieutenant of the artillery, sworn to the constitution; but desiring to die in the bosom of the Church and in the same faith that I have professed, which I confess to be the only true religion, I retract with my whole soul the said oath, repenting sincerely for having taken it, and for the bad example that I have given." See "Retractaciones," *La Cruz* 5, no. 15 (August 20, 1857): 519.

42. Quoted in Sinkin, *The Mexican Reforma*, 134n5.

43. Writing twenty years after these events, the historian reflected that in the present state of religious indifference it would be almost inconceivable for anyone to forfeit their financial wellbeing for religious principles, "preferring misery to the sacrifice of one's Catholic beliefs." But at that time, he recalled wistfully, Mexican society was highly religious "and the religious ideal had deep roots in the heart of the inhabitants." Zamacois, *Historia de Méjico*, 14:521–22.

44. Díaz López, *Versión francesa de México*, 406.

45. Pérez Verdía, *Historia particular*, 2:419.

46. According to Vigil, there were rumors of a plot to break open the jail to liberate conservative prisoners in San Luis Potosí during Holy Week, but it never materialized. In Puebla, however, the clergy created a minor scandal by their refusal to accept donations offered by government officials during the high holy days. Vigil, *La Reforma*, 236.

47. The thirty-seven-year-old Baz became a follower of Gómez Farías when he was only eighteen and for the next twenty years waged a tireless campaign against the clerical *fuero* and ecclesiastical property and in favor of religious toleration. Appointed governor of the Federal District by Gómez Farías in 1846, he was a chief instigator of the attempt to confiscate Church wealth during the war with the US. Reappointed to this position by General Álvarez in 1855, he was also responsible for the demolition at the Franciscan Convent in 1856.

48. Because the eucharistic liturgy is never celebrated on Good Friday, very early the custom arose of reserving the consecrated species from the Mass of Maundy Thursday in a special tabernacle in order to provide a Host for the celebrant to receive during the celebration of the Passion of Christ, the so-called "Mass of the Pre-Sanctified," the following day and to provide viaticum for anyone in danger of death during this period. Typically, this temporary tabernacle was placed on a highly decorated "altar of repose," which also became an object of special prayer and devotion. Although the Church repeatedly forbade handing over the key to this tabernacle to any layman, the custom was tolerated in Mexico because of its antiquity. Rome had issued decrees forbidding this practice in 1610, 1642, 1673, 1684, and 1745. However, the Archbishop of Mexico City had ruled in 1841 that the practice could continue, "it being the

custom." See *Breve tratado de las ceremonias que se han de observer en los dias de semana santa, sacado de los mejores autores que se iran citando en sus lugares respectivos: compuesto por un aficionado* (Mexico City: Luis Abaniano y Valdes, 1841), 14–15. After the events of April 9, 1857, the liberal press argued that handing over the key to a secular authority during this ceremony was always a symbolic recognition of the *patronato*. Conservatives, however, responded that this was a fanciful interpretation since the rank and office of the participating layman had always varied from year to year.

49. As Pesado later explained, such customs were natural where the temporal power protected the interests of Church. But "the pretension of honor in the temples" was simply incompatible with the reality of the current political situation. José Joaquín Pesado, "Sucesos de la semana santa en la capital de la republica," *La Cruz* 4, no. 17 (April 16, 1857): 583–84. Liberal newspapers, on the other hand, sided with Baz by quoting the words of Christ: "Give to Caesar what is Caesar's." The conservative press responded by completing the quotation: "but give to God what is God's." "Al Cesar lo que es del Cesar," *Diario de Avisos*, May 4, 1857.

50. The entire correspondence between Baz and Garza was published the following week in Pesado, "Sucesos de la semana santa," 584–88. It may also be found in the appendix to Emilio del Castillo Negrete, *Mexico en el siglo XIX* (Mexico City: Imprenta del Editor, 1892), 26:262–72. According to Gabric, "Baz had the audacity of insisting on obtaining the key to the tabernacle without receiving Holy Communion, which is one of the conditions for the metropolitan chapter handing it over." According to Gabriac, Comonfort, "anticipating his arrogance," ordered him not to insist on being received in the cathedral. But the governor "followed his anti-Catholic impulses and threw down the gauntlet," in order to provoke a scene that he hoped would humiliate the clergy. Díaz López, *Versión francesa de México*, 412. Similar situations occurred on Maundy Thursday in Juchilpila (Zacatecas) and in Tlaxcala (Tlaxcala). See Brian Connaughton, "1856–1857," 433–35. Portilla, however, reported that the traditional ceremonies were carried out with civic involvement at the Basilica of Our Lady of Guadalupe and other places without incident. Portilla, *Méjico en 1856 and 1857*, 204.

51. Before the restoration of the rites of Holy Week undertaken by Pope Pius XII in 1955, the chief liturgies of the Easter Triduum (Maundy Thursday, Good Friday, and Holy Saturday) were celebrated early in the morning of each day.

52. See Portilla, *Méjico en 1856 and 1857*, 200–5; Zamacois, *Historia de Méjico*, 14:533–40; and Malo, *Diario de sucesos notables*, 2:485–86. Only Zamacois records the improbable number of lights in his detailed description of the ornaments displayed that night.

53. See "El C. Juan José Baz gobernador del Distrito á los habitantes de el," in Castillo Negrete, *Mexico en el siglo XIX*, 26:268.

54. Pesado, "Sucesos de la semana santa," 581; and Díaz López, *Versión francesa de México*, 1:412–13.

55. The entire poem may be found in Aguilar y Marocho, *La familia enferma*, 151–62.

56. For example, the semi-official *El Estandarte Nacional* argued that the clergy who were present had not only failed to contain the anti-government riot inside the cathedral but had refused to leave the sanctuary to pacify the mob after they heard shouts and gunshots outside. Quoted in Vigil, *La Reforma*, 235.

57. This sentiment and the government's charges against the archbishop and his canons were included in an indictment drawn up on Easter Sunday. "Suprema órden de 12 de Abril de 1857, sobre estrañamiento y llevadera prisión del Arzobispo Garza y canónigos, cuyo castigo pidió D. Juan José Baz, á quien desairaon," in Castillo Negrete, *Mexico en el siglo XIX*, 26:269–72.

58. For the debate in the constituent congress on stole fees, see Zarco, *Historia del congreso*, 1262–65. A plan to abolish stole fees was also drawn up by Lafragua, as interior minister, in early 1856, but its implementation was delayed for tactical reasons. The final *Ley de Obvenciones Parroquiales*, also known as the *Ley Iglesias* for the minister who issued it, was advertised as a concession to the poor, who liberals believed were oppressed by the current sacramental fee schedule. See Silvestre Villegas Revueltas, "Los obispos y la reforma liberal," *Metapolítica* 6, no. 22 (March–April 2002): 97–98. According to O'Hara, the new law had colonial precedents. O'Hara, *A Flock Divided*, 219.

59. For the complete text of the law, see "Señala los aranceles parroquiales para el cobro de derechos y obvenciones" in Pérez Lugo, *La cuestión religiosa*. 191–92. The archbishop issued an official response to this new challenge on April 17, in which he declared that the Church, "by the institution of Jesus Christ, is free, sovereign and independent of all human powers." See "Circular del Illmo. Sr. Arzobispo de México," *La Cruz* 4, no. 18 (April 23, 1857): 627–28. The text of the new law was also printed in this issue, 625–26. For a discussion of the ensuing debate in the press, see José María Roa Bárcena, "Revista de la prensa," *La Cruz* 4, no. 19 (April 30, 1857): 635–38.

60. In his correspondence with the archbishop, Iglesias indicated that deportation was the most fitting punishment for his "crime." However, in consideration of his age and infirmities, the president had commuted this sentence to house arrest until further notice. Only five canons were eventually arrested, as the rest had gone into hiding after their escape from the cathedral. Furthermore, as soon as their arrest and that of the archbishop was known, the apostolic delegate went to see the president at his residence in Tacubaya to obtain their release. Ultimately, thanks to Msgr. Clementi's intervention, they were held only two days in a room at the city hall. Díaz López, *Versión francesa de México*, 1:412; and Rivera, *Anales Mexicanos*, 22. Garcia Ugarte indicates that Mariano Riva Palacios, a *moderado*, also played a role in the archbishop's release. García Ugarte, *Poder político y religioso*, 1:680–82. However, the police continued to pursue the three canons that had evaded arrest in order to make them serve the same sentence. See Malo, *Diario de sucesos notables*, 2:486–87.

61. Because the politicians and officers involved were anxious to justify their own actions, the official reports vary and contain some conflicting detail. Although the troops later claimed that they were provoked, it does appear that they fired first. Pompa y Pompa, *Coleccción de documentos*, 22–26, 60–64. Zamacois reported that because of the defections that occurred during the subsequent fighting, only two officers, two scribes, and ten soldiers were remaining in the company that withdrew on April 13. Zamacois, *Historia de Méjico*, 14:559–60.

62. Here the political officer was stoned while reading the constitution. Afterward mobs destroyed the platform where the ceremony had just occurred, assaulted the military

barracks, sacked various government buildings, and opened the jail. Pompa y Pompa, *Coleccción de documentos,* 57–60.

63. For other examples, see Connaughton, "1856–1857," 432–42. Detailed military dispatches relating to the various disorders occasioned by the promulgation of the constitution are published in Pompa y Pompa, *Coleccción de documentos,* 20–88. Also see "La nueva constitucion," *La Cruz* 4, no. 18 (April 23, 1857): 616–17; Zamacois, *Historia de Méjico,* 14:557–60; and Vigil, *La Reforma,* 232.

64. Un Católico [Remigo Tovar], *Crimenes de la demogogía: El colegio apostolico de Guadalupe en Zacatecas* (Mexico City: J.M. Lara, 1860). 76–77.

65. The commander at Lagos also wrote, "I can assure you that a very insignificant part of the lowest class of the city got mixed up in the trouble." Pompa y Pompa, *Coleccción de documentos,* 64. On the other hand, in Zamora and Mascota we know that the rebellions were at least directed by *gente de bien.*

66. The federal army that attacked Mascota consisted of 450 troops, 15 cavalry, and two pieces of artillery arrayed against a force of 400 rebel defenders. Rocha claimed that he lost no men on this campaign, which proved that "the excommunications that the bad priests pronounce against us are worth nothing." Pompa y Pompa, *Coleccción de documentos,* 27–29. The rebels, however, reported that 32 federal soldiers and a "concubine" who had accompanied the general to the front lines were killed. Un Católico, *Crimenes de la demogogía,* 76–77n2. Tovar, a conservative journalist, was the actual leader of the Mascota revolt. See also Zamacois, *Historia de Méjico,* 14:558; and Pérez Verdía, *Historia particular,* 2:422–23.

67. See Pompa y Pompa, *Coleccción de documentos,* 39–41, 57–60; and Rivera, *Anales Mexicanos,* 23n5.

68. Like most liberals, Portilla attributed this problem to a false consciousness, "for by ignorance or deceit they have been made to believe that their religious beliefs are attacked in [the constitution]." Another liberal, José de la Luz Morena, wrote that "the authorities and the majority of the population of this district and principally of this town, seduced and deceived by the iniquitous deductions and threats of the secular and regular clergy that unfortunately abound in this town, have openly refused [to take the oath] under the pretext of being afraid they would not be absolved in the tribunal of penance." Pompa y Pompa, *Coleccción de documentos,* 67–81.

69. Pompa y Pompa, 67–69.

70. García Ugarte, *Poder político y religioso,* 1:672–73.

71. Díaz López, *Versión francesa de México,* 1:406.

72. These comments are taken from a petition submitted to President Comonfort by the municipal officials of Coyoacán and San Angel (suburbs of Mexico City), who had themselves already taken the oath. It asked him to use his executive power to suspend the constitutional articles that offended Catholics, arguing that the nonjuring crisis was causing the financial ruin of many Mexicans and leading to "a religious civil war." See "La nueva constitucion," *La Cruz* 4, no. 18 (April 23, 1857): 616.

73. [Francisco de P. Campa], "Caso de conciencia: la cuestión del juramento," *El Siglo Diez y Neuve,* September 1, 1857. This long letter to the editor was signed "The priest of a town of Jalisco."

74. Un Jalisciense, *Tendencia de la demagogia*, 26–27n2.

75. See "Retractaciones," *La Cruz* 5, no. 15 (August 20, 1857): 519. This article also stated that liberal newspapers like *La Trait d'Union* rejoiced in reports of false retractions, "since such individuals make a mockery of the clergy." The editors of *La Cruz*, however, countered that such sacrilege only highlighted the basic immorality of the enemies of the Church.

76. Similar cases were also reported in Guanajuato and Colima. The details of these episodes are recorded in Rivera, *Anales Mexicanos*, 29n10. Because Fr. Rivera was a prosecutor in the ecclesiastical tribunal of Guadalajara, he had first-hand knowledge of such cases. According to Catholic teaching, the bride and groom, not the priest, confer the sacrament of matrimony on one another by their consent to be married. But in order to eliminate secret or forced marriages, the Council of Trent had decreed that this intention must be expressed in the presence of a priest and two witnesses. That is why the "clandestine marriages" in Mexico were eventually judged "illicit, but valid" by the ecclesiastical authorities. See "Decree on the Reformation of Marriage" (November 11, 1563) in Waterworth, *Canons and Decrees*, 196–99.

77. The latter case was reported along with the story that baptism had been denied to a workingman's infant daughter. This event was denied by the *Diario de Avisos*, which pointed out that canon law allowed no impediments for the baptism of innocent children. Since both cases were based on anonymous rumors, the article concluded that "the demagogic newspapers" published any unsubstantiated calumny as long as it was injurious to religion and the clergy. "Dos cases de juramentados," *Diario de Avisos*, May 27, 1857. Another reported case involved a priest, "similar to many," who was said to have refused to bury an infant whose poor parents could not pay for the funeral. Liberals eagerly sought out such stories and publicized as many as they could find to support their anticlerical narrative. Mallon, *Peasant and Nation*, 93.

78. According to Gabric, plans for this mission began almost as soon as the allocution appeared, but Comonfort had to delay its implementation for almost three months due to a lack of funds. Díaz López, *Versión francesa de México*, 1:403.

79. See Luis Medina Ascensio, SJ, *La iglesia y el estado liberal, 1836–1867*, vol. 2 of *México y el Vaticano* (Mexico City: 1984, Editorial Jus), 211–18.

80. Díaz López, *Versión francesa de México*, 1:417.

81. Some Mexican Catholics, in fact, found this pragmatism hard to believe. The anonymous priest of Jalisco claimed that telegraph dispatches from Rome claiming that Montes had been officially received at the Vatican or that the Holy Father had approved the actions of the Mexican government must have been forged. "No one pays any attention to them," he wrote. Un Jalisciense, *Tendencias de la demagogia*, 34.

82. Although most other religious institutions were also to be abolished, Montes also offered to preserve the colleges run by the Congregation for the Propagation of the Faith, which prepared priests for the Indian missions.

83. [Manuel Baranda], *Apuntamientos sobre derecho público eclesiástico* (Mexico City: Imprenta de Ignacio Cumplido, 1857), 76 pages.

84. Gabriac wrote on May 11, 1857: "Not having dared to directly combat or refute the allocution of the Holy Father, Comonfort's cabinet delegated this task to a certain

Manuel Baranda, a jurist famous for his abilities as well as his degeneracy; but the response of the Mexican lawyer was published anonymously. It is said that his great [financial] misery forced him to sell himself to the government." Díaz López, *Versión francesa de México*, 417.

85. Díaz López, 417.

86. *Ligeras reflexiones sobre un cuaderno anónimo intitulado "Apuntamientos sobre derecho publico eclesiastico"* (Mexico City: J. M. Andrade y F. Escalante, 1847), 28 pages. This pamphlet was also published as a supplement to *La Cruz* 5, no. 3 (May 28, 1857).

87. Un catolico mexicano [José Julián Tornel y Mendívil], "Examen de los apuntamientos sobre derecho publico eclesiastico" *La Cruz* 5, no. 9 (July 9, 1857): 217 to 7, no. 24 (July 29, 1858): 792 passim. The work was originally published under a pseudonym, but the author's name was revealed after the fall of the liberal regime. The final installment of the series was included in the last issue of *La Cruz*, which ceased publication at the end of July 1858. The entire work was also published that year as a 385-page book. José Julian Tornel y Mendivil, *Apuntamientos sobre derecho público eclesiástico* (Mexico City: Andrade y Escalante, 1858). Tornel, an eminent jurist, was the brother of the *santanista* general and politician, José María Tornel y Mendívil. For biographical information on the former, see María del Carmen Rovira, ed., *Pensamiento filosófico mexicano del siglo XIX y primeros años del XX* (Mexico City, Universidad Nacional Autónoma de México, 2001), 3:43–44.

88. José Joaquín Pesado, "Reflexiones sobre la iglesia y el estado," *La Cruz* 5, no. 8 (July 2, 1857):234 to 5, no. 13 (August 6, 1857): 416 passim.

89. Juan Nepomuceno Rodríguez de San Miguel, *"Reforma del clero, o sean declamaciones sobre su corrupción y sus riquezas* (1848; repr., Morelia: I. Arango, 1856), 10 pages. For biographical information, see "Rodríguez de San Miguel, Juan N." in Francisco Sosa, *Biografias de mexicanos destinguidos* (Mexico City: Oficina Tipografica de la Secretaria de Fomento, 1884), 911–15. For this author's other accomplishments, see María del Refugio González Domínguez, "Juan N. Rodríguez de San Miguel, jurista conservador mexicano" in *Estudios jurídicos en homenaje a Marta Morineau*, ed. Nuria González Martín (Mexico City: UNAM, Instituto de Investigaciones Jurídicas, 2016), 1:233–49.

90. Juan Nepomuceno Rodríguez de San Miguel, *Varias observaciones contra un opúsculo titulado Aputamientos sobre derecho público eclesiástico* (Mexico City: J. M. Lara, 1857). 52 pages. This work was signed on May 25, 1857, and published June 1.

91. This comment appears in a manuscript note on a copy of the pamphlet held in the Lafragua Collection in Mexico City (LAF 1060). The handwriting has been identified as that of Agustín Rivera, later author of *Anales Mexicanos*.

92. Bernardo Couto, *Discurso sobre la constitutción de la iglesia* (Mexico City: Andrade y Escalante, 1857), 84 pages. The booklet initially appeared as a supplement to *La Cruz* 5, no. 9 (July 9, 1857).

93. Hale, *Mexican Liberalism*, 128.

94. Couto publicly defended his change of heart in a letter to the editor of *La Cruz* in January 1858. "El Sr. Lic. D. Bernardo Couto," *La Cruz* 6, no. 16 (January 14,1858): 524–25. Biographical information may be found in "Noticia del autor," in *Obras del*

Doctor D. José Bernardo Couto (Mexico City: V. Agüeros, 1898), v–xxvii; and Ricardo Couto, *José Bernardo Couto* (Mexico City: Editorial Citlaltepetl, 1961), 5–30.

95. One such writer declared that "This writing will immortalize its author in the annals of the Mexican Church since in it is manifested not only his profound knowledge and erudition in both law, in history, and theological science, but above all, his unblemished Catholicism." Un Jalisciense, *Tendendcias de la demagogia*, 25n1.

96. The Durango proclamation, dated September 19, 1857, was reprinted in "Voto de gracias al autor del *Discurso sobre la constitucion de la iglesia*," *La Cruz* 6, no. 2 (October 8, 1857): 78–79.

97. Alejandro Arango y Escandon, *Epístola dirigida a mi maestro y amigo el Doctor D. José Bernardo Couto, con motivo de la publicación de su "Discurso sobre la constitucion de la iglesia"* (Mexico City: n.p., n.d.), 8 pages. Arango y Escandon, a fellow-member of the literary Academia de Letrán, was a former clerk in Couto's law practice. He was also the author of the scholarly *Estudio sobre Fray Luis de Leon*, serialized in the pages of *La Cruz* during 1855 and 1856.

98. Norberto Pérez Cuyado [pseud.], *Disertación sobre la naturaleza y límites de la authoridad eclesiástica* (Mexico City: n.p. 1825); "Las ideas religiosas del Sr. Lic. D. Bernardo Couto, puestas en evidencia,"and "Independencia de los gobiernos demonstrada por el Lic. D. Bernardo Couto y Pérez," *El Monitor Republicano*, August 23 and 24, 1857.

99. This series denied the infallibility of the pope and bishops in non-religious matters and argued that there were no anti-religious elements in the new constitution. See [José Manuel T. Alvires], "Juramento," *El Siglo Diez y Nueve*, April 14, 15, 16, 17, 18, 19, 27 and May 2, 1857. The articles were later collected and published as J. Manuel T. Alvires, *Reflexiones sobre los decretos episcopales que prohiben el juramento constitucional* (Mexico City: N. Chávez, 1857).

100. Alvires pointed out that since the Ten Commandments did not proscribe political oaths, it was "unjust" and "despotic" to refer to this matter as a sin. Alvires, *Reflexiones sobre los decretos episcopales*, 8. Catholic apologists responded that according to the definitions in Padre Ripalda's catechism, an oath to this particular constitution violated both the second and the eighth commandments: "Thou shalt not take the name of the Lord thy God in vain" and "Thou shalt not bear false witness."

101. Aguilar y Marocho, *La familia enferma*, 51.

102. José Joaquin Pesado, "Contestación a las *Reflexiones sobre los decretos episcopales*," *La Cruz* 5, nos. 5–7 (June 11, 18, 25, 1857): 129–36, 161–69, 193–203.

103. Agustin de la Rosa, *Contestacion al Sr. Alvires, autor del cuaderno titulado "Reflexiones sobre los decretos episcopales, etc."*(Guadalajara: Rodriguez, 1857).

104. Salinas, *Dudas de un estudiante*, 21. In his sympathetic biography of Comonfort, Portilla claimed that conservatives had viciously attacked Alvires, calling him "schismatic, heretical, scandalous, a public sinner, excommunicated, impious and even an atheist." Portilla, *Méjico en 1856 and 1857*. 239. Zamacois, however, stated that he could find no documentary evidence of such slander. It is true that most of the replies to Alvires adopted a civil tone. But although Salinas did not accuse Alvires directly in his polemic, all these charges were not-so-subtly implied. See Zamacois, *Historia de Méjico*, 14:585.

105. Since Alvires also held a doctorate in canon law, it is almost certain that he was personally acquainted with both José Guadalupe Romero and Ramón Camacho García, professors of canon law and theology at the Conciliar Seminary in Morelia, who coauthored the series of articles denouncing his work. See "Camacho y García, Ramón" and "Romero y López, José Guadalupe," in Real Ledezma, *Enciclopedia histórica y biográfica de la Universidad de Guadalajara: Los Universitarios entre el Instituto y la Universidad.*

106. Alvires published these additions in *El Siglo Diez y Nueve* under the original title. The collected articles were later reprinted as José Manuel T. Alvires. *Reflexiones sobre los decretos episcopales que prohiben el juramento constitucional. Segunda parte: En la que se responde a las objeciones* and *Tercera parte: En la que se hacen esplicaciones importantes* (Mexico City: N. Chávez, 1857).

107. Alvires, *Tercera parte,* 50–55.

108. Aguilar y Marocho, *La familia enferma,* 53.

109. Reprinted in "Palabras y hechos," *Diario de Avisos,* June 22, 1857.

110. "Apuntes sobre el juramento de la constitución," *La Cruz* 5, no. 3 (May 28, 1857): 72–73.

111. See [Campa], "Caso de conciencia."

112. Clemente de Jesús Munguía, *Opúsculo escrito por el Illmo. Sr. Obispo D. Clemente de Jesús Munguía, en defensa de la soberanía, derechos y libertades de la iglesia atacados en la constitución civil de 1857 y en otros decretos expedidos por el actual gobierno de la nación* (Morelia: Ignacio Arango, 1857), 40–41.

113. Aguilar y Marocho, *La familia enferma.* 52. See also "Asuntos eclesiásticos en Oajaca" *La Cruz* 5, no. 15 (August 20, 1857): 501–3. After the sacraments were denied to a dying man in Jalapa (Zacatecas), *El Heraldo* solemnly declared that "the priest should not be allowed to continue his ministry." *La Cruz* analyzed the details of this case in "El Señor Presbitero D. José María Mora," *La Cruz* 5, no. 7 (June 25, 1857): 224.

114. Fr. Carrillo, the priest in question, was exiled for his "crime." Malo, *Diario de sucesos notables,* 2:491; and Francisco Vera, "Destierro de un sacerdote," *La Cruz* 5, no. 12 (July 30, 1857): 408. Juárez also demanded exile for a priest that refused the sacrament to the mayor of Tarehua (Oaxaca). Connaughton, "1856–1857," 447.

115. The newspaper was *El Tiempo.* Quoted in Portilla, 257–58. See also Connaughton, "1856–1857," 450. There were rumors that the priest had also demanded an exorbitant fee for the interment, but the conservative press denied this.

116. See Malo, *Diario de sucesos notables,* 2:494; Aguilar y Marocho, *La familia enferma,* 54; Zamacois, *Historia de Méjico,* 14:635–38; and Vigil, *La Reforma,* 242–3. Vigil's notes also include the deposition made by the military chaplain, Fr. Vicente Guevara, on September 1. Forced burials by liberals also occurred in Sayula (Jalisco) and Villa de Concordia (San Luis Potosí.) See Connaughton, "1856–1857," 443, 445–46.

117. José Joaquín Pesado, "Los cementerios cristianos," *La Cruz* 5, no. 19 (September 17, 1857): 625–31.

118. See "Revista del interior y del esterior," La Cruz 5, no. 18 (September 10, 1857): 623. On November 13, the Archbishop of Mexico issued a circular reaffirming that Christian burial was to be denied to anyone who refused to restore adjudicated ecclesias-

tical property or to abjure the oath. Furthermore, the clergy were to offer no prayers or masses for the repose of their souls, nor accept any donations on their behalf. See "Nego el clero sepultura a los que juraron la constitución y compraron bienes de manos muertas," in Pérez Lugo, *La cuestión religiosa*, 324–25.

119. An article in *Diario de Avisos* detailed the lives and work of the exiled priests, concluding that most were popular and exemplary ministers of religion. Un amigo de la verdad [pseud.], "Obras son amores y no buenas razones," *Diario de Avisos*, September 17, 1857.

120. The details of this story, including a summary of articles from Monterrey newspapers and transcriptions of official documents relating to the case, may be found in "Asuntos eclesiasticos en Nuevo León y Coahuila" and "Sucesos de Coahuila y Nuevo León," *La Cruz* 6, nos. 1, 2 (October 1 and 8, 1857): 18–27 and 41–47.

CHAPTER SEVEN

1. Historical narratives of the war include Manuel Cambre, *La Guerra de Tres Años: apuntes para la historia de la Reforma* (Guadalajara: José Cabrera, 1904); Alfonso Trueba, *La Guerra de Tres Años*, 2nd ed. (Mexico City: Editorial Campeador, 1954); and Fowler, *Guerra de Tres Años*. For the continuing debate on the dates that the war began (in 1857 or 1858) and ended (in 1860 or 1861), see Fowler, *Grammar of Civil War*, 208–9.

2. "Tacubaya, Plan de (December 1857)" in Marley, *Mexico at War*, 381–83. See also Trueba, *Guerra de Tres Años*, 5–7.

3. The full document is available in Cambre, *Guerra de Tres Años*, 13–19. Later, writing from his exile in New York City, Comonfort confessed that the constitution was neither what the country wanted or needed in 1857. "That constitution, which should have been a rainbow of peace and fountain of health, that ought to have resolved all questions and put an end to all disturbances, went on to raise up one of the worst storms that has ever afflicted Mexico . . . its observation was impossible, its unpopularity was palpable." "Manifesto" (July 1858), quoted in Rivera, *Anales Mexicanos*, 42.

4. General Zuloaga was a supporter of the Comonfort administration and had led federal troops against the conservative revolts in Puebla in 1856 and 1857. Other moderate liberals participating in the coup included Manuel Payno, Manuel Silicio, Ignacio de la Llave, and Miguel de María Echeagaray. Even the radical Juan José Baz joined. See García Ugarte, *Polder político y religioso*, 1:708; and Fowler, *Guerra de Tres Años*, 25–26.

5. Fowler, *Guerra de Tres Años*, 30. In 1861, conservatives who had served in the conservative administration after Comonfort fled were indicted for "usurping power." In their defense, they pointed out that the constitution had already been overthrown by the liberal coup so they could not be blamed for forming a new government. José María Cuevas, *Informe de Licenciado J. M. Cuevas ante la primera sala del Tribunal Superior en el punto sobre competencia del Juzgado de Distrito, para conocer de la causa que se instruye al Sr. D. Luis C. Cuevas, por haber sido ministro de relaciones en la administracion establecida en enero de 1858* (Mexico City: J. M. Lara, 1861), 37–39.

6. The States of Puebla, Tlaxcala, Mexico, Chiapas, Tabasco, San Luis Potosi, and Veracruz supported Comonfort, although Veracruz switched sides on December 30.

7. In this three-sided contest, conservatives held the Ciudadela and San Agustín Church, while Comonfort and his supporters held the presidential palace. The *puro* faction occupied the Churches of San Francisco (after incarcerating the friars) and the Santísima.

8. Comonfort met Benito Juárez on the night of December 15 to elicit his support for the upcoming coup, but Juárez refused. Rivera, *Anales Mexicanos*, 31. Comonfort left Mexico City on January 31 and sailed from Veracruz on February 7, 1858, aboard the *Tennessee*. He arrived in New Orleans on February 10 and eventually settled in New York City. He returned to Mexico to fight the French in 1862.

9. Rivera, 33–34. General Parra was named the new Minister of War.

10. Malo, *Diario de sucesos notables*, 2:509.

11. Cambre, *Guerra de Tres Años*, 33–34. Pope Pius IX sent his apostolic blessing to the Zuloaga government on March 18. "Relaciones entre México y Roma," *La Cruz* 7, no. 3 (March 4, 1858): 94–96; and "Mexico y Roma," *La Cruz* 7, no 13 (May 13, 1858): 415–16.

12. J. H., *El liberalismo y sus efectos en la República Mexicana* (Mexico City: Andres Boix, 1858), 11.

13. "La festividad nacional de San Felipe de Jesus" and "Festividad religiosa," *La Sociedad*, February 6, 1858; and Malo, *Diario de sucesos notables*, 2:510.

14. "Honres fúnebres," *La Sociedad*, February 17, 1858; Malo, *Diario de sucesos notables*, 2:511.

15. "Nuesta Señora de los Remedios," *La Cruz* 7, no. 2 (February 25, 1858): 63.

16. Letter of Nicolás Cuevas to Juan Pérez de la Llana (April 8, 1858) in Salado Álvarez, *Episodios Nacionales*, 164.

17. "La ultima semana santa," *La Cruz* 7, no. 8 (April 8, 1858): 252–3; Malo, *Diario de sucesos notables*, 2:515–16.

18. "Funcion Religiosa," *La Cruz* 7, no. 9 (April 15, 1858): 287.

19. This was Joaquin Orihuela, executed on December 11, 1856. Rivera, *Anales Mexicanos*, 18. The conservatives later named a battalion in his honor.

20. Aguilar y Marocho, *La familia enferma*, 58.

21. The murders occurred in San Miguel Canoa (Puebla) at the end of the second Puebla revolt in November 1856. See "Asesinatos," "Importate causa criminal," "Exhumacion de los cadaveres de los Sres. Benitez y Castillero," and "Mas sobre la muerte de Benitez y Castillero," *Diario de Avisos*, March 9, 10, 20, and 25, 1857. In some reports, Benitez's first name is given as Ignacio. A third, unidentified body was also found but determined not to be that of a servant as initially supposed. The outcome of the trial of the priest and his accomplices is unknown, but the story was included in Portilla's biography of Comonfort to show the inhumanity of the "reactionaries." Portilla, *Mejico en 1856 y 1857*, 354–57. Fowler also uses Portilla's version as evidence for the attitudes of "fanatical priests." Fowler, *The Grammar of Civil War*, 120. Coincidentally, another famous "lynching" also occurred in San Miguel Canoa in 1968. Again, the priest and mayor were implicated in the deaths of two outsiders, this time mistaken

for communist agitators. A thoughtful analysis of this later incident, with a recognition of the problems of memory and "competing narratives," is found in Kevin M. Chrisman, "Community, Power, and Memory in Díaz Ordaz's Mexico: The 1968 Lynching in San Miguel Canoa, Puebla," (Master's thesis, University of Nebraska, 2013), 59, https://digitalcommons.unl.edu/historydiss/59.

22. In the Bible (1 Maccabees), Judas Macabee and his four brothers led a revolt (167–160 BCE) against the Hellenistic rulers who attempted to eradicate traditional Jewish practices in Palestine. The annual festival of Hanukkah celebrates their victory.

23. José Maria Roa Bárcena, "Honras funebres celebradas en Puebla," *La Cruz* 7, no. 2 (February 25, 1858): 53–60; Pablo Antonio del Niño Jesus, *Oración fúnebre en memoria y honor de los valientes militares que sucumbieron en la lucha contra la demagogia* (Puebla: José Maria Rivera, 1858), 17 pages.

24. See Ugarte García, *Poder político y religioso*, 1:721. The liberal forces also had some experienced commanders, such as fifty-three-year-old General Anastasio Parrodi, a veteran of the war in Texas and the US-Mexican War and General de la Llave. But radical politicians like Melchor Ocampo, Santos Degollado and Miguel Cruz-Aedo also commanded troops, often with disastrous results.

25. This was the *Plan del Hospicio*, which started in Guadalajara. See "Márquez Araujo, Leonardo (1820–1913)" in Marley, *Mexico at War*, 207–12.

26. See Brian Hamnett, "Mexican Conservatives, Clericals, and Soldiers: The 'Traitor' Tomás Mejía through Reform and Empire, 1855–1867," *Bulletin of Latin American Research* 20, no. 2 (April 2001): 187–209.

27. The Military College, founded in 1822, was initially located in the former buildings of the Inquisition. It was moved to Chapultepec Castle in 1840. Both Osollo and Miramón were among the "niños héroes" (boy heroes) that defended the castle during the American attack.

28. See Rosaura Hernández Rodriguez, *El general conservador Luis G. Osollo* (Mexico City: Editorial Jus, 1959); and "Osollo Pancorbo, Luis Gonzaga (1828–1858)" in Marley, *Mexico at War*, 277–82.

29. See "Miramón Tarelo, Miguel Gregorio de la Luz Atenógenes (1831–1867)" in Marley, *Mexico at War*, 227–35.

30. Cambre, *Guerra de Tres Años*, 48.

31. "Despedida de los redactors de 'La Cruz,'" *La Cruz* 7, no. 24 (July 29, 1858): 793–94.

32. Daniel S. Haworth, "Desde los baluartes conservadores: La ciudad de México y la guerra de Reforma (1857–1860)," *Relaciones: Estudios de Historia y Sociadad* (El Colegio de Michoacán) 21, no. 84 (Autumn 2000): 122–24.

33. This was the same day that Zuloaga rescinded the Juárez, Lerdo and Iglesias laws. The abrogation of the *Ley Lerdo* and the return of some Church property and rents would offset some of this cost, but this process was slow and confusing. García Ugarte, *Poder político y religioso*, 1:751–54.

34. Haworth, "Desde los baluartes conservadores," 112–13.

35. The Archdiocese of Mexico City and the Diocese of Puebla were the most promising sources of funds since they remained in conservative hands throughout the war. García Ugarte, *Poder político y religioso*, 1:751, 768.

36. The conflict caused by conservative efforts to extract money from the Church in Oaxaca is described in Berry, *La Reforma in Oaxaca*, 68–72.

37. These conflicts were exacerbated by the fact that much of the rural population in these states supported the Church, but the urban centers were controlled by liberal politicians. Hamnett, "Mexican Conservatives," 194.

38. Pérez Verdía, *Historia particular*, 3:129. The historian Luis Pérez Verdía y Villaseñor was born in Guadalajara in 1857. His father, Antonio Pérez Verdía, had been a member of the Student Phalanx in Guadalajara in the 1850s.

39. Pérez Verdía, *Historia particular*, 3:129. See also Cornejo Franco, *De la independencia a la reforma*, 19–24; and Enrique de Olavarría y Ferrari, *Reseña histórica del teatro en México*, 2nd ed. (Mexico City: La Europa, 1895), 319.

40. This happened in Teocaltiche (Jalisco) when Antonia Ceballos, a liberal supporter, grabbed Antonia García, lifted her green skirts and spanked her in front of a crowd of men. Cornejo Franco, *De la independencia a la reforma*, 21–23.

41. Pérez Verdía, *Historia particular*, 3:129. "*Hacheros*" ("hatchets") was a derogatory nickname for the liberals. It originated during the Ayutla revolt, when liberal troops used hatchets to break open and loot private homes and shops during an attack on Guadalajara in January 1856. [Villalvazo], *D. Santos Degollado*, 5; and Cambre, *Guerra de Tres Años*, 22–23. For the other nicknames for the liberals and conservatives and their origins, see Salado Álvarez, *Episodios Nacionales*, 187n1.

42. Cambre, *Guerra de Tres Años*, 23–24.

43. As had occurred in Puebla in 1856, anxious crowds surrounded the episcopal palace to protect the bishop when this news spread. "Guadalajara," *El Siglo Diez y Nueve*, February 13, 1858.

44. Cambre, *Guerra de Tres Años*, 50–61; and Pérez Verdía, *Historia particular*, 3:4–23. According to Cambre, the rallying cry was: "Long live the Army! Death to the National Guard! Death to the constitution!"

45. "Guadalajara," *La Sociedad*, March 25, 1858. Alfonso Trueba claims that the story that Guillermo Prieto intervened to prevent the execution of Juárez is a liberal myth. Trueba, *Guerra de Tres Años*, 13. The Prieto legend is included in Rivera, *Anales Mexicanos*, 35–36; and Cambre, *Guerra de Tres Años*, 56.

46. Rivera, *Anales Mexicanos*, 37–38.

47. Pérez Verdía, *Historia particular*, 3:33.

48. Cambre, *Guerra de Tres Años*, 81–84.

49. Thirty-eight-year-old Zuazua had joined the military during the US invasion and fought in both the regular army and as a guerilla. It has been said that his ruthlessness reflected his experience fighting Indian tribes on the frontier. He was killed during an internecine struggle between liberal chiefs on July 30, 1859. See "Zuazua Esparza, Juan Nepomuceno (1820-1860)" in Marley, *Mexico at War*, 470–75.

50. Trueba, *Guerra de Tres Años*, 15–16. Huitzilopochtli (called Huichilobos by the Spanish conquistators) was the Aztec god of war and the sun who required large numbers of human sacrifices to remain powerful. Pérez Verdía called this the "first example of inhumanity" in the war. Pérez Verdía, *Historia particular*, 3:34. One conservative report stated that the prisoners were held three days without food and were denied the

consolations of religion before they were beheaded. [R. G. H.], *Memoria sobre la propie-dad eclesiástica; riqueza pública destruida y víctimas hechas por los demagogos de 858 hasta junio de 863* (Mexico City: Literaria, 1864), 26. However, it is more likely that they were shot, since one of the victims, the conservative mayor Pedro Gallardo, was later found to be still alive and was hidden by a priest until he recovered from his wounds. Rivera, *Anales Mexicanos*, 39–40n13.

51. Herrera y Cairo was also a distinguished physician. In 1856, as Governor of Jalisco, he had once arrested and intimidated the superiors of the major religious orders for preaching against the liberal government. On May 20, 1858, Gen. Francisco G. Casa-nova sent Lieutenant Colonels Manuel Piélago and Aniceto Monayo to the ex-governor's hacienda to arrest him. Apparently, this was the result of an "intrigue" by one of his personal enemies, a Dr. Liceaga, although many others were also blamed for his death. He and another prisoner were shot without trial the next day. A few months later the liberal government declared him a national hero ("benemerito") and created a "Herrera y Cairo Battalion" in his honor. See "Herrera y Cairo, José Ignacio," in Real Ledezma, *Enciclopedia histórica y biográfia de la Universidad de Guadalajara*.

52. Statement of General Parra (minister of war), May 29, 1858. Quoted in "Fusilamien-tos en Jalisco," *La Sociedad*, June 5, 1858. The conservative press contrasted this re-sponse with the praise heaped on Col. Zuazua by Santos Degollado after his execution of prisoners in Zacatecas. "Lo que hace el supremo gobieo y lo que hacen los con-stitucionalistas." and "La enerjía debe aliarse con la justicia," *La Sociedad*, June 7, 1858.

53. Trueba, *Guerra de Tres Años*, 18. When the City of Veracruz rejected the Tacubaya Plan, the conservative government had created a new state capital in Xalapa. Malo, *Diario de sucesos notables*, 2:513, 520.

54. García Ugarte, *Poder político y religioso*, 1:771.

55. For an example of a priest who joined the liberal forces, see Zachary Brittsan, *Popular Politics*, 42.

56. [R. G. H.], *Memoria de la propiedad eclesiástica*, 32. García Ugarte states that although priests were handled roughly by the liberals, "nevertheless, few were killed." She cites only one priest executed in the State of Mexico, although others died later from the beating and wounds they received, including one priest attacked with machetes. García Ugarte, *Poder político y religioso*, 1:814. For the State of Jalisco, Rivera gives the names of five priests shot, one hanged and one beheaded by the constitutionalists. Rivera, *Anales Mexicanos*, 79n21.

57. Aguilar y Marocho, *La familia enferma*, 70.

58. "El asesinato del Sr. cura Ortega," *La Sociedad*, April 29, 1859; "Algo sobre el asesinato del Sr. cura Ortega," *La Sociedad*, May 6, 1859; "Remitidos," and "Soneto dedicada á la muerte del llamado cura de Zacapoaxtla, presbítero D. Francisco Ortega y García," *Diario de Avisos*, November 9, 1859; Aguilar y Marocho, *La familia enferma* 82; and [R. G. H.], *Memoria sobre la propiedad eclesiástica*, 32.

59. Pérez Verdía, *Historia particular*, 3:40; Rivera, *Anales Mexicanos*, 41; and [Villalvazo], *D. Santos Degollado*, 48.

60. Fanny Calderón described the cathedral during her visit to Morelia in 1841: "The high altar is dazzling with gold and silver; the railing which leads from it to the choir is of

pure silver, with pillars of the same metal; the two pulpits, with their stairs, are also covered with silver." Calderón de la Barca, *Life in Mexico*, 588.

61. Fanny Calderón had remarked in 1841 that the cathedral "is still wonderfully rich, notwithstanding that silver to the amount of thirty-two thousand marks has been taken from it during the civil wars." Calderón de la Barca, 588.

62. The cathedral remained closed until March 23, 1861. Malo, *Diario de sucesos notables*, 2:606.

63. Trueba, *Guerra de Tres Años*, 20–21; García Ugarte, *Poder político y religioso*, 1:733–34; Rivera, *Anales Mexicanos*, 43n17; Aguilar y Marocho, *La familia enferma*, 72; and Malo, *Diario de sucesos notables*, 2:524. The estimated value of the silver was around a half million pesos. In December, conservatives uncovered around fifty bars of silver, valued at 70,000 pesos, still buried at the former residence of the US ambassador, John Forsyth, in Tacubaya, a suburb of Mexico City. Rivera, *Anales Mexicanos*, 46; Aguilar y Marocho, *La familia enferma*, 77; and Malo, *Diario de sucesos notables*, 2:530.

64. Un ingenio de esta villa [pseud.], *Porfirio ó El héroe de la crujia* (Mexico City: Vicente Segura, 1858), 5, 12.

65. *Porfirio*, 33.

66. *Porfirio*, 12, 32. Potosí Mountain, today in Bolivia, was once the major source of silver from colonial Latin America.

67. *Porfirio*, 8, 16.

68. *Porfirio*, 67. This was the Italian officer named Moretto who was attached to Blanco's command. The anticlerical Giuseppe Mazzini (1805–1872) was an important Italian revolutionary.

69. *Porfirio*, 69. A footnote on this page informs the reader that such a toast had actually been made in one of the usual liberal "orgies."

70. *Porfirio*, 73. This final scene may have been inspired by a report from Morelia in which a well-known liberal was pressured to return silver candlesticks and thuribles that he had received from Huerta. His wife came down with a fever, which she believed was because of his connection to this "sacrilegious robbery." In her delirium, she demanded that he "get that silver out of the house . . . it burns, don't touch it!" "Hechos de los demagagos," *Diario de Avisos*, December 19, 1858.

71. The hospice was built in 1805 by Bishop Juan Cruz Ruiz de Cabañas as a refuge for orphans, the handicapped and the elderly. The neoclassical buildings were designed by the famous architect, Manuel Tolsá. Today it is a UN World Heritage site: https://whc.unesco.org/en/list/815/.

72. [Villalvazo], *D. Santos Degollado*, 51, 54–55. Colonel Joseph M. Chessman played a role in many actions under Degollado's command. See Cambre, *Guerra de Tres Años*, 111–12, 116, 142, 379. In 1859, an American newspaper boasted that in a recent battle a "church soldier" (a term for conservative combatants used by anti-Catholic newspapers in the US) seized Chessman by the throat, but the American drew his six-shooter and killed all six of his assailants. "Among the officers under Mexican Degollado," *Athens (TN) Post*, March 25, 1859. Villalvazo refered to him as an "executioner" and Rivera called him a "Yankee bandit." Rivera, *Anales Mexicanos*, 45. On October 19, 1859, Juárez raised him to the rank of general. Aguilar y Marocho, *La familia enferma*, 138.

73. The complete lyrics of the song are printed in Cambre, *Guerra de Tres Años*, 114n1. The first verse has been translated as: "Cassocks and cowls, / Predominate everywhere, / Wise men in their high hats, / Shall make us all happy." CHORUS: "Like crabs following the lead, / Let's all march backward, / Zis, zis y zás / Let's all march backward." "Cangrejos, Marcha de los (1854–1867)" in Marley, *Mexico at War*, 68.

74. See "Guadalajara, Sieges of (1858–1860)" in Marley, *Mexico at War*, 157–58.

75. The cause of the "cerebral" fever is uncertain. In various sources it has been attributed to cholera, typhoid fever, and even scarlet fever.

76. Malo, *Diario de sucesos notables*, 2:520–21; "Fallecimiento del Señor General Osollo," *La Cruz* 7: no. 20 (July 1, 1858): 640.

77. "Honres fúnebres en Guadalajara," *La Sociedad*, July 9, 1858.

78. "Un recuerdo del simpatico General Luis G. Osollo" and "Retrato del General Osollo" (advertisements), *La Sociedad*, July 16, 1858.

79. Malo, *Diario de sucesos notables*, 2:528.

80. Trueba, *Guerra de Tres Años*, 21; Pérez Verdía, *Historia particular*, 3:49–53; Rivera, *Anales Mexicanos*, 45; Aguilar y Marocho, *La familia enferma*, 74; [R. G. H.], *Memoria sobre la propiedad eclesiástica*, 28–29; and Fowler, *Guerra de Tres Años*, 41–42. Although Santos Degollado endorsed the execution of Monayo and Piélago, he immediately denounced the murder of General Blancarte and placed Rojas "outside the law." He also authorized a pension for Blancarte's widow and orphans. Cambre, *Guerra de Tres Años*, 162–63. However, Degollado exonerated Rojas and restored him to his previous rank on May 9, 1859. "El último decreto de Degollado relative al cabecilla Rojas," *La Sociedad*, August 3, 1859; Trueba, *Guerra de Tres Años*, 22; and Rivera, *Anales Mexicanos*, 50.

81. All those targeted for execution, along with Bishop Espinosa and Canon Rafael Tovar, had been accused by liberals of plotting Herrera y Cairo's death inside the bishop's palace, the very place where the hangings occurred. After his death, a local pharmacist had removed Herrera y Cairo's heart, which was venerated as a relic by some liberals and eventually enshrined in a Masonic temple in San Francisco, California, indicating that he held some high rank in the lodge. See Cambre, *Guerra de Tres Años*, 100n1, 103, 159, and 217–18.

82. Father Agustín Rivera witnessed some of these attacks from an upstairs window before he was denounced and arrested himself. As a liberal sympathizer, he was later released by his former seminary classmate, Cruz-Aedo. Rivera, *Anales Mexicanos*, 45n21. Other specific cases of assault are described in [Villalvazo], *D. Santos Degollado*, 66–69.

83. A detailed inventory of the loot taken from each location is included in [Villalvazo], 71–78.

84. [Villalvazo], 75–77; and Rivera, *Anales Mexicanos*, 45–46n22.

85. Cambre, *Guerra de Tres Años*, 170.

86. [Villalvazo], *D. Santos Degollado*, 65.

87. [Villalvazo], 56–58. The address was delivered to liberal troops in San Pedro Tlaquepaque (Jalisco), and later repeated in Guadalajara. Vallarta was referring to the Franciscan convent in Zapópan and the textile factory nearby. In October 1860 forty-eight friars from this monastery were taken prisoner by liberals but later released. Cambre, *Guerra de Tres Años*, 539.

88. The plaza was named Plaza Núñez in honor of General José Silverio Núñez, who died during the recent siege. Official reports denied rumors that he had been drugged to prevent him from retracting his oath in order to receive the last rites. Instead, they insisted that he was "chloroformed" only to reduce the pain of his wounds. They also insisted that he had in fact received absolution before his death from the hospital chaplain, who did not question him about the oath. Cambre, *Guerra de Tres Años*, 150–51, and 171. He was buried from the cathedral on November 4, the last civic funeral held by liberals before these were outlawed by the Reforma laws. Pérez Verdía, *Historia particular*, 3:54.

89. The Carmelite community was a particular target of the liberals because its superior was believed to have encouraged the revolt of March 19. At one point, Colonel Refugio González even decapitated the statues in this church in an iconoclastic frenzy, but it is not clear when this occurred. Pérez Verdía, *Historia particular*, 3:5, 54, 129. Ultimately, all the property of the monastery was seized and its library was given to the state. [Villalvazo], *D. Santos Degollado*, 79–80. After taking the city, liberals searched diligently for the prior of the community, but Fray Joaquín de San Alberto had escaped the city in secret and eventually reached Querétaro. Rivera, *Anales Mexicanos*, 44n20.

90. Individuals had to be paid to demolish the buildings and clear away the rubble, although some of the material was salvaged and sold. [Villalvazo], *D. Santos Degollado*, 79.

91. Aguilar y Marocho, *La familia enferma*, 76, 84.

92. In the play *Porfirio*, Governor Huerta refers to the infirmity of "*calle-abre-manía.*" *Porfirio*, 8. The term is also used in a poem mocking liberal leaders, where Huerta, presented as a follower of King Henry VIII, orders the tearing down of monasteries, "systematizing the *calle-abre-manía.*" "Los heroes de mi patria," *La Sociedad*, December 22, 1858.

93. Aguilar y Marocho, *La familia enferma*, 75, 78. Some church bells were melted down by General Uraga, leader of the conservatives, after the *Plan del Hospicio* in 1852. Agustín Rivera, *Anales Mexicanos: La reforma i el segundo imperio*, 6th ed. (Lagos de Moreno, MX: Lopez Arce, 1904), 95n1. This note does not appear in the 1891 edition of the book.

94. The liberals were defeated at the San Miguel Ranch near Poncitlán (Jalisco) on December 14. Miramón entered Guadalajara on December 15. Trueba, *Guerra de Tres Años*, 22; and "Guadalajara" in Marley, *Mexico at War*, 159. Miramón won another victory at the Battle of San Joaquín (Colima) on December 26, 1858.

95. They escaped from the ruins by climbing down ropes. Cambre, *Guerra de Tres Años*, 200–205; and Rivera, *Anales Mexicanos*, 47. Although the explosion was generally believed to have been an accident, some conservatives blamed it on the American Chessman, "the sapper of Guadalajara and its palace." "Curiosidades constitucionalistas," *La Sociedad*, August 2, 1859.

96. Cambre, *Guerra de Tres Años*, 207–9. Pérez Verdía and Rivera indicate that this was the occasion for a famous oration by Fr. Ignacio de Cabrera in honor of the general delivered in the chapel at the Belen Hospital. Pérez Verdía, *Historia particular*, 3:62; and Rivera, *Anales Mexicanos*, 47. However, this panegyric, in which Blancarte was compared to Moses, occurred during the more elaborate celebrations on the first an-

niversary of the general's death (October 31, 1859). Cambre, *Guerra de Tres Años.* 328–29. For the sermons preached on that day and other commemorative poems, see *Grato recuerdo á los martires de Guadalajara sacrificados en los meses de Setiembre y Octubre de 1858 por la demagogia.* (Guadalajara: Luis P. Vidaurri, 1859). Because he had referred to the constitutionalists as "Philistines," Father Cabrera was exiled to the United States when liberals next occupied the city. Rivera, *Anales Mexicanos*, 47n1.

97. Miramón had retaken San Luis Potosí on September 29 and Márquez had retaken Zacatecas on October 24.

98. Despite its liberal reputation, there were some conservatives remaining in the city. At one point the governor, Manuel Gutiérrez Zamora, ordered that all the houses of conservatives be marked with red, and later black, crosses. "Veracruz," *La Sociedad*, March 19, 1858.

99. Plan of Ayotla (December 20, 1858), "The Pronunciamiento in Independent Mexico 1821–1876," University of Saint Andrews, https://arts.st-andrews.ac.uk/pronuncia mientos/search.php?searchString=Ayotla&pid=1340.

100. Plan of Navidad (December 23, 1858), "The Pronunciamiento in Independent Mexico 1821–1876," University of Saint Andrews, https://arts.st-andrews.ac.uk/pronun ciamientos/search.php?searchString=Robles&pid=1008.

101. Malo, *Diario de sucesos notables*, 2:537–38. He was referring to a comet (named after Charles V) whose appearance in Mexico he recorded on October 5, 1858. Malo, 2:525.

102. García Ugarte, *Poder político y religioso*, 1:807. Conservative elites also held a banquet for Miramón on February 7 at the Minería. In his toast to the substitute president, Aguilar y Marocho noted that "Divine Providence has placed the fate of the entire republic in the hands of a single man."

103. Malo, *Diario de sucesos notables*, 2:539.

104. Only this American was executed when Miramón captured over one hundred prisoners after a brief battle at the Soledad River en route to Veracruz. Trueba, *Guerra de Tres Años*, 26; and Malo, *Diario de sucesos notables*, 2:540. Aguilar y Marocho claims that the financial loss due to the destruction of the bridges, some built during the colonial period, was over 800,000 pesos. Aguilar y Marocho, *La familia enferma*, 81.

105. Trueba, *Guerra de Tres Años*, 28–29.

106. This campaign, led by General Miguel Blanco, had been requested and financed by frustrated liberals within Mexico City. See Haworth, "Desde los baluartes conservadores," 102.

107. In response, government officials posted notices identifying the location of cisterns, wells, and artesian springs in the city. Malo, *Diario de sucesos notables*, 2:541.

108. Trueba, *Guerra de Tres Años*, 29.

109. "Tacubaya, Battle of (1859)" in Marley, *Mexico at War*, 383–86. Throughout the campaign, Degollado was expecting a popular uprising in Mexico City that never materialized.

110. *Los Demagogos y sus escritos, Contestacion al cuaderno titulada: "Los asesinatos de Tacuba,"* (Guadalajara: Díoniso Rodríguez, 1859), 12.

111. Haworth, "Desde los baluartes conservadores," 103. Concepción Lombardo de Miramón (1835–1921) married Miguel on October 24, 1858.

112. Malo, *Diario de sucesos notables*, 2:544.

113. Of the two hundred liberal prisoners taken, conservatives reported that fourteen or sixteen were shot. See Haworth, "Desde los baluartes conservadores," 103; *Los Demagogos y sus escritos*, 10. Miramón accepted responsibility for some of the executions. In later years Márquez stated that he was only following the orders of the president when he ordered the prisoners shot. Miramón, for his part, admitted that he ordered the execution of captured officers but not civilians. See Fowler, *Guerra de Tres Años*, 270–80; and Rivera, *Anales Mexicanos*, 49n6.

114. [Francisco Zarco], *Los asesinatos de Tacubaya* (Mexico City: n.p., 1859), 8 pages. The executions occurred late on April 11. Remarkably, Zarco's pamphlet was already in publication just two days later. Fowler, *Guerra de Tres Años*, 271.

115. [Zarco], *Los asesinatos de Tacubaya*, 5–6. The teenagers were said to fifteen- and seventeen-year-old brothers, sons of an American engineer named Smith and his Mexican wife.

116. [Zarco], 7.

117. *Los Demagogos y sus escritos*, 27 pages.

118. For American readers, the most extreme version of these events was included in Hubert Howe Bancroft's *The History of Mexico*, vol. 5, *1824–1861* (San Francisco: A. L. Bancroft & Company, 1885), 763–64.

119. For example, in the City of Durango (Durango), military outposts had been given the names of various conservative martyrs. "Durango," *La Sociedad*, July 11, 1858.

120. [Zarco], *Los asesinatos de Tacubaya*, 5.

121. "Circular del Ministerio de Gobernación—Excita á los gobernadores de los Estados, con motive de los fusilamientos de Tacubaya" (April 23, 1859) in Manuel Dublan and José María Lozano, eds., *Legislación Mexicana ó colección completa de las disposiciones legislativas expendidas desde la Independencia de la República* (Mexico City: Imprenta del Comercio, 1904), 8:667–69. Degollado issued a circular on May 21, 1859, establishing a pension for the widows and orphans of the victims and promising that a monument declaring "Glory and Honor to the Martyrs Immolated at Tacubaya" would be erected on the spot. Printed in Cambre, *Guerra de Tres Años*, 250–51. The first official commemoration there was held on April 15, 1861. Malo, *Diario de sucesos notables*, 2:610. The monument, an obelisk, is still standing.

122. Juan Pérez de la Llana added some new details to Zarco's account in a letter to Prieto on April 18, 1859. "De Juan Pérez de la Llana a Don Guillermo Prieto" in Salado Álvarez, *Episodios Nacionales*, 254–59.

123. Aurelio Luis Gallardo, *Los Mártires de Tacubaya: Drama histórico en cinco actos*, 1859. Quoted in María Guadalupe Sánches Robles, "Él personaje histórico en la dramaturgia de Aurelio Luis Gallardo," *Sincronía* 13, no. 48 (Fall 2008), http://sincronia.cucsh.udg.mx/sanchezotono08.htm.

124. Cornejo Franco, *De la independencia a la reforma*, 35–36. In 1866, during the French Intervention, the play was publicly burned in the Plaza de Armas in Guadalajara, and Gallardo was exiled to the United States.

125. On the other hand, when General Márquez returned to Guadalajara on May 15, he was received as a conquering hero and a Te Deum was celebrated in the cathedral in his honor. Rivera, *Anales Mexicanos*, 50–51; and Pérez Verdía, *Historia particular*, 3:67.

126. Rivera, *Anales Mexicanos*, 51. The impact of the Tacubaya executions was also probably the reason for Degollado's rehabilitation of Rojas on May 9, 1859. Rojas would go on to shoot one hundred and sixty more prisoners on January 27, 1860, at Toma de Teal (Zacatecas) and another twenty-two at Tepic (Nayarit) on May 10, 1860. (59, 61).

127. Information about the phantom American doctors was probably conveyed by Ocampo. The deaths of other American mercenaries were not mentioned. "Third Annual Message to Congress on the State of the Union," https://www.presidency. ucsb.edu/documents/third-annual-message-congress-the-state-the-union.

128. The US had designs on the States of Chihuahua, Sonora, Sinaloa, and Baja California. It also wanted transit rights across the Tehuantepec Peninsula. Trueba, *Guerra de Tres Años*, 16.

129. Olliff, *Reforma Mexico*, 68.

130. The diplomatic mission officially ended on June 21, 1858, but ex-consul John Black continued to supply liberals in Veracruz with vital intelligence from the capital.

131. According to Olliff, Buchanan's policies toward Mexico were always dictated by his territorial ambitions, perhaps hoping that enlarging US territory would distract the nation from the looming sectional conflict. Olliff, *Reforma Mexico*, 150–51, 155.

132. "El Gobierno Constitucional á la Nacíon," reproduced in Ocampo, *Obras completas*, 2:113–42. Ruiz was the administration's minister of justice, public education, and ecclesiastical affairs, and Lerdo was currently the minister of finance and public works for the Juárez regime.

133. The radicals had been debating and planning these laws for months, although the main ideas were already present in a letter that Lerdo sent to Santa Anna in 1853. Rivera, *Anales Mexicanos*, 51n8; and Olliff, *Reforma Mexico*, 135.

134. Ocampo, *Obras Completas*, 2:136.

135. Ocampo, 2:114–15.

136. Ocampo, 2:117.

137. Olliff reports that obtaining US loans was the primary motive for these measures. Olliff, *Reforma Mexico*, 135–36. Lerdo was immediately sent to New Orleans and New York with the good news. García Ugarte, *Poder político y religioso*, 1:821.

138. "Ley de nacionalización de bienes eclesiásticos" (July 12, 1859) in Dublan and Lozano, *Legislación Mexicana*, 8:680–83. This law provided only thirty days for those who had obtained Church property under the *Ley Lerdo* to verify their previous purchases. That meant the deeds to property in conservative-held territory, where such declarations were not possible or where the titles had already been returned to the clergy, could also be offered as collateral. Naturally, holding such mortgages greatly increased American interest in a liberal victory.

139. "Veracruz," *La Sociedad*, July 27, 1859. After this, "Juárez continued selling the churches of Veracruz, ensuring that the buyers were foreigners, principally Yankees, so that they would never return to Church control." Aguilar y Marocho, *La familia enferma*, 107, 110.

140. As it happened, all remaining convents were closed by a new exclaustration decree in February 1863.

141. García Ugarte, *Poder político y religioso*, 820. There had been one hundred and forty-four religious communities (monasteries and friaries) for men and fifty-eight

convents for women in Mexico in 1856. Rivera, *Anales Mexicanos*, 52n9. The history and fate of each is detailed in Luis Alfaro y Peña, *Relacion descriptiva de la fundacion, dedicacion, etc., de las iglesias y conventos de Mexico: Con una reseña de la variacion que han sufrido durante dl gobierno de D. Benito Juarez* (Mexico City: M. Villanova, 1863).

142. "Ley de matrimonio civil" (July 27, 1859) in Dublan and Lozano, *Legislación Mexicana*, 8:691–95. Although the marriage rules and restrictions based on canon law were discarded, marriage was still considered indissoluble at this time. President Venustiano Carranza legalized divorce in Mexico in 1915.

143. In a government circular issued on August 6, the new law was blamed on the "growing intolerance and despotism of the clergy," who had forced "honorable" and "patriotic" citizens to choose between obeying their lawful government and the "sometimes ignorant and always arbitrary" rulings of the religious authorities in order to have a church wedding. Dublan and Lozano, *Legislación Mexicana*. 8:707.

144. Ocampo, *Obras Completas*, 2:123.

145. "Ley orgánica del registro civil" (July 28, 1859) in Dublan and Lozano, *Legislación Mexicana*, 8:696–702. This also included the recording of adoptions and the legal separation of spouses.

146. "Decreto del gobierno—Declara que cesa toda intervención del clero en los cementerios y camposantos" (July 29, 1859) in Dublan and Lozano, 8:702–5.

147. "Resolucion del Ministerio de Relaciones—Se manda retirar la legacion de México, cerca del gobierno Pontificio" (August 3, 1859) in Dublan and Lozano, 8:705. Manuel Castilla Portugal was head of the liberal Mexican delegation. On January 31, 1860, President Miramón had named Bishop Labastida, still in exile, as his minister plenipotentiary to the Holy See. García Ugarte, *Poder político y religioso*, 2:1693.

148. "Decreto del gobierno—Declara qué dias deben tenerse como festivos, y prohibe la asistencia official á las funciones de iglesia" (August 11, 1859), in Dublan and Lozano, *Legislación Mexicana*, 8:710.

149. The major Marian feasts of Candlemas (February 2), the Assumption (August 15) and the Immaculate Conception (December 8) were no longer recognized. In a speech that Ocampo gave on August 16, he supposedly proclaimed that the Virgin of Guadalupe "is no longer the patroness of Mexico" and denounced her miraculous image as a fraud. Aguilar y Marocho, *La familia enferma*, 118. In 1861, February 5 was restored to the calendar, rechristened as "Constitution Day." Malo, *Diario de sucesos notables*, 2:594.

150. This was decreed on July 31, 1859. See Sinkin, *The Mexican Reforma*, 140. "Exclaustration" (from the convent) means the return of a monk or nun to secular life.

151. Aguilar y Marocho, *La familia enferma*, 105, 110, 111, 113, 114.

152. For the history of the college, founded in 1702, see Alfaro y Peña, *Relacion descriptiva*, 314–16.

153. Aguilar y Marocho reports that twelve were left dead on this night and another thirty were imprisoned, one of these being executed later. Aguilar y Marocho, *La familia enferma*, 112–13. However, García Ugarte indicates that the disturbance occurred the night before the expulsion. This was preceded by negotiations with the governor that attempted to spare this institution since it did not belong to a particular religious

order. General Márquez invited the exiled clerics, and all other displaced religious, to take refuge in Guadalajara. García Ugarte, *Poder político y religioso*, 1:835–38. For a contemporary reaction to the destruction of the institute, see Un Católico, *Crimenes de la demogogía*.

154. After the Franciscans were expelled from Zacatecas, their chapel was turned into a gunpowder factory and their cells were used as a brothel. Aguilar y Marcho, *La familia enferma*, 115. The Augustinian monastery was acquired by Governor González Ortega, who turned it into a hotel. See Bernardo del Hoyo Calzada, "Los conventos de Zacatecas," *History of the Diocese of Zacatecas* (blog), Jan. 7, 2015, https://historiadela diocesisdezacatecas.blogspot.com/2015/01/los-conventos-de-zacatecas.html.

155. Aguilar y Marocho, *La familia enferma*. 111. Liberals later turned this monastery into a school of arts and crafts. "San Luis Potosí," *La Sociedad*, July 31, 1859.

156. This monastery was sold by Governor Huerta "for two or three thousand pesos to a Yankee." Aguilar y Marocho, *La familia enferma*, 135. The buildings were finally demolished in 1860. Alfaro y Peña, *Relacion descriptiva*, 237–38.

157. Aguilar y Marocho, *La familia enferma*, 103.

158. The five pastoral letters were issued on July 29, August 5, 12, 19 and September 7, 1859. García Ugarte, *Poder político y religioso*, 823–28.

159. Around August 21, 1859, however, the archbishop allowed the Miramón government to set up a special office to receive voluntary donations of precious metals and jewels from religious communities and corporations to help meet the emergency needs of the government. Rivera, *Anales Mexicanos*, 53–54; and García Ugarte, *Poder político y religioso*, 823. José Ramon Malo, who was in charge of this operation, kept a complete inventory of the proceeds. Malo, *Diario de sucesos notables*, 572–76.

160. The other bishops included Bishop Espinosa (Guadalajara), Bishop Munguía (Michoacán—in exile), Verea (Linares/Nueva León—in exile), and Bishop Barajas (San Luis Potosí—in exile). Father Francisco Serrano represented the Diocese of Puebla, whose bishop (Labastida) was still in exile outside the country. Bishop José María Guerra y Rodríguez of the Diocese of Yucatán, on the other hand, simply appealed to Juárez as the president for an exemption from the new laws. García Ugarte, *Poder político y religioso*, 828–35. He would be rewarded for this deference when the other bishops were punished after the conservative defeat.

161. Jaime Olveda, "El punto de vista de la iglesia sobre las leyes de la reforma" in *México durante la Guerra de Reforma*, vol. 2, *Contextos, prácticas culturales, imaginarios y representaciones*, ed. Celia del Palacio Montiel (Xalapa, MX: Universidad Veracruzana, 2011), 84–93.

162. Civil marriage was called the *"ley de amancebamiento civil"* in Aguilar y Marocho, *La familia enferma*, 109.

163. Agustín de la Rosa Serrano was a well-known theologian and accomplished professor of languages at the seminary in Guadalajara. Agustín de la Rosa, *El matrimonio civil, considerado en su relacions con la religion, la familia y la sociedad* (Guadalajara: Rodriguez, 1859), 14.

164. Aguilar y Marocho, *La familia enferma*, 111, 124; and "Protestas contra las leyes demagogias," *La Sociedad*, August 5, 1859.

165. Printed in Cambre, *Guerra de Tres Años*, 312–14.

166. The reference to communism probably reflects the call for land redistribution that was included in the July 7 manifesto. Ocampo, *Obras Completas*, 2:138. Márquez was one of the generals that signed this document, which referenced the expulsion of the religious from Zacatecas as proof liberal perfidy. "El primer cuerpo de ejercito y la guarnicion de Guadalajara protestan contra el manifiesto del Lic. Benito Juarez—19 de Agosto de 1859," in García Cantú, *El pensamiento de la reacción mexicana*, 539–42.

167. Francisco Zúñiga, *Discurso pronunciado el 16 de Setiembre de 1859, en la Alameda de esta ciudad por el Sr. consejero de gobierno del departamento, Lic. Don Francisco Zúñiga* (Toluca, MX: Tipografía del Instituto Literario, 1859), 12 pages. Toluca, about forty miles southwest of Mexico City, is the capital of the State of Mexico.

168. The battle took place on September 29, 1858, and was won by conservative troops under Generals Miramón and Márquez. The liberal General Zuazua, wounded in a brawl, was temporarily replaced by Jordan. See "Ahualulco de los Pinos, Battle of (1858)" and "Zaragoza Seguín, Ignaico" in Marley, *Mexico at War*, 11–13 and 461.

169. Luis Gonzaga Cuevas, "Juicio sobre el estado politico de México en 1860," Appendix 2, *Porvenir de México* (1851; repr. Mexico City: Cien de México, 1992), 600. Aguliar y Marocho also recorded that "Yankee arms, money and officers solicited by Degollado" arrived in San Luis Potosí on August 13, 1859. Aguilar y Marocho, *La familia enferma*, 116.

170. "Curiosidades constitucionalistas," *La Sociedad*, August 2, 1859. A newspaper in Zacatecas confirmed on August 25, 1859, that four thousand American soldiers passed through Tampico on their way to Veracruz. Aguilar y Marocho, *La familia enferma*, 122–23.

171. Olliff, *Reforma Mexico*, 139.

172. "Estancia de las Vacas, Battle of (1859)" in Marley, *Mexico at War*, 140–42. The participation of American gunners was noted by the liberal newspaper, *La Reforma*, in Veracruz on August 19, 1859. Aguilar y Marocho, *La familia enferma*, 144.

173. The treaty was signed in Paris by Juan Nepomuceno Almonte (Zuloaga's minister) and Alejandro Mon y Menéndez (Queen Isabel II's representative). Relations between Mexico and Spain had been broken in December 1856 after the murder of some Spaniards on the haciendas of San Vicente, Chiconcuac and Dolores (Morelos) by partisans of Juan Álvarez. See Ramona Falcón, "Discontento campesino e hispanofobia. La tierra caliente a mediados del siglo XIX," *Historia Mexicana* 44, no. 3 (January–March 1995): 491–95. The Mon-Almonte treaty reestablished ties with Spain and committed Mexico to the payment of an indemnity for these and other Spanish losses. It also revived the conventions of 1853 related to previous debts owed to Spain. Rivera, *Anales Mexicanos*, 55.

174. The treaty consisted of two separate agreements: the "Treaty of Transits and Commerce" and the "Convention to Enforce Treaty Stipulations and to Maintain Order and Security in the Territories of Each of the Two Republics." Two million dollars would be delivered to Mexico once the treaty was ratified but the rest was to remain in US hands to pay for American claims. Olliff, *Reforma Mexico*, 141–44. The US senate voted against the treaty (27 to 18) on May 31, 1860. See Pearl T. Ponce, "As Dead

as Julius Caesar: The Rejection of the McLane-Ocampo Treaty," *Civil War History* 53, no. 4 (December 2007): 342–78.

175. During the summer, a Guadalajara newspaper published a table showing all battles of the war, divided into first, second, and third "order" conflicts. According to this table, conservatives had won a total of seventy-one battles while the liberals could claim only sixteen victories. Reprinted in "Documento curioso," *La Sociedad*, August 2, 1859.

176. There was also a dispute over funds that Márquez had seized to pay his troops. Trueba, *Guerra de Tres Años*, 33.

177. Miramón occupied Colima (Colima) on December 22 and defeated the liberal forces at Tonila (Jalisco), twenty miles away, on December 24. Trueba, 33.

178. Malo, *Diario de sucesos notables*, 2:557.

179. Both liberals and conservatives called him the *"joven Macabeo."* See "joven Macabeo" in Marley, *Mexico at War*, 188–89.

180. The verse (from Psalm 89:20) belonged to the chants related to the liturgical feast for King David ("Common of a Confessor not a Bishop"). But the liberal priest, Agustín Rivera, who read a description of the service later, noted with derision the use of this text and other common invocations from the Litany of the Saints. He also complained about a prayer addressed to God for "your servant, our president Miguel," since to him it sounded similar to the term "Servant of God," officially used only in prayers for an emperor. Rivera, *Anales Mexicanos*, 57–58. His long diary entry about this event is probably the source for Luis Pérez Verdía's inaccurate report that the choir had chanted "the Servant of God Miguel, anointed of God" and that Miramón had therefore been given "royal honors." Pérez Vedia, *Historia particular*, 3:87–88. Clearly, the Miramón cult greatly annoyed those who did not fully support the conservative cause.

181. The "Himno a Miramón" carried the dedication "Al Exco. Sr. President de la República D. Miguel Miramón en su entrada a México después de la campaña de Colima." Francisco González Bocanegra (1824–1861) wrote the lyrics to Mexico's national anthem in 1853. The song was chosen by a jury that included José Joaquín Pesado, José Bernardo Couto, and Manuel Carpio. During the Miramón administration Bocanegra served as "Censor of Theaters." Joaquín Antonia Peñalosa, *Francisco González Bocanegra: vida y obra*, 2nd ed. (San Luis Potosí: Universidad Autónoma de San Luis Potosí, 1998), 35, 283.

182. Veracruz earned this title for enduring Spanish bombardment in 1823 and French bombardment in 1837.

183. On March 20, Degollado reported that conservative bombardment had already caused considerable damage in the city. García Ugarte, *Poder político y religioso*, 2:1694.

184. The USS *Saratoga* was the third US naval ship by this name. It had a complement of 210 officers and men onboard and was armed with four 8-inch shell guns and eighteen 32-pounders. "Saratoga III (Sloop-of-War)," Naval History and Heritage Command, Sept. 2, 2015, https://www.history.navy.mil/content/history/nhhc/research/histories/ship-histories/danfs/s/saratoga-iii.html.

185. José Fuentes Mares, *Juárez y los Estados Unidos*, 4th edition (Mexico City: Editorial Jus, 1964), 176–78.

186. Trueba, *Guerra de Tres Años*, 35–39; "Veracruz, Conservative Sieges of (1859–1860)" in Marley, *Mexico at War*, 427–29. The ships were sold in New Orleans on January 19, 1861, and later became part of the Confederate Navy. Malo, *Diario de sucesos notables*, 2:596.

187. Olliff, *Reforma Mexico*, 147. The battle may also have helped derail the McLane-Ocampo Treaty, since US senators became wary of future interventions in Mexico.

188. General González Ortega confiscated the silver on January 6, 1860. Rivera, *Anales Mexicanos*, 58.

189. The action was remarkable for the lack of vengeance against the captured conservative officers. Cambre, *Guerra de Tres Años*, 423–32.

190. Zuloaga was also behind an anonymous publication that had earlier criticized Miramón's conduct during the war. He would remain Miramón's captive until his escape on the night of August 2–3, 1860. See "Zuloaga Trillo, Félix María" in Marley, *Mexico at War*, 475–81.

191. "Silao, Battle of (1860)" in Marley, *Mexico at War*, 375–78. Miramón only escaped this battle because he was not recognized in the chaos by the liberal soldiers intent on the capture of his palomino stallion named *"Dorado"* (Golden one).

192. Trueba, *Guerra de Tres Años*, 41.

193. Rivera, *Anales Mexicanos*, 63; and "Márquez" in Marley, *Mexico at War*, 212.

194. "Guadalajara" in Marley, *Mexico at War*, 160–61. Trueba gives the conservative number as 3,000. Trueba, *Guerra de Tres Años*, 43. Rivera reports it as 7,000. Rivera, *Anales Mexicanos*, 65.

195. Tables showing the placement of the liberal artillery units and their guns is included in Cambre, *Guerra de Tres Años*, 543–46.

196. Pérez Verdía, *Historia particular*, 3:120.

197. Cambre, *Guerra de Tres Años*, 542.

198. This occurred on September 23. Precious metals were also requisitioned from other religious houses on October 2, together yielding a total of 35,798 pesos. Pérez Verdía, *Historia particular*, 3:110, 114; and Cambre, *Guerra de Tres Años*, 537–38.

199. Rivera, *Anales Mexicanos*, 64.

200. Ignacio Zaragoza Seguín (1829–1862) was only thirty-one years old when he was promoted to general in González Ortega's army. Zaragoza was placed in command of the campaign when Ortega became ill.

201. Márquez was only twenty-two miles away, but the surrender agreement had already been signed on October 30. He escaped after the battle, leaving behind three thousand men and eighteen cannons.

202. Quoted in Haworth, "Desde los baluartes conservadores," 127.

203. Rivera, *Anales Mexicanos*, 65–66.

204. Ocampo, *Obras Completas*, 2:119.

205. "Ley sobre libertad de cultos" (December 4, 1860), in Dublan and Lozano, *Legislación Mexicana*, 8:762–66.

206. This law also abolished the right of sanctuary (asylum) in churches. Catholic clergy now had no special privileges, although ministers of any denomination were exempt from military service. García Ugarte, *Poder político y religioso*, 1:891–92.

207. Rivera, *Anales Mexicanos*, 66. Benito Gómez Farias was the son of the deceased *puro* politician, Valentín Gómez Farias. Degollado had been relieved of his commands by Juárez in September and was later attached to Berriozábel's army. Despairing of a liberal victory at the last siege of Guadalajara, he had attempted to negotiate a separate peace through the British Minister, George Matthew. He had also acted without authorization in the case of silver confiscated from foreign-owned mines. See Scholes, *Mexican Politics*, 41–42.

208. "Calpulalpan, Battle of (1860)" in Marley, *Mexico at War*, 62–65; Trueba, *Guerra de Tres Años*, 45–46; and Cambre, *Guerra de Tres Años*, 566–70.

209. Malo, *Diario de sucesos notables*, 2:583. Cambre states that liberal chiefs saw the flags as an insult, since they suggested that the federal troops were considered uncivilized. They disappeared after General González Ortega issued a decree promising respect for property. Cambre, *Guerra de Tres Años*, 570–71.

210. Roa Bárcena, *Biografía*, 115–16. Pesado himself died of pneumonia on March 3, 1861. Rivera, *Anales Mexicanos*, 74. Malo wrote that he also felt compelled to go into hiding "for the first time in my life" to avoid arrest "for my opinions." Malo, *Diario de sucesos notables*, 2:581.

211. Florencio María del Castillo's ecstatic account of the festivities is included in Cambre, *Guerra de Tres Años*, 573–79. Other liberal newspapers, like *La Reforma* in Guadalajara, published similar glowing reports of the festivities. "¡Gloria á la libertad! / ¡Honra al progreso!" *La Reforma*, January 1, 1861.

212. Ramirez Aparicio, *Los conventos suprimidos en México*, v.

213. Pedro Rosas, *El Clero y las revoluciones* (Mexico City: L. Inclan, 1861), 10. The purpose of this work, written in March 1861, was to prove that the clergy were not responsible for the political upheavals in Mexico.

CHAPTER EIGHT

1. This fact was highlighted in all of Mexico's constitutions before 1857.

2. Malo, *Diario de sucesos notables*, 2:584.

3. Apparently, this day was chosen for Juárez's formal entry since it was the third anniversary of the conservative coup against Comonfort in 1858. Malo, 2:587–88; Rivera, *Anales Mexicanos*, 69.

4. Some members of the cabinet, like Melchoir Ocampo and Ignacio de la Llave, tendered their resignations at this action, arguing that the emergency powers that Juárez had enjoyed were now expired and that the congress should decide the fate of the prelates. Malo, *Diario de sucesos notables*, 2:589–90; and Rivera, *Anales Mexicanos*, 70. Justo Sierra later wrote that some liberals like Manuel Altamirano were demanding much harsher punishments. García Ugarte, *Polder político y religioso*, 1:905.

5. Rivera, *Anales Mexicanos*, 71. Bishop Labastida (Puebla) was already in exile in Rome. Bishop Verea had not been named in the deportation decree but chose to join his brother bishops in exile. Bishop Joaquín Fernández Madrid y Canal (1801–1861) was a native of Tlaxcala. He was consecrated in Rome as titular bishop of Tanagra (Greece) in 1834. Bishop Guerra Rodríguez of the distant Diocese of

Yucatán was also not affected by the decree. García Ugarte, *Poder político y religioso*, 1:908–10.

6. García Ugarte, 1:9056–57.

7. From the report of the Spanish ambassador, quoted in Rivera, *Anales Mexicanos*, 72. According to witnesses, the riot was organized by two men, Joaquín Villalobos from Mexico City, and an Italian, possibly one of the professional agitators who left Europe after the failure of the 1848 revolutions. "Los prelados Mexicanos" and "Veracruz," *El Párajo Verde*, May 2 and June 2, 1861; "El motin de Veracruz," *El Constitucional*, July 2, 1861.

8. "El atentado de Veracruz," *El Párajo Verde*, February 7, 1861. *El Párajo Verde* was published by Mariano Villanueva y Francesconi from January 5 to June 4, 1861, when a liberal mob destroyed its presses. It was revived from 1863 to 1877.

9. Arturo Camacho Becerra, "De la imagen sagrada al arte secular: Artistas ante las leyes de Reforma," in *México durante la Guerra de Reforma*, vol. 2, *Contextos, prácticas culturales, imaginarios y representaciones*, ed. Celia del Palacio Montiel (Xalapa, MX: Universidad Veracruzana, 2011), 245.

10. Gabriela Díaz Patiño, *Católicos, liberales y protestantes*, 126.

11. Rivera, *Anales Mexicanos*, 70; and [R. G. H.], *Memoria sobre la propiedad eclesiástica*, 12. A monstrance is a receptacle used to display the consecrated Host for the veneration of the faithful. The one taken from the cathedral was traditionally used in the annual Corpus Christi procession. Over the years, family jewels had been donated to adorn the monstrance as a sign of devotion to the presence of Christ in the Eucharist. An inventory of the immense treasure confiscated from the cathedral is included in Alfaro y Peña, *Relacion descriptive*, 14–15. Malo states that the commission left behind only the bare minimum of sacred vessels needed for the divine service, but the cathedral was searched again on the night of March 6, 1861. Malo, *Diario de sucesos notables*, 2:589, 603. More confiscations were made on August 7 and August 11. García Ugarte, *Poder político y religioso*, 1:904.

12. A Señora Barron paid 72,000 pesos to rescue the monstrance. Alfaro y Peña, *Relacion descriptiva*, 14n1.

13. The gold, pearls and diamonds from the monstrance were found in a clockmaker's shop. The shop owner and the agent who delivered the monstrance were both arrested, although no specific punishment was reported. Malo, *Diario de sucesos notables*, 2:604.

14. An inventory of the items confiscated on both dates is included in Alfaro y Peña, *Relacion descriptiva*, 31n1, 32n1.

15. Most of the chapels were destroyed, although what remained of the main church was eventually sold to American Episcopalians in 1869, who removed most of its historic images. Jean-Pierre Bastian, *Los Disidentes: Sociedades protestantes y revolución en México, 1872–1911* (Mexico City: El Colegio de México, 1989), 38; and Díaz Patiño, *Católicos, liberales y protestantes*, 123. For a time, a circus occupied the monastery's atrium and some buildings were turned into a military barracks. For the fate of the historic buildings and recent plans for partial restoration, see Raúl Nieto Garcia, "El convento grande de San Francisco de la ciudad de México," *Bitácora Architectura*, no. 3 (Summer 2000): 12–19.

16. Alfaro y Peña, *Relacion descriptiva*, 64, 87.

17. Malo, *Diario de sucesos notables*, 2:613.

18. [R. G. H.], *Memoria sobre la propiedad eclesiástica*, 13. According to the Reforma decree, books, manuscripts, art, and antiques were supposed to be transferred to public institutions. However, the author claims that less than ten percent of the volumes survived.

19. Alfaro y Peña, *Relacion descriptiva*, 75n2; [R. G. H.], *Memoria sobre la propiedad eclesiástica*, 13–14; and Díaz Patiño, *Católicos, liberales y protestantes*, 105–25. In some cases, important cult images that had been the focus of devotion for generations were lost.

20. Malo reports that the walnut choir stalls from the Augustinian monastery, embellished with two hundred and fifty-four carved reliefs, were sold for just 3,000 pesos, although the cathedral canons had once offered the monks their own stalls plus 15,000 pesos in exchange for them. Malo, *Diario de sucesos notables*, 2:615.

21. [R. G. H.] *Memoria de la propiedad eclesiástica*, 7–8.

22. Díaz Patiño, *Católicos, liberales y protestantes*, 125–27.

23. At this time there also appeared a satirical work (in verse) called the "Catechism of Machiavellian-Clerical Doctrine, or Father Ripalda's Catechism as observed and preached by the Mexican Clergy." Pedro T. Echeverria, *Catecismo de la doctrina clero-maquiavelica o sea del Padre Ripalda segun lo observa y predica el clero mexicano* (Mexico City: Imprenta de la Reforma, 1861), 26 pages.

24. Nicolás Pizarro, *Catecismo politico constitucional*, 2nd ed. (Mexico City: Ana Echeverria de Pizarro e hijas, 1861), 21. The minister of justice and public education appointed this book for use in all schools on March 15, 1861.

25. "Los frailes y la ley de esclaustracion," *La Reforma*, January 3, 1861.

26. Malo, *Diario de sucesos notables*, 2:601; Alfaro y Peña, *Relacion descriptiva*, 63–64; Ramirez Aparicio, *Los conventos suprimidos en México*, 14–15; and Díaz Patiño, *Católicos, liberales y protestantes*, 340. Among these mummies was the body of the famous Fray Servando Teresa de Mier, OP (1763–1822), one of the fathers of Mexican Independence. The mummies were later sold to an Italian circus owner, who planned to exhibit them in Buenos Aires and Europe. They were last seen at a fair in Belgium but disappeared long ago. Susana Rotker, ed., *The Memoirs of Fray Servando Teresa de Mier*, trans. Helen Lane (Oxford: Oxford University Press, 1998), xix, xxxvii.

27. On February 24, 1861, the Conciliar Seminary was relocated to the suppressed Convent of San Camilo and the original buildings destroyed. Malo, *Diario de sucesos notables*, 2:591, 600.

28. See Elsa Malvido, "Los hospitales en México en el siglo xix en el marco de la secularización. De la caridad a la salud pública," in *Secularización del Estado y la sociedad*, ed. Patricia Galeana de Valadés (Mexico City: Siglo XXI, 2010), 255–67; Guillermo Fajardo Ortiz, "México 1861. Perspectiva histórica de la secularización de los hospitales," *Revista de la Facultad de Medicina de la UNAM* 55, no. 5 (September–October 2012): 44–47.

29. For example, the previous requirement that patients pray and take part in religious exercises was dropped. This change was noted at the San Lazaro hospital on September 14, 1861. Malo, *Diario de sucesos notables*, 2:639.

30. The Hospital del Terceros, once part of the Franciscan complex, was reestablished as a maternity hospital in November 1861. However, the project never materialized, so

the building was sold and became the "Railroad Hotel" instead. Ramírez Aparicio, *Los conventos suprimidos en México*, 354–55.

31. Malvido, "Los hospitales en México," 265–66. Two days before this decree, the house of the Daughters of Charity in Mexico City was searched and money that individuals had left there for safekeeping was confiscated. Malo, *Diario de sucesos notables*, 2:598. In Mexico City, the community of thirty-three sisters was in charge of the Divino Salvador, San Pablo, San Andreas, and San Juan de Dios hospitals. Alfaro y Peña, *Relacion descriptiva*, 128–29.

32. "Charácter que les reconoce el supremo gobierno á las hermanas de la caridad y padres paulinos" (May 28, 1861) in Dublan and Lozano, *Legislación Mexicana*, 9:222–23. In addition, this circular addressed the priests of the related Vincentian order ("Padres Paulinas"), also known for their charitable work. A decree dissolving the congregation was issued on October 23, 1861. Malo, *Diario de sucesos notables*, 2:654. The Spiritu Santo convent and church associated with the Vincentians were destroyed in February 1862. Alfaro y Peña, *Relacion descriptiva*. 84. The remaining four hundred Daughters of Charity were expelled from Mexico in 1872 by Sebastián Lerdo.

33. There were five hundred and seventy-eight nuns in Mexico City in 1861. For a list of the communities and the numbers in each, see Malo, *Diario de sucesos notables*, 2:607–8.

34. Rivera, *Anales Mexicanos*, 74; Malo, *Diario de sucesos notables*, 2:597–99. A typhus outbreak started in Mexico City following the arrival of liberal troops from Guadalajara in January 1861. Malo, 2:588–89. See also Josefina Muriel, "Desamortización de los colegios de niñas: Los colegios femeninos y la exclaustración de 1856," in *Memoria del I Coloquio Historia de la Iglesia en el Siglo XIX*, ed. Manuel Ramos Medina (Mexico City: Centro de Estudios de Historia de México Condumex, 1998), 290–94. Muriel also describes the negative impact of this suppression on female education in Mexico, since many convents conducted schools for girls. Eventually even those staffed by lay teachers were closed since they had been sponsored by religious confraternities.

35. Even the antiquarian Manuel Ramírez Aparicio, although an enthusiastic supporter of the Reforma, regretted the rough treatment of the nuns, necessarily perpetrated under the cover of darkness. Ramírez Aparicio, *Los conventos suprimidos en México*, vi–vii.

36. Malo, *Diario de sucesos notables*, 2:601; Jesús Joel Peña Espinosa, "Crisis, agonía y restauración del monasterio de Santa Mónica de la ciudad de Puebla, 1827–1943," *Boletín de Monumentos Históricos* 3, no. 30 (January–April 2014): 289–90. There were approximately three hundred and twenty nuns in Puebla at this time.

37. Malo, *Diario de sucesos notables*, 2:611.

38. A newspaper later reported that Ignacio Ramírez, the minister of justice and public education, was awarded the contract for tearing down the churches and convents in the city. He was paid 6,000 pesos for each and granted rights to all the debris, which could also be salvaged and sold. Malo, *Diario de sucesos notables*, 2:617. At times, this process included disinterring the bodies of the religious from their cemeteries, as happened at the Jésus María Convent on the night of August 25, 1861. Malo, 2:632; and Alfaro y Peña, *Relacion descriptiva*, 93–94.

39. Malo, 2:600; Alfaro y Peña, 108–9.

40. There may have been some demonstrations against the removal of the nuns after the fact, since on February 18 Malo reported that signs were posted in Mexico City threating violence against the clergy, who were charged with inciting some recent protests. Malo, *Diario de sucesos notables*, 2:598–9.

41. Malo, 2:656–57.

42. Under Juárez, the government "began to interfere directly not only in the relations between Church and State, but also in matters of daily worship, that is to say, in the sphere of collective and private piety." Adrian A. Bantjes Aróstegui, "Religión popular y revolución en México: Una perspectiva de larga duración," in *México a la luz de sus revoluciones: volumen 2*, ed. Laura Rojas and Susan Deeds (Mexico City: El Colegio de México, 2014), 59–60.

43. Díaz Patiña, *Católicos, liberals y protestantes*, 139–40.

44. Malo, *Diario de sucesos notables*, 2:587; Rivera, *Anales Mexicanos*, 69. Viaticum is the Holy Communion administered to the dying. For this purpose, the consecrated Host was carried by the priest from the church in a pyx. In Catholic countries, this process was surrounded by ceremonies showing respect for the presence of Christ in the Blessed Sacrament.

45. For example, in 1824 an American cobbler living in Mexico City was killed by an angry crowd for refusing to kneel when the Blessed Sacrament passed by. Tomás S. Goslin, *Los evangélicos en la América Latina* (Buenos Aires: La Aurora, 1956), 92.

46. Malo, *Diario de sucesos notables*, 2:593.

47. Malo, 2:595–96. The following month, perhaps in retaliation for this petition, the government confiscated sacred vessels and jewels from the parish and its priest. Alfaro y Peña, *Relacion descriptiva*, 50.

48. Malo, *Diario de sucesos notables*, 2:608.

49. See Díaz Patino, *Católicos, liberales y protestantes*, 137.

50. "Decreto por la secretaría de justice y fomento" (August 30, 1862), in Basilio José Arrillaga, ed., *Recopilacion de leyes, decretos, bandos, reglamentos, circulares y providencias de los supremos poderes y otras autoridades de la Republica Mexicana: Junio de 1862* (Mexico City: A. Boix, 1862), 76–77. This decree also abolished all ecclesiastical cabildos and imposed a prison sentence of one to three years for any clergyman who criticized the government.

51. See Díaz Patiña, *Católicos, liberales y protestantes*, 104.

52. Malo, *Diario de sucesos notables*, 2:654; For the list of churches closed and those allowed to remain open, see "Bando de gobierno del Distrito" (October 24, 1861) in Dublan and Lozano, *Legislación Mexicana*, 9:322.

53. Alfaro y Peña, *Relacion descriptiva*, 41n5. See Díaz Patiño, *Católicos, liberales y protestantes*, 136–38.

54. Malo, *Diario de sucesos notables*, 2:617.

55. The banned letter was titled "The Public Good." See "Puebla," *Siglo Diez y Nueve*, May 16, 1861; and Alfaro y Peña, *Relacion descriptiva*, 203n1. According to Alfaro y Peña, the official ordered the priest to stop reading the letter on May 10. Malo, who added that the priest was physically removed from the pulpit, reported the event on

May 15. Both sources point out that the official did not remove his hat in church. Irigoyen and Mr. Guevara, his secretary, were deported from the state on May 12. Malo, *Diario de sucesos notables*, 2:613–15.

56. Malo, 2:600.

57. The churches were La Señora de Merced, Santisma Trinidad, San Hipólito and the old chapel the Bethlehemites. Malo, 2:601.

58. See Bastian, *Los Disidentes*, 32–35; Díaz Patiño, *Católicos, liberales y protestantes*, 169–71; Abraham Téllez Aguilar, "Una iglesia cismática mexicana en el siglo xix," *Estudios de historia moderna y contemporánea de México*, 13, no. 13 (1990), 253–56.

59. "Aviso a los catolicios," *El Monitor*, February 24, 1861. *El Monitor* tended to report favorably on the new church, since its editor was a member.

60. The local curate was blamed for the incident and deported. Malo, *Diario de sucesos notables*, 2:609.

61. Ocampo, who had retired to his hacienda near Maravatío (Michoacán), was captured by conservative guerillas and executed at Tepejí del Rió (Hidalgo) on June 3, 1861. Manuel Payno, "Ocampo," in *El Libro Rojo: 1520–1867* (Mexico City: A. Pola, 1906), 2:168–71.

62. See Joel Morales Cruz, *The Mexican Reformation: Catholic Pluralism, Enlightenment Religion, and the* Iglesia de Jesús *Movement in Benito Juárez's Mexico (1859–72)* (Eugene, OR: Pickwick Publications, 2011), 150–86; Bastian, *Los Disidentes*, 35–40.

63. Malo, *Diario de sucesos notables*, 2:776.

64. Bishop Labastida had been exiled from his diocese in Puebla on May 21, 1856. The exiled Archbishop de la Garza died in Barcelona on March 11, 1862, and Labastida was made Archbishop of Mexico City in Rome on March 19, 1863. He and Bishop Munguía returned to Mexico under French protection on September 17. Malo, 2:779. The other members of the Regency were José Mariano Salas and Juan Nepomuceno Almonte.

65. For example, on February 8, 1864, twenty-five sisters returned to the part of the Convent of Jesús María that had been recovered. Malo, 2:783–84.

66. As usual, the Mexican bishops insisted that only Rome could resolve the question of church property. When negotiations with the Holy See stalled, Maximilian reaffirmed the nationalization of church property on February 26. 1865. Rivera, *Anales Mexicanos*, 206.

67. Maximilian's government even licensed a bookstore that sold Protestant Bibles and anti-Catholic tracts. Rivera, 207n7.

68. The animosity of the emperor and his wife toward "the clerical party" led to police surveillance of its supposed leaders, Labastida, Munguía, and the new apostolic delegate, Pier Francesco Meglia. Rivera, 203.

69. In spite of its opposition to the French project, the United States, sidelined by its own civil war, was initially unable to intervene in Mexico. With the defeat of the Confederacy in May 1865, substantial material support was given to the forces of Juárez and diplomatic pressure helped convince Napoleon III, already facing a threat from Prussia, to remove French troops in 1866.

70. For example, the Augustinian convent of Santa Monica survived in Puebla until it was denounced by an informer in 1934. Today the building houses the Museo de Arte

Religioso–Ex Convento de Santa Mónica. For the post-Reforma history of the nuns of the convent of the Purísima Concepción in Michoacán, see the epilogue in Margaret Chowning, *Rebellious Nuns: The Troubled History of a Mexican Convent, 1752–1863* (Oxford: Oxford University Press, 2005), 263–70.

71. Although the first lady received a Catholic funeral, some liberals complained that she had not been given a state funeral in the cathedral. The incongruity of this demand in secular Mexico was explained in "Acusacion al clero" *La Voz de Mexico*, January 10, 1871.

72. This nostalgia is present in his 1871 novel, *Navidad en las montanas.*

73. For example, Edward Wright-Rios's study of post-Reforma Oaxaca shows that "Catholicism remained vibrant" there. "The state failed to uproot Catholicism's solid historical foundations and never countered the value much of the population placed upon the spiritual mediation offered by the church." Wright-Rios, *Revolutions in Mexican Catholicism*, 281.

74. See Brian Stauffer, *Victory on Earth or in Heaven: Mexico's Religionero Rebellion* (Albuquerque: University of New Mexico Press, 2020).

75. See Paul Vanderwood, *The Power of God against the Guns of Government: Religious Upheaval in Mexico at the Turn of the Nineteenth Century* (Stanford, CA: Stanford University Press, 1998).

76. The war is also known as the "Cristiada." The term "Cristero" comes from the battle cry of the rebels: *"¡Viva Cristo Rey!"* ("Long live Christ the King!"). Meyer estimates that 60,000 federal soldiers and 40,000 Cristeros were killed during the war. He also indicates that 5,000 Cristeros were murdered by the government after their surrender. The civilian losses were also massive. Meyer, *The Cristero Rebellion*, 178, 201–202. The complexities of this conflict are examined in Ramón Jrade, "Inquiries into the Cristero Insurrection against the Mexican Revolution," *Latin American Research Review* 20, no. 2 (1985): 53–69.

Bibliography

Acle Aguirre, Andrea. "Amigos y Alliados: José Bernardo Couto (1803–1862) y José Joaquín Pesado (1801–1861)." *Historia Mexicana* 61, no. 1 (2011): 163–230.

Aguilar y Marocho, Ignacio. *La familia enferma.* 1860. Reprint, Mexico City: Editorial Jus, 1960.

Alamán, Gil. *Sermon predicado por el padre Don Gil Alamán, presbitero de la congregación del Oratorio de San Felipe Neri de México, el día 17 de junio de 1855, primero de los tres días en que celebró solemnemente la misma congregación en su iglesia la declaración dogmatica de la Inmaculada Concepción de la Santisima Virgen María, Madre de Dios.* Mexico City: Andrade y Escalante, 1856.

Alamán, Lucas. *Disertaciones sobre la Historia de la República Mexicana.* 3 vols. Mexico City: Lara, 1844–1849.

———. *Historia de México, desde los primeros movimientos que prepararon su independencia en el año de 1808, hasta la época presente.* 5 vols. Mexico City, Lara, 1849–1852.

Alfaro y Peña, Luis. *Relacion descriptiva de la fundacion, dedicacion, etc., de las iglesias y conventos de Mexico: Con una reseña de la variacion que han sufrido durante de gobierno de D. Benito Juarez.* Mexico City: M. Villanova, 1863.

Álvarez, Ignacio. *Revolucion de la Reforma.* Vol. 6 of *Estudios sobre la historia general de Mexico.* Zacatecas: Timoteo Macias, 1877.

[Álvarez, Manuel, SJ]. *El fanal de la juventud, ó sean breves avisos á las personas que por su sencillez ó falta de instrucción, se hallan mas espuestas á padecer naufragio.* Mexico City: Imprenta de Abadiano, 1860.

Alvires, Manuel Toribio. *Reflexiones sobre los decretos episcopales que prohíben el juramento constitucional.* Mexico City: N. Chávez, 1857.

———. *Segunda parte: En la que responde a las objeciones.* Mexico City: N. Chávez, 1857.

———. *Tercera parte: En la que se hacen esplicaciones importantes.* Mexico City: N. Chávez, 1857.

Amador, Elias. *Bosquejo historico de Zacatecas.* Vol. 2. Zacatecas: Tipografía de Hospico de Niños en Guadalupe, 1912.

Anderson, Margaret Lavinia. "The Divisions of the Pope: The Catholic Revival and Europe's Transition to Democracy." In *The Politics of Religion in an Age of Revival: Studies in Nineteenth-Century Europe and Latin America,* edited by Austen Ivereigh, 22–42. London: Institute of Latin American Studies, 2000.

Aranda y Carpinteiro, Diego de. *Carta pastoral en la que se hace saber a todo el venerable clero secular y regular de la diócesis de Guadalajara la encíclica de N.S.P. el Sr. Pío IX sobre el interesante asunto de la Inmaculada Concepción de María Sma.* Guadalajara: Rodríguez, 1849.

Arango y Escandon, Alejandro. *Epístola dirigida a mi maestro y amigo el Doctor D. José Bernardo Couto, con motivo de la publicación de su "Discurso sobre la constitucion de la iglesia."* Mexico: n.p., 1857.

Arenal Fenochio, Jaime del. "La historiografía conservadora mexicana del siglo xix." *Metapolítica* 6, no. 22 (March–April 2002): 47–55.

Argudín, Yolanda. *Historia del perodismo en México desde el virreinato hasta nuestros días.* Mexico City: Panorama, 1987.

Aróstegui, Adrian A. Bantjes. "Religión popular y revolución en México: Una perspectiva de larga duración." In *México a la luz de sus revoluciones: volumen 2,* edited by Laura Rojas and Susan Deeds, 55–66. Mexico City: El Colegio de México, 2014.

Arrillaga, Basilio José, ed. *Recopilacion de leyes, decretos, bandos, reglamentos, circulares y providencias de los supremos poderes y otras autoridades de la Republica Mexicana: Junio de 1862.* Mexico City: A. Boix, 1862.

Arrom, Silvia Marina. "Catholic Philanthropy and Civil Society: The Lay Volunteers of Saint Vincent de Paul in Nineteenth-Century Mexico." In *Philanthropy and Social Change in Latin America,* edited by Cynthia Sanborn and Felipe Portocarrero. 31–62. Cambridge, MA: Harvard University Press, 2005.

———. *The Women of Mexico City, 1790–1857.* Stanford, CA: Stanford University Press, 1985.

Arteta, Begoña. "José María Roa Bárcena." In *En busca de un discurso integrado de la nación, 1848–1884,* edited by Antonia Pi-Suñer Llorens, 241–56. Mexico City: Universidad Nacional Autónoma de México, 1996.

Ayuntamiento, á quien se ha pasado de preferencia y con recomendación del Supremo Gobierno, para que informe lo conveniente. Mexico City: Imprenta del Catolico, 1846.

Balmes, Jaime Luciano. *El protestantismo comparado con el catolicismo en sus relaciones con la civilización europea.* 4 vols. Barcelona: Antonio Brusi, 1844.

Bancroft, Hubert Howe. *The History of Mexico.* Vol. 5, *1824–1861.* San Francisco: A. L. Bancroft & Company, 1885.

[Baranda, Manuel]. *Apuntamientos sobre derecho público eclesiástico.* Mexico City: Ignacio Cumplido, 1857.

Barker, Nancy Nichols. *The French Experience in Mexico, 1821–1861.* Chapel Hill: University of North Carolina Press, 1979.

Bastian, Jean-Pierre, "Una ausencia notoria: la francmasonería en la historiografía mexicanista." *Historia Mexicana* 44, no. 3 (January–March 1995): 439–460.

———. *Los Disidentes: sociedades protestantes y revolución en México, 1872–1911.* Mexico City: El Colegio de México, 1989.

Bazant, Jan. *Alienation of Church Wealth in Mexico: Social and Economic Aspects of the Liberal Revolution, 1856–1875.* Cambridge: Cambridge University Press, 1971.

———. *Antonio Haro y Tamariz y sus aventuras políticas, 1811–1869.* Mexico City: El Colegio de México, 1985.

——. "Tres revoluciones mexicanas." *Historia Mexicana* 10, no. 2 (October–December 1960): 220–242.

Berry, Charles R. *La Reforma in Oaxaca, 1856–57.* Lincoln: University of Nebraska Press, 1981.

Borutta, Manuel. "Anti-Catholicism and the Culture War in Risorgimento Italy." In *The Risorgimento Revisited: Nationalism and Culture in Nineteenth-Century Italy,* edited by Silvana Patriarca and Lucy Riall, 191–213. New York: Palgrave Macmillan, 2012.

Brading, D. A. *Church and State in Bourbon Mexico: The Diocese of Michoacán, 1749–1810.* Cambridge: Cambridge University Press, 1994.

——. "Liberal Patriotism and the Mexican Reforma." *Journal of Latin American Studies* 20, no. 1 (May 1988): 27–48.

——. *Mexican Phoenix: Our Lady of Guadalupe: Image and Tradition across Five Centuries.* Cambridge: Cambridge University Press, 2001.

——. *The Origins of Mexican Nationalism.* Cambridge: Cambridge University Press, 1985.

——. "Tridentine Catholicism and Enlightened Despotism in Bourbon Mexico," *Journal of Latin American Studies* 15, no. 1 (May 1983): 1–22.

——. "Ultramontane Intransigence and the Mexican Reform: Clemente de Jesús Munguía." In *The Politics of Religion in an Age of Revival: Studies in Nineteenth-Century Europe and Latin America,* edited by Austen Ivereigh, 115–42. London: Institute of Latin American Studies, 2000.

Bravo Ugarte, José, SJ. *Munguía: Obispo y arzobispo de Michoacán (1810–1868), su vida y su obra.* Mexico City: Editorial Jus,1967.

——. *Periodistas y periodicos mexicanos hasta 1935.* Mexico City: Editorial Jus, 1966.

Breve tratado de las ceremonias que se han de observer en los dias de semana santa, sacado de los mejores autores que se iran citando en sus lugares respectivos: Compuesto por un aficionado. Mexico City: Luis Abaniano y Valdes, 1841.

Brittsan, Zachary. *Popular Politics and Rebellion in Mexico: Manuel Lozada and La Reforma, 1855–1876.* Nashville, TN: Vanderbilt University Press, 2015.

Bushnell, David. "Assessing the Legacy of Liberalism." In *Liberals, Politics, and Power: State Formation in Nineteenth-Century Latin America,* edited by Barbara A. Tenenbaum and Vincent C. Peloso, 278–300. Athens: University of Georgia Press, 1996.

Cahill, David. "Popular Religion and Appropriation: The Example of Corpus Christi in Eighteenth-Century Cuzco." *Latin American Research Review* 31, no. 2 (1996): 67–110.

Calderón de la Barca, Fanny. *Life in Mexico.* Edited by Howard T. Fisher and Marion Hall Fisher. New York: Doubleday, 1966.

Callcott, Wilfrid Hardy. *Church and State in Mexico: 1822-1857.* Durham, NC: Duke University Press, 1926.

Camacho Becerra, Auturo. "De la imagen sagrada al arte secular: Artistas ante las leyes de Reforma." In *Contextos, prácticas culturales, imaginarios y representaciones,* 207–73. Vol. 2 of *México durante la Guerra de Reforma,* edited by Celia del Palacio Montiel. Xalapa, MX: Universidad Veracruzana, 2011.

Cambre, Minuel. *La Guerra de Tres Años: Apuntes para la historia de la Reforma.* Guadalajara: José Cabrera, 1904.

Carlen, Claudia, ed. *The Papal Encyclicals: 1740–1878*. Vol. 1. McGrath, NH: McGrath Publishing Co., 1981.

Carmona Dávila, Doralicia. "Juárez lamenta la suspensión del periódico 'Siglo XIX,'" Memoria política de México, March 3, 2021. https://memoriapoliticademexico.org/Efemerides/9/20091858.html.

Carrion, Antonio. *Historia de la Ciudad de Puebla de los Angeles*. Puebla: Colegio Salesiano, 1897.

Castillo Negrete, Emilio del. *Mexico en el siglo XIX*, vol. 26. Mexico City: Imprenta del Editor, 1892.

Un Católico [Tovar, Remigo]. *Crimenes de la demagogia: El colegio apostolico de Guadalupe en Zacatecas*. Mexico City: J. M. Lara, 1860.

Chasen-López, Francie. "Guerra, nación y género: Las oaxaqueños en la Guerra de Tres Años." In *Contextos, prácticas culturales, imaginarios y representaciones*, vol. 2 of *México durante la Guerra de Reforma*, edited by Celia del Palacio Montiel, 97–137. Xalapa, MX: Universidad Veracruzana, 2011.

Chowning, Margaret. *Catholic Women and Mexican Politics*. Princeton, NJ: Princeton University Press, 2023.

———. *Rebellious Nuns: The Troubled History of a Mexican Convent, 1752–1863*. Oxford: Oxford University Press, 2005.

———. *Wealth and Power in Provincial Mexico: Michoacán from the Late Colony to the Revolution*. Stanford, CA: Stanford University Press, 1999.

Chrisman, Kevin M. "Community, Power, and Memory in Díaz Ordaz's Mexico: The 1968 Lynching in San Miguel Canoa, Puebla." Master's thesis, University of Nebraska, 2013. https://digitalcommons.unl.edu/historydiss/59.

Clark, Christopher. "The New Catholicism and the European Culture Wars." In *Culture Wars: Secular-Catholic Conflict in Nineteenth-Century Europe*, edited by Christopher Clark and Wolfram Kaiser, 11–47. Cambridge: Cambridge University Press, 2009.

Clark, Christopher, and Wolfram Kaiser. Introduction to *Culture Wars: Secular-Catholic Conflict in Nineteenth-Century Europe*, 1–10. Edited by Christopher Clark and Wolfram Kaiser. Cambridge: Cambridge University Press, 2009.

Comunicaciones cambiadas entre el Excmo. Sr. ministro de Justicia y Negocios eclesiásticos, y el illmo. Sr. obispo de Guadalajara, con motivo de la ley de desamortización sancionada en 25 de junio de 1856. Guadalajara: Rodríguez, 1857.

Connaughton, Brian. "1856–1857: Conciencia religiosa y controversia ciudadana." In *Prácticas populares, cultura política y poder en México, siglo xix*, edited by Brian Connaughton, 395–464. Mexico City: Universidad Autónoma Metropolitana, 2008.

———. *Clerical Ideology in a Revolutionary Age: The Guadalajara Church and the Idea of the Mexican Nation, 1788–1853*. Calgary, AB: University of Calgary Press, 2003.

———. Introduction to *Iglesia, religión y leyes de la Reforma*, 15–38. Vol. 1 of *México durante la Guerra de Reforma*, edited by Brian Connaughton. Xalapa, MX: Universidad Veracruzana, 2011.

———. "La larga cuesta del conservadurismo mexicano, del disguso resentido a la propuesta partidaria, 1789–1854." In *El conservadurismo mexicano en el siglo xix*

(1810–1910), edited by Humberto Morales and William Fowler, 169–86. Puebla: Benemérita Universidad Autónoma de Puebla, 1999.

———. *La mancuerna discordante: La república católica liberal en México hasta La Reforma.* Mexico City: Universidad Autónoma Metropolitana, Unidad Iztapalapa, 2019.

Contestaciones habidas entre el Illmo. Señor Arzobispo y el Ministerio de Justicia con motivo de la ley sobre administracion de ese ramo. Mexico City: José Mariano Fernández de Lara, 1855.

Contestaciones habidas entre el illmo. Sr. arzobispo de México, Dr. D. Lázaro de la Garza y Ballesteros, y el Exmo. Sr. ministro de justicia, negocios, eclesiásticos e instrucción pública, Lic. D. Ezequiel Montes, con motivo de la ley espedida en 25 de junio de 1856, sobre la desamortización de los bienes de las corporaciones civiles y eclesiásticas de la República. Mexico City: José A. Godoy, 1856.

Coppa, Frank J. *The Modern Papacy since 1789.* New York: Longman, 1998.

Cornejo Franco, José. *De la independencia a la reforma.* Guadalajara: Ediciones del Gobierno del Estado, 1959.

Costeloe, Michael P. "The Administration, Collection and Distribution of Tithes in the Archbishopric of Mexico, 1800–1860." *The Americas* 23, no. 1 (July 1966): 3–27.

———. *Church and State in Independent Mexico: A Study in the Patronage Debate, 1821–1857.* London: Royal Historical Society, 1978.

———. *Church Wealth in Mexico: A Study of the 'Juzgado de Capellanias' in the Archbishopric of Mexico, 1800–1856.* Cambridge: Cambridge University Press, 1967.

———. "*Hombres de bien* in the Age of Santa Anna." In *Mexico in the Age of Democratic Revolutions, 1750–1850*, edited by Jaime E. Rodriguez O., 243–57. Boulder, CO: Lynne Reinner Publishers, 1994.

Couto, José Bernardo. *Discurso sobre la constitución de la iglesia.* Mexico City: Andrade y Escalante, 1857.

———. *Obras del Doctor D. José Bernardo Couto.* Mexico City: V. Agüeros, 1898.

Couto, Ricardo. *José Bernardo Couto.* Veracruz: Editorial Citlaltepetl, 1961.

Covo, Jacqueline. "Los clubes políticos en la Revolución de Ayutla." *Historia Mexicana* 26, no. 3 (January–March 1977): 438–55.

———. *Las ideas de la Reforma en México (1855–1861).* Mexico City: Universidad Nacional Autónoma de México, 1983.

"Cox, Jeffrey. "Secularization and Other Master Narratives of Religion in Modern Europe." *Kirchliche Zeitgeschichte* 14, no. 1 (2001): 24.

Creed, J. L., ed. and trans. *Lactantius: De Mortibus Persecutorum.* Oxford: Oxford University Press, 1984.

La Cruz: Periódico esclusivamente religioso. Mexico City: November 1, 1855–July 29, 1858.

Cruz-Aedo, Miguel. *Discurso pronunciado en el salon principal del Instituto del Estado, el 17 de Setiembre de 1855, aniversario de las víctimas de la patria, por el C. Miguel Cruz-Aedo, miembro el la sociedad literaria, "La Esperanaza."* Guadalajara: Tipografía del Gobierno, 1855.

———. *Los pobrecitos estudiantes del seminario de Guadalajara* (Mexico City: R. Rafael, 1852).

Cuevas, José María. *Informe de Licenciado J. M. Cuevas ante la primera sala del Tribunal Superior en el punto sobre competencia del Juzgado de Distrito, para conocer de la causa que se instruye al Sr. D. Luis C. Cuevas, por haber sido ministro de relaciones en la administracion establecida en enero de 1858.* Mexico City: J. M. Lara, 1861.

Cuevas, Mariano, SJ. *Historia de la iglesia en México*, 6th ed., vol. 5. Mexico City: Editorial Porrúa, 1992.

Davis, Thomas B., and Amando Ricon Virulegio. *The Political Plans of Mexico*. Lanham, MD: University Press of America, 1987.

Decorme, Gerado, SJ. *Historia de la Compañía de Jesús en la Republica Mexicana durante el siglo xix*. Vol. 2. Guadalajara: J. M. Yguiniz, 1921.

Decreto concediendo el pase al breve en que se nombre Delegado Apostolico á Monseñor Luis Clementi; Dicatmen sobre la admission del misma breve. Mexico City: Ignacio Cumplido, 1853.

Delpar, Helen, ed. *Encyclopedia of Latin America*. New York: McGraw-Hill, 1974.

Los Demagogos y sus escritos, Contestacion al cuaderno titulada: "Los asesinatos de Tacuba." Guadalajara: Díoniso Rodríguez, 1859.

Diálogo entre Martin y Juan Diego. Parts 1 and 2. Mexico City: V. Segura Argüelles, 1855. Parts 2 and 3. Mexico City: Tomás S. Gardida, 1855.

Diario de Avisos: Publicación de literatura, industria, ciencias y artes. Mexico City: November 6, 1856–January 1, 1861.

Díaz López, Lilia, trans. and ed. *Versión francesa de México: Informes diplomáticos (1853–1858)*. Vol. 1. Mexico City: El Colegio de México, 1963.

Díaz Patiño, Gabriela. *Católicos, liberales y protestantes: El debate por las imágenes religiosas en la formación de una cultura nacional (1848–1908)*. Mexico City: El Colegio de México: 2016.

Diccionario Porrúa: Historia, biografía, y geografía de México, 6th ed. Mexico City: Editorial Porrúa, 1995.

Dublan, Manuel, and José María Lozano, eds., *Legislación Mexicana ó colección completa de las disposiciones legislativas expendidas desde la Independencia de la República*. Vols. 8, 9, and 10. Mexico City: Imprenta del Comercio, 1904.

Duffy, Eamon. *The Stripping of the Altars: Traditional Religion in England 1400–1580*. New Haven, CT: Yale University Press, 1992.

Echeverria, Pedro T. *Catecismo de la doctrina clero-maquiavelica o sea del Padre Ripalda segun lo observa y predica el clero mexicano*. Mexico City: Imprenta de la Reforma, 1861.

Espinosa y Dávalos, Pedro. *A N. M. I. V. S. Dean y cabildo, al V. clero secular y regular y á todos los fieles de esta Diócesis.* Guadalajara, n.p., 1854.

——. *Carta pastoral del Illmo. Sr. Obispo de Guadalajara en que se inserta la alocución de Su Santidad.* Guadalajara: Rodríguez, 1858.

——. *El Illmo. Señor Obispo de Guadalajara en union con su cabildo, representa al supreme gobierno pidiendo la modificación o derogación de algunos artículos de la ley sobre Registro Civil.* Guadalajara: Rodríguez, 1857.

——. *Protesta del Illmo. Sr. Obispo de Guadalajara contra la ley de 25 de junio de 1856.* Guadalajara: n.p., 1856.

——. *Quinta carta pastoral que el Illmo. Señor Obispo de Guadalajara, dirije a sus diocesanos.* Guadalajara: Rodríguez, 1855.

Fajardo Ortiz, Guillermo. "México 1861. Perspectiva histórica de la secularización de los hospitals." *Revista de la Facultad de Medicina de la UNAM* 55, no. 5 (September–October 2012): 44–47.

Falcón, Ramona. "Discontento campesino e hispanofobia. La tierra caliente a mediados del siglo XIX." *Historia Mexicana* 44, no. 3 (January–March 1995): 461–98.

Farriss, N. M. *Crown and Clergy in Colonial Mexico, 1759–1821.* London: Athlone Press, 1968.

Fernández Fernández, Iñigo. "El liberalismo católico en la prensa mexicana de la primera mitad del siglo XIX (1833–1857)." *Historia 396* (Pontificia Universidad Católica de Valparaiso, Chile) 4, no. 1 (2014): 59–74.

Fowler, Will. "Dreams of Stability: Mexican Political Thought during the 'Forgotten Years': An Analysis of the Beliefs of the Creole Intelligentsia (1821–1853)." *Bulletin of Latin American Research* 14, no. 3 (1995): 287–312.

———. *The Grammar of Civil War: A Mexican Case Study, 1857–61.* Lincoln: University of Nebraska Press, 2022.

———. *La Guerra de Tres Años, 1857–1861: El conflicto del que nacio el estado laico mexicano.* Mexico City: Critica, 2020.

———. *Independent Mexico: The Pronunciamiento in the Age of Santa Anna, 1821–1858.* Lincoln: University of Nebraska Press, 2016.

———. *Mexico in the Age of Proposals, 1821–1853.* Westport, CT: Greenwood Press, 1998.

———. *Tornel and Santa Anna: The Writer and the Caudillo, Mexico 1795–1853.* Westport, CT: Greenwood Press, 2000.

Fraile, G. "Balmes, Jaime Luciano." In *The New Catholic Encyclopedia*, 2nd ed. 2:232–33. Detroit, MI: Gale Group, 2003.

Fuentes Mares, José. *Juárez y los Estados Unidos*, 4th ed. Mexico City: Editorial Jus, 1964.

Fuentes Díaz, Vicente. *Santos Degollado, La victoria de la República.* Mexico City: Secretaría de Educación Pública, 1967.

Galeana de Valadés, Patricia. "Los liberales y la iglesia." In *The Mexican and Mexican American Experience in the 19th Century*, edited by Jaime E. Rodríguez O., 44–54. Tempe, AZ: Bilingual Press, 1989.

Galvan Rivera, Mariano, *Guia de forasteros en la ciudad de México para el año de 1854.* Mexico City: Santiago Perez, 1854.

Gamboa, José M. *Leyes constitucionales de México durante el siglo xix.* Mexico City: Oficina Tipografía de la Secretaría de Fomento, 1901.

García Cantú, Gastón, ed. *El pensamiento de la reacción mexicana: Historia documental, 1810–1962.* Mexico City: Empresas Editorials, 1965.

García Gutiérrez, Jesús, SJ. *Apuntamientos de historia eclesiástica Mejicana.* Mexico City: Victoria, 1922.

García Ugarte, Marta Eugenia. *Liberalismo e iglesia católica en México, 1824–1855.* Mexico City: Instituto Mexicano de Doctrina Social Cristiana, 1999.

———. *Poder político y religioso: México siglo XIX.* 2 vols. Mexico City: Universidad Nacional Autónoma de México, 2010,

Gilbert, David A. "Finding Faith in the Nineteenth Century: Fanny Calderón de la Barca's Journey to the Catholic Church (via Mexico)," *The Catholic Social Science Review* 23 (2018): 141–55.

Gonzaga Cuevas, Luis. *Porvenir de México.* 1851. Reprinted with appendices, Mexico City: Cien de México, 1992.

González Domínguez, María del Refugio. "Juan N. Rodríguez de San Miguel, jurista conservador mexicano." In *Estudios jurídicos en homenaje a Marta Morineau.* Edited by

Nuria González Martín, 1:233–49. Mexico City: UNAM, Instituto de Investigaciones Jurídicas, 2016.

Goslin, Tomás S. *Los evangélicos en la América Latina.* Buenos Aires: La Aurora, 1956.

Grato recuerdo á los martires de Guadalajara sacrificados en los meses de Septiembre y Octubre de 1858 por la demagogia. Guadalajara: Luis P. Vidaurri, 1859.

Greenberg, Amy S. *A Wicked War: Polk, Clay, Lincoln, and the 1846 U.S. Invasion of Mexico.* New York: Alfred A. Knopf, 2012.

Grew, Raymond. "Liberty and the Catholic Church in Nineteenth-Century Europe." In *Freedom and Religion in the Nineteenth Century,* edited by Richard Helmstadter, 196–232. Stanford, CA: Stanford University Press, 1997.

Guame, Jean. *Histoire de la société domestique chez tous les peoples anciens et modernes, ou influence du Christianisme sur la famille.* 2 vols. Paris: Guame Freres, 1844.

Guardino, Peter, F. *Peasants, Politics, and the Formation of Mexico's National State: Guerrero, 1800-1857.* Stanford, CA: Stanford University Press, 1996.

Gutiérrez Casillas, José, SJ. *Jesuitas en México durante el siglo xix.* Mexico City: Biblioteca Porrúa, 1972.

Gutiérrez Negrón, Sergio. "Estética, polémica y Dios: aestesis teológica en el semanario mexicano *La Cruz (1855–1858)*." In *Sensibilidades conservadores: el debate cultural sobre la civilización en América Latina y España durante el Siglo XIX,* edited by Kari Soriano Salkjelsvik, 353–72. Madrid: Iberoamericana, 2021.

Hale, Charles A. *Mexican Liberalism in the Age of Mora, 1821-1853.* New Haven, CT: Yale University Press, 1968.

——. "The War with the United States and the Crisis in Mexican Thought." *The Americas* 14, no. 1 (October 1957): 153–73.

Hammond, John Hays. "José María Roa Bárcena: Mexican Writer and Champion of Catholicism." *The Americas* 6, no. 1 (July 1949): 45–55.

Hamnett, Brian. "The Comonfort Presidency, 1855-1857." *Bulletin of Latin American Research* 15, no. 1 (January 1996): 81–100.

——. "Mexican Conservatives, Clericals, and Soldiers: The 'Traitor' Tomás Mejía through Reform and Empire, 1855–1867." *Bulletin of Latin American Research* 20, no. 2 (April 2001): 187–209.

——. *Reform, Rebellion and Party in Mexico, 1836–1861.* Cardiff, UK: University of Wales Press, 2022.

Harrington, Raymond Patrick. "The Secular Clergy in the Diocese of Merida de Yucatán: 1780–1850." PhD diss., The Catholic University of America, 1983.

Haworth, Daniel S. "Desde los Baluartes Conservadores: La Ciudad de México y la Guerra de Reforma (1857–1860)." *Relaciones: Estudios de Historia y Sociadad* (El Colegio de Michoacán) 21, no. 84 (Autumn 2000): 97–131.

Hempton, David. "Established Churches and the Growth of Religious Pluralism: A Case Study of Christianisation and Secularisation in England since 1700." In *The Decline of Christendom in Western Europe, 1700-2000,* edited by Hugh McLeod and Werner Ustorf, 81–98. Cambridge: Cambridge University Press, 2003.

Hernández Rodriguez, Rosaura. *El General Conservador Luis G. Osollo.* Mexico City: Editorial Jus, 1959.

Hunter, James Davison. *Before the Shooting Begins: Searching for Democracy in America's Culture War.* New York: The Free Press, 1994.

——. *Culture Wars: The Struggle to Define America.* New York: Basic Books, 1991.

——. "Reflections on the Culture War Hypothesis." In *America at War with Itself: Cultural Conflict in Contemporary Society,* edited by James L. Nolan, Jr., 243–56. Greenwich, CT: JAI Press, 1995.

——. "Response to Davis and Robinson: Remembering Durkheim." *Journal for the Scientific Study of Religion* 35, no. 3 (September 1996): 246–48.

Un ingenio de esta villa [pseud.]. *Porfirio ó El héroe de la crujia.* Mexico City: Vicente Segura, 1858.

Intervalo lucido de Miguel Cruz-Aedo. Mexico City: Segura Arguelles, 1855.

Ivereigh, Austen. Introduction to *The Politics of Religion in an Age of Revival: Studies in Nineteenth-Century Europe and Latin America,* 1–21. Edited by Austen Ivereigh, London: Institute of Latin American Studies, 2000.

Un Jalisciense [pseud.]. *Tendencias de la demagogia mejicana, manifestadas por sus propios hechos.* Guadalajara: Rodríguez, 1857.

Jrade, Ramón. "Inquiries into the Cristero Insurrection against the Mexican Revolution." *Latin American Research Review* 20, no. 2 (1985): 53–69.

Juárez, José Roberto. "La lucha por el poder a la caída de Santa Anna." *Historia Mexicana* 10 (1960): 72–93.

——. Review of *La famila enferma,* by Ignacio Aguilar y Marocho, *Hispanic American Historical Review* 51, no. 2 (May 1971): 367–68.

Knowlton, Robert J. *Church Property and the Mexican Reform, 1856-1910.* DeKalb: Northern Illinois University Press, 1976.

——. "Clerical Response to the Mexican Reform, 1855–1875." *Catholic Historical Review* 50, no. 4 (January 1965): 509–28.

Krause, Enrique. *La historia cuenta.* Mexico City: Tusquets Editores, 1998.

——. "La Reforma: 'Tiempo-eje' de México." In *Las Leyes de Reforma y el Estado laico: importancia história y validez contemporánea,* edited by Roberto Blancarte, 21–35. Mexico City: El Colegio de México, 2013.

Lannon, Francis. "1898 and the Politics of Catholic Identity in Spain." In *The Politics of Religion in an Age of Revival: Studies in Nineteenth-Century Europe and Latin America,* edited by Austen Ivereigh, 56–73. London: Institute of Latin American Studies, 2000.

Lara, Jaime. *Christian Texts for Aztecs: Art and Liturgy in Colonial Mexico.* Notre Dame, IN: University of Notre Dame Press, 2008.

Larkin, Brian. *The Very Nature of God: Baroque Catholicism and Religious Reform in Bourbon Mexico City.* Albuquerque: University of New Mexico Press, 2010.

Lerdo de Tejada, Miguel. *Cuadro Sinóptico de la República Mexicana en 1856.* Mexico City: Ignacio Cumplido, 1856.

[J. H.] *Liberalismo y sus efectos en la República Mexicana.* Mexico City: Andres Boix, 1858.

Ligeras reflexiones sobre un cuaderno anónimo intitulado "Apuntamientos sobre derecho publico eclesiastico." Mexico City: J. M. Andrade y F. Escalante, 1857.

Los Reyes, Guillermo de. "El impacto de la masonería en los orígenes del discurso secular, laico y anticlerical en México." In *Secularización del Estado y la Sociedad*, edited by Patricia Galeana, 101–126. Mexico City: Siglo XXI Editores, 2010

Macaulay, Thomas Babington. *The History of England from the Accession of James II*. 5 vols. London: Longman, Brown, Green, and Longmans, 1848.

Magaña Ocaña, Itzel. "Pelagio Antonio de Labastida y Dávalos, Obispo y Arzobispo de México frente a la Reforma y el Segundo Imperio." Thesis, Universidad Nacional Autónoma de México, 1993.

Mallon, Florencia E. *Peasant and Nation: The Making of Postcolonial Mexico and Peru*. Berkeley: University of California Press, 1994.

Malo, José Ramón. *Diario de sucesos notables*. Edited by Mariano Cuevas, SJ. 2 vols. Mexico: Editorial Patria, 1948.

Malvido, Elsa. "Los hospitales en México en el siglo xix en el marco de la secularización. De la caridad a la salud pública." In *Secularización del Estado y la sociedad*, edited by Patricia Galeana de Valadés, 255–67. Mexico City: Siglo XXI, 2010.

Manning, William R., ed. Diplomatic Correspondence of the United States: Inter-American Affairs, 1831–1860. Vol. 9. Mexico: 1848 (mid-year)–1860.Washington, DC: Carnegie Endowment for International Peace, 1937.

Marley, David F. *Mexico at War: From the Struggle for Independence to the 21st-Century Drug Wars*. Santa Barbara, CA: ABC-CLIO, 2014.

Martinez Báez, Antonio, ed. *Representaciones sobre la tolerancia religiosa*. Mexico City: Colección "El Siglo XIX," 1959.

Matson, Robert W. "Church Wealth in Ninetenth-Century Mexico: A Review of the Literature." Catholic Historical Review 64, no. 4 (October 1979): 600–609.

[Maximilian of Hapsburg]. *Los traidores pintados por si mismos. Libro secreto de Maximiliano, en que aparece la idea que tenía de sus servidores*. Mexico City: Imprenta del Gobierno, 1867.

McGowan, Gerald. *Prensa y poder, 1854–1857*. Mexico City: El Colegio de Mexico, 1978.

McMillan, James F. "Religion and Politics in Nineteenth-Century France: Further Reflections on Why Catholics and Republicans Couldn't Stand Each Other." In *The Politics of Religion in an Age of Revival: Studies in Nineteenth-Century Europe and Latin America*, edited by Austen Ivereigh, 43–55. London: Institute of Latin American Studies, 2000.

Medina Ascensio, Luis, SJ. *La iglesia y el estado liberal: 1836-1867*. Vol. 2 of *México y el Vaticano*. Mexico City: Editorial Jus, 1984.

[R. G. H.] *Memoria sobre la propiedad eclesiástica; riqueza pública destruida y víctimas hechas por los demagogos de 858 hasta junio de 863*. Mexico City: Literaria, 1864.

Meyer, Jean A. *The Cristero Rebellion: The Mexican People Between Church and State, 1926-1929*. Translated by Richard Southern. Cambridge: Cambridge University Press, 1976.

Mijangos y González, Pablo. "Clemente de Jesús Munguía y el fracaso de los liberalismos católicos en México (1846–1861)." In *Iglesia, religión y Leyes de Reforma*, 167–198. Vol. 1 of *México durante la Guerra de Reforma*, edited by Brian Connaughton, Xalapa, MX: Universidad Veracruzana, 2011.

———. *The Lawyer of the Church: Bishop Clemente de Jesús Munguía and the Clerical Response to the Mexican Liberal Reforma*. Lincoln: University of Nebraska Press, 2015.

———. *La Reforma, Herramientas para la Historia*. Mexico City: Fondo de Cultura Económica, 2018.

El Monitor Republicano: Diario de política, artes, industria, comercio, modas, literatura, teatros, variedades y anuncios. Mexico City: August 17, 1855–December 31, 1856.

Montalembert, Charles de. *Du Devoir des Catholiques dans la Question de la Liberté d'Enseignement.* Paris: Au bureau de l'Univers, 1843.

Moody, Joseph N. *The Church as Enemy: Anticlericalism in Nineteenth-Century French Literature.* Washington, DC: Corpus Books, 1968.

Morales, Francisco, OFM. "Mexican Society and the Franciscan Order in a Period of Transition." *The Americas* 54, no. 3 (January 1998): 323–256.

———. "Procesos internos de reforma en las órdenes religiosas: Propuestas y obstáculos." In *Historia de la Iglesia en el Siglo XIX*, edited by Manuel Ramos Medina, 149–77. Mexico City: Centro de Estudios de Historia de México Condumex, 1998.

Morales, Huberto, and William Fowler. Introduction to *El conservadurismo mexicano en el siglo xix (1810–1910)*, edited by Humberto Morales and William Fowler, 11–36. Puebla: Benemérita Universidad Autónoma de Puebla, 1999.

Morales, J[uan] B[atista]. *Disertacion contra la tolerancia religioso.* Mexico City: Galvan, 1831.

Morales Cruz, Joel. *The Mexican Reformation: Catholic Pluralism, Enlightenment Religion, and the Iglesia de Jesús Movement in Benito Juárez's Mexico (1859–72).* Eugene, OR: Pickwick Publications, 2011.

Moreno, Juan Carlos, and Jaime Ros. "Mexico's Market Reforms in Historical Perspective." *CEPAL Review* 84 (December 2004): 35–56.

Morgan, Ronald J. *Spanish American Saints and the Rhetoric of Identity, 1600-1810.* Tucson: University of Arizona Press, 2002.

Mörner, Magnus, ed. *The Expulsion of the Jesuits from Latin America.* New York: Alfred A Knopf, 1965.

Munguía, Clemente de Jesús. *Opúsculo escrito por el Illmo. Sr. Obispo D. Clemente de Jesús Munguía, en defensa de la soberanía, derechos y libertades de la iglesia atacados en la constitución civil de 1857 y en otros decretos expedidos por el actual gobierno de la nación.* Morelia: Ignacio Arango, 1857.

Muriel, Josefina. "Desamortización de los colegios de niñas: Los colegios femeninos y la exclaustración de 1856." In *Memoria del I Coloquio Historia de la Iglesia en el Siglo XIX*, edited by Manuel Ramos Medina, 290–94. Mexico City: Centro de Estudios de Historia de México Condumex, 1998.

Nieto Garcia, Raúl. "El convento grande de San Francisco de la ciudad de México." *Bitácora Architectura*, no. 3 (Summer 2000): 12–19.

El Nuncio Apostólico en México: Monseñor Luis Clementi, Arzobispo impartibus di Damsco. [Mexico City?], 1854.

Ocampo, Melchor. *Obras Completas.* 3 vols. Mexico City: F. Vázquez, 1900–01.

O'Hara, Matthew D. *A Flock Divided: Race, Religion and Politics in Mexico, 1749–1857.* Durham, NC: Duke University Press, 2010).

Olavarría y Ferrari, Enrique de. *Reseña histórica del teatro en México.* 2nd ed. Mexico City: La Europa, 1895.

Olea Franco, Rafael. "*La Quinta Modelo* de Roa Bárcena en el debate cultural." In *Contextos, prácticas culturales, imaginarios y representaciones*, 289–309. Vol. 2 of *México durante la Guerra de Reforma*, edited by Celia del Palacio Montiel. Xalapa, MX: Universidad Veracruzana, 2011.

Olliff, Donathon C. *Reforma Mexico and the United States: A Search for Alternatives to Annexation, 1854–1861*. Tuscaloosa: University of Alabama Press, 1981.

Olveda, Jaime. "El punto de vista de la iglesia sobre las leyes de la reforma." In *Contextos, prácticas culturales, imaginarios y representaciones*, 84–93. Vol. 2 of *México durante la Guerra de Reforma*, edited by Celia del Palacio Montiel. Xalapa, MX: Universidad Veracruzana, 2011.

Orozco Farias, Rogelio. *Fuentes históricas: México 1821–1867*. 2nd ed. Mexico City: Editorial Progreso, 1965.

Pablo Antonio del Niño Jesus. *Oración fúnebre en memoria y honor de los valientes militares que sucumbieron en la lucha contra la demagogia*. Puebla: José Maria Rivera, 1858.

El Pájaro Verde: Religión, política, literatura, artes, ciencias, industria, comercio, medicina, tribunales, agricultura, minería, teatros, modas, revista general de la prensa de Europa y del Nuevo-Mundo. Mexico City: January 5–June 7, 1861.

Palacio Montiel, Celia del. Preface to *Iglesia, religión y leyes de la Reforma*, 7–12. Vol. 1 of *México durante la Guerra de Reforma*, edited by Brian Connaughton. Xalapa, MX: Universidad Veracruzana, 2011

———. "La prensa de la Reforma." In *Contextos, prácticas culturales, imaginarios y representaciones*, 155–206. Vol. 2 of *México durante la Guerra de Reforma*, edited by Celia del Palacio Montiel. Xalapa, MX: Universidad Veracruzana, 2011.

———. *La Primera Generación Romántica en Guadalajara: El Falange de Estudio*. Guadalajara: Editorial Universidad de Guadalajara, 1993.

Pani, Erika. "Iglesia, Estado y Reforma: Las complejidades de una ruptura." In *Iglesia, religión y Leyes de Reforma*, 41–71. Vol. 1 of *México durante la Guerra de Reforma*, edited by Brian Connaughton. Xalapa, MX: Universidad Veracruzana, 2011.

———. Prologue to *La Reforma: Herramientas para la Historia*, by Pablo Mijangos y González, 11–14. Mexico City: Fondo de Cultura Económica, 2018.

El partido conservador en México. Mexico: J. M. Andrade y F. Escalante, 1855.

Pasquel, Leonardo. "Numero dedicado al General Ignacio de la Llave en el primer centenario de su muerte, 1863-1963." *Revista Jarocha* 5, no. 25 (June 1963): 3–27.

Payno, Manuel. "Ocampo." In *El Libro Rojo: 1520–1867*, vol. 2, 168–71. Mexico City: A. Pola, 1906.

Peña Espinosa, Jesús Joel. "Crisis, agonía y restauración del monasterio de Santa Mónica de la ciudad de Puebla, 1827–1943." *Boletín de Monumentos Históricos* 3, no. 30 (January–April 2014): 283–303.

Peñalosa, Joaquín Antonia. *Francisco González Bocanegra: vida y obra*. 2nd ed. San Luis Potosí: Universidad Autónoma de San Luis Potosí, 1998.

Perales Ojeda, Alicia. *Las asociaciones literarias mexicanas*. 2nd revised ed. Mexico City: Universidad Nacional Autónoma de México, 2000.

Pérez Cuyado, Norberto [Jóse Bernardo Couto]. *Disertación sobre la naturaleza y límites de la authoridad eclesiástica*. Mexico: n.p., 1825.

Pérez Lugo, J. [Joaquín Ramírez Cabañas]. *La cuestión religiosa de México*. Mexico City: Publicaciones del Centro Cultural "Cuauhtemoc," 1926.

Pérez Verdía, Luis. *Historia particular del Estado de Jalisco desde los primeros tiempos de que hay noticia, hasta nuestros días*. 3 vols. Guadalajara: Escuela de Artes y Oficios del Estado, 1910–11.

Perrone, Giovanni, SJ. *Il Protestantsimo e la regola di fede*. Turin, Italy: Giacinto Marietti,1854.

Pinheiro, John C. *Missionaries of Republicanism: A Religious History of the Mexican-American War*. New York: Oxford University Press, 2014.

Pizarro, Nicolás. *Catecismo politico constitucional*. 2nd ed. Mexico City: Ana Echeverria de Pizarro e hijas, 1861.

Plasencia de la Parra, Enrique. *Independencia y nacionalismo a la luz del discurso conmemorativo (1825–1867)*. Mexico City: Consejo Nacional para la Cultura y las Artes, 1991.

Pola, Angel. "Santos Degollado." In *El Libro Rojo: 1520–1867*. Vol. 2, 360–96. Mexico City: A. Pola, 1906.

Pompa y Pompa, Antonio, ed. *Colección de documentos inéditos o muy raros relativos a la Reforma en México*. Vol. 1. Mexico City: Institutio Nacional de Antropologia y Historia, 1957.

Ponce, Pearl T. "As Dead as Julius Caesar: The Rejection of the McLane-Ocampo Treaty." *Civil War History* 53, no. 4 (December 2007): 342–78.

Portilla, Anselmo de la. *Méjico en 1856 and 1857: Gobierno de General Comonfort*. New York: S. Hallet, 1858.

Prieto, Guillermo. *Memorias de mis tiempos*. 2 vols. Mexico City: Editorial Patria, 1948.

———. *Oración civica pronunciada por el ciudadano Guillermo Prieto en la Alameda de México, el día 16 de septiembre de 1855, aniversario del glorioso grito de "¡Independencia!" dado por el cura de Dolores en 1810*. Mexico City: Ignacio Cumplido, 1855.

Protesta que hacen los poblanos, en favor del fuero eclesiastico. Puebla: José María Rivera, 1855.

Quirarte, Martín. *El problema religioso en México*. Mexico City: Institutio Nacional de Antropología, 1967.

Ramirez Aparicio, Manuel. *Los conventos suprimidos en México*. Mexico City: J. M. Aguilar, 1861.

Real Aguila, José. *Sermon que en el aniversario de la definición dogmatica sobre la Inmaculada Concepción de María Santisma predicó en la santa iglesia catedral de Durango, el Dr. José Real Aguila . . . el día 8 de diciembre de 1855*. Durango: Imprenta del Gobierno, 1855.

Real Ledezma, Juan, ed. *Enciclopedia histórica y biográfica de la Universidad de Guadalajara: Los universitarios entre el instituto y la Universidad*. June 2017. http://enciclopedia.udg.mx/capitulos/los-universitarios-entre-el-instituto-y-la-universidad.

———, ed. *Historia: La confrontación de la Universidad de Guadalajara y el Instituto de Ciencias del Estado de Jalisco, 1821–1861*. October 2013. https://www.udg.mx/es/nuestra/presentacion/historia/periodos/periodo-ii.

Reglamento de la sociedad conservadora de las garantías sociales. [Mexico City?]: 1859.

Los religiosos de San Francisco y su convento de México. [Mexico City?]: 1858.

Representación al soberano congreso contra el art. 15 del proyecto de constitución sobre la tolerancia religiosa. Mexico City: Andrade y Escalante, 1856.

Representación que al soberano congreso constituyente hacen los vecinos del pueblo de Tlalnepantla Cuautenca. Mexico City: L. Inclan, 1856.

Representación que eleven al soberano congreso, los vecinos de las municipalidades de Cuautilan, Tepotzolan, Huehuetoca, San Miguel, Tultepec, Tultitlan, y Teoloyucan, pidiendo se repruebe el art. 15 del proyecto de constitución sobre tolerancia de cultos. Mexico City: Vicente Segura, 1857.

Representación que hace el vecindario de Querétaro al soberano congreso, para que no sea admitida la tolerancia de cultos propuesta en el proyecto de constitución. Querétaro: Mariano Rodríguez Velazquez, 1856.

Representación que hacen al congreso constituyente various dueños de finacas rusticas y urbanas en Michoacán, Guanajuato y Guerrero. Morelia: I. Arango, 1856.

Representación que hacen al congreso constituyente varios dueños de propiedades territoriales, contra algunos artículos de los proyectos de leyes fundamentales que se discuten actualmente. Mexico City: Ignacio Cumplido, 1856.

La Revolución: Periódico democrático independiente. (Guadalajara) 28 August 28–December 15, 1855.

Ricker, Dennis Paul. "The Lower Secular Clergy of Central Mexico: 1821–1857." PhD diss., University of Texas, 1982.

Rivera, Agustín. *Anales Mexicanos: La Reforma y el Segundo Imperio.* 1891. Reprint, Mexico City: Universidad Nacional Autónoma de México, 1994.

———. *Anales Mexicanos: La reforma i el segundo imperio.* 6th ed. Lagos de Moreno, MX: Lopez Arce, 1904.

Riviere d'Arc, Helene. *Guadalajara y su region: Influencias y dificultades de una metropolis mexicana.* Translated by Carlos Montemayor and Josefina Anaya. Mexico City: SepSetentris, 1973.

Roa Bárcena, José María. *Biografía de D. José Joaquín Pesado.* Mexico City: Editorial Jus, 1962.

———. *La Quinta Modelo.* Mexico City: Instituto Nacional de Bellas Artes, 1984.

Rocafuerte, Vincente. *Ensayo sobre tolerancia religiosa por el ciudadano.* 2nd. ed. México City: Imprenta de Martin Rivera, 1831.

Rodíguez, Jaime Javier. *The Literature of the U.S.-Mexican War: Narrative, Time, and Identity.* Austin: University of Texas Press, 2010.

Rodríguez Piña, Javier. "La defensa de la Iglesia ante la legislación liberal en el periodo 1855–1861." *Secuencia* 39 (September/December 1997): 73–82.

———. "Conservatives Contest the Meaning of Independence, 1846–1855." In ¡*Viva Mexico! ¡Viva La Independencia! Celebrations of September 16,* edited by Wiliam H. Beezley and David E. Lorey, 101–129. Wilmington, DE: SR Books, 2001.

Rodríguez de San Miguel, Juan Nepomuceno. *Reforma del clero, o sean declamaciones sobre su corrupción y sus riquezas.* 1848. Reprint, Morelia: I. Arango, 1856.

———. *Varias observaciones contra un opúsculo titulado Aputamientos sobre derecho público eclesiástico.* Mexico City: J. M. Lara, 1857.

Rosa, Agustin de la. *Contestacion al Sr. Alvires, autor del cuaderno titulado "Reflexiones sobre los decretos episcopales, etc."* Guadalajara: Rodriguez, 1857.

———. *El matrimonio civil considerado en sus relaciones con la religion, la familia y la sociedad.* Guadalajara: Rodríguez, 1859.

Rosas, Pedro. *El Clero y las revoluciones.* Mexico City: L. Inclan, 1861.

Rossi, Ernest E., and Jack C. Plano. *Latin America: A Political Dictionary.* Santa Barbara, CA: ABC-CLIO, 1992.

Rotker, Susana, ed. *The Memoirs of Fray Servando Teresa de Mier.* Translated by Helen Lane. Oxford: Oxford University Press, 1998.

Rovira, María del Carmen, ed. *Pensamiento filosófico mexicano del siglo XIX y primeros años del XX.* 3 vols. Mexico City, Universidad Nacional Autónoma de México, 2001.

Ruiz Castañeda, María del Carmen. *Periodismo politico de la Reforma en la cuidad de México,1854–1861.* Mexico City: Instituto de Investigaciónes Sociales, 1954.

———. *La prensa periodica en torno a la Constitución de 1857.* Mexico City: Instituto de Investigaciones Sociales, 1959.

Ruiz Guerra, Rubén. "Los dilemas de la conciencia: Juan Bautista Morales y su defensa liberal de la iglesia." In *Historia de la Iglesia en el Siglo XIX,* edited by Manuel Ramos Medina, 411–22. Mexico City: Centro de Estudios de Historia de México Condumex, 1998.

Salado Álvarez, Victoriano. *Episodios Nacionales: Santa Anna, la reforma, la intervención, el Imperio.* 1904. Reprint, Mexico City: Editorial Porrúa, 1984.

Salinas, Juan N. *Dudas de un estudiante con motivo de las reflexiones del Sr. Alvires sobre los decretos episcopales que prohiben el juramento constitucional.* Morelia: Ignacio Arango, 1857.

Sánchez Flores, Ramón. *Zacapoaxtla: República de indios y villa de españoles.* 2nd ed. Zacapoaxtla, MX: n.p., 1984.

Sánchez, José. *Anticlericalism: A Brief History.* South Bend, IN: University of Notre Dame Press, 1972.

Sánchez, José M. *Doctrina cristiana del Jerónimo de Ripalda é intento bibliográfico de la misma. Años 1591–1900.* Madrid: Imprenta Alemana, 1909.

Sánches Robles, María Guadalupe. "El personaje histórico en la dramaturgia de Aurelio Luis Gallardo." *Sincronía* 13, no. 48 (Fall 2008). http://sincronia.cucsh.udg.mx/sanchezotono8.htm.

Schivelbusch, Wolfgang. *The Culture of Defeat: On National Trauma, Mourning, and Recovery.* New York: Metropolitan Books, 2003.

Scholes, Walter V. "Church and State at the Mexican Constitutional Convention, 1856–1857." *The Americas* 4, no. 2 (October 1947): 151–174.

———. *Mexican Politics During the Juárez Regime, 1855-1872.* Columbia: University of Missouri Press, 1969.

Sierra, Justo. *Evolución política del pueblo mexicano.* 2nd ed. Edited by Edmundo O'Gorman. Mexico City: Universidad Nacional Autónoma de México, 1957.

El Siglo Diez y Nueve: Periódico político, literario y de avisos. Mexico City: June 1, 1848–September 12, 1856, and October 1, 1856–July 31, 1858.

Sinkin, Richard. *The Mexican Reforma, 1855–1876: A Study in Liberal Nation Building.* Austin: University of Texas Press, 1979.

Smith, Benjamin T. *The Roots of Conservatism in Mexico: Catholicism, Society, and Politics in the Mixteca Baja, 1750–1962.* Albuquerque: University of New Mexico Press, 2012.

La Sociedad: Periódico político y literario. Mexico City: December 1, 1855–July 1856, December 26, 1857–1867.

Sosa, Francisco. *Biografias de mexicanos distinguidos.* Mexico City: Oficina Tipográfica de la Secretaría de Fomento, 1884.

Staples, Anne. "Clerics as Politicians: Church, State, and Political Power in Independent Mexico." In *Mexico in the Age of Democratic Revolutions, 1750–1850*, edited by Jaime E. Rodríguez O., 223–41. Boulder, CO: Lynne Rienner Publishers, 1994.

———. "La educación como instrumento ideológico del estado. El conservadurismo educativo en el México decimonónico." In *El conservadurismo mexicano en el siglo xix (1810-1910)*, edited by Huberto Morales and William Fowler, 103–114. Puebla: Benemérita Universidad Autónoma de Puebla, 1999.

———. "Secularización: Estado y iglesia en tiempos de Gómez Farías." *Estudios Modernos y Contemporáneos de México* 10, no. 10 (1986): 109–23.

Stauffer, Brian. *Victory on Earth or in Heaven: Mexico's Religionero Rebellion.* Albuquerque: University of New Mexico Press, 2020.

Steinfels, Peter. "The Failed Encounter: The Catholic Church and Liberalism in the Nineteenth Century." In *Catholicism and Liberalism: Contributions to American Public Policy*, edited by R. Bruce Douglass and David Hollenbach, 19–44. Cambridge: Cambridge University Press, 1994.

Sullivan-González, Douglass. *Piety, Power, and Politics: Religion and Nation Formation in Guatemala, 1821–1871.* Pittsburgh: Pittsburgh University Press, 1998.

Taylor, William B. *Magistrates of the Sacred: Priests and Parishioners in Eighteenth-Century Mexico.* Stanford: CA, Stanford University Press, 1996.

———. *Shrines and Miraculous Images: Religious Life in Mexico Before the Reforma.* Albuquerque: University of New Mexico Press, 2019.

Tecuanhuey Sandoval, Alicia. "Antes del conflicto general: Puebla, 1855–1860." In *Iglesia, religión y Leyes de Reforma*, 199–244. Vol. 1 of *México durante la Guerra de Reforma*, edited by Brian Connaughton, Xalapa, MX: Universidad Veracruzana, 2011.

Téllez Aguilar, Abraham. "Una iglesia cismática mexicana en el siglo xix." *Estudios de historia moderna y contemporánea de México*, 13, no. 13 (1990): 253–56.

Tennenbaum, Barbara A. "Development and Sovereignty: Intellectuals and the Second Empire." In *Los intelectuales y el poder en México*, edited by Roderic A. Camp, Charles A. Hale, and Josefina Zoraida Vázquez, 77–88. Los Angeles: UCLA Latin American Center Publications, 1991.

Thomas, Emory M. *Robert E. Lee: A Biography.* New York: Norton, 1995.

Thomson, Guy P. C. "La contrarreforma en Puebla, 1854–1886." In *El conservadurismo mexicano en el siglo xix (1810-1910)*, edited by Humberto Morales and William Fowler, 239–63. Puebla: Benemérita Universidad Autónoma de Puebla, 1999.

———. "Popular Aspects of Liberalism in Mexico, 1848–1888." *Bulletin of Latin American Research* 10, no. 1 (1991): 265–92.

Thomson, Guy P. C., and David LaFrance. *Patriotism, Politics, and Popular Libealism in Nineteenth-Century Mexico.* Wilmington, DE: Scholarly Resources, 1999.

Tornel y Mendivil, José Julian. *Apuntamientos sobre derecho público eclesiástico.* Mexico City: Andrade y Escalante, 1858.

El Tribuno del Pueblo. (Mexico City) August 19, 1856–January 10, 1857.

Trueba, Alfonso. *La Guerra de Tres Años.* 2nd ed. Mexico City: Editorial Campeador, 1954.

Valadés, José C. *Alamán: Estadista e Historiador.* Mexico City: Universidad Nacional Autónoma de México, 1987.

Valdovinos, Mucio (sic). *La Sociedad de los trece; ó, los conservadores por dentro: juguete cómico en un acto.* Mexico City: V. Segura Argüelles (sic), 1859.

Vallarta, Ignacio Luis. *Discurso que en el solemne aniversario del día 16 de septiembre de 1810, leyó en la plaza principal de Guadaljara el C. Ignacio L. Vallarta, miembro de la sociedad literaria "La Esperanza."* Guadalajara: Tipografía del Gobierno, 1855.

Van Young, Eric. "Popular Religion and the Politics of Insurgency in Mexico, 1810–1821." In *The Politics of Religion in an Age of Revival,* edited by Austen Ivereigh, 74–114. London: Institute of Latin American Studies, 2000.

Vanderwood, Paul. *The Power of God Against the Guns of Government: Religious Upheaval in Mexico at the Turn of the Nineteenth Century.* Stanford, CA: Stanford University Press, 1998.

Vásquez Mellado, Alfonso. *La Ciudad de los Palacios: Imágenes de cinco siglos.* Mexico City: Editorial Diana, 1990.

Vigil, José María. *La Reforma.* Vol. 5 of *México a través de los siglos,* edited by Vicente Riva Palacio. Barcelona: Espasa y Compañia, 1888.

[Villalvazo y Rodríguez, Germán Ascensión]. *D. Santos Degolado considerado como gobernador de Jalisco, y como general en jefe de las fuerzas que sitiaron.* Guadalajara: Tipografía del Gobierno, 1859.

Villegas Revueltas, Silvestre. *El liberalismo moderado en México: 1852–1864.* Mexico City: Universidad Nacional Autónoma de México, 1997.

———. "Los obispos y la reforma liberal." *Metapolítica* 6, no. 22 (March–April 2002): 91–103.

Voekel, Pam. *Alone Before God: The Religious Origins of Modernity in Mexico.* Durham, NC: Duke University Press, 2002.

Waterworth, J., trans. *The Canons and Decrees of the Sacred and Oecumenical Council of Trent.* London: C. Dolman, 1848.

Werner, Michael S., ed. *Encyclopedia of Mexico: History, Society and Culture.* Chicago: Fitzroy Dearborn Publishers, 1997.

West, Ty. "La familia enferma: el liberalismo como enfermedad (México, 1857–1864)." In *Sensibilidades conservadores: el debate cultural sobre la civilización en América Latina y España durante el Siglo XIX,* edited by Kari Soriano Salkjelsvik, 189–213. Madrid: Iberoamericana, 2021.

Wheat, Raymond C. *Francisco Zarco: El portavoz liberal de la Reforma.* Mexico City: Editorial Porrúa, 1957.

Wolcott, Roger. *The Correspondence of William Hickling Prescott, 1833–1847.* Boston: Houghton Mifflin, 1925.

Wright-Rios, Edward. *Revolutions in Mexican Catholicism: Reform and Revelation in Oaxaca, 1887–1934.* Durham, NC: Duke University Press, 2009.

Zalce y Rodríguez, Luis J. *Apuntes para la historia de la masonería en México.* Mexico City: Talleres Tipográficos de la Penitenciaría del Distrito Federal, 1950.

Zamacois, Niceto de. *Historia de Méjico, desde sus tiempos mas remotos hasta nuestros dias,* vols. 14 and 15. Mexico City: J. F. Parres, 1880.

Zarco, Francisco. *Actas oficiales y minutario de decretos del congreso extraordinario constituyente de 1856–1857.* Mexico City: El Colegio de México, 1957.

[Zarco, Francisco]. *Los asesinatos de Tacubaya*. Mexico City: n.p., 1859.

———. *Historia del congreso extraordinario constituyente (1856–1857)*. 1857–61. Reprint, Mexico City: El Colegio de México, 1956.

Zerón-Medina, Fausto. *Felicidad de México*. Mexico City: Editorial Clío, 1995.

Zúñiga, Francisco. *Discurso pronunciado el 16 de Setiembre de 1859, en la Alameda de esta ciudad por el Sr. consejero de gobierno del departamento, Lic. Don Francisco Zúñiga*. Toluca, MX: Tipografía del Instituto Literario, 1859.

Index

Printed in the USA
CPSIA information can be obtained
at www.ICGtesting.com
CBHW032131100424
6737CB00003B/114

9 780826 506436